D1320841

HARBRACE
COLLEGE
HANDBOOK
FOR CANADIAN WRITERS

HARBRACE COLLEGE HANDBOOK

FOR CANADIAN WRITERS

FOURTH EDITION

John C. Hodges
Late of the University of Tennessee

Mary E. Whitten
North Texas State University

Judy Brown/Jane Flick
University of British Columbia

HARCOURT
BRACE
CANADA

Harcourt Brace & Company, Canada
Toronto Montreal Orlando Fort Worth San Diego
Philadelphia London Sydney Tokyo

Canadian Cataloguing in Publication Data
  Main entry under title:

  Harbrace college handbook for Canadian writers

  4th ed.
  First ed. published under title: Harbrace college
  handbook. Canadian ed.
  Includes index.
  ISBN 0-7747-3266-0

  1. English language – Grammar.
  2. English language – Rhetoric. I. Hodges, John C., 1892-1967.

  PE1112.H6 1994   808'.042   C94-930205-8

Publisher: Heather McWhinney
Editor and Marketing Manager: Michael J. Young
Director of Publishing Services: Jean Davies
Editorial Manager: Marcel Chiera
Production Manager: Sue-Ann Becker
Manufacturing Co-ordinator: Denise Wake
Copy Editor: Nancy Flight
Cover Design: Brett Miller
Typesetting and Assembly: Bergman Graphics Limited
Printing and Binding: Best Gagné Book Manufacturers

∞ This book was printed in Canada on acid-free paper.
  3 4 5   98 97

Preface

The Harbrace College Handbook for Canadian Writers is both a reference guide for individual writers and a textbook for use in the classroom. It is a comprehensive yet concise summary of the principles of good writing. The purpose of the text is to help students become more effective writers. The handbook is a practical approach and aims to proffer advice clearly and concisely. Throughout the book, students will find abundant specific examples demonstrating principles of writing applicable to professional tasks as well as course work. Whether they are in the classroom studying the textbook with an instructor or working through parts of the text independently, students will find an easily mastered system of reference.

This edition of *The Harbrace College Handbook for Canadian Writers,* like the last, aims to reflect the Canadian context while preserving the organization and methods that have proven so successful in the many earlier American editions. In revising the text, we have used the third Canadian edition and have also drawn on the eleventh American edition by Hodges, Whitten et al. (1990). Throughout this book, we have emphasized examples from the work of Canadian writers and from the Canadian milieu. The sample research paper features Canadian as well as British and American resources, as do the reference works illustrating bibliographical practices for MLA- and APA-style papers.

Readers will find that spelling conventions in the text follow those of the *Gage Canadian Dictionary,* with only two significant exceptions, represented by our preference for *-our* over *-or* and *-yze* over *-yse.* Units of measurement appear in metric. (Notice, however, that quoted excerpts do not always follow these practices. We have respected original spellings, units of measurement, regional usage, and punctuation in quoted examples.)

The text begins with a review of the essentials of grammar, to be used as needed to introduce subsequent sections of the book, and ends with a glossary of frequently used grammatical terms—a useful reference for students throughout the course. The endpapers give a helpful overview. Instructors will find these efficient guides in marking papers, and students will find them useful as aids to revision. The time-tested organization of the handbook gives great flexibility to instructor and student alike. Depending on the needs and interests of their students, instructors may choose to teach sections of the book in any order. For example, some instructors may want to begin with Section **33** (The Whole Composition) or Section **32** (The Paragraph); others may prefer to start with Sections **19–30,** which deal with diction and sentences. Students learning on their own may choose to begin with a specific problem in grammar or a principle in composition, or they may prefer to work their way through a whole section. In every section, the large number and wide variety of exercises make possible the selection of activities appropriate to the needs of a particular class or student. Supplementary exercises designed to give students additional practice are available for Sections **1–32** in the ancillary to this book—*The Harbrace College Workbook for Canadian Writers* (originally prepared to accompany the third edition).

The fourth Canadian edition is an extensive revision of the third Canadian edition. With instructors' and students' needs in mind, we have thoroughly reviewed Sections **1–31** to clarify exposition, add fresh examples, set examples in rhetorical context where possible, rewrite exercises where necessary, and remove unnecessary cross-referencing. In most chapters we have added new exercises cast in paragraphs. We intend these paragraph exercises to give students practice beyond the usual style of separate sentences by having them work through examples within paragraphs. In Section **19** we have introduced a discussion of sexist and biased language, with accompanying exercises designed to help students recognize and avoid such language. Section **32** (The Paragraph) contains new examples of paragraphs and, in particular, paragraphs illustrating detailed development. Section **33** (The Whole Composition) features more discussion of the composition process. It stresses the importance of purpose and audience as it fully describes the process of planning, writing, and revising. New outlines and two student essays provide illustration.

The two most heavily revised sections in the handbook are Sections **34** (The Research Paper) and **35** (Writing for Special Purposes). The chapter on the research paper contains greater coverage of both MLA and APA styles of documentation and includes new student research papers that illustrate both forms. A brief comment on documentation styles of other disciplines also appears in this section. Section **35** is greatly expanded. In addition to giving students guidance in writing letters and memos and preparing résumés, it now addresses analysis of and writing about literature and provides student essays on works of fiction, poetry, and drama.

Although extensive, the changes are not radical. The character of *The Harbrace College Handbook for Canadian Writers,* familiar to users of the third edition, remains intact. The changes and additions do not overshadow the solid, proven coverage of earlier editions.

Finally, we would like to thank the reviewers of the third Canadian edition whose suggestions contributed to this revision: Rebecca Bersagel, University of Alberta; Garry Engkent, University of Toronto; Ann Klinck, University of New Brunswick; Raymond St. Jacques, University of Ottawa; and Kathleen Scherf, University of New Brunswick.

Judy Brown and Jane Flick
University of British Columbia

A Note from the Publisher

Thank you for selecting *Harbrace College Handbook for Canadian Writers, 4/e.* The authors and publisher have devoted considerable time to the careful development of this book. We appreciate your recognition of this effort and accomplishment.

We want to hear what you think about *Harbrace College Handbook for Canadian Writers, 4/e.* Please take a few minutes to fill in the stamped reply card at the back of the book. Your comments and suggestions will be valuable to us as we prepare new editions and other books.

To the Student

Numbers or Symbols / A number or a symbol written in the margin of your paper indicates a need for correction or improvement and calls for revision. If your instructor uses a number, turn directly to the corresponding number at the top of the page in the handbook. If your instructor uses a symbol, first consult the alphabetical list of symbols inside the back cover to find the number of the section to which you should turn. An appropriate letter after a number or symbol (such as **2b** or **frag/b**) will refer you to a specific part of a section.

References / Your instructor will ordinarily refer you to the number or symbol (**2** or **frag, 9** or **cap, 18** or **sp, 28** or **ref**) appearing at the head of one of the thirty-four sections of the handbook. The rule given in colour at the beginning of each section covers the whole section. One of the more specific rules given within the section will usually guide you in revision. Study the section to which you have been referred— the whole of the section if necessary—and master the specific part of the section that applies to your writing.

Correction and Revision / After you have studied the rules called to your attention, revise your paper carefully, as directed by your instructor. One method of revision is explained and illustrated in Section **8,** pages 111–14.

Contents

MECHANICS

PUNCTUATION

12 The Comma

13 Superfluous Commas

14 The Semicolon

Contents

Contents

LARGER ELEMENTS

34   The Research Paper

Contents

GRAMMAR

Sentence Sense

1

Master the essentials of the sentence to aid clear thinking and effective writing.

A key to good writing is to have sentence sense. Sentence sense is the awareness of what makes a sentence—the ability to recognize its grammatical essentials and to understand the relationships among its parts. A close study of this section will help you not only to develop or sharpen your sentence sense but also to make intelligent use of other sections of this handbook. (For explanations of unfamiliar grammatical terms, see **Grammatical Terms,** beginning on page 657.)

In each of the following sentences, the plus sign connects the two basic grammatical parts of the sentence: the subject and the predicate. The first part functions as the complete subject (the simple subject and all the words associated with it), and the second part functions as the complete predicate (the verb and all the words associated with it). The grammatical subject (or simple subject) and the verb (or simple predicate) are in boldface.

> The hijacked **plane + has landed** safely.
> **Sandra +** thoughtfully **gave** us three house plants.

These **trees + should have been planted** in March.
The **tomato + is** a fruit. **It + tastes** good in salads.

The pattern of these sentences is **Subject + Predicate**, the basic order of sentences in English.

1a
Learn to recognize verbs.

A verb functions as the predicate of a sentence or as an essential part of the predicate.

> ### Subject + PREDICATE.

Colleen   **drives.**
Colleen   usually **drives** her car to work.

Predicates may be compound:

> Colleen usually **drives** her car to work and nearly always **arrives** on time. [compound predicate]

You can learn to recognize a verb by observing its *meaning* and its *form.* Often defined as a word expressing action, occurrence, or existence (a state of being), a verb is used to make a statement, to ask a question, or to give a command or direction.

They **moved** to Toronto.   **Is** this true?
The rain **stopped.**   **Consider** the options.

In the present tense, all verbs change form for the third-person singular.

SINGULAR		PLURAL
1st person	I ask, I eat, I walk	We ask, we eat, we walk
2nd person	You ask, you eat, you walk	You ask, you eat, you walk
3rd person	She **asks,** he **eats,** it **walks**	They ask, they eat, they walk

When converted from the present to the past tense, nearly all verbs change form: *ask—asked; eat—ate*. (See also Section **7**.)

PRESENT TENSE		PAST TENSE
I **ski**. Kay **skis**.		I **skied**.
You **win**. She **wins**.		You **won**.
We **quit**. He **quits**.	BUT	He **quit**.

When used with *have, has,* or *had,* most verbs end in *-d* or *-ed* (*have moved, had played*), but some have a special ending (*has eaten*). All progressive verbs, which denote continuous action, are used with a form of *be* and end in *-ing,* as in *was eating*.

Tom **has moved**.	They **have taken** the tests.
He **is moving**.	We **had been taking** lessons.

As these examples show, a verb may consist of two or more words, a unit often referred to as a verb phrase or an expanded verb.

Auxiliaries   A phrase like *have eaten, was helped,* or *did eat* follows this pattern: **auxiliary + verb**. Since auxiliaries, or helping verbs, precede the verb, they are often called verb markers.

The fight **had started**.   He **will be studying** late.
Amy **ought to decide** now. [Compare "Amy *should decide* now."]

The following words are commonly used as auxiliaries:

have, has, had	do, does, did
be, am, are, is, was, were, been	
will, shall, can	would, should, could
may, might, must	ought to, has to, have to, had to, used to

Other words may intervene between the auxiliary and the verb:

Have the members **paid** their dues? I **have** not **paid** mine.

Computer disks **will** never completely **replace** books.

Although not a verb, the contraction for *not* may be added to many auxiliaries: *haven't, doesn't, aren't, can't*. The full word *not* following an auxiliary is written separately; an exception is *cannot*.

■ **Exercise 1**   Underline the verbs, including any auxiliaries, in the following sentences.

1. Helen Archer will be coming to the convention.
2. I came early for registration and for orientation.
3. Arthur said he would like a dinner meeting, if possible.
4. He quoted some old saying that we must eat to live.
5. I hope Helen will have time to visit the bicycle centre.
6. When the factory runs well, it can produce a hundred bicycles a day.
7. Perhaps Helen hasn't arrived yet because she missed the train.
8. She might have been able to take an earlier train.
9. I hope she will be staying for a few extra days.
10. We ought to enjoy the opportunity to learn and the break from studies.

Phrasal verbs   Sometimes a verb combines with a particle such as *across, away, down, for, in, off, out, up,* or *with* to create a phrasal verb that has a different meaning from that of the verb as a single word. For example, the meaning of the verb "turned," even when the adverb "out" occurs nearby, is different from the meaning of the combination "turned out." The meanings of "turned" and "turned out" are both different from the meaning of "turned" and "out" when they are separated by an object. Some phrasal verbs use more than one particle, as, for example, *turn out* *for* in the sense of *attend*, or *put up with* in the sense of *tolerate*. Consider the following examples:

> He **turned** the corner. [moved in a particular direction]
> He **turned** away from Carole. [moved in a contrary direction]
> He **turned out** an impressive soufflé. [produced]
> She **turned out** her handbag on the counter. [emptied]
> He **turned** his son **out** of the house. [threw out, evicted]
> She **turned** the cake **out** onto the tray. [inverted]
> I hope everything **turns out** well. [ends]
> They all **turned out for** the annual meeting. [attended]

Phrasal verbs function grammatically in exactly the same ways that single-word verbs do.

> He **ran** across the street. [single-word verb and adverbial phrase]
> He **ran across** an old diary. [phrasal verb and object] [Compare "He *found* an old diary."]
> Ron **put up** the peaches for the winter, and he made jam. [phrasal verb and object]
> Ron **put** the peaches *up* on the shelf. [single-word verb and adverb]
> The rocket **blew up.** [phrasal verb] The balloon **blew** *up* and *into* the trees. [single-word verb and adverbial modifiers]

Note that other words may intervene between the verb and the particle:

> We **looked** Yvon **up.** Felomina **handed** her report **in.**

■ **Exercise 2**   Underline the phrasal verbs in the following sentences. (Be sure to include particles separated from the main verb by other words.)

1. Tom and Yoshi brought up their children to behave well and respect others.

2. Even when they were very small, Sue and Tim cleaned up after themselves.
3. They also tidied up their own rooms.
4. Their parents also handed down to them little traditions from both sides of the family.
5. For example, Yoshi's parents always took off their shoes when they visited.
6. Yoshi taught the children to take their shoes off too and turn them around on the top step.
7. Tom's parents always put on their best clothes for Sunday dinner.
8. The whole family, including the children, dressed up for Sunday visits.
9. Tim and Sue grew up feeling that they took after their grandparents.
10. They always looked forward to holidays and visits with their grandparents.

■ **Exercise 3**   Underline the complete verbs in the following sentences. Identify any auxiliaries and particles.

1. In 1992, the extramarital activities of members of Britain's royal family drew the world's attention.
2. People everywhere were discussing the failing marriage of the Prince and Princess of Wales.
3. To the dismay of Prince Charles, the London tabloids published a transcript of an intimate conversation.
4. The British media had, according to many, overstepped the boundaries of taste.
5. In the view of staunch monarchists, the press had delivered the Prince a cruel blow by invading his privacy.
6. Many Britons, defending their "right to know," gobbled up scraps of gossip.
7. Interestingly, the coverage led to a widespread debate about freedom of the press.
8. Some politicians were suffering attacks by the press and were seeking a way to fight back.
9. The treatment of Prince Charles gave them their opportunity.

10. They seized on the issue of privacy, whipped up public debate, and demanded new censorship controls.

1b
Learn to recognize subjects and objects of verbs.

SUBJECTS OF VERBS

All grammatically complete sentences, except for imperatives (commands or requests), contain stated subjects of verbs. In the following sentences, the subjects are in boldface, and the verbs are in italics.

> **Ontario** *produces* delicious corn.
> *Does*n't **Iowa** also *grow* corn?
> *Take,* for example, Ontario and Iowa. [imperative]

Subjects of verbs may be compound:
> **Ontario** and **Iowa** grow corn. [compound subject]

To identify the grammatical subject of a sentence, first find the verb; then use the verb in a question beginning with *who* or *what,* as shown in the following examples:

The two dogs in the cage ate.	The shack was built by Al.
Verb: **ate**	Verb: **was built**
WHO or WHAT ate?	WHAT was built?
The dogs	**The shack**
(not the cage) **ate.**	(not Al) **was built.**
Subject: **dogs**	Subject: **shack**

Subjects of verbs are nouns or pronouns (or word groups serving as nouns).

Subjects usually precede verbs in sentences. Common exceptions to the *subject + verb* pattern occur when subjects are used in questions and after the expletive *there* (which is never the subject).

Was the **statement** true? [verb + subject]
Did these **refugees survive?** [auxiliary + subject + verb]
There **were** no **objections.** [expletive + verb + subject]

OBJECTS OF VERBS

Verbs denoting action often require objects to complete the meaning of the predicate. When they do so they are called *transitive* verbs. In the following sentences, the objects are in boldface.

The clerk sold **him** the expensive **briefcase.** [direct object: *briefcase*—indirect object: *him*]
Kim met the **mayor** and her **husband.** [compound direct object]
I mailed **Ruth** and **him** four tickets. [compound indirect object]

Like the subjects of verbs, direct and indirect objects of verbs are generally nouns or pronouns.

To identify a direct object, find the subject and the verb; then use them in a question ending with *whom* or *what*, as shown in the following example:

Karen completely ignored the reporters.
Subject and verb: **Karen ignored**
Karen ignored WHOM OR WHAT? **reporters**
Direct object: **reporters**

Notice that direct objects in sentences like the following are directly affected by the action of the verb.

A tornado levelled a city in West Texas. [*tornado,* the subject, acts; *city,* the object, receives the action]

Knowing how to change an active verb to the passive voice can also help you to identify an object, since the object of an active verb can usually be made the subject of a passive verb.

ACTIVE   The Expos finally **defeated** the **Mets.**
[*Mets* is the direct object of *defeated.*]
PASSIVE   The **Mets were** finally **defeated** by the Expos.
[*Mets* is the subject of *were defeated.*]

Notice that a form of *be* (such as *is, are, was*) is added when an active verb is changed to a passive. A passive verb form indicates that the grammatical subject is not the doer or the agent but the object, receiver, or effect of the action.

Some verbs (such as *give, offer, bring, take, lend, send, buy,* and *sell*) may have both a direct object and an indirect object. An indirect object generally states *to whom* or *for whom* (or *to what* or *for what*) something is done.

Richard sent Sajida an invitation.
Subject + verb + direct object: **Richard sent invitation**
Richard sent an invitation TO WHOM? **Sajida**
Indirect object: **Sajida**

Word order   Becoming thoroughly aware of the meaningfulness of English word order—normally **Subject + Verb + Object**—will help you to recognize subjects and objects. Carefully study three of the most commonly used sentence patterns, observing the importance of word order—especially in Pattern 2—in determining meaning. (For patterns with subject and object complements, see **4b.**)

PATTERN 1

> ### SUBJECT + VERB.

The **children did** not **listen.**
The **lights** on the patrol car **flashed** ominously.

PATTERN 2

> ### SUBJECT + VERB + OBJECT.

Mice frighten **elephants.**
Elephants frighten **mice.**
Our **team won** the gold **medal.**

PATTERN 3

> ### SUBJECT + VERB + INDIRECT OBJECT
> ### + DIRECT OBJECT.

Mark baked Fred a **cake.**
The **company will** probably **send me** a small **refund.**

In some sentences—especially questions—the direct object does not always take the position indicated by these basic patterns.

What **medal** did our team win?
[direct object + auxiliary + subject + verb]

■ **Exercise 4**   Circle the subjects of the verbs in Exercise 3 on pages 7–8. Label direct objects *DO* and indirect objects *IO*.

■ **Exercise 5**   Circle all subjects and underline all objects of verbs in the quotations below. Prepare for a class discussion of the use of the three basic sentence patterns.

1. Art and games need rules, conventions, and spectators.
                                        —MARSHALL McLUHAN
2. We do not own our images and life stories the way we own a bicycle or a house.   —BARBARA AMIEL
3. We all know, I think, that Nature gave man whiskers and a mustache with the quaint idea in mind that these would prove attractive to the female.   —JAMES THURBER

4. Canada has earned the right to be heard, in peacetime and in war.   —PIERRE TRUDEAU
5. Save the fleeting minute: learn gracefully to dodge the bore.   —SIR WILLIAM OSLER
6. The people never give up their liberties but under some delusion.   —EDMUND BURKE
7. When you educate a man, you educate an individual; but when you educate a woman, you educate a family.
   —AGNES KRIPPS
8. A diploma can't get you work in the theatre, but a part can.
   —GENEVIEVE BUJOLD.

1c
Learn to recognize all the parts of speech.

Two methods of classifying words in a sentence are illustrated in the chart below. The first method classifies words according to their function in a sentence; the second, according to their part of speech. Notice that one part of speech—the noun (a naming word with a typical form)—is used as a subject, a direct object, a modifier, and an object of a preposition.

Waiters usually offer us free coffee at Joe's cafe.

	FUNCTION	PART OF SPEECH
Waiters	subject	noun
usually	modifier	adverb
offer	verb of predicate	verb
us	indirect object	pronoun
free	modifier	adjective
coffee	direct object	noun
at	preposition	preposition
Joe's	modifier	noun
cafe	object of preposition	noun

Words are traditionally grouped into eight classes or parts of speech: *verbs, nouns, pronouns, adjectives, adverbs, prepositions, conjunctions,* and *interjections.* Verbs, nouns, adjectives, and adverbs (called *vocabulary* or *lexical* words) make up more than 99 percent of all words listed in the dictionary. But pronouns, prepositions, and conjunctions—although small in number—are important because they are used over and over in our speaking and writing. Prepositions and conjunctions (called *function* or *structure* words) connect and relate other parts of speech.

Of the eight word classes, only three—prepositions, conjunctions, and interjections—do not change their form. For a summary of the form changes of the other parts of speech, see **inflection,** page 668.

Carefully study the forms, meanings, and functions of each of the eight parts of speech listed in the following pages. For additional examples or more detailed information, see the corresponding entries in **Grammatical Terms,** beginning on page 657.

VERBS *notify, notifies, is notifying, notified*
        write, writes, is writing, wrote, has written

A verb functions as the predicate of a sentence or as an essential part of the predicate: see **1a.**

> Herman **writes.**
> He **has written** five poems.
> He **is** no longer **writing** those dull stories.

Two frequently used verb-forming suffixes are *-ize* and *-ify:*

> *terror* (noun)—*terrorize, terrify* (verbs)

Note: Verbals (infinitives, participles, and gerunds) cannot function as the predicate of a sentence: see **1d,** pages 19–20.

NOUNS   *woman, women; kindness, kindnesses*
           nation, nations; nation's, nations'
           Carthage, Singapore, William, NDP
           the *money,* an *understanding,* a *breakthrough*

Nouns function as subjects, objects, complements, appositives, and modifiers, as well as in direct address and in absolute constructions. See **noun,** pages 671–72. Nouns name persons, places, things, ideas, animals, and so on. The articles *a, an,* and *the* signal that a noun is to follow (a *chair,* an *activity,* the last *race*).

    McKinney drives a **truck** for the **Salvation Army.**

Endings such as *-ance, -ation, -ence, -ism, -ity, -ment, -ness,* and *-ship* are called noun-forming suffixes:

    relax, depend (verbs)—*relaxation, dependence* (nouns)
    kind, rigid (adjectives)—*kindness, rigidity* (nouns)

Note: Words like *father-in-law, Labour Day, swimming pool,* and *breakthrough* are generally classified as *compound nouns.*

PRONOUNS   *I, me, my mine, myself; they, you, him, it*
             this, these; who, whose, whom; which, that
             one, ones, one's; everybody, anyone

Pronouns serve the function of nouns in sentences:
    They bought **it** for **her. Everyone** knows **this.**

ADJECTIVES *shy, sleepy, attractive, famous, historic*
              three men, *this* class, *another* one
              young, younger, youngest
              good, better, best

The articles *a, an,* and *the* are variously classified as adjectives, determiners, or function words. Adjectives modify or qualify nouns and pronouns (and sometimes gerunds). Adjectives are generally placed near the words they modify.

> **These difficult** decisions, whether **right** or **wrong,** affect all of us.
> **Alpine** flowers are most **beautiful** in July.

In the second of these two examples, *beautiful* is a predicate adjective (subject complement), a word that modifies the subject and helps to complete the meaning of a linking verb (*be, am, is, are, was, were, been, seem, become, feel, look, smell, sound, taste,* and so on): see **4b.**

Suffixes such as *-al, -able, -ant, -ative, -ic, -ish, -less, -ous,* and *-y* may be added to certain verbs or nouns to form adjectives:

> *accept, repent* (verbs)—*acceptable, repentant* (adjectives)
> *angel, effort* (nouns)—*angelic, effortless* (adjectives)

ADVERBS   *rarely* saw, call *daily, soon* left, left *sooner*
very short, *too* angry, *never* shy, *not* fearful
practically never loses, *nearly always* cold

As the examples show, adverbs modify verbs, adjectives, and other adverbs. In addition, an adverb may modify a verbal, a phrase, a clause, or even the rest of the sentence in which it appears:

> I noticed a plane **slowly** circling overhead.
> **Honestly,** Ben did catch a big shark.

The *-ly* ending nearly always converts adjectives to adverbs:

> *rare, honest* (adjectives)—*rarely, honestly* (adverbs)

PREPOSITIONS   *on* a shelf, *between* us, *because of* rain
to the door, *by* them, *before* class

A preposition always has an object, which is usually a noun or a pronoun. The preposition links and relates its object to some other word in the sentence. The preposition with its object (and any modifiers) is called a *prepositional phrase.*

Byron expressed **with great force** his love **of liberty.**

The preposition may follow rather than precede its object, and it may be placed at the end of the sentence:

What was he complaining **about?** [*What* is the object of the preposition.]

Words commonly used as prepositions:

about	besides	inside	since
above	between	into	through
across	beyond	like	throughout
after	but	near	till
against	by	of	to
along	concerning	off	toward
among	despite	on	under
around	down	onto	underneath
at	during	out	until
before	except	outside	up
behind	excepting	over	upon
below	for	past	with
beneath	from	regarding	within
beside	in	round	without

Phrasal prepositions (two or more words):

according to	due to	on account of
along with	except for	out of
apart from	in addition to	up to
as for	in case of	with regard to
as regards	in front of	with reference to
as to	in lieu of	with respect to
because of	in place of	with the
by means of	in regard to	exception of
by reason of	in spite of	
by way of	instead of	

CONJUNCTIONS   cars *and* trucks, in the boat *or* on the pier
will try *but* may lose, *neither* Amy *nor* Bill
I worked, *for* Dad needed money.
The river rises *when* the snow melts.

Conjunctions serve as connectors. The co-ordinating conjunctions (*and, or, nor, for, so,* and *yet*), as well as the correlatives (*both—and, either—or, neither—nor, not only—but also, whether—or*), connect sentence elements (words, phrases, or clauses) of equal grammatical rank. See also Section **26.** The subordinating conjunctions (such as *because, if, since, till, when, where, while*) connect subordinate clauses with main clauses: see **1d,** pages 23–26.

Note: Words like *consequently, however, nevertheless, then,* and *therefore* (see the list on page 45) are used as conjunctive adverbs (or adverbial conjunctions):

Don seemed bored in class; **however,** he did listen and
learn.

INTERJECTIONS   *Wow! Oh,* that's a surprise.

Interjections are exclamations. They may be followed by an exclamation point or by a comma.

A dictionary labels words according to their part of speech. Some words have only one classification—for example, *notify* (verb), *sleepy* (adjective), *practically* (adverb). Other words have more than one label because they can function as two or more parts of speech. Each classification depends on the use of a word in a given sentence. The word *living,* for instance, is first treated as a form of the verb *live* (as in *are living*) and is then listed separately and defined as an adjective (*a living example*) and as a noun (*makes a living*). Another example is the word *up:*

> They dragged the sled **up** the hill. [preposition]
> She follows the **ups** and downs of the market. [noun]
> "They **have upped** the rent again," he complained. [verb]
> Kelly **ran up** the bill. [part of phrasal verb]
> The **up** escalator is jerking again. [adjective]
> Hopkins says to look **up,** to "look **up** at the skies!" [adverb]

■ **Exercise 6**   Using your dictionary as an aid if you wish, classify each word in the following sentences according to its part of speech.

1. He struts with the gravity of a frozen penguin. —TIME
2. Neither intelligence nor integrity can be imposed by law. —CARL BECKER
3. Speak up, gentlemen; I am not opposed to male participation in government.   —CHARLOTTE WHITTON
4. Of all persons, adolescents are the most intensely personal; their intensity is often uncomfortable to adults.
   —EDGAR Z. FRIEDENBERG
5. We can remember minutely and precisely only the things which never really happened to us. —ERIC HOFFER
6. Bureaucracy, the rule of no one, has become the modern form of despotism. —MARY McCARTHY
7. Skeptical scrutiny is the means, in both science and religion, by which deep thought can be winnowed from deep nonsense. —CARL SAGAN

8. If baseball evokes the civility of a national pastime, football provokes the slam-bang unruliness of passion.
—DIANNE BRADY

9. Self-help books are the feeble effort of the publishing business to fill a vacuum created by the rush of change.
—ROBERT FULFORD

10. The worst thing that has happened to science education is that the great fun has gone out of it. —LEWIS THOMAS

1d

Learn to recognize phrases and subordinate clauses.

Observe how a short simple sentence may be expanded by adding modifiers—not only single words but also word groups that function as adjectives or adverbs.

The hijacked plane has landed.

[subject (noun phrase) + predicate (verb phrase)]

Expansion:

The **first** hijacked plane has landed **safely.** [single-word modifiers added]

The first hijacked plane **to arrive at this airport** has landed safely **on the south runway.** [phrases added]

The first hijacked plane **that we have ever seen** at this airport has landed safely on the south runway, **which has been closed to traffic for a year.** [subordinate clauses added]

A word group used as a single part of speech (noun, verb, adjective, or adverb) is either a phrase or a subordinate clause.

PHRASES

A phrase is a sequence of grammatically related words without a subject and a predicate.

the hijacked plane [noun phrase—no predicate]

has landed [verb phrase—no subject]

at this airport; on the south runway; to traffic; for a year [prepositional phrases—neither subject nor predicate]

For a list of types of phrases with examples, see **phrase,** page 675.

As you learn to recognize phrases, give special attention to verb forms in word groups used as a noun, an adjective, or an adverb. Such verb forms (called *verbals* and classified as participles, gerunds, and infinitives) are much like verbs in that they have different tenses, can take subjects and objects, and can be modified by adverbs. They cannot function as the predicate of a sentence, however.

VERBAL PHRASES IN SENTENCES

Shoppers **milling around** did not buy much. [participial phrase (see page 674) modifying the noun *shoppers*]

Some people win arguments by **just remaining silent.** [gerund phrase (page 667), object of the preposition *by*]

The group arrived in a van **loaded with heavy equipment.** [participial phrase modifying the noun *van*]

Vernon went to Ottawa **to visit relatives.** [infinitive phrase (see page 668) modifying the verb *went*]

As the examples illustrate, participial, gerund, and infinitive phrases function as single parts of speech and are therefore only parts of sentences.

(1) Phrases used as nouns

Gerund phrases are always used as nouns. Infinitive phrases are often used as nouns (although they may also function as modifiers). Occasionally a prepositional phrase functions as a noun (as in "*After supper* is too late!").

NOUNS	PHRASES USED AS NOUNS
The **decision** is important.	**Choosing a major** is important. [gerund phrase—subject]

She likes the **job**.	She likes **to do the work**. [infinitive phrase—direct object]
He uses my room for **storage**.	He uses my room for **storing all his auto parts**. [gerund phrase —object of a preposition]
He wants two things: **money** and **power**.	He wants two things: **to make money** and **to gain power**. [infinitive phrases in a compound appositive—see page 63]

■ **Exercise 7**   Underline the gerund phrases and the infinitive phrases (including any modifiers) used as nouns in the following sentences.

1. Writing solely for the purpose of attacking others is cynical.

2. To perceive praise for one's achievements is sometimes embarrassing but always gratifying.

3. Angry and proud, Claire decided to fight back.

4. All laboratory procedures—especially the mixing of chemicals after measuring or heating them—require care.

5. The art department has been increasing its classes by encouraging students to take evening courses in sculpting and drawing from live models.

6. He thinks that studying at the last minute will get him through.

7. Antonio intended to win distinction for his college group.

8. Suzanne can't bear taking criticism from others.

9. To argue for the preservation of parkland is not enough; one must act.

10. Putting all of your eggs in one basket may be tempting fate.

(2) Phrases used as modifiers

Prepositional phrases nearly always function as adjectives or adverbs. Infinitive phrases are also used as adjectives or adverbs. Participial phrases are used as adjectives. Absolute phrases are used as adverbs.

ADJECTIVES	PHRASES USED AS ADJECTIVES
It was a **sorrowful** day.	It was a day **of sorrow.** [prepositional phrase]
Appropriate language is best.	Language **to suit the occasion** is best. [infinitive phrase]
Destructive storms lashed the Prairies	**Destroying many crops of corn and oats,** storms lashed the Prairies. [participial phrase containing a prepositional phrase]
The **icy** bridge was narrow.	The bridge **covered with ice** was narrow. [participal phrase containing a prepositional phrase]

ADVERBS	PHRASES USED AS ADVERBS
Drive **carefully.**	Drive **with care on wet streets.** [prepositional phrases]
I nodded **respectfully.**	I nodded **to show respect.** [infinitive phrase]
Consequently, we could hardly see the road.	**The rain coming down in torrents,** we could hardly see the road. [absolute phrase—see page 657]

These examples illustrate how phrases function in the same way as single-word modifiers. But phrases are not merely substitutes for single words: they can express far more than can be conveyed in one word:

The gas fluttered **from empty to full.**
He telephoned his wife **to tell her of his arrival.**
The firefighters **hosing down the adjacent buildings** had
very little standing room.

■ **Exercise 8**   In the following sentences, underline each phrase
used as a modifier. Then state whether the phrase functions as an
adjective or as an adverb.

1. They worked fast, Elinor preparing the soil and Daniel
planting the seedlings.
2. An enormous ribbon of seaweed drifting above the
swimmer unnerved him for a moment.
3. Not caring to eat with the rest of us, she chose to sit by
herself and read.
4. He took the course to get more practice in drafting and to
prepare himself for studies in architecture.
5. My sister bought a laptop computer, small but enough
for her needs.
6. The competitors to watch closely are the ones practising
on the west court.
7. Crawling through the underbrush, I suddenly remembered the coil of rope left on top of the truck.
8. A singing voice like that one comes along only once in a
generation.
9. Elated by Wayne Gretzky's return to play, the Los
Angeles fans gave him a rousing welcome.
10. I wrote the letter to support his application.

SUBORDINATE CLAUSES

A clause is a sequence of related words containing both a
subject and a predicate. Unlike a main clause (an independent unit—see **1e**), a subordinate clause is grammatically
dependent; it is used as a single part of a speech. A subordinate clause functions within sentences as an adverb, an
adjective, or a noun.

Gary was my first and only blind date **because I married him.** [adverb clause]

Simple illustrations, **which the instructor drew on the board,** explained the process. [adjective clause]

Geologists know **why earthquakes occur.** [noun clause—direct object]

The following conjunctions are commonly used to introduce, connect, and relate subordinate clauses to other words in the sentence.

Words commonly used as subordinating conjunctions:

after	inasmuch as	supposing [that]
although	in case [that]	than
as	in order that	that
as [far/soon] as	insofar as	though
as if	in that	till
as though	lest	unless
because	no matter how	until
before	now that	when, whenever
even if	once	where, wherever
even though	provided [that]	whether
how	since	while
if	so that	why

The relative pronouns also serve as markers of subordinate clauses:

that, what, which; who, whoever; whom, whomever; whose

(1) Subordinate clauses used as nouns

NOUNS	NOUN CLAUSES
The **news** may be false.	**What the newspapers say** may be false. [subject]
I do not know his **address.**	I do not know **where he lives.** [direct object]
Give the tools to **Amir.**	Give the tools to **whoever can use them best.** [object of a preposition]

The conjunction *that* before a noun clause may be omitted in some sentences:

> I know **she is right.** [Compare "I know *that she is right.*"]

(2) Subordinate clauses used as modifiers

Two types of subordinate clauses, the adjective clause and the adverb clause, are used as modifiers.

Adjective clauses   Any clause that modifies a noun or a pronoun is an adjective clause. Adjective clauses, which nearly always follow the words modified, usually begin with relative pronouns but may begin with such words as *when, where,* or *why.*

ADJECTIVES	ADJECTIVE CLAUSES
Everyone needs **loyal** friends	Everyone needs friends **who are loyal.**
The **golden** window reflects the sun.	The window, **which shines like gold,** reflects the sun.
Peaceful countrysides no longer exist.	Countrysides **where one can find peace of mind** no longer exist.

If it is not used as a subject, the relative pronoun in an adjective clause may sometimes be omitted:

> He is a man **I admire.** [Compare "He is a man whom I admire."]

Adverb clauses   An adverb clause usually modifies a verb but may modify an adjective, an adverb, or even the rest of the sentence in which it appears. Adverb clauses are ordinarily introduced by subordinating conjunctions.

ADVERBS	ADVERB CLAUSES
Soon the lights went out.	**When the windstorm hit,** the lights went out.
No alcoholic beverages are sold **locally.**	No alcoholic beverages are sold **where I live.**
The price is **too** high for me.	The price is higher **than I can afford.**
Speak **very** distinctly.	Speak as distinctly **as you can.**

Some adverb clauses may be elliptical. See also **25b.**

> If I can save enough money, I'll go to France next summer. **If not,** I'll take a trip to Montreal. [Omitted words are clearly implied.]

■ **Exercise 9**   In the following sentences, underline the subordinate clauses. Identify the clauses by writing the labels NOUN, ADJECTIVE, or ADVERB above each.

1. Political scientists have observed that increases in global economic problems are contributing to international instability.
2. That many nations are committed to maintaining stability is evident.
3. Among those who actively work for peace are Canada's peacekeeping forces.
4. What Canada's troops did or tried to do in the Balkans was restore social order and guarantee security of person for those who were left in small villages.
5. Most citizens saw that Canadian soldiers were trying to help them, but some saw them simply as interlopers who wore army uniforms.
6. If Canadian peacekeeping forces are to do their jobs well, the government must be prepared to spend more on their training than it has done in the past.
7. Public polls, which have become important to policy makers, show support for Canada's role as a peacekeeping nation.
8. Because the polling of public opinion has become important in election campaigns, candidates are demanding

that pollsters reveal their questioning procedures and the number of persons polled.

9. When pollsters, who are unelected, become powerful figures in the shaping of government policy, the public must be concerned.

10. While debates rage about the use and misuse of polls, Canadians continue to be fascinated by samplings that reflect public opinion.

1e

Learn to recognize main clauses and the various types of sentences.

Since both are independent units of expression, a main clause and a simple sentence have the same grammatical structure: **subject + predicate.** Generally, however, the term *main clause* refers to an independent part of a sentence containing other clauses.

SIMPLE SENTENCES
I had lost my passport.
I did not look for it.

MAIN CLAUSES IN SENTENCES
I had lost my passport, but **I did not look for it.** [A coordinating conjunction links the two main clauses.]
Although I had lost my passport, **I did not look for it.** [A subordinate clause precedes the main clause.]

Sentences may be classified according to their structure as *simple, compound, complex,* or *compound-complex.*

1. A simple sentence has only one subject and one predicate (either or both of which may be compound):
   Dick started a coin collection. [SUBJECT, VERB, OBJECT.]

2. A compound sentence consists of at least two main clauses:

Dick started a coin collection, and his friend bought an album of rare stamps. [MAIN CLAUSE, and MAIN CLAUSE. See **12a.**]

3. A complex sentence has one main clause and at least one subordinate clause:

As soon as Dick started a coin collection, his friend bought an album of rare stamps. [ADVERB CLAUSE, MAIN CLAUSE. See **12b.**]

4. A compound-complex sentence consists of at least two main clauses and at least one subordinate clause:

As soon as Dick started a coin collection, his friend bought an album of rare stamps; on Christmas morning they exchanged coins and stamps. [ADVERB CLAUSE, MAIN CLAUSE; MAIN CLAUSE. See **14a.**]

Sentences may also be classified according to their purpose and are punctuated accordingly:

DECLARATIVE	He refused the offer. [statement]
IMPERATIVE	Refuse the offer. [request or command]
INTERROGATIVE	Did he refuse the offer? He refused, didn't he? He refused it? [questions]
EXCLAMATORY	What an offer! He refused it! Refuse it! [exclamations]

■ **Exercise 10**   Underline the main clauses in the following sentences. Put subordinate clauses in brackets. (Noun clauses may be an integral part of the basic pattern of a main clause, as in the second sentence.)

1. Canada has often participated in the United Nations' peacekeeping operations, and its efforts have generally been successful.
2. Acid rain poses a threat to the environment, and some scientists say it is destroying the maple sugar industry in Quebec.

3. The planet Mars has two satellites, which were discovered by Asaph Hall in 1877.
4. The film reached its climax as the hero, acting more decisively than she had ever done before, confronted her accusers.
5. Mount Logan is the highest peak in Canada; it reaches an altitude of almost six thousand metres.
6. Because it entrenches and increases the power of Canada's provinces, the agreement redefines the nature of Confederation.
7. In 1993, researchers made several attempts to isolate the causes of Alzheimer's disease, but when they tested their hypotheses, the results were inconclusive.
8. An argument may be supported or refuted by appeals to logic or emotion, as rhetoricians show.
9. Visitors to the Gaspé Peninsula frequently stop at Percé Rock, a landmark that draws many amateur photographers every year.
10. We know that recessions mean unemployment; unfortunately, those laid off first are often rehired last.

■ **Exercise 11** Classify the sentences in Exercise 10 as *compound* (there are two), *complex* (five), or *compound-complex* (three).

■ **Exercise 12** First, identify the main and subordinate clauses in the sentences in the following paragraph; then classify the sentences according to their purpose (*declarative, imperative, interrogative,* or *exclamatory*). Your instructor may also wish you to classify the sentences according to structure.

¹Jim angrily called himself a fool, as he had been doing all the way to the swamp. ²Why had he listened to Fred's mad idea? ³What did ghosts and family legends mean to him, in this age of computers and solar-energy converters? ⁴He had enough mysteries of his own, of a highly complex sort, which

involved an intricate search for values. ⁵But now he was chasing down ghosts, and this chase in the middle of the night was absurd. ⁶It was lunacy! ⁷The legends that surrounded the ghosts had horrified him as a child, and they were a horror still. ⁸As he approached the dark trail that would lead him to the old mansion, he felt almost sick. ⁹The safe, sure things of every day had become distant fantasies. ¹⁰Only this grotesque night—and whatever ghosts might be lurking in the shadows—seemed hideously real.

■ **Exercise 13** Classify the sentences in the following paragraph as *compound, complex,* or *compound-complex.* You may wish to review Exercise 9 before you begin.

¹The ancient Chinese believed that in the features of the natural landscape one could glimpse the mathematically precise order of the universe and all the beneficial and harmful forces that were harmoniously connected according to the principle of Tao—the Way. ²This was not a question of metaphor: the topography did not represent good or evil; it really was good or evil. ³Under these circumstances, locating a building in the landscape became a decision of momentous proportions that could affect an individual and a family for generations to come. ⁴The result was *feng-shui,* which means "wind and water," and which was a kind of cosmic surveying tool. ⁵Its coherent, scientific practice dates from the Sung dynasty (960-1126), but its roots are much older than that. ⁶It was first used to locate grave sites—the Chinese worshipped their ancestors, who, they believed, influenced the good fortune of their descendants. ⁷Eventually, it began to be used to locate the homes of the living; and, indeed, the earliest book on *feng-shui,* published during the Han dynasty (202 B.C.–A.D. 220), was entitled *The Canon of the Dwellings.*

—WITOLD RYBCZYNSKI

Sentence Fragments

2

As a rule, do not write sentence fragments.

The term *fragment* refers to a non-sentence beginning with a capital letter and ending with a period. Although written as if it were a sentence, a fragment is only a part of a sentence—such as a phrase or a subordinate clause.

FRAGMENTS

My father always planting a spring garden.

Because he likes to eat vegetables.

That help the body to combat infection.

For example, yellow and green ones.

SENTENCES

My father always plants a spring garden.

He likes to eat vegetables.

He likes to eat vegetables that help the body to combat infection—for example, yellow and green ones.

As you study the preceding examples, notice that the first fragment is converted to a sentence by substituting *plants* (a verb) for *planting* (a participle) and the second by omitting *because* (a subordinating conjunction). The last two fragments (a subordinate clause and a phrase) are made into parts of a sentence.

Similarly, you can eliminate any fragment in your own papers (1) by making it into a sentence or (2) by making it a part of a sentence. If you cannot easily distinguish structural differences between sentences and non-sentences, study Section **1**, especially **1d**.

Test for a sentence Before handing in a composition, proofread each word group written as a sentence. First, be sure that it has at least one subject and one predicate.

> FRAGMENTS WITHOUT A SUBJECT, A PREDICATE, OR BOTH
> And for days tried to change my mind. [no subject]
> Water sparkling in the moonlight. [no predicate]
> Without the slightest hesitation. [no subject, no predicate]

Next, be sure that the word group is not a dependent clause beginning with a subordinating conjunction or a relative pronoun (see page 24).

> FRAGMENTS WITH SUBJECT AND PREDICATE
> When he tried for days to change my mind. [subject and verb: *he tried*; subordinating conjunction: *when*]
> Which sparkles in the moonlight. [subject and verb: *which sparkles*; relative pronoun: *which*]

Not all fragments are to be avoided. Written dialogue that mirrors speech habits often contains grammatically incomplete sentences or elliptical expressions within the quotation marks: see **9e**. Answers to questions are often single words, phrases, or subordinate clauses written as sentences.

> Where does Peg begin a mystery story? **On the last page.**

Occasionally, writers deliberately use fragments for effect.

The job calls for extensive travel, for numerous trips to developing countries. **Better to examine the problems of the Third World in person than to observe them from continents away. Better to meet the people themselves than to study official reports about them.** [Note the effective repetition and the parallel structure in the two fragments.]

Even though they are suitable for some purposes, sentence fragments are comparatively rare in formal expository writing. In formal papers, sentence fragments are to be used—if at all—sparingly and with care.

2a
Do not capitalize and punctuate a phrase as you would a sentence.

Phrases containing verbals:

FRAGMENT	He will have a chance to go home next weekend. **And to meet his new stepfather.** [infinitive phrase]
REVISED	He will have a chance to go home next weekend and to meet his new stepfather. [fragment included in the preceding sentence]
FRAGMENT	Astronauts venturing deep into space may not come back to earth for fifty years. **Returning only to discover an uninhabitable planet.** [participial phrase]
REVISED	Astronauts venturing deep into space may not come back to earth for fifty years. They may return only to discover an uninhabitable planet. [fragment made into a sentence]
FRAGMENT	The children finally arrived at camp. **Many dancing for joy, and some crying for their parents.** [absolute phrases]
REVISED	The children finally arrived at camp. Many were dancing for joy, and some were crying for their parents. [fragment made into a sentence]

Prepositional phrase:

FRAGMENT   Soon I began to work for the company. **First in the rock pit and later on the highway.**

REVISED   Soon I began to work for the company, first in the rock pit and later on the highway.

Part of a compound predicate:

FRAGMENT   Sarah was elected president of her class. **And was made a member of Canada World Youth.**

REVISED   Sarah was elected president of her class and was made a member of Canada World Youth.

Appositive:

FRAGMENT   The new lawyer needed a secretary. **Preferably someone with intelligence and experience.**

REVISED   The new lawyer needed a secretary, preferably someone with intelligence and experience.

■ **Exercise 1**   Eliminate each fragment below by including it in the adjacent sentence or by making it into a complete sentence.

1. Haiti has a long history of political upheaval. As recounted by Robert and Nancy Heinl in their book, *Written in Blood.*
2. She went out with her friends to celebrate. Her final physics labs written up and handed in.
3. The media spent untold hours reporting on the Constitutional Referendum. The single issue creating the most controversy being the so-called Quebec Question.
4. I wanted a break from the winter doldrums. Definitely one that would allow me to get outdoors for exercise.
5. She returned home with a heavily laden book bag. Only to realize that she had left her handbag in Elena's car.
6. They left the dance when the flickering lights signalled the closing. But danced down the steps and along the streets under the moonlight.
7. Throwing aluminum pop cans into the garbage. That was what angered him most.

8. They hiked back to their campsite. And found that bears had strewn all the food they had not hung up in the trees.
9. He killed seven flies at one swat. Against the law of averages, but possible.
10. A muffled roar. The sound coming from the neighbour's chain saw grew more and more irritating.

2b

Do not capitalize and punctuate a subordinate clause as you would a sentence.

FRAGMENT — Thousands of young people became active workers in the community. **After these appeals had changed their apathy to concern.** [detached adverb clause]

REVISED — Thousands of young people became active workers in the community after these appeals had changed their apathy to concern. [fragment included in the preceding sentence]

FRAGMENT — No one knew where he came from. **Or who he was.** [detached noun clause, part of a compound object]

REVISED — No one knew where he came from or who he was. [fragment included in the preceding sentence]

FRAGMENT — We were trying to follow the directions. **Which were confusing and absurd.** [detached adjective clause]

REVISED — We were trying to follow the directions, which were confusing and absurd. [fragment included in the preceding sentence]

OR

We tried to follow the directions. They were confusing and absurd. [fragment made into a sentence]

OR

We tried to follow the confusing, absurd directions. [fragment reduced to adjectivals that are included in the preceding sentence]

■ **Exercise 2**   Eliminate each fragment below by including it in the preceding sentence or by making it into a sentence.

1. Bob faints whenever he sees medical operations on TV. And even when the doctor takes his blood pressure reading.
2. I am making a study of cigarette advertisements. That appeal specifically to young children through pop culture images and catchy phrases and jingles.
3. Jennifer thinks that all schoolchildren should wear uniforms. Whether they attend public schools or private schools.
4. Hari decided to give diving a try. After he watched a clubs' day demonstration in the student union.
5. Her parents think that she spends too much time with her best friend. And that her studies are being adversely affected by too much social activity.

■ **Exercise 3**   Some of the following examples are correct sentences, and others include fragments. Note which are complete sentences, and make necessary changes in the others to create complete sentences.

1. From Cornwall in far southeast England, Celtic miners took their mining skills all over the world. Known as "Cousin Jacks" from their habit of inquiring whether there were any jobs "for Cousin Jack in the old country."
2. Helena managed to keep her temper. She even smiled through the filming. Though she really felt that TV exposure was unlikely to help their cause.
3. Streptomycin was discovered by isolating a chicken-disease fungus. The two isolated cultures for the research coming from the throat of a sick chicken and the other from field soil.
4. Henri, knowing that the interview would decide whether he got the job, determining to appear calm and confident. His determination paid off.

5. With exams coming up soon and only two full weekends for study. John became nervous.

6. Why she had gone to the trouble of repainting the wall he didn't understand. He hadn't himself seen anything wrong with the colour.

7. The town dump in Bella Coola has become a rather sad local attraction. Not only for the bears who forage there, but for the townspeople who take their visitors there to watch the bears.

8. Some photographs were not intended as works of art—for example the portraits of well-to-do Montrealers taken by William Notman in the last century. They are now collected by art museums, however.

9. The Notman photographs are valued not only because they are visual records of the nineteenth-century merchant class. But also because they are images featuring beautiful composition in black and white.

10. Pinball machines have developed from relatively primitive electronic games into computerized wonders. Complicated story lines, two or three playing levels, and devices to send balls rocketing at remarkable speed are features of the new machines.

■ **Exercise 4** Each of the following paragraphs has *nine* fragments. Find the fragments. Revise each fragment by attaching it logically to an adjacent sentence or by rewriting the fragment so that it stands as an independent sentence.

(a) ¹The little paperback almanac I found at the newsstand has given me some fascinating information. ²Not just about the weather and changes in the moon. ³There are also intriguing statistics. ⁴A tub bath, for example, requires more water than a shower. ⁵In all probability, forty or forty-five litres more, depending on how dirty the bather is. ⁶And one of the Montezumas downed fifty jars of cocoa every day. ⁷Which seems a bit exaggerated to me. ⁸To say the least. ⁹I also learned that an average beard has thirteen thousand whiskers. ¹⁰That, in the course of a lifetime, a man could shave off more than eight metres of whiskers, over eight hundred centimetres. [11]If my math is correct. [12]Some other interesting facts in the almanac. [13]Suppose a person was born on Sunday, February 29, 1976. [14]Another birthday not celebrated on Sunday until the year 2004. [15]Because February 29 falls on weekdays till then—twenty-eight birthdays later. [16]As I laid the almanac aside, I remembered that line in *Slaughterhouse Five:* "So it goes."

(b) [1]Roger and Simone discussed the problem of junk mail as they put out the trash on Saturday, both of them increasingly irritated by the sea of paper flooding in. [2]Roger told Simone that he had read that paper comprises up to 35 percent of the garbage generated in major cities. [3]This certainly seemed to be true. [4]In their household. [5]Knowing the papers were bound for the blue boxes. [6]They sorted them for recycling, the newspaper flyers going into one pile and the other papers into a "mixed paper" pile. [7]Resentful of the time spent sorting and tying and carrying. [8]They began to consider what they could do. [9]"Of course, we could use less paper ourselves," said Roger. [10]"True," said Simone, "but that wouldn't solve the problem with the junk mail. [11]Our real problem." [12]They considered incinerating junk mail for home heat. [13]Not enough to make a difference in the winter and not a useful suggestion for the summer. [14]Burning the trash was a fantasy, however. [15]Since much printed matter contains lead-based ink, plastic, and residual dioxins from bleaching paper. [16]Such materials are not environmentally suited for indiscriminate burning, appropriate disposal facilities being needed. [17]Simone proposed another method for ridding themselves of some junk mail. [18]Not only safer, but one that would send a message to those generating the mail. [19]Determined to deal with at least some of the nuisance. [20]They put a plan into action. [21]They picked out all the business-reply-mail envelopes supplied for return responses. [22]They would send back to the point of origin any mail with a return. [23]A sense of victory—very small and very personal—cheering them on in their cleaning efforts. [24]They returned to the sorting.

Comma Splice and Fused Sentence

3

Do not link two main clauses with only a comma (comma splice) or run two main clauses together without any punctuation (fused sentence).

The terms *comma splice* and *fused sentence* (also called *comma fault* and *run-on sentence*) refer to errors in punctuation that occur only in compound (or compound-complex) sentences.

COMMA SPLICE
The current was swift, he could not swim to shore. [only a comma between main clauses]

FUSED SENTENCE
The current was swift he could not swim to shore. [no punctuation between the main clauses]

You can correct either a comma splice or a fused sentence without changing your meaning by (1) placing a period after the first main clause and writing the second main clause as a sentence, (2) using a semicolon to separate the main clauses, or (3) using a comma before you insert an appropriate co-ordinating conjunction (*and, but, or, nor, for, so, yet*) to link and relate the main clauses.

> REVISIONS
> The current was swift. He could not swim to shore.
> The current was swift; he could not swim to shore.
> The current was swift, **so** he could not swim to shore.

When you use the second method of revision, keep in mind that the semicolon separates two grammatically equal units of thought: **Subject + predicate; subject + predicate.** As you proofread your papers to check for comma splices and as you make revisions, do not overuse the semicolon or use it between parts of unequal grammatical rank: see **14c.**

Often a more effective way to revise a comma splice or fused sentence is to make one clause subordinate to the other: see **24b.**

> REVISIONS
> The current was so swift that he could not swim to shore.
> Because the current was swift, he could not swim to shore.

A subordinate clause may be reduced to a phrase and used as a part of a simple sentence: "*Because of the swift current,* he could not swim to shore."

If you cannot always recognize a main clause and distinguish it from a phrase or a subordinate clause, study Section **1,** especially **1d** and **1e.**

3a

Use a comma between main clauses only when they are linked by the co-ordinating conjunctions *and, but, or, for, nor, so,* or *yet*. See also **12a.**

COMMA SPLICE   Canada observed its centennial in 1967, the United States celebrated its bicentennial in 1976.

REVISED   Canada observed its centennial in 1967, **and** the United States celebrated its bicentennial in 1976. [the co-ordinating conjunction *and* added after the comma]
OR
Canada observed its centennial in 1967; the United celebrated its bicentennial in 1976. [A semicolon separates the main clauses: see **14a.**]

COMMA SPLICE   Her first novel was not a bestseller, it was not a complete failure either.

REVISED   Her first novel was not a bestseller, **nor** was it a complete failure. [Note the shift in the word order of subject and verb after the co-ordinating conjunction *nor.*]
OR
Her first novel was **neither** a bestseller **nor** a complete failure. [a simple sentence with a compound complement]

COMMA SPLICE   The old tree stumps grated against the bottom of our boat, they did not damage the propeller.

REVISED   The old tree stumps grated against the bottom of our boat, **but** they did not damage the propeller. [the co-ordinating conjunction *but* added after the comma]
OR
Although the old tree stumps grated against the bottom of our boat, they did not damage the propeller. [Addition of *although* makes the first clause subordinate: see **12b.**]

Caution: Do not omit punctuation between main clauses not linked by *and, but, or, for, nor, so,* and *yet.*

FUSED SENTENCE She brought him a novel he read it in single afternoon.

REVISED She bought him a novel. He read it in a single afternoon. [each main clause written as a sentence]
OR
She bought him a novel; he read it in a single afternoon. [main clauses separated by a semicolon: see **14a.**]

Note 1: Either a comma or a semicolon may be used between short main clauses not linked by *and, but, or, for, nor, so,* or *yet* when the clauses are parallel in form and unified in thought:

School bores them, preaching bores them, even television bores them. —ARTHUR MILLER
One is the reality; the other is the symbol. —NANCY HALE

Note 2: The comma is used to separate a statement from a tag question:

He votes, doesn't he? You can't change it, can you?

■ **Exercise 1** Connect each pair of sentences below in two ways, first with a semicolon and then with one of these co-ordinating conjunctions: *and, but, for, or, nor, so,* or *yet.*

EXAMPLE
I could have walked up the steep trail. I preferred to rent a horse.
  a. *I could have walked up the steep trail; I preferred to rent a horse.*
  b. *I could have walked up the steep trail,* **but** *I preferred to rent a horse.*

EXAMPLE

They should have bought a good-quality tent fly. It would have guaranteed them a dry place to sleep.

a. *They should have bought a good-quality tent fly; it would have guaranteed them a dry place to sleep.*

b. *They should have bought a good-quality tent fly, **for** it would have guaranteed them a dry place to sleep.*

1. The stakes were high in the political game. She played to win.
2. The belt was too small for him. She had to exchange it.
3. At the cineplex, they watched the musical comedy in one theatre. We enjoyed the horror movie in another.
4. He never allows himself the luxury of a break. He doesn't seem to understand why others may need one.
5. He may be very demanding about practice at the barre. He also has the best interests of the ballet company at heart.
6. Some call him a crackpot. Others think he is a visionary.
7. She's not an accomplished painter. You have to admit she uses colour very well.
8. I enjoy her lectures. Most of what she presents is new to me.
9. I decided to take a nap before proofreading my essay. I knew I had to be very alert to check it carefully.
10. He claims to be an activist. He refuses to participate in any public protest.

■ **Exercise 2**   Use a subordinating conjunction (see the list on page 24) to combine each of the ten pairs of sentences in Exercise 1. For the use of the comma, refer to **12b.**

EXAMPLE

Although *I could have walked up the steep trail, I preferred to rent a horse.*

EXAMPLE

Because it would have guaranteed them a dry place to sleep, a good-quality tent fly would have been a wise purchase.

■ **Exercise 3**   Proofread the following sentences. Place a check mark after a sentence with a comma splice and an X after a fused sentence. Do not mark correctly punctuated sentences.

1. In the former Soviet Union, old ghosts of nationality and ideology have risen, Armenians have been set against the Kazakhs, for example.
2. Canada needs new markets for its exports those markets may lie in the Pacific Rim.
3. Alfred Nobel established the Nobel prizes, which are awarded each year in the categories of physics, chemistry, medicine, economics, literature, and peace.
4. The telephone woke me up twice last night after midnight I decided to leave it off the hook.
5. Historical guilt is the root of many problems today for those who need an excuse for hatred, blaming today's German youth for Nazi atrocities is convenient.
6. When a virus enters a computer system, it attacks and destroys memory.
7. The rains fell for three days straight, by the fourth day the road was blocked by several mudslides.
8. The Chinese New Year begins with the first moon in Aquarius, and so it falls between 21 January and 19 February in any given year.
9. The history that we studied in school was inadequate in one respect, it failed to focus on the culture and heritage of Native peoples.
10. I once thought that poetry was incomprehensible, a puzzle to be solved only by experts, but now I can read it with pleasure and without puzzlement.

■ **Exercise 4**   Use various methods of revision as you correct the comma splices or fused sentences in Exercise 3.

3b

Be sure to use a semicolon before a conjunctive adverb or transitional phrase placed between main clauses. See also **14a.**

COMMA SPLICE	TV weather maps have various symbols, for example, a big apostrophe means drizzle.
REVISED	TV weather maps have various symbols; for example, a big apostrophe means drizzle. [MAIN CLAUSE; transitional expression, MAIN CLAUSE.]
FUSED SENTENCE	The tiny storms cannot be identified as hurricanes therefore they are called neutercanes.
REVISED	The tiny storms cannot be identified as hurricanes; therefore they are called neutercanes. [MAIN CLAUSE; conjunctive adverb MAIN CLAUSE.]

Below is a list of frequently used conjunctive adverbs and transitional phrases.

CONJUNCTIVE ADVERBS

also	incidentally	nonetheless
anyway	indeed	otherwise
besides	instead	still
consequently	likewise	then
finally	meanwhile	therefore
furthermore	moreover	thus
hence	nevertheless	
however	next	

TRANSITIONAL PHRASES

after all	even so	in the second place
as a result	for example	on the contrary
at any rate	in addition	on the other hand
at the same time	in fact	
by the way	in other words	

Unlike a co-ordinating conjunction, which has a fixed position between the main clauses it links, many conjunctive adverbs and transitional phrases may either begin the second main clause or take another position in it.

She doubted the value of daily meditation; **however,** she decided to try it. [The conjunctive adverb begins the second main clause. See also **14a,** pages 174–75.]

She doubted the value of daily meditation; she decided, **however**, to try it. [The conjunctive adverb (set off by commas) appears later in the clause.]

COMPARE   She doubted the value of daily meditation, **but** she decided to try it. [The co-ordinating conjunction has a fixed position.]

■**Exercise 5**   Write five correctly punctuated compound sentences using various conjunctive adverbs and transitional phrases to connect and relate main clauses.

3c
Do not let a divided quotation trick you into making a comma splice.

COMMA SPLICE   "Who won the lottery?" he asked, "how much money was in the jackpot?"

REVISED   "Who won the lottery?" he asked. "How much money was in the jackpot?"

COMMA SPLICE   "Injustice is relatively easy to bear," says Mencken, "It is justice that hurts."

REVISED   "Injustice is relatively easy to bear," says Mencken; "it is justice that hurts."

■**Exercise 6**   Divide the following quotations without creating a comma splice, as shown in the example below.

EXAMPLE
Oscar Wilde once wrote, "Anyone can make history. Only a great man can write it."
"Anyone can make history," Oscar Wilde once wrote. "Only a great man can write it."

1. "Those who talk about the future are scoundrels. It is the present that matters," wrote Louis Ferdinand Céline.
2. It was Barbara Tuchman who said, "Books are the carriers of civilization. Without books, history is silent, literature dumb, science crippled, thought and speculation at a standstill."
3. Bernard Shaw once said, "I must have been an insufferable child; all children are."
4. "I am saddest when I sing. So are those who hear me," Artemus Ward commented.
5. Auguste Rodin said, "I invent nothing. I rediscover."

■ **Exercise 7**   Correct the comma splices and fused sentences in the following paragraph. Do not revise a correctly punctuated sentence.

[1]"Age is just a frame of mind," Annie often says, "you're as old or as young as you think you are." [2]Does she really believe this, or is she just making conversation? [3]Well, when she was seventeen, her father said, "Annie, you're not old enough to marry Johnny, besides he's a city boy." [4]So Annie ran away from her Melville, Saskatchewan, home in Toronto she found another city boy, Frank, and married him. [5]When Annie was thirty-nine, Frank died. [6]A year later she shocked everyone by marrying William, he was a seventy-seven-year-old veteran of the Boer War. [7]"Billy thinks young," Annie explained, "and he's just as young as he thinks he is." [8]Maybe she was right that happy marriage lasted eighteen years. [9]Annie celebrated her seventieth birthday by going to Australia, there she married Tom, who in her opinion was a youngster in his late sixties. [10]But her third marriage didn't last long because Tom soon fell ill and died, still Annie went on with her life. [11]In 1980, when Annie was eighty-three, she found and finally married her childhood sweetheart, then eighty-seven-year-old Johnny whisked her away to his home in Montreal. [12]Annie's fourth wedding made front-page news in Melville, and then the whole town echoed Annie's words: "Life doesn't begin at sixteen or at forty. It begins when you want it to, age is just a frame of mind."

■ **Exercise 8** First, review Section **2** and study Section **3.** Then proofread the following for sentence fragments, comma splices, and fused sentences. Make appropriate revisions. Put a check mark after each sentence that needs no revision.

1. Lily first visited the museum, then she strolled through the park.
2. The plaza was originally designed to attract office workers tourists use it now. Not to mention vendors and street musicians.
3. They wish to help the homeless, however, they are not prepared to pay higher taxes for the purpose.
4. The Canadian Club hosts political figures, it is not, however, a partisan political organization.
5. Pierre Trudeau attended the London School of Economics, where he studied modern economic theory.
6. In 1988, some Canadians expressed concern about the Canada–U.S. Free Trade Agreement. The reason being that social programs might be threatened by the pact.
7. Our choir will go to Holland in May, when the tulip gardens are especially beautiful.
8. A long article in the magazine describes botulism, this is just another name for food poisoning.
9. That is absurd. It's nonsense. An argument that is riddled with stupid assumptions.
10. After class, I often drop by the college bookstore. Usually buying bestselling paperbacks, then never getting around to reading any of them.

Adjectives and Adverbs

4

Distinguish between adjectives and adverbs and use the appropriate forms.

Adjectives and adverbs are modifiers. Modifiers qualify or limit the meaning of other words. As you study the following examples, observe that (1) the adjectives modify nouns or pronouns and (2) the adverbs modify verbs, adjectives, or other adverbs.

ADJECTIVES	ADVERBS
the **sudden** change	changed **suddenly**
a **brief, dramatic** one	a **briefly** dramatic one
armed squads	**very heavily** armed squads
She looked **angry.**	She looked **angrily** at me.
He made the cheque **good.**	He made the speech **well.**

Adverbs may also modify verbals (gerunds, infinitives, participles) or even whole clauses.

The *-ly* ending can be an adjective-forming suffix as well as an adverb-forming one.

NOUNS TO ADJECTIVES	earth—earthly, ghost—ghostly
ADJECTIVES TO ADVERBS	rapid—rapidly, lucky—luckily

A number of words ending in *-ly* (such as *deadly, cow-ardly*), as well as many not ending in *-ly* (such as *far, fast, little, well*), may function either as adjectives or as adverbs. Some adverbs have two forms (such as *quick, quickly; slow, slowly; loud* and *clear, loudly* and *clearly*).

When in doubt about the correct use of a given modifier, consult your dictionary. Look for the labels *adj.* and *adv.,* for comparative and superlative forms, for examples of usage, and for any usage notes.

4a
Use adverbs to modify verbs, adjectives, and other adverbs.

> NOT   Jack Nicholson played Jimmy Hoffa just perfect.
> BUT   Jack Nicholson played Jimmy Hoffa just **perfectly.**
> [The adverb modifies the verb *played.*]

> NOT   The plane departs at a reasonable early hour.
> BUT   The plane departs at a **reasonably** early hour. [The adverb modifies the adjective *early.*]

Most dictionaries still label the following as informal usage: *sure* for *surely, real* for *really,* and *good* for the adverb *well.*

> INFORMAL   The Flames played **real good** during the first period.
> GENERAL   The Flames played **extremely well** during the first period. [appropriate in both formal and informal usage—see also **19b.**]

■ **Exercise 1** In each phrase, convert the adjective into an adverb, following the pattern of the examples.

EXAMPLE
abrupt reply—*replied abruptly* [OR *abruptly replied*]

1. brave defence   3. casual remark   5. prompt response
2. calm behaviour   4. particular notice   6. sincere belief

EXAMPLE
complete happiness—*completely happy*

7. near possibility	9. sudden popularity	11. excessive suspicion
8. unusual anger	10. strange sadness	12. significant absence

■ **Exercise 2** In the following sentences, convert any non-standard or informal modifier into an adverb form. Put a check mark after each sentence that needs no revision.

1. He sure could tune a carburetor good.
2. Everyone there was surprised by how sweet she sang in the solo part.
3. Last night the stars seemed exceptionally clear and bright.
4. Ella's mother commented on how strange her friend Alan dressed.
5. They treat the visiting singing teacher in a real respectful way, for she had been the voice coach of Luciano Pavarotti for several years.
6. Although they don't get together very regular, they chat as if they were continuing a conversation begun the day before.
7. My notes are hard to read when I have to write that rapid.
8. They act as though they are special privileged in some way.
9. Of course, the trains in the loading yard bang about pretty badly sometimes.
10. They are an international known accounting firm, specializing in film finances.

4b

Distinguish between adverbs used to modify the verb and adjectives used as a subject complement or an object complement.

NOT   The honeysuckle smells sweetly in the morning. [The adverb *sweetly* does not modify the verb *smells*.]

BUT   The honeysuckle smells **sweet** in the morning. [The adjective *sweet* is a subject complement.]

NOT   We painted the sign careful. [The adjective *careful* does not modify the noun *sign*.]

BUT   We painted the sign **carefully.** [The adverb *carefully* modifies the verb *painted*.]

Subject complements (usually adjectives, nouns, or pronouns) refer to the subject, but they are part of the predicate and help to complete the meaning of linking verbs—such as *feel, look, smell, sound, taste,* and forms of the verb *be.* When used as subject complements, adjectives always modify the subject.

```
SUBJECT + LINKING VERB + SUBJECT COMPLEMENT.
```

The speech sounded **bold.**
The soup tastes **different** with these herbs in it.

Object complements (usually adjectives or nouns) refer to, identify, or qualify the direct object as they help to complete the meaning of such verbs as *make, name, elect, call, find, consider.* When used as object complements, adjectives always modify the object.

```
SUBJECT + VERB + DIRECT OBJECT + OBJECT COMPLEMENT.
```

These herbs make the soup **different.**
He considered the speech **bold.**

Either an adverb or an adjective may follow a direct object; the choice depends on meaning, on the word modified:

> He considered Jane **angrily.** [The adverb *angrily* modifies the verb *considered*.]
>
> He considered Jane **angry.** [An object complement, *angry* modifies the noun *Jane.*]

Caution: Do not omit the *-d* or *-ed* of a past participle used as an adjective. (See also **7a,** pages 89–90.)

> NOT   The diver was experience.
>
> BUT   The diver was **experienced**. [Compare "an experienced diver."]

■ **Exercise 3**   Using adjectives as complements, write two sentences that illustrate each of the following patterns.

Subject + linking verb + subject complement.
Subject + verb + direct object + object complement.

■ **Exercise 4**   Look up each pair of modifiers in your dictionary. Give special attention to specific examples of usage and to any usage notes. Then write sentences of your own to illustrate the formal use of each modifier.

> EXAMPLE
> bad, badly—*I felt bad. I played badlly.*

1. slow, slowly	3. awful, awfully	5. most, almost
2. real, really	4. good, well	6. quick, quickly

4c

Use the appropriate forms of adjectives and adverbs for the comparative and the superlative. See also **22c.**

Many adjectives and adverbs change form to indicate degree. As you study the following examples, notice that the term *positive* refers to the simple, uncompared form of the adjective or adverb.

POSITIVE	COMPARATIVE	SUPERLATIVE
cold	colder	coldest
warmly	more warmly	most warmly
sturdy	sturdier	sturdiest
helpful	more helpful	most helpful
fortunate	less fortunate	least fortunate
good, well	better	best
bad, badly	worse	worst
far	farther, further	farthest, furthest
little	less OR littler	least OR littlest

In general, many of the shorter adjectives (and a few adverbs) form the comparative degree by the addition of *-er* and the superlative by the addition of *-est*. Some two-syllable adjectives, especially those ending in a vowel sound (like *dirty, shallow*), regularly take the *-er* and *-est* endings. The longer adjectives and most adverbs form the comparative by the use of *more* (or *less*) and the superlative by the use of *most* (or *least*). A few modifiers have irregular comparatives and superlatives.

(1) Use the comparative to denote a greater degree or to refer to two in a comparison.

The metropolitan area is much **bigger** now than it once was.

Bert can run **faster** than his father.
Dried apples are **more** nutritious per kilogram than fresh apples. [a comparison of two groups]

With the use of *other,* the comparative form may refer to more than two.

Surinder can run **faster** than the *other* players.

(2) Use the superlative to denote the greatest degree or to refer to three or more in a comparison.

The interests of the family are **best** served by open com-
munication.
Kate is the **fastest** of the three runners.
OR Kate is the **fastest** runner of all.

The superlative occasionally refers to two, as in "Put your
best foot forward!" and "Both of us had a cold, but mine
was the *worst.*"

Note: Current usage, however illogical it may seem,
accepts comparisons of many adjectives or adverbs with
absolute meanings, such as "a *more perfect* society," "the
deadest campus," and "*less completely* exhausted." But
many writers make an exception of *unique*—using "*more
nearly* unique" rather than "more unique." They consider
unique an absolute adjective—one without degrees of
comparison.

(3) **Do not use a double comparison.**

NOT   Our swimming hole is much more shallower than
       Lake Louise. [double comparative: *-er* and *more*]
BUT   Our swimming hole is much **shallower** than Lake
       Louise. [deletion of the comparative *more*]
NOT   That was the most funniest situation. [double superla-
       tive: *-est* and *most*]
BUT   That was the **funniest** situation. [deletion of the
       superlative *most*]

■ **Exercise 5**   Give the comparative and superlative of each
adjective or adverb.

1. dangerous	5. mellow	9. thick
2. enthusiastically	6. restrictive	10. thickly
3. frightened	7. scared	11. wise
4. hungry	8. sedately	12. wittily

■ **Exercise 6** Fill in each blank by using the appropriate comparative or superlative form of the modifier given at the beginning of each sentence.

1. *good*   Francis Ford Coppola's *Dracula* was decidedly the _____ of all the films made of Bram Stoker's novel.

2. *scary*   He thought that parts of *Beauty and the Beast* were more disturbing than the _____ bits in *Fantasia.*

3. *zany*   A _____ comedy ensemble than Newfoundland's Codco is hard to imagine.

4. *hollow*   As the barrel goes from half empty to empty, the sound grows _____.

5. *bad*   Of the two, this choice seems the _____.

6. *mature*   Naturally, a person's outlook on life is _____ at eighteen than at sixteen.

7. *useful*   The _____ tool of all is a screwdriver.

8. *little*   Some smokers are _____ considerate than others.

9. *strong*   Who in that quartet has the _____ voice?

10. *patient*   A _____ adviser you cannot expect to find.

4d

Avoid awkward or ambiguous use of a noun form as an adjective.

Many noun forms are used to modify other nouns (as in *reference* manual, *capital gains* tax, *Food and Agriculture* Organization), especially when appropriate adjectives are not available. But such forms should be avoided when they are either awkward or confusing.

AWKWARD	Many candidates entered the mayor race.
BETTER	Many candidates entered the mayoral race.
CONFUSING	The George Bush North American Free Trade Agreement was already signed when Bill Clinton took office in 1993.
BETTER	George Bush had already signed the North American Free Trade Agreement when Bill Clinton took office in 1993.

4e
Do not use the double negative.

The term *double negative* refers to the use of two negatives to express a single negation. Like the double comparison, the double negative is grammatically redundant.

NON-STANDARD	He did not keep no records. [double negative: *not* and *no*]
STANDARD	He did not keep any records. [one negative: *not*]
	OR
	He kept no records. [one negative: *no*]

If used with an unnecessary negative like *not, nothing,* or *without,* the modifiers *hardly, barely,* and *scarcely* are still considered non-standard.

NON-STANDARD	I couldn't hardly quit in the middle of the job.
STANDARD	I **could hardly** quit in the middle of the job.
NON-STANDARD	Hardly nothing was in its right place.
STANDARD	**Hardly anything** was in its right place.
NON-STANDARD	The motion passed without scarcely a protest.
STANDARD	The motion passed **with scarcely** a protest.

The use of two negatives to express a positive is acceptable and can be effective.

> We can**not** afford to stand by and do **nothing** about child abuse. [a positive meaning: We have to do something about it.]

■ **Exercise 7**   Eliminate double negatives in the following sentences.

1. They don't have no home.
2. It was so noisy I couldn't hardly hear myself think.
3. We never do nothing but talk about the weather.
4. We needed gas but couldn't buy none.
5. The club didn't scarcely have any money left.
6. The muffin I ate for breakfast was so large that I won't hardly need any lunch.
7. They didn't have no place to go.
8. Even though we lined up on the first day of sales, we couldn't get no tickets for the concert.
9. Rachel and Alex didn't scarcely have any money left after buying all their course books.
10. The food looked good, but she couldn't eat none of it because she was nervous.

■ **Exercise 8**   After you have reread rules **4a** through **4e** and have studied the examples, correct all errors in the use of adjectives or adverbs in the following sentences. Also eliminate any awkward use of nouns as adjectives. Put a check mark after any sentence that needs no revision.

1. The magazine has been published continuous since 1951, but it does not sell good now.
2. Adding chopped onions and jalapeños to the chili makes it taste real well.
3. According to Environment Canada, December is supposed to be our most wettest month, but we've barely received a drop of rain.
4. It was easily the largest deficit in history.

5. Because it was filled to capacity with abandon dogs, the shelter was more noisier than usual.
6. The repair estimates mechanic was out to lunch.
7. Our class enjoyed writing autobiography compositions.
8. My sister seems much more happier now that she has returned to college.
9. It was a really interesting hockey game between a well-coached team and a group of naturally good athletes.
10. A favourite device of detective novels authors is to cast suspicion on seeming innocent characters.

■ **Exercise 9** Correct all errors in the use of adjectives or adverbs in the following paragraph and eliminate awkward use of nouns for adjectives. Make a note of any sentence that needs no revision.

¹The Action News Service was a distinguished one, for it had provided stories continuous since World War II. ²It had a reputation for providing coverage that was unbias. ³When Erin saw Action's advertisement for a reporter in the trade paper, she was excited, and even more excited when she got the job. ⁴After working for *Happy Families* magazine for three years, she was real happy to get a job with Action. ⁵She was sure she would be more contenter there than at the magazine. ⁶However, she was given the rather dull task of checking biography details for features. ⁷She hadn't barely worked there a month when she began to worry that she would not be much more happier at all. ⁸Then her editor gave her the seeming innocent task of interviewing a candidate intending to run for public office in a small town. ⁹He was most reluctant to be interviewed. ¹⁰She finally persuaded him that he needed an opportunity to convince voters that he was much the better of the three candidates. ¹¹What she was not supposed to discover she discovered in just two days of real exciting investigation: his entry into the mayor campaign was being financed by a crime organization. ¹²His small town was to become a safe centre for drug distribution. ¹³Erin's interview became national news. ¹⁴She couldn't have had no better break as a beginning news reporter.

Case

5

Choose the case form that shows the function of nouns and pronouns in sentences.

Case refers to the form of a noun or pronoun that shows its relation to other words in a sentence. For example, the different case forms of the boldfaced pronouns below, all referring to the same person, show their different uses.

> **I** [the subject] believe that **my** [adjectival] uncle will help **me** [direct object].

I is in the subjective (or nominative) case; *my,* in the possessive (or genitive); *me,* in the objective.

Nouns and some indefinite pronouns have a distinctive form only in the possessive case: a student**'s** opinion, the students**'** opinions, everyone**'s** vote. See **15a.**

As you study the following tables, observe that the pronouns *I, we, he, she, they,* and *who* have distinctive forms for all three cases.

PERSONAL PRONOUNS

Notice that some of the personal pronouns listed in the following table—*my, our, your, him, her, it,* and *them*—are also used as parts of *-self* pronouns. (Formal English does not, however, accept *myself* as a substitute for *I* or *me*. See **intensive/reflexive pronoun,** page 669.)

	SUBJECTIVE	POSSESSIVE	OBJECTIVE
Singular			
1st person	I	my, mine	me
2nd person	you	your, yours	you
3rd person	he, she, it	his, her, hers, its	him, her, it
Plural			
1st person	we	our, ours	us
2nd person	you	your, yours	you
3rd person	they	their, theirs	them

THE RELATIVE PRONOUNS *WHO* AND *WHICH*

	SUBJECTIVE	POSSESSIVE	OBJECTIVE
Singular OR	who	whose	whom
Plural	which	whose	which

Although *who, whose,* and *whom* ordinarily refer to people, the possessive pronoun *whose* (in lieu of an awkward *of which*) sometimes refers to things: "The poem, *whose* author is unknown, has recently been set to music."

The subject of a verb and a subject complement are in the subjective case.

SUBJECTIVE   **We** left early. **Who** noticed? [subjects of verbs]
That was **he** at the door. [subject complement]

The possessive case indicates ownership or a comparable relationship: see **15a** Nouns and pronouns in the possessive case ordinarily serve as adjectivals, but a few pronouns (such as *mine* and *theirs*) take the position of nouns and function as subjects, objects, and so on. The possessive is used before a gerund (an *-ing* verbal serving as a noun).

POSSESSIVE **Their** cat likes **its** new leash. [adjectivals]
I resent **his** confusing one example with proof.
[before gerund]

The object of a verb, verbal, or preposition and the subject of an infinitive are in the objective case.

OBJECTIVE Hans blamed **me.** [direct object]
Feeding **them** is a nuisance. [object of verbal.]
I fried **her** two eggs. [indirect object]
To **whom** was it addressed? [object of preposition]
I didn't want **him** to fail. [subject of infinitive]

APPOSITIVES

Appositives are nouns or pronouns placed next to or very near other nouns or pronouns to identify them, explain them, or supplement their meaning. An appositive has the same case as the word that it refers to.

SUBJECTIVE Some people—for example, **he** and **I**—did not agree. [*He* and *I* refer to *people,* the subject.]
OBJECTIVE The officer ticketed both drivers, **Rita** and **him.** [*Rita* and *him* identify *drivers,* the object.]

5a

Do not let a compound construction trick you into choosing inappropriate forms of pronouns.

I noticed **she and Margaret** carried the chairs.
NOT
I noticed **her and Margaret** carried the chairs.

You will need to decide which form of pronoun is appropriate for what you mean to say. *I noticed **her and Margaret** carried the chairs* is incorrect because *she and Margaret* are the subjects of the verb *carried,* not the objects of *I noticed.*

Subjects, subject complements:

> **She and her brother** play golf on Saturday mornings.
> I thought **he or Dad** would come to my rescue.
> It was **Maria and I** who solved the problem. [See **5f.**]

Objects of prepositions:

> between **you and me**   to **the chef and her**
> except **David and him**   with **Carla and me**

Objects of verb or verbal, subjects of infinitive:

> Rajiv may appoint **you or me.** [direct object]
> They lent **Tom and her** ten dollars. [indirect object]
> He gets nowhere by scolding **Rae or him.** [object of gerund]
> Dad wanted **Sue and me** to keep the old car. [subject of infinitive]

Appositives:

> Two members of the cast, **he and I,** assisted the director [Compare "*He and I,* two members of the cast, assisted the director."]

> The director often calls on her two assistants: **him and me.** [Compare "The director often calls on *him and me,* her two assistants."]

> "Let us, just **you and me,**" he drawled, "sit down and reason together." [Informal English accepts the expression *Let's you and I.*]

Note 1: Do not let an appositive following *we* or *us* cause you to choose the wrong form.

> NOT Us students need this. Don told we students about it.
> BUT **We** students need this. Don told **us** about it.

Note 2: As a rule, speakers and writers place first-person pronouns last in a compound construction—usually as a matter of courtesy (rather than for emphasis).

■ **Exercise 1**   Choose the correct pronoun within the parentheses in each of the following sentences.

1. Everyone except for Sandra and (she, her) plans to go to Casa Loma on Sunday.
2. The director has promised a part in the musical to Michael and (I, me).
3. Are Henry Leung and (they, them) still planning to open an autobody shop?
4. In his opinion, between Leonard Cohen and (he, him) there is a friendly rivalry.
5. Leaving Elizabeth and (he, him) at the library, Martin went on to the computer centre to do his assignment.
6. Either Sylvie Frechette or (he, him) will be there to present the medals to the winners, Eileen and (she, her).
7. When choosing to become engineers, young women like Kimberley and (I, me) have more support than women students had even ten years ago.
8. It was Awneet and (she, her) who invited Claude and (he, him), two of the hottest drummers in town.
9. (He Him) and (I, me) edited the video for our communications class.
10. Since we had only played small parts before, Mack and (I, me) expected Luc and (she, her) to beat us out at the auditions.

5b

Determine the case of each pronoun by how it is used in its own clause.

(1) Who or whoever as the subject of a clause

The subject of a verb in a subordinate clause takes the subjective case, even when the whole clause is used as an object:

I forget **who** won the World Series in 1992. [In its own clause, *who* is the subject of the verb *won*. The complete clause *who won the World Series in 1992* is the object of the verb *forget*.]

He has respect for **whoever** is in power. [*Whoever* is the subject of *is*. The complete clause *whoever is in power* is the object of the preposition *for*.]

(2) Who or whom before *I think, he says*, and so on

Such expressions as *I think, he says, she believes,* and *we know* may follow either *who* or *whom*. The choice depends on the use of *who* or *whom* in its own clause:

Gene is a man **whom** we know well. [*Whom* is the direct object of *know*. Compare "We know him well."]

Gene is a man **who** we know is honest. [*Who* is the subject of the second *is*. Compare "We know that Gene is a man *who* is honest."]

(3) Pronoun after *than or as*

In sentences such as the following, which have implied (rather than stated) elements, the choice of the pronoun form is important to meaning:

She admires Kurt more than **I.** [meaning "more than I do"]

She admires Kurt more than **me.** [meaning "more than she admires me"]

He talks about food as much as **she.** [meaning "as much as she does"]

He talks about food as much as **her.** [meaning "as much as he talks about her"]

Formal usage still requires the use of the subjective case of pronouns in sentences such as the following:

Mr. Chow is older than **I.** [Compare "older than I am."]

Aristotle is not so often quoted as **they.** [Compare "as they are."]

■ **Exercise 2**   Using the case form in parentheses, convert each pair of sentences below into a single sentence.

EXAMPLES

I admire the woman. She cycled from Prince Edward Island to British Columbia. (*who*)
I admire the woman who cycled from Prince Edward Island to British Columbia.

Evelyn consulted an astrologer. She had met him in San Francisco. (*whom*)
Evelyn consulted an astrologer whom she had met in San Francisco.

1. Surely you must remember the name of the French General. He met his death on the Plains of Abraham in 1758. (*who*)
2. Hercule Poirot is a famous detective. Agatha Christie finally kills him off in *Curtain*. (*whom*)
3. Jay and his friends are the ones. According to the dorm supervisor, they have been playing late-night pranks in the dining hall. (*who*)
4. He invited the three Barclay sisters to audition. One of them got the part. (*whom*)
5. Willie de Wit was one of Canada's most outstanding amateur boxers. He won the silver medal in the 1984 Olympics at Los Angeles. (*who*)
6. Annie Oakley was a real person. The life of this western legend inspired the musical *Annie Get Your Gun*. (*whom*)
7. Jack sent the information to every Canadian movie reviewer he could reach. He believed they would make or break his film's reception. (*who*)
8. Some parents make an introvert of an only child. They think they are protecting their offspring. (*who*)
9. The gymnastics instructor knew very well how to prepare her students for international competition. She was trained in Europe. (*who*)
10. Chung scored the winning goal in last night's game. I have told you about him before. (*whom*)

■ **Exercise 3**   In sentences 1 to 5 below, insert *I think* after each *who;* then read each sentence aloud. Notice that *who,* not *whom,* is still the correct case form.

1. George Eliot, who was a woman, wrote *Adam Bede.*
2. It was Margaret Laurence who served for three years as chancellor of Trent University.
3. Maugham, who was an Englishman, died in 1965.
4. I was delighted by the public support for Salman Rushdie, who has received too little in recent years.
5. Pavel Bure, who deserves the adulation of hockey fans, is a fine model for young hockey players.

■ **Exercise 4**   In the sentences below, complete each comparison by using first *they* and then *them.* Prepare to explain the differences in meaning.

1. My roommate likes you as much as _____.
2. The director praised her more than _____.
3. He finds the blue period paintings more interesting than _____.
4. Trina thinks about problems in the Middle East more than _____.
5. The women heroes in the novels were more inspiring than _____.

5c

As a rule, use *whom* for all objects. *See also* **5b.**

In sentences:

> **Whom** do they recommend? [object of the verb *do recommend*]
>
> For **whom** did the board of directors vote? [object of the preposition *for*]
>
> Danny told Beth **whom** to call. Danny told Beth to call **whom?** [object of the infinitive *to call*—see also **5e.**]

In subordinate clauses:

> The artist **whom** she admired has gone away. [object of the verb *admired* in the adjective clause]
>
> This is a friend **whom** I write to once a year. [object of the preposition *to* in the adjective clause]

Formal and informal English accept the omission of *whom* in sentences such as the following:

> The artist she admired has gone away.
>
> This is a friend I write to once a year.

Note: Informal English accepts *who* rather than *whom*, except after a preposition:

> Who do they recommend?   She told me who to call.

■ **Exercise 5** Formalize usage by changing *who* to *whom* when the pronoun functions as an object. Put a check mark after sentences containing *who* correctly used as the subject of a verb or as a subject complement.

1. Who do they intend to send?
2. Who of those present could doubt that?
3. He knows who they will nominate.
4. He knows who will be nominated.
5. You will never guess who I saw at the airport.
6. Everyone knows who they are and what they stand for.
7. I told you that she knows who to call first for help in a crisis.
8. The student who the teacher questioned next had prepared a full answer.
9. To find out who blackmailed who, be sure to watch the last part of *A Life in Ruins.*
10. It seemed during registration week that whoever I asked for directions gave me a map of the campus.

5d

As a rule, use the possessive case immediately before a gerund.

I resented **his** criticizing our every move. [Compare "I resented his criticism, not him."]

Harry's refusing the offer was a surprise. [Compare "Harry's refusal was a surprise."]

The *-ing* form of a verb can be used as a noun (gerund) or as an adjective (participle). The possessive case is not used before participles:

Caroline's radioing the Ski Patrol solved our problem. [*Radioing* is a gerund. Compare "*Her action* solved our problem."]

The **man** sitting at the desk solved our problem. [*Sitting* is a participle. Compare "*He* solved our problem."]

Note: Do not use an awkward possessive before a gerund.

AWKWARD   The board approved of something's being sent to the poor overseas.

BETTER   The board approved of sending something to the poor overseas.

5e

Use the objective case for the subject or the object of an infinitive.

They expected Nancy and **me** to do the scriptwriting. [subject of the infinitive *to do*]

I did not want to challenge Pierre or **him**. [object of the infinitive *to challenge*]

5f

Especially in formal writing, use the subjective case for the subject complement.

> That certainly could be **she** sitting near the front.
> It was **I** who first noticed the difference. [Compare "I was the one who first noticed the difference."]

Informal English accepts *It's me* (*him, her, us,* and *them*).

■ **Exercise 6**   Find and revise all case forms that would be inappropriate in formal writing. Put a check mark after each sentence that needs no revision.

1. As for I and my wife, we prefer the mountains to the seashore, but she likes to camp out more than I.
2. There was no one who would listen to us, no one whom we could turn to for help.
3. It was Al and he who I blamed for me not making that sale.
4. Jack's racing the motor did not hurry Terry or me.
5. It is true that the Americans produce more goods than us, but we usually export more than them.
6. Do Tracy and she want you and me to help them paint the car?
7. Let's you and me tell Harvey who to put in charge of the organization.
8. Just between you and me, I think that her family and she could do these things for themselves.
9. We students wanted higher standards in high school, but most of us graduating seniors did not speak up much.
10. The clerk wanted us—Pierre-Marc and I—to choose one of the newer classical recordings.

■ **Exercise 7**   Find and revise all case forms that would be inappropriate in formal writing. Underline each sentence that needs no revision.

¹Stories of individualists always captivate we readers, and since the appearance of *Crocodile Dundee,* the remarkable

characters of Oz have grabbed our imaginations. [2]Ben Carlin was an Australian who, after seeing an amphibious jeep in action in India during World War II, felt challenged to modify one and drive him around the world—oceans and all. [3]After the war he found a wrecked jeep and spent years rebuilding it himself. [4]The task was probably unthinkable to anyone but he. [5]It was him, a tireless worker who amazed his friends with his dogged efforts, who figured out how to adapt jeep fuel tanks to equip themselves for long-range travel.

[6]In 1950 Carlin and his wife, Elinore (who he had recently married), drove into the sea off the coast of Nova Scotia. [7]Elinore and him made it across the Atlantic to North Africa, though not uneventfully. [8]They survived many trials in their crossing, accounts of which may be found in his book, *Half-Safe*. [9]Perhaps the most unnerving experience that Elinore and himself weathered was a hurricane. [10]After crossing the Mediterranean to Gibraltar, they had a hilarious struggle with the British police, who they encountered at the RAF seaplane ramp. [11]In a scene that wouldn't be out of place in a Monty Python skit, the police demanded the Carlins provide them with proper credentials before being allowed to drive their aquatic jeep onto the Rock. [12]The Carlins tell of the encounter with officers who, they were later to recall, had no curiosity about a jeep's driving up out of the sea or about people as adventurous as them. [13]They seemed interested only in their jobs, specifically in dealing with whomever broke a rule.

[14]The Carlins slowly journeyed to the Channel and across itself to England. [15]In the next three years Ben rebuilt the vehicle and wrote his book. [16]They began to feel strains in their marriage, especially Elinore—though few women seem as patient as her. [17]In 1954 they drove back into the Channel, to go overland to India. [18]Elinore called it quits in India, but Ben continued with an Australian who they had met along the way. [19]They went as far as Japan together. [20]For the drive across the Pacific and on to Anchorage, an American signed on with him. [21]Ben's companion, of who little is known, left him in Alaska. [22]Himself determined to continue, the remarkable Australian completed his circuit of the globe by jeep with a solo trip across Canada.

Agreement

6

Make a verb agree in number with its subject; make a pronoun agree in number with its antecedent.

A verb and its subject or a pronoun and its antecedent agree when their forms indicate the same number or person. Notice below that the singular subject takes a singular verb and that the plural subject takes a plural verb. (If you cannot easily recognize verbs and their subjects, study **1a** and **1b.**)

> SINGULAR   The **car** in the lot **looks** shabby. [car *looks*]
> PLURAL   The **cars** in the lot **look** shabby. [cars *look*]

Lack of subject-verb agreement occurs chiefly in the use of the present tense. Except for forms of *be* and *have* (*you were, he has eaten*), verbs in other tenses do not change form to indicate the number or person of their subjects. For a list of various forms of *be* and the subjects they take, see page 87.

When a pronoun has an antecedent (the word the pronoun refers to), the two words usually agree in number. (See also Section **28.**)

SINGULAR	A **wolf** has **its** own language. [*wolf—its*]
PLURAL	**Wolves** have **their** own language. [*wolves—their*]

Note: A pronoun also agrees with its antecedent in gender. Agreement in gender is usually easy and natural:

the **boy** and **his** mother [masculine]
the **girl** and **her** mother [feminine]
the **garden** and **its** weeds [neuter]

Subject and Verb

6a
Make a verb agree in number with its subject.

As you study the following rules and examples, remember that *-s* (or *-es*) marks plural nouns but singular verbs (those present-tense verbs with third-person singular subjects).

subject + *s*   OR   **verb +** *s*

Whistles blow at noon   A whistle blows at noon.
The egotists like attention.   The egotist likes attention.

(1) **Do not be misled by nouns or pronouns intervening between the subject and the verb or by subjects and verbs with endings that are not clearly sounded.**

The **repetition** of the drumbeats **helps** to stir emotions.
Every **one** of you **is invited** to the panel discussion.
Scientists sift the facts.
The **scientist asks** several pertinent questions.

As a rule, the grammatical number of the subject is not changed by the addition of expressions beginning with such words as *accompanied by, along with, as well as, in addition to, including, no less than, not to mention, together with.*

> **Unemployment** as well as taxes **influences** votes.
> **Taxes,** not to mention unemployment, **influence** votes.

(2) Subjects joined by *and* are usually plural.

> My **parents** and my **uncle do** not **understand** this.
> The **band** and the **team were leading** the parade.
> **Skiing in the Rockies** and **windsurfing at Maui** are similar in several ways. [gerund phrases—compare "Two activities are similar."]

Exceptions: Occasionally, such a compound subject takes a singular verb because the subject denotes one person or a single unit.

> The **inventor** and chief **producer** of the snowmobile was a native of Quebec, Henri Bombardier.
> **Hooting** and **jeering** at public rallies is characteristic of political life in many democracies.

Every or *each* preceding singular subjects joined by *and* calls for a singular verb:

> Every silver knife, fork, and spoon **has** to be counted.
> Each cat and each dog **has** its own toy.

Placed after a plural subject, *each* does not affect the verb form:

> The cats each **have** their own toys.

Some writers use a singular verb when *each* follows a compound subject:

> The cat and the dog each **have** their own toys. [Or, sometimes, "The cat and the dog each *has* its own toy."]

(3) **Singular subjects joined by *or, either . . . or,* or *neither . . . nor* usually take a singular verb.**

Paula or her secretary **answers** the phone on Saturday.
Either the mayor or the premier **is** the keynote speaker.
Neither praise nor blame **affects** her.

If one subject is singular and one is plural, the verb usually agrees with the nearer subject:

Neither the quality nor the prices **have** changed.
Neither the prices nor the quality **has** changed. [Compare "The prices *and* the quality *have* not changed."]

The verb also agrees with the nearer subject in sentences like the following.

Either Pat or **you were** ready for any emergency call.
Either you or **Pat was** ready for any emergency call.

(4) **Do not let inverted word order (VERB + SUBJECT) or the structure *there* + VERB + SUBJECT cause you to make a mistake in agreement.**

VERB + SUBJECT
Hardest hit by the budget cuts **were** Canadian **fishers.**

Among our grandest and longest-lived illusions **is** the **notion** of the noble savage.   — JOHN PFEIFFER

Neither **do drugstores** sell only drugs. [Here *neither* is a conjunction meaning *nor yet.*]

THERE + VERB + SUBJECT
There **is** a **photograph** on the desk.
There **are** several **photographs** on the desk.
There **are light** and **shadow** in the photograph. [Singular subjects joined by *and* usually take a plural verb.]
There **is a child** and **an old man** in the photograph. [If the noun immediately following the verb is preceded by *a* or *an,* the verb often appears in the singular. This usage is considered to be informal.]

(5) **A relative pronoun (*who, which, that*) used as subject has the same number as its antecedent.**

It is the **pharmacist who** often **suggests** a new brand.
Tonsillitis is among those **diseases that are** curable.
This is one of the **local papers that print** a daily horoscope.
[The antecedent of *that* is *local papers*, NOT *one;* several papers print horoscopes.]

BUT

This is the only **one** of the local papers **that prints** a daily horoscope. [*That* refers to *one:* only one paper prints a daily horoscope; the other papers do not. Compare "This is the only local paper that prints . . . "]

It is not better things but better **people that make** better living. —CARLL TUCKER [Compare "Better people (not better things) make better living."]

(6) **When used as subjects, such words as *each, either, neither, one, everybody,* and *anyone* regularly take singular verbs.**

Neither likes the friends of the other.
Each of them **does have** political ambitions.
Everybody in the office **has** tickets.

Subjects such as *all, any, half, most, none,* and *some* may take a singular or a plural verb; the context generally determines the choice of the verb form.

Aiko collects stamps; **some are** worth a lot. [Compare "Some of them are worth a lot."]
The honey was marked down because **some was** sugary. [Compare "Some of it was sugary."]

(7) **Collective nouns (and phrases denoting a fixed quantity) take a singular verb when they refer to the group as a unit and take a plural verb when they refer to individuals or parts of the group.**

Singular (regarded as a unit):

> My **family has** its traditions.
> **The number** of books **is** very small.
> A **billion dollars is** a lot of money.
> The **majority** of food **was** wasted.
> **Two-thirds** of this road **has** been finished.

Plural (regarded as individuals or parts):

> A **number** of students **were** absent.
> The **majority** of us **are** for it.
> **Two-thirds** of these roads **have** been finished.
> The **media have** shaped public opinion. [The use of *media*
> as a singular subject is questionable.]

The use of *data* as a singular noun has gained currency in recent years; many writers, however, prefer to use *data* only as a plural noun.

> PREFERRED   The **data were** accurate.

(8) A linking verb agrees with its subject, not with its complement (predicate noun).

> His **problem is** frequent headaches.
> Frequent **headaches are** his problem.

Note: Because the number of the pronoun *what* depends on the number of the word (or word group) referred to, the verb does agree with its complement in sentences like these:

> What I do, at these times, **is** to change the way the system
> works.   —LEWIS THOMAS [Compare "That is what I do."]

> Of course, what you see in the final commercial **are** pretty
> pictures—the bear in a canoe, the bear in a Jeep, the bear
> padding behind the man.   —JONATHAN PRICE [Compare
> "Pretty pictures are what you see."]

(9) Nouns plural in form but singular in meaning usually take singular verbs. In all doubtful cases, consult a good dictionary.

Nouns that are regularly treated as singular include *economics, electronics, measles, mumps, news,* and *physics.*

> News **is** travelling faster than ever before.
> Physics **has** fascinated my roommate for months.

Some nouns ending in *-ics* (such as *athletics, politics, statistics,* and *tactics*) can be either singular or plural:

> Statistics **is** an interesting subject.
> Statistics **are** often misleading.

(10) The title of a single work or a word spoken of as a word, even when plural in form, takes a singular verb.

> *Thelma and Louise* **sticks** in the memory. [The movie, not the characters, sticks in the memory.]
> "Autumn Leaves" **is** a beautiful song.
> *Kids* **is** informal for *children.*

■**Exercise 1** The following sentences are all correct. Read them aloud, stressing the italicized words. If any sentence sounds wrong to you, read it aloud two or three more times so that you will gain practice in saying and hearing the correct forms.

1. *Doesn't it* make sense?
2. *Neither* employee *observes* the dress code.
3. A *number* in this group *are* affected.
4. The *timing* of these protests *was* poorly *planned.*
5. There *are* several *books* and three *maps* in the car.
6. Neither his *hat* nor his walking *stick was* missing.
7. Every *one* of her students, including Mark, *thinks* she is friendly.
8. Al was the *only one* of the speakers *who was* interesting.

9. There *were* several *excuses* for his behaviour.
10. The *data* for the experiment *were collected* over a period of two years.

■ **Exercise 2** Correct any errors in agreement of subject and verb. Put a check mark after any sentence that needs no correction.

1. The futility of the searches are becoming obvious.
2. There is a cap and two scarves in the box.
3. A woollen cap and a warm scarf are essential.
4. Any one of the proposals—even those with sketchy drawings—were better than no submissions at all.
5. The only one of the painters who were offended by the criticism was Dravinsky.
6. He asked, "Doesn't that allow enough travel time?"
7. I think each of the students have useful suggestions.
8. Every one of the glasses in those shipments is flawed.
9. The media, in his opinion, is wrong to invade the couple's privacy.
10. Bread and peanut butter, his favourite of all snacks, are fattening.

■ **Exercise 3** Choose the correct form of the verb within parentheses in each of the following sentences. Make sure that the verb agrees with its subject according to the rules of formal English.

1. Neither of them (know, knows) when to stop.
2. There (come, comes) to my mind now the names of the two or three people who were most influential in my life.
3. The Lotto prize (was, were) four million dollars.
4. A motel, as well as a lodge and a marina, (serve, serves) fishing crews.
5. Neither Professor Barr nor Professor Neill (think, thinks) that the problem is solved.
6. Attitudes about responsibility, of course, (vary, varies).
7. Every one of the items (was, were) inventoried this month.
8. An understanding of mathematics (is, are) facilitated by a knowledge of number theory.

9. A low wall and a high hedge (provide, provides) privacy for the entrance.
10. Such computers, which (store, stores) personal data, (jeopardize, jeopardizes) the privacy of millions.

Pronoun and Antecedent

6b

Make a pronoun agree in number and gender with its antecedent.

SINGULAR	A lawyer represents **his** or **her** clients.
PLURAL	Lawyers represent **their** clients.
FEMININE	A lawyer represents **her** clients.
MASCULINE	A lawyer represents **his** clients.

(1) Such singular antecedents as *man, woman, person, everybody, one, anyone, each, either, neither, sort*, and *kind* are usually (but not always) referred to by a singular pronoun.

Each of these companies had **its** books audited. [NOT their]
One has to live with **oneself.** [NOT themselves]
A **man** or a **woman** has a duty to follow **his** or **her** conscience. [a pair of antecedents]

Note: Avoid the use of pronouns that exclude either gender or that stereotype male and female roles:

SEXIST	As a person grows up, he must assume responsibility. [excludes females]
SEXIST	As a person grows up, *she* must assume responsibility. [excludes males]
RECAST	As people grow up, they must assume responsibility. [includes both genders]
SEXIST	As a person grows up, *he* must assume *financial* responsibility. [excludes females *and* assumes that male responsibilities are *financial*]
SEXIST	As a person grows up, *she* must assume *domestic* responsibilities. [excludes males *and* assumes that female responsibilities are *domestic*]

RECAST   As people grow up, they must assume domestic and financial responsibility. [includes both genders]

The following sentences illustrate obvious stereotyping of male and female roles:

A *professor* should be thoroughly familiar with *his* materials.

A *primary teacher* must encourage *her* pupils so that they will develop confidence.

A good *secretary* shows *her* excellent skills of organization in many ways.

Include both sexes by using one of the following options:

A professor should be thoroughly familiar with his or her materials. [substitute compound phrase]

Primary teachers must encourage their pupils if they are to develop confidence. [recast in plural]

A good secretary uses excellent skills of organization in many ways. [recast to avoid the pronoun altogether]

Any of these options may change your meaning. Many people consider the compound phrase *his or her* stylistically awkward; many also find the forms *his/her* and *he/she* ugly and bureaucratic. You can almost always rewrite your sentences to avoid them. The most effective options are to recast the sentence in the plural or to avoid the pronoun altogether. Consider the following sentence:

A **person** needs to see **his** dentist once a year.

This sentence can be recast in the following ways:

A person needs to see **the** dentist twice a year.

People need to see **their** dentists twice a year.

Increasingly, however, writers are using plural pronouns to refer to singular antecedents that denote both sexes or either sex.

In fact, the fear of growing old is so great that every aged **person** is an insult and a threat to the society. **They** remind us of our own death.   —SHARON CURTIN

Although avoided in formal writing, the use of a plural pronoun to refer to a singular antecedent is natural or sensible when the gender is unknown or when a singular pronoun would not fit the meaning. Wherever possible, however, recast the sentence to avoid this agreement problem.

INFORMAL   If **anyone** calls while I'm gone, ask **them** to leave a message.

RECAST   While I'm gone, ask **anyone who calls** to leave a message.

INFORMAL   **Everyone** was invited to lunch, but **they** had already eaten.

RECAST   **All** of them were invited to lunch, but **they** had already eaten.

As you make choices about pronouns referring to singular antecedents such as *everyone* and *a person,* consider not only your own preferences but those of your audience.

(2) **Two or more antecedents joined by *and* are referred to by a plural pronoun; two or more singular antecedents joined by *or* or *nor* are referred to by a singular pronoun.**

Andrew and Mikis lost **their** self-confidence.
Did **Andrew or Mikis** lose **his** self-confidence?

If one of two antecedents joined by *or* or *nor* is singular and one is plural, the pronoun usually agrees with the nearer antecedent:

Neither the **package nor** the **letters** had reached **their** destination. [*Their* is closer to the plural antecedent *letters.*]

Stray **kittens or** even an abandoned grown cat has **its** problems finding enough food to survive long. [*Its* is closer to the singular antecedent *cat.*]

(3) Collective nouns are referred to by singular or plural pronouns, depending on whether the collective noun has a singular or plural sense. See also **6a(7).**

Special care should be taken to avoid treating a collective noun as both singular and plural within the same sentence.

INCONSISTENT	The choir **is** writing **their** own music. [singular verb, plural pronoun]
CONSISTENT	The choir **is** writing **its** own music. [both singular]
CONSISTENT	The group of students **do** not agree on methods, but **they** unite on basic aims. [both plural]

■ **Exercise 4**   Make the language of the following sentences inclusive rather than sexist.

1. A doctor who treats his own child shows poor judgement.
2. The nurse is very skilled, keeping track of her patients' improvements in an unobtrusive way.
3. Every lawyer should make sure his receptionist knows which parking place is hers.
4. The child's teacher gave her report to the social worker, who put it on her desk so that she would have it ready for the psychiatrist to use in his testimony.
5. The policeman asked the little old lady if the robber had put her money in his pocket.

■ **Exercise 5**   Following the rules of formal usage, choose the correct pronoun or verb form in parentheses in each sentence.

1. A number of writers (has, have) expressed (his, her and his, his/her, their) concern about sexist usage.

2. If any one of the sisters (needs, need) a ride to school, (she, they) can call Trudy.
3. Neither the pilot nor the flight attendants mentioned the incident when (he, they) talked to reporters.
4. The basketball team (was, were) opportunistic; (it, they) took advantage of every break.
5. If the board of directors (controls, control) the company, (it, they) may vote (itself, themselves) bonuses.

■**Exercise 6** All of the following sentences are correct. Change them as directed in parentheses, revising other parts of the sentence to secure agreement of subject and verb, pronoun and antecedent.

1. A sign in the lab reads: "This computer does only what you tell it to, not what you want it to." (Change *This computer* to *These computers.*)
2. Perhaps this sign was put up by some frustrated students who were having trouble with their computer manuals. (Change *some frustrated students* to *a frustrated student.*)
3. The sign in the lab reminds me of similar problems. A chef, for example, whose vegetables or casserole is ruined in a microwave might think: "This oven reads buttons, not minds." (Change *vegetables or casserole* to *casserole or vegetables.* Change *This oven* to *These ovens.*)
4. All too often what comes out of our mouths is the very opposite of what we intend to say but exposes what we really think. (Change *what* to *the words that.* Change *our* to *one's.*)
5. Two of my instructors, together with a few of my classmates, were talking about such Freudian slips the other day. (Change *Two* to *One.*)
6. Who knows what kind of label is attached to one's computer errors! (Change *kind* to *kinds.*)
7. Then there is the mirror. (Change *the mirror* to *mirrors.*) There are times when people don't like to face mirrors. (Change *people* to *a person.*)
8. At such times a person has to face how he or she actually looks, not how he or she wants to look. (Change *a person* to *people.*)

9. There is another thought that comes to mind. (Change *another thought* to *other thoughts*.)
10. Mirrors reflect images in reverse, so not even in a mirror do we ever see ourselves as we really are. (Change *we* to *one*.)

■ **Exercise 7** In the paragraph below, cross out those verbs that do not agree with their subjects. Replace each verb with the correct form.

¹An accurate record of the number of people in a nation are essential for government planners and policy makers. ²At regular intervals the government conduct a census, asking its citizens to participate in a nationwide "snapshot." ³The name for the statisticians who do such population studies are demographers. ⁴Demographers who work on the census depends on complete and honest answers to the questions on the forms. ⁵Finding out how many people actually live in a location and how many in a particular, defined area of that place require diligence. ⁶Almost everybody, young people as well as older people, have some story about somebody's being missed in the great counting up. ⁷"Be sure to count your visitors," says the directions, but many people forget to do this when the time to fill in the forms actually come. ⁸They tend to fill in the number of people in the house on census day as the same number on a "usual day"—even though two or three visitors to the house is there, and even though one of the children are away at college. ⁹Among the most challenging problems population counters face are the inclination of some individuals to escape detection in the society. ¹⁰Some persons, for example, wishes to evade the notice of immigration officials. ¹¹Others wishes personal details about marital status to remain private. ¹²Falsely answering such questions are illegal, of course, but many citizens do not realize this. ¹³Census Canada, however, have been making greater efforts to tell its participants that information is confidential. ¹⁴After all, as the news tell us, a million dollars are a lot to spend to get faulty information.

Verb Forms

7

Use the appropriate form of the verb.

The forms of verbs and auxiliaries may indicate not only the number and person of their subjects (see **6a**) but also tense, voice, and mood. A change in the form of a verb shows a specific meaning or a grammatical relationship to some other word or group of words in a sentence.

Regular and irregular verbs The way a verb changes form determines its classification as regular or irregular. A regular verb takes the *-d* or *-ed* ending to denote the past tense.

> REGULAR *believe (believes), believed, believing*
> *attack (attacks), attacked, attacking*

Irregular verbs do not take the *-d* or *-ed* ending. They are inflected in various other ways to indicate past tense: see **irregular verb,** page 669.

> IRREGULAR *run (runs), ran, running*
> *eat (eats), ate, eaten, eating*

A few irregular verbs (like *cut* or *hurt*) have the same form in the present and the past tense.

Forms of the verb *be* The most irregular verb in the English language is *be*. It has eight forms: *am, are, is, was, were, be, been, being.*

That may **be** true.   He **was being** difficult.

Below is a list of forms of *be* used with various subjects in the present and the past tense.

PRESENT	I am	you are	he/she/it is	[singular]
	we are	you are	they are	[plural]
PAST	I was	you were	he/she/it was	[singular]
	we were	you were	they were	[plural]

A form of *be* is used with the present participle to form the progressive: **is** *attacking, will* **be** *eating.* A form of *be* is used with a past participle to form the passive: **was** *attacked, had* **been** *eaten.*

Tense *Tense* refers to the form of the verb that indicates time. There are different ways of classifying the number of tenses in English. If you consider only the form changes of single-word verbs, there are only two tenses (present and past); if you consider progressive forms and certain auxiliaries, there are twelve. The usual practice, however, is to distinguish six tenses. Of these six, one refers to the present time, three to the past, and two to the future.

Time	**Tense**	**Verb**
Present:	PRESENT	try, give
Past:	PAST	tried, gave
	PRESENT PERFECT	have tried, have given
	PAST PERFECT	had tried, had given

Time	**Tense**	**Verb**
Future:	FUTURE	will (OR shall) try
		will (OR shall) give
	FUTURE PERFECT	will (OR shall) have tried
		will (OR shall) have given

The forms of the verb used in the following synopsis are
see (sees), saw, seen, seeing (called the principal parts: see
7a).

	Active	*Passive*
PRESENT	see/sees	am/is/are seen
Progressive	am/is/are seeing	am/is/are being seen
PAST	saw	was/were seen
Progressive	was/were seeing	was/were being seen
FUTURE	will see	will be seen
Progressive	will be seeing	will be being seen
PRESENT PERFECT	have/has seen	have/has been seen
Progressive	have/has been seeing	have/has been seen
PAST PERFECT	had seen	had been seen
Progressive	had been seeing	had been being seen
FUTURE PERFECT	will have seen	will have been seen
Progressive	will have been seeing	will have been being seen

The preceding verb forms—the most frequently used for
making assertions or asking questions—are in the indicative mood. In the imperative mood (used for commands or
requests), verbs have only present tense (*see, be seen*). For
verb forms in the subjunctive mood, see **7c**. See also **conjugation,** pages 663–64.

Note: Verbals (including their progressive forms) have
voice and tense.

	Infinitives
PRESENT	to see, to be seen, to be seeing
PRESENT PERFECT	to have seen, to have been seen, to have been seeing
	Participles
PRESENT	seeing, being seen
PAST	seen
PRESENT PERFECT	having seen, having been seen

Gerunds

PRESENT   seeing, being seen
PRESENT PERFECT   having seen, having been seen

7a

Avoid misusing the principal parts of verbs and confusing similar verbs.

NOT   Has the prime minister spoke to the press about this? [misuse of a principal part of the verb *speak*]

BUT   **Has** the prime minister **spoken** to the press about this?

NOT   The hand-carved birds laid on the shelf for years. [confusion of past forms of the similar verbs *lie* and *lay*]

BUT   The hand-carved birds **lay** on the shelf for years.

(1)   Avoid misusing the principal parts of verbs.

The principal parts of a verb include the present form (*see*), which is also the stem of the infinitive (*to see*); the past form (*saw*); and the past participle (*seen*). (See "Principal Parts of Verbs" on pages 90–91.) The present participle (*seeing*) is often considered a fourth principal part.

The *present* form may function as a single-word verb or may be preceded by words such as *do, will, may, could, have to,* or *used to.*

I **ask,** he **does ask,** we **will begin,** it **used to begin**

The *past* form functions as a single-word verb.

He **asked** a few questions.
The show **began** at eight.

When used as part of a simple predicate, the *past participle* as well as the *present participle* always has at least one auxiliary.

He **has asked** them. I **was asked.** I **will be asking** questions.
They **have begun. Had** he **begun?** It **is beginning** to snow.

Both the past and the present participle serve not only as parts of a simple predicate but also as adjectivals: "pastries *baked* last week," "heat waves *rising* from the road." Nouns modified by participles are not sentences: see **2a**.

Caution: Do not omit a needed *-d* or *-ed* because of the pronunciation. For example, although it is easy to remember a clearly pronounced *-d* or *-ed* (*added, repeated*), it is sometimes difficult to remember to add a needed *-d* or *-ed* in such expressions as *had priced them* or *opened it*. Observe the use of the *-d* or *-ed* in these sentences:

> Yesterday I ask**ed** myself: "Is the judge prejudice**d**?"
> He use**d** to smoke. I am not suppose**d** to be the boss.

The following list of principal parts includes both regular and irregular verbs that are sometimes misused.

Principal Parts of Verbs

PRESENT	PAST	PAST PARTICIPLE
arise	arose	arisen
ask	asked	asked
attack	attacked	attacked
awaken	awakened	awakened
become	became	become
begin	began	begun
blow	blew	blown
break	broke	broken
bring	brought	brought
burst	burst	burst
choose	chose	chosen
cling	clung	clung
come	came	come
creep	crept	crept
dive	dived OR dove	dived
do	did	done
drag	dragged	dragged
draw	drew	drawn
drink	drank	drunk OR drank

PRESENT	PAST	PAST PARTICIPLE
drive	drove	driven
drown	drowned	drowned
eat	ate	eaten
fall	fell	fallen
fly	flew	flown
forgive	forgave	forgiven
freeze	froze	frozen
give	gave	given
go	went	gone
grow	grew	grown
happen	happened	happened
know	knew	known
ride	rode	ridden
ring	rang	rung
rise	rose	risen
run	ran	run
see	saw	seen
shake	shook	shaken
shrink	shrank OR shrunk	shrunk OR shrunken
sing	sang	sung
sink	sank OR sunk	sunk
speak	spoke	spoken
spin	spun	spun
spring	sprang	sprung
steal	stole	stolen
sting	stung	stung
stink	stank OR stunk	stunk
swear	swore	sworn
swim	swam	swum
swing	swung	swung
take	took	taken
tear	tore	torn
throw	threw	thrown
wake	woke OR waked	waked OR woken
wear	wore	worn
wring	wrung	wrung
write	wrote	written

Note: Mistakes with verbs sometimes involve spelling errors. Use care when you write troublesome verb forms such as the following:

PRESENT	PAST	PAST PARTICIPLE	PRESENT PARTICIPLE
lead	led	led	leading
loosen	loosened	loosened	loosening
lose	lost	lost	losing
pay	paid	paid	paying
study	studied	studied	studying

■ **Exercise 1**   Respond to the questions in the past tense with a past-tense verb; respond to the questions in the future tense with a present-perfect verb (*have* or *has* + a past participle). Follow the pattern of the examples.

EXAMPLES   Did she criticize Don? *Yes, she criticized Don.*
Will they take it? *They have already taken it.*

1. Did he give it away?
2. Will you run a kilometre?
3. Did the man drown?
4. Will they begin that?
5. Did the wind blow?
6. Will she choose it?
7. Did it really happen?
8. Will the river rise?
9. Did you do that?
10. Will they bring it?
11. Did you spin your wheels?
12. Will they freeze it?
13. Did he cling to that belief?
14. Will they go to the police?
15. Did she know them?
16. Will the fire alarm ring?
17. Did the sack burst?
18. Will he eat it?
19. Did you grow these?
20. Will Bert speak out?

(2) Do not confuse *set* with *sit* or *lay* with *lie*.

Sit means "be seated," and *lie down* means "rest in or get into a horizontal position." To *set* or *lay* something down is to place it or put it somewhere.

Learn the distinctions between the forms of *sit* and *set* and those of *lie* and *lay*.

PRESENT (INFINITIVE)	PAST	PAST PARTICLE	PRESENT PARTICIPLE
(to) sit	sat	sat	sitting
(to) set	set	set	setting
(to) lie	lay	lain	lying
(to) lay	laid	laid	laying

As a rule, the verbs (or verbals) *sit* and *lie* are intransitive; they do not take objects. *Set* and *lay* are usually transitive and therefore take objects. Transitive verbs may be passive as well as active. (If you cannot easily recognize objects of verbs, see **1b**.)

Sit down. **Sitting** down, I thought it over. He **sat** up.

Lie down. I **lay** down. It **was lying** here. **Has** it **lain** here long?

Somebody **had set** the pup in the cart. It **had been set** there.

We **ought to lay** these aside. These **should be laid** aside.

◼ **Exercise 2** Substitute the correct forms of *sit* and *lie* for the italicized word in each sentence. Follow the pattern of the example. Do not change the tense of the verb.

> EXAMPLE I *remained* in that position for twenty minutes.
> I ***sat*** *in that position for twenty minutes.*
> I ***lay*** *in that position for twenty minutes.*

1. Jacques doesn't ever want to *get* down.
2. The dog *stayed* near the luggage.
3. The toy car has been *rusting* in the yard.
4. He often *sleeps* on a park bench.
5. Has it *been* there all along?

◼ **Exercise 3** Without changing the tense of the italicized verb, substitute the correct form of one of the verbs in parentheses at the end of each sentence.

1. Last week we *put* down the new tiles in the hall. (lie/lay)
2. I often *stand* there and watch the tide come in. (sit/set)
3. After lunch Hanna decided to *plop* down for a nap (lie/lay)
4. Dan was *sprawling* on the picnic table. (sit/set)
5. Dan was *putting* up the picnic table. (sit/set)

7b

Learn the meaning of tense forms. Use logical tense forms in sequence.

(1)   Learn the meaning of tense forms.

Although tense refers to time (see page 87), the tense forms do not always agree with divisions of actual time. The present tense, for example, is by no means limited to the present time. As you study the following examples, observe that auxiliaries as well as single-word verbs indicate time.

PRESENT TENSE

I **see** what you meant by that remark. [now, present time]

Maureen **uses** common sense. [habitual action]

Mistakes **are** often **made.** [passive verb, habitual action]

Blind innocence **sees** no evil. [universal or timeless truth]

In 1939 Hitler **attacks** Poland. [historical present]

Conrad **writes** about what he **sees** in the human heart. [literary present]

Officially winter **begins** next week. [present form, used with the adverbial *next week* to denote future time]

I **am learning** from my mistakes. [a progressive form denoting past, present, and (probably) future]

PAST TENSE—past time, not extending to the present

I **saw** the accident. [at a definite time before now]

They **used** makeshift tools. [action completed in the past]

We **were enjoying** our reunion. [a progressive form denoting continuing action in the past]

The accident **was seen** by two people. [passive]

Westerns **used to be** more popular. [Compare "*were* more popular then."]

FUTURE TENSE—at a future time, sometime after now

He **will see** his lawyer.

Shall we **use** a different strategy?

He **will be seeing** his lawyer. [progressive]

A different strategy **will be used.** [passive]

PRESENT PERFECT TENSE—sometime before now, up to now

I **have seen** the movie. [sometime before now]

She **has used** her savings wisely. [up to now]

Has Kevin **been using** his talents?

Deer **have been seen** in those woods.

PAST PERFECT TENSE—before a specific time in the past

Carla **had talked** to me before the game started.

After he **had used** his savings, he applied for a loan.

Had they **been sailing** along the coast before the storm?

At his death their home **had been** on the market for ten years.

FUTURE PERFECT TENSE—before a specific time in the future

The top executive **will have seen** the report by next week.

By the year 2000 I **will have been seeing** my dreams in action. [a rarely used passive, progressive, future-perfect verb]

Note: Sometimes the simple past is used for the past perfect:

Carla **talked** to me before the game started.

Far more frequently the simple future replaces the future perfect:

The top executive **will see** the report by next week.

By the year 2000 I **will be seeing** my dreams in action.

■ **Exercise 4** Prepare to discuss differences in the meaning of the tense forms separated by slashes.

1. It *has rained / had rained* for days.
2. Mary *waxed / did wax / was waxing* the car.
3. Min Hua *teaches / is teaching* Chinese.
4. I *spoke / have spoken* to him about this.
5. The Singers *had sold / will have sold* their house by then.
6. Time *passes / does pass / has passed / had been passing* rapidly.
7. In 1840 Thomas Carlyle *calls / called* time a great mystery, a miracle.

(2) Use logical tense forms in sequence.

Verbs

Notice in the following examples the relationship of each verb form to actual time:

> When the speaker **entered,** the audience **rose.** [Both actions took place at the same definite time in the past.]
>
> I **have ceased** worrying because I **have heard** no more rumours. [Both verb forms indicate action at some time before now.]
>
> When I **had been** at camp four weeks, I **received** word that my application **had been accepted.** [The *had* before *been* indicates a time before that of *received.*]

Infinitives

Use the present infinitive to express action occurring at the same time as, or later than, that of the main verb; use the present-perfect infinitive for action before that of the main verb:

> I am pleased **to meet** you. [present infinitive—for the same time as that of the main verb]
>
> He wanted **to meet** you. He wants **to meet** you. [present infinitives—for time later than *wanted* or *wants*]
>
> He seems **to have met** her before. [present-perfect infinitive—for time before that of the main verb]

Participles

Use the present form of participles to express action occurring at the same time as that of the main verb; use the present perfect form for action before that of the main verb:

> **Walking** along the streets, he met many old friends. [The walking and the meeting were simultaneous.]

> **Having climbed** that mountain, they felt a real sense of achievement. [The climbing took place first; then came their sense of achievement.]

■ **Exercise 5**   Choose the verb form inside parentheses that is the logical tense form in sequence.

1. When the fire sale (ended, had ended), the store closed.
2. Fans cheered as the goal (had been scored, was scored)
3. The team plans (to celebrate, to have celebrated) tomorrow.
4. We should have planned (to have gone, to go) by bus.
5. (Having finished, Finishing) the test, Leslie left the room.
6. (Having bought, Buying) the tickets, Mr. Leung took the children to the circus.
7. The president had left the meeting before it (had adjourned, adjourned).
8. It is customary for ranchers (to brand, to have branded) their cattle.
9. Marilyn had not expected (to see, to have seen) her cousin at the rally.
10. The pond has begun freezing because the temperature (dropped, has dropped).

■ **Exercise 6**   In the following paragraph, fill in the correct form and tense of the verbs inside parentheses.

> EXAMPLE: Although a few other geologists (work) on the Burgess Shale after Walcott's death, major work (do) not (begin) again for another thirty years.

> SOLUTION: Although a few other geologists **worked** on the Burgess Shale after Walcott's death, major work **did** not begin again for another thirty years.

¹The Burgess Shale, located on a breathtaking slope of Mount Wapta in the Rockies, (be) arguably the world's most important fossil formation. ²Three quarries in this band of rock (yield) the fossilized remains of small sea creatures not seen on earth for 530 million years. ³Their age and location (be) not the only reasons these fossils (fascinate) the scientists now working the shale and its specimens. ⁴Up to the present, scientists (be) unable to identify many of the fossil animals. ⁵Numbers of Burgess Shale creatures (belong) to no known family of animals, though the scientist who (stumble) upon the shale in 1909 and (work) on it until his death in 1927 (classify) all of the more than 60,000 specimens he (find) in the shale he (pry) loose. ⁶Today a controversy about classification (rage) among paleontologists. ⁷The fossil animals that Charles Doolittle Walcott (discover) and that other paleontologists (discover) in the shale quarries every summer since 1966 (reveal) a world of weird wonders. ⁸Not surprisingly, the Burgess Shale (be) at the centre of scientists' searches for answers to puzzling questions about early life on earth and even questions about the mechanisms of evolution.

7c

Use the appropriate form of the verb for the subjunctive mood.

Although the subjunctive mood is alive in such fixed expressions as *far be it from me, be that as it may, as it were,* and *God bless you,* it has been largely displaced by the indicative. But a few distinctive forms for the subjunctive still occur.

For the verb *be:*

> *Present,* singular or plural: **be**
> *Past,* singular or plural: **were**

(Contrast the indicative forms of *be* with various subjects on page 87.)

For all other verbs with third-person singular subjects:

> *Present,* singular only: **see** [The *-s* ending is dropped.]
>
> EXAMPLES
> It is necessary that I **be** on time.
> Suppose he **were** to die before she does.
> One debater insisted that the other not **avoid** the question
>
> ALTERNATIVES
> I **have to be** on time.
> Suppose he **dies** before she does.
> One debater urged the other not **to avoid** the question.

Should and *would* (past forms of *shall* and *will*) are also used for the subjunctive.

(1) **Use the subjunctive in *that* clauses after such verbs as *demand, recommend, urge, insist, request, suggest, move.***

> I move that the report **be** approved.
> The counsellor suggested that he **discover** the library.
> OR
> The counsellor told him *to discover* the library.

Note: Use the subjunctive in *that* clauses that are preceded by the construction *it is* and adjectives such as *important/essential/imperative/vital/necessary/desirable* or others used to express the idea that something must be done.

> *It is essential that* every student *complete* the medical form.
> *It is important that* you *be* there at the beginning.

(2) **Especially in formal English, use the subjunctive to express wishes or (in *if* or *as if* clauses) a hypo-**

thetical, highly improbable, or contrary-to-fact condition.

I wish I **were** in London. **Would I were** there now!
If I **were** you, I would accept the offer.
Act as if every other person on the stage **were** a member of your family.

Especially in formal English, *should* is still used in conditional clauses:

If she **should** resign, we **would** have grave difficulty locating a competent replacement.

OR

If she *resigns,* we *will* have grave difficulty locating a competent replacement.

The indicative is displacing this use of the subjunctive, just as *will* is displacing *shall*—except in questions such as *"Shall we tell?"*

(3) Do not use *would have* for *had* in an *if* clause that expresses an imagined condition.

NOT   If he would have arrived earlier, he wouldn't have lost the sale.

BUT   If he **had** arrived earlier, he wouldn't have lost the sale

OR

Had he arrived earlier, he wouldn't have lost the sale.

■ **Exercise 7** Prepare to explain the use of the subjunctive in the following sentences.

1. Rudolf Nureyev conducted the dance rehearsal as though he were just any ballet master.
2. The diver acts if she were a champion already.
3. It is essential that we be prepared for an earthquake.

4. The shareholders insist that he call a meeting within a week.
5. If I were you, I would switch my major to political science.
6. We demand that he be set free.
7. This year's cuts to library funding require that we be rigorous in collecting fines for overdue books.
8. If there should be any delay in the ferry's departure, we would have to arrange for the hotel to send a bus.
9. I wish that the children had had more practice in reading aloud.
10. Had Paula Gomez been at the door, Mike's parents would have been admitted in time for them to see the whole of his performance.

■ **Exercise 8**   Compose five sentences illustrating various uses of the subjunctive.

7d

Avoid needless shifts in tense or mood. See also **27a.**

INCORRECT	She **stood** up to her opponents in the debate and **tries** to score a victory. [shift in tense from past to present]
CORRECT	She **stood** up to her opponents in the debate and **tried** to score a victory.
INCORRECT	It is necessary to restrain foolhardy park visitors. If a female bear **were** to mistake their friendly intentions and **supposes** them a menace to her cubs, such visitors would be in trouble. [shift in mood from subjunctive to indicative] But females with cubs **were** only one of the dangers. [a correct sentence if standing alone, but here inconsistent with present tense of preceding sentence and therefore misleading] All bears are wild animals and not domesticated pets. It **is** therefore an important part of the park

ranger's duty to watch the tourists and above all
don't let anyone try to feed the bears. [shift in
mood from indicative to imperative]

CORRECT   It is necessary to restrain foolhardy park visitors. If a female bear **were** to mistake their
friendly intentions and **suppose** them a menace
to her cubs, such visitors would be in trouble.
But females with cubs **are** only one of the dangers. All bears are wild animals and not domes-
ticated pets. It **is** therefore an important part of
the park ranger's duty to watch the tourists and
above all not to let anyone try to feed the bears.

■ **Exercise 9** In the following passages correct all errors and
inconsistencies in tense and mood as well as any other errors in
verb usage. Put a check mark after any sentence that is satisfactory as it stands.

(a) ¹Charles Dickens creates many memorable characters in
David Copperfield. ²He give many of his characters names
that suggest their personalities. ³Mr. Murdstone is unfeeling,
Little Emily is shy, and Dr. Strong is virtuous. ⁴Dickens also
tags his characters with recurring peculiarities of speech;
these may even call their trademarks. ⁵For example, Barkis
continues to have proposed marriage with these words:
"Barkis is willin'." ⁶The proud Uriah Heep, a hypocrite, keeps
calling himself a humble man. ⁷Over and over Mr. Micawber
rambled on and concludes, "In short—." ⁸When he owed
debts this character shrugs off what he terms his "pecuniary
difficulties." ⁹With cheerful certainty, he repeats his favourite
prophecy: "Something is bound to turn up." ¹⁰Set down and
read *David Copperfield* through to become acquainted with
these interesting people.

(b) ¹Across the Thames from Shakespeare's London lay the
area known as the Bankside, probably as rough and
unsavoury a neighbourhood as ever laid across the river from
any city. ²And yet it was to such a place that Shakespeare and
his company had to have gone to build their new theatre. ³For

the Puritan government of the city had set up all sorts of prohibitions against theatrical entertainment within the city walls. [4]When it became necessary, therefore, for the company to have moved their playhouse from its old location north of the city, they obtain a lease to a tract on the Bankside. [5]Other theatrical companies had went there before them, and it seemed reasonable to have supposed that Shakespeare and his partners would prosper in the new location. [6]Apparently the Puritans of the city had no law against anyone's moving cartloads of lumber through the public streets. [7]There is no record that the company met with difficulty while the timbers of the dismantled playhouse are being hauled to the new site. [8]The partners had foresaw and forestalled one difficulty: the efforts of their old landlord to have stopped them from removing the building. [9]Lest his presence complicate their task and would perhaps defeat its working altogether, they waited until he had gone out of town. [10]And when he came back, his lot was bare. [11]The building's timbers were all in stacks on the far side of the river, and the theatre is waiting only to be put together. [12]It is a matter of general knowledge that on the Bankside Shakespeare continued his successful career as a showman and went on to enjoy even greater prosperity after he had made the move than before.

MECHANICS

Manuscript Form

8

Put your manuscript in acceptable form. Revise and proofread with care.

8a
Use the proper materials.

Unless you are given other instructions, follow these general practices:

(1) **Handwritten papers** Use regular looseleaf paper, size 21.6 cm × 27.9 cm (8½ × 11 inches), with widely spaced lines. (Narrow spaces between lines do not allow enough room for corrections.) Use black or blue ink. Write on only one side of the paper.

(2) **Typewritten papers** Use regular white typing paper (not sheets torn from a spiral notebook), size 21.6 cm × 27.9 cm (8½ × 11 inches). Or use a good grade of bond paper (not onionskin). Use a black ribbon. Double-space between lines. Type on only one side of the paper.

(3) **Word-processed papers** Check with your instructor to make sure the typeface and the paper you plan to

use will be satisfactory. Letter-quality print from a good daisy-wheel or laser printer is always acceptable. If you have a dot matrix printer, set the word-processing program (or the printer) for near-letter-quality print; most readers find print that shows the separate dots hard to read. Use good-quality, letter-sized cut sheets or equally good quality pin-feed paper that separates cleanly on all edges. Make sure the printer ribbon is fresh enough to type clear, dark characters.

8b

Arrange your writing in clear and orderly fashion on the page.

(1) **Margins** Leave wide enough margins—about 2.5 cm on all sides—to prevent a crowded appearance. The ruled vertical line on looseleaf paper marks the left margin.

(2) **Indention** Indent the first lines of paragraphs uniformly, about 2.5 cm in handwritten copy and five spaces in typewritten copy.

(3) **Paging**   Use Arabic numerals—without parentheses or periods—in the upper right-hand corner to mark all pages.

(4) **Title**   Do not put quotation marks around the title or underline it (unless it is a quotation or the title of a book), and use no period after the title. Capitalize the first and last words of the title and all other words except articles, co-ordinating conjunctions, prepositions, and the *to* in infinitives. See also **9c**.

When you do not use a title page, centre the title on the page about 3.8 cm from the top or on the first ruled line. Leave one blank line between the title and the first paragraph. When you do use a separate title page, include the following information attractively spaced: the title of your paper, your name, the course title and number, the instructor's name, and the date.

(5) **Quoted lines**   When you quote over four lines of another's writing to explain or support your ideas, set the quotation off by indention; see **16a(3)**. Acknowledge the source of quotations: see Section **34,** pages 497–520.

(6) **Punctuation**   Never begin a line with a comma, a colon, a semicolon, a hyphen, a dash, or a terminal mark of punctuation; never end a line with the first of a set of brackets, parentheses, or quotation marks.

(7) **Identification**   Usually papers carry the name of the student, the course title and number, the instructor's name, and the date. Often the number of the assignment is given.

(8) **Binding**   Unless your instructor tells you otherwise, staple or paper clip the pages of your paper; do not use pins, brads, or plastic folders.

8c
Write or type your manuscript so that it can be read easily and accurately.

(1) **Legible handwriting**   Form each letter clearly; distinguish between *o* and *a*, *t* and *l*, *b* and *f*, and between capital and lower-case letters. Use firm dots, not circles, for periods. Make each word a distinct unit. Avoid flourishes.

(2) **Legible typing/clean printout**   Before typing or printing out your final draft, check the quality of the ribbon or tape and the cleanness of the type. Double-

space between lines. If you are using a typewriter, do not strike over an incorrect letter; make neat corrections. Leave one space after a comma or semicolon; one or two after a colon; two after a period, a question mark, or an exclamation point. To indicate a dash, use two hyphens without spacing before, between, or after. Use a pen to insert marks or symbols that are not on your typewriter or in your word-processing system, such as accent marks, mathematical symbols, or brackets. If you are using a word processor connected to a laser printer and have a choice of typefaces and sizes, check whether your instructor has any preferences or special requirements for these elements.

8d

Avoid dividing a word at the end of a line. Make such divisions only between syllables and according to standard practice.

You will seldom need to divide words if you do not leave too wide a right margin. Remember that the reader expects a somewhat uneven right margin but may be distracted or slowed down by a series of word divisions at the ends of consecutive lines. (If you are using a word-processing system, avoid right-margin justification or alignment.)

When you do need to divide a word at the end of a line, use a hyphen to mark the separation of syllables. In college dictionaries, dots usually divide the syllables of words:

| **re • al • ly** | **pre • fer** | **pref • er • ence** |
| **sell • ing** | **set • ting** | |

But not every division between syllables is an appropriate place for dividing a word at the end of a line. The following principles are useful guidelines:

(1) **One-letter syllables**   Do not put the first or last letter of a word at the end or beginning of a line. Do not divide *o • mit, a • ble, spunk • y, bo • a.*

(2) **Two-word endings**   Do not put the last two letters of a word at the beginning of a line. Do not divide *dat • ed, does • n't, safe • ly, grav • el, tax • is.*

(3) **Misleading divisions**   Do not make divisions that may cause a misreading: *sour • ces, on • ions, an • gel, colo • nel, re • ally.*

The vertical lines in the following examples mark appropriate end-of-line divisions.

(4) **Hyphenated words**   Divide hyphenated words only at the hyphen.

   mass-| produced
   father-| in-law OR **father-in-| law**

(5) **-ing words**   Divide words ending in -ing between those consonants that you double when adding -ing.

   set-| ting   **jam-| ming**   **plan-| ning**
   [Compare sell-| ing.]

(6) **Consonants between vowels**   Divide words between two consonants that come between vowels—except when the division does not reflect pronunciation.

   pic-| nic   **dis-| cuss**   **thun-| der**   BUT **co-| bra**

(7) **Abbreviations and acronyms**   Do not divide abbreviations, initials, or capitalized acronyms.

   B.A. [degree]   **O.E.C.D.**   **CBC**   **UPEI**   **UNESCO**

(8) **Caution:**   Do not divide one-syllable words, such as *twelfth, through, or grabbed.*

Note: Many word-processing programs include an automatic hyphenation feature, but these features sometimes hyphenate words incorrectly. Check each hyphenation and make corrections as needed.

■ **Exercise 1**   First put a check mark after the words that should not be divided at the end of a line; then, with the aid of your dictionary, write out the other words by syllables and insert hyphens followed by a vertical line to indicate appropriate end-of-line divisions.

1. cross-reference
2. economic
3. fifteenth
4. GATT
5. gripped
6. gripping
7. guessing
8. against
9. present (now)
10. present (give)

11. seacoast
12. eventual
13. recline
14. C.P.A.
15. magical
16. CHUM-FM
17. matches
18. dissolve
19. cobwebs
20. patron

8e
Revise and proofread your manuscript with care.

(1) Revise and proofread your paper before submitting it to the instructor.

When doing out-of-class papers, write a first draft, put the paper aside for a few hours or a day, and then revise it. As you revise, focus your attention on content and style. Use the Reviser's Checklist on page 465–67 in Section **33**.

If only a few changes are needed, the paper may be handed in—after clear, legible corrections have been made—without rewriting. If extensive changes are necessary on any page, make a full, clean copy of it to submit to the instructor.

When doing in-class papers, use the last few minutes for proofreading and making corrections. As you proofread, focus your attention on manuscript form—on mechanics, punctuation, spelling. Watch for the items noted in the Proofreader's Checklist on page 117. For examples of how to make corrections, see pages 113–14.

(2) **Revise your paper after the instructor has marked it.**

Become familiar with the numbers or abbreviations used by your instructor to indicate specific errors or suggested changes.

Unless directed otherwise, follow this procedure as you revise a marked paper:

(a) In this handbook find the exact principle that deals with each error or recommended change.
(b) After the instructor's mark in the margin, write the letter designating the appropriate principle, such as **a** or **c**. If your instructor uses abbreviations rather than numbers, you can identify the appropriate principles by number and letter.
(c) If your instructor's suggestions involve more than mechanical corrections, rewrite the composition. If only minor changes are needed, make them on the marked paper using a no. 2 pencil or a pen of a different colour from the original so that they will stand out.

This method of revision will help you understand why a change is desirable and avoid repeating the same mistakes.

Following are examples of a paragraph marked by an instructor and the same paragraph corrected by a student. Examine the corrected paragraph to see how deletions of words, corrections of misspelling, substitutions of words, and changes in capitalization and punctuation are made.

Notice also the use of a caret (^) at the point in the line where an addition is made.

A Paragraph Marked by an Instructor

9   Drug pushers affect Society directly and

9   indirectly. They affect Society directly because

20   they break the law and sell dangerous drugs to

3   innocent victims simply to make money, the indi-

23   rect effect is because the people who become

18   addicted to the drugs that these pushers sell

13   loose the ability to make rational decisions,

20   and will probably become criminals themselves

2   to support their habits. Thus contributing to

9   the explosion of crime in Society today. The

32   pushers therefore jeopardize their own safety

20   and also the safety of the innocent public.

The Paragraph Being Revised by the Student

Drug pushers affect Society directly and

indirectly. They affect Society directly because
jeopardizing their own safety as well as that of their victims,
they break the law and ^sell dangerous drugs ~~to~~
solely for profit. They affect Society indirectly
~~innocent victims simply to make money, the indirect~~
buy these drugs usually
~~effect is~~ because the people who ^become addicted,
lose
~~to the drugs that these pushers sell loose~~ the

ability to make rational decisions, and ~~will~~
often
~~probably~~ become criminals themselves to support

their habits. Thus, ~~contributing to~~ drug pushers are a major catalyst in the explosion

of crime~~, in Society today. The pushers therefore~~

~~jeopardize their own safety and also the safety of~~

~~the innocent public.~~

The Paragraph Resubmitted by the Student

Drug pushers affect society directly and
indirectly. They affect society directly because
they break the law and, jeopardizing their own
safety as well as that of their victims, sell
dangerous drugs solely for profit. They affect
society indirectly because the people who buy
these drugs usually become addicted, lose the
ability to make rational decisions, and often
become criminals themselves to support their
habits. Thus, drug pushers are a major catalyst
in the explosion of crime.

8f

Keep a record of your revisions to help you improve your writing.

To monitor your progress toward mastery of writing, your instructor may want you to record and analyze your errors. You can record the marks your instructor makes on each paper by grouping them in columns corresponding to each of the seven major divisions of this handbook, as the following Record of Revisions illustrates. In the spaces for Paper No. 1 are the numbers and letters from the margin of the revised paragraph. In the spelling column is the correctly spelled word rather than **18c.** You may wish to add to your record sheet other columns for date, grade, and instructor's comments.

RECORD OF REVISIONS

Paper No.	Grammar 1-7	Mechanics 8-11	Punctuation 12-17	Words Misspelled 18	Diction 19-22	Effectiveness 23-30	Larger Elements 31-34
1	2a 3a	9f	13b	lose	20c	23d	32b

8g
Use a word processor effectively.

A word-processing program can make the writing process easier and help you produce a clear, tidy, error-free paper. These programs allow you to insert and delete whole paragraphs or even pages. Word processing can make the mechanics of revision easier because it allows you to rearrange words and blocks of writing by moving them to a part of the composition where you think they will be most effective. And word processing allows you to do this without having to retype everything. The computer simply makes room on the screen where you need it and takes space away where you don't.

When you have completed your drafting and revising, you can use the search function of the program to help ensure consistency in your use of terms and to show you if you have been repetitious. Style-checking programs can highlight many kinds of grammatical errors and mannerisms that may distract your reader from the point you are trying to make. You can also verify your spelling and find typographical errors with the spelling checkers most word-processing programs include, but be aware that no program can catch the use of one correctly spelled word for another: of, say, *hole* for *whole*, or *compliant* for *complaint*. Usually these proofreading programs operate by highlighting or otherwise isolating on the screen the part of your composition that may contain a problem. Word processing makes revision easier, but you still must choose which revisions you need to make.

Word processors will lay out pages of your manuscript exactly to your specifications. You can have the computer number your pages; produce single, double, or other spacing; print a certain number of lines per page; underline or print words and phrases in boldface; and hyphenate words at the ends of lines. Unless your printer has proportional spacing, do not take advantage of the computer's capability to justify (align) the right margin. Justification inserts spaces between words so that every line is the same length. The odd spacing that results in the lines of the text makes reading more difficult.

Word processors are not foolproof. Because inserting and deleting are so easy, you can create strange kinds of errors by inadvertently leaving in parts of old sentences you have abandoned or by mistakenly taking out parts of sentences you want to keep but have been tinkering with, and you can lose all of it if you forget to save, or back-up, the document regularly. And because word processors are easy to use, they can make a wordy writer even wordier, a terse writer even less fluent. Finally, using word-processing programs does not make careful proofreading unnecessary; indeed, proofreading your final copy is essential. Word-processing programs are only a mechanical means for manipulating language you create yourself. They cannot think for you; they only remind you to think for yourself.

Proofreader's Checklist

1. **Title** Is there any unnecessary punctuation in the title? Is it centred on the line? Are key words capitalized? See **8b(4)**.

2. **Indention** Is the first line of each paragraph indented? Is any lengthy quoted passage set off from the text? See **8b(2)** and **16a(3)**.

3. **Sentences** Does each sentence begin with a capital and end with the appropriate end mark? Are there any fragments, comma splices, or fused sentences? See **9e, 17a–c,** and Sections **2–3**.

4. **Spelling, mechanics** Are there any misspellings or mistakes in typing or handwriting? Are capitals and underlining (italics) used correctly? Should any abbreviations or numbers be spelled out? See **8c** and Sections **9–11** and **18**.

5. **Punctuation** Have any end marks been omitted? Are apostrophes correctly placed? Are there any superfluous commas? See Sections **12–17**.

■ **Exercise 2** Proofread the following composition. Circle the mistakes that you find and prepare to discuss in class the changes you would make to correct the text.

Programmed People.

A lot of people in the workaday-world is a machine—an insensitive, unhearing, unseeing, unthinking, unfeeling mechanism. They act like they are programmed, all their movements or responses triggered by clocks. . Take, for example, my brother. At 7:30 A.M. he automatically shuts off the alarm, then for the next hour he grumbles and sputter around like the cold, sluggish motor that he is.

On the way to work he did not see the glorious sky or notice ambulance at his neighbour's house. At 8:20 he unlocks his store and starts selling auto parts; however, all mourning long he never once really sees a customers' face. While eating lunch at Joe's cafe, the same music he spent a half dollar for yesterday is playing again. he does not hear it. At one o'clock my brother is back working with invoices and punching at a calculator; The clock and him ticks on and on.

When the hour hand hits five, it pushes the "move" button of my brother: lock store, take bus, pet dog at front door, kiss wife and baby, eat supper, read paper, watch TV, and during the 10-o'clock news he starts his nodding. His wife interrupts his light snoring to say that thier neighbour had a mild heart attach while mowing the lawn. My brother jerks and snorts. Then he mumbles, "Tell me tomorrow. I'm to tired now."

Capitals

9

Capitalize words according to standard conventions. Avoid unnecessary capitals.

A study of the principles in this section should help you use capitals correctly. When special problems arise, consult a good recent college dictionary. Dictionaries list not only words and abbreviations that begin with capitals but also acronyms that adopt full capitals:

Halloween, World War II, Hon., Ph.D., ICAO, FORTRAN

If usage is divided, dictionaries also give options:

Old Guard OR old guard, Nos. OR nos., Mountie OR mountie

A recent dictionary is an especially useful guide when the capitalization of a word depends on a given meaning: "*mosaic* pictures" but "*Mosaic* laws," "on *earth*" but "the planet *Earth*," "a *prairie* dog" but "the *Prairies*."

9a
Capitalize proper names and, usually, their derivatives and their shortened forms (abbreviations and acronyms).

PROPER NAMES

As you study the following examples, observe that common nouns like *college, company, memorial, park,* and *street* are capitalized when they are essential parts of proper names.

(1) **Names and nicknames of persons or things, trademarks**

Gandhi, Henry V, Lucy Maud Montgomery, T.S. Eliot, Vui Nguyen; Honest Abe, the Great One, the Grey Fox, John Bull, the Material Girl; Flight 41D, Gemini Award, Noah's Ark, Olympics, the Peace Tower, Skydome; Cabbagetown, Fort Book, the Jolly Roger, Lotus Land, the Main, the Rock; Apple II, Birks, Bombardier, Dentyne, Jeep Cherokee, Nike, Snow Cat

(2) **Geographical names**

Continents and geographical groups

Asia, Australia, Europe, South America; the Americas, the Balkans

Countries, states, provinces, cities, towns and villages

America, Canada, Zaire; New Brunswick, Tasmania, Texas, Yukon; Barcelona, The Hague, New York, Quebec City; Elmtown, Greenwich Village

Mountains, islands, lakes, rivers, falls, bodies of water

the Himalayas, the Rocky Mountains, the Smokies, Mount Blanc, Mount Waddington; the Philippines, the Hebrides, Baffin Island, Isle St. Louis; the Great Lakes, Lac St-Jean, Lake Titicaca; the Amazon, the Danube (OR the River Danube), the Fraser (OR the Fraser River); the Angel Falls, Niagara Falls; the Pacific Ocean, the Gulf of St. Lawrence, the Strait of Hormuz, English Bay

Deserts, forests, peninsulas, archipelagos
the Kalahari, the Black Forest, the Iberian Peninsula, the Malay Archipelago

Geographical names drawn from points of the compass, points on the globe, topographical features of the globe
the Middle East, the Orient, the South; the Arctic Circle, the North Pole, the Equator, the 49th parallel; the Barren Grounds, the Great Divide, the Lake District, the Pacific Northwest, the Mindanao Trench

Note: The definite article *the* that forms part of many of these names is not capitalized. Capitalize *north, south, east,* and *west* when they refer to a specific region (e.g., Canada's North, the mysterious East).

(3) Peoples and languages
American, Aztec, Filipino, Finn, Indian (fr. India), Inuit, Kuwaiti, Métis, Native American, Pole, Salish, Scot, Somali, Zambian
Arabic, English, French, Greek, Inuktituk, Latin, Polish, Russian, Spanish, Swahili, Urdu

(4) Organizations, government agencies, institutions, companies
AIDS Vancouver, the Toronto Blue Jays, Canadian Press, the Red Cross, the United Nations; Canada Post, the Commons Justice Committee, the National Film Board, the Royal Canadian Mounted Police, the Senate, the Supreme Court; Acadia University, the Ryerson Institute, Seneca College; CP Express, Fujitsu, Hydro Québec, Telestat Canada
Option: *the Liberal Party* or *the Liberal party*

(5) Days of the week, months, holidays
Tuesday, October, Good Friday, Groundhog Day, Remembrance Day, Thanksgiving

Note: Do not capitalize names of the seasons: spring, summer, autumn, fall, winter.

(6) Historical documents, periods, movements, events
the Charter of Rights and Freedoms, the Child Care Act, the Free Trade Agreement, the Magna Carta; the Ming Dynasty, the Middle Ages, the Stone Age; the Enlightenment, the Romantic Movement; Confederation, the Conquest, the Russian Revolution; the Commonwealth Conference, the Economic Summit

(7) Religions and their adherents, holy books, holy days, words denoting the god or gods of a religion, religious premises
Buddhism, Christianity, Hinduism, Islam, Judaism, Bahaism, Shinto, Taoism
Buddhists, Christians, Hindus, Muslims, Jews, Anglicans, Catholics, Mennonites
Buddhist Scriptures, the Bible, the Veda, the Koran, the Torah, the Talmud
Buddha Day, Easter, Christmas, Lent, Diwali, Festival of Id, Ramadan, Hanukkah, Yom Kippur
Buddha, Christ, Brahma, Allah, Yahweh, the Deity, God, Messiah, the Supreme Being
Chan Quang Buddhist Society, First Baptist Church, Holy Rosary Cathedral, St. Andrew's Wesley Church, Shiva Temple, Akali Singh Sikh Temple, Temple Sholom

Option: Some writers always capitalize pronouns (except *who, whom, whose*) referring to God. Other writers capitalize such pronouns only when the capital is needed to prevent ambiguity, as in "The Lord commanded the prophet to warn *His* people."

(8) Personifications. See also **20a(4).**
I could feel Old Man Time breathing down the back of my neck.   —PATRICK McMANUS

Note: Occasionally, a common noun is capitalized for emphasis or clarity, as in "The motivation for many politicians is Power."

DERIVATIVES: WORDS ORIGINATING IN PROPER NAMES

[verbs] Americanize, Balkanize, Frenchify [*largely pejorative*], Romanize; [nouns] an Acadian, Christmas, Fenianism, a Highlander, an Israelite, Marxism; [adjectives] Chaplinesque, Finnish, Germanic, Machiavellian, Peter Pan (collar), Samsonite (luggage), Shakespearean

When proper names and their derivatives become names of a general class, they are no longer capitalized.

zipper [originally a capitalized trademark]
chauvinistic [derived from *Nicholas Chauvin*]
bowdlerize [derived from *Dr. Thomas Bowdler*]
mackinaw [derived from the Ojibway name
    Michilimackinac, which was shortened to *Mackinac* and
    then *Mackinaw*]

Note: Capitalization of prefixes with words derived from proper names is not consistent. Consult a dictionary for capitals and hyphens for a particular word. The following examples illustrate:

Pre-Cambrian, but *pre-Socratic; Pre-Loyalist,* but *pre-Confederation;* and *Anti-Confederate,* but *anti-Confederate* activities

ABBREVIATIONS AND ACRONYMS

These shortened forms of capitalized words are derived from the initial letters of capitalized word groups. See also **17a(2)**.

B.C.   L.A. OR LA   D.O.T.   NFB   CBC   DST
CRTC   OPEC   UNESCO   NATO   RCMP   MADD

Common exceptions: B.C., A.D., A.M. OR a.m., P.M. OR p.m.

9b

Capitalize titles of persons that precede the name of the title holder.

Aunt Mae	BUT Mae, my aunt
Captain Holt	BUT Holt, the captain in charge
Dean Joe Ghiz	BUT Joe Ghiz, the dean
Premier Catherine Callbeck	BUT Catherine Callbeck, our premier

When the title acts as a modifier, treat it as an adjective and use lower case:

American president Bill Clinton, law faculty dean Lynn Smith

Note: Usage is divided regarding the capitalization of titles of high rank or distinction when not followed by a proper name: the Prime Minister (OR prime minister) of Canada.

Words denoting family relationship are usually capitalized when serving as substitutes for proper names: "Tell Mother I'll write soon."

9c

In titles and subtitles of books, plays, student papers, and so on, capitalize the first and last words and all other words except articles, co-ordinating conjunctions, prepositions, and the *to* in infinitives.

The articles are *a, an, the*; the co-ordinating conjunctions are *and, but, or, nor, for, so, yet.* (Formerly, longer prepositions like *before, between,* or *through* in titles were capitalized; the style today, however, favours lower-cased prepositions, whatever the length.)

All Creatures Great and Small
"What It Takes to Be a Leader"

"Why Women Are Paid Less Than Men" [The subordinating conjunction *than* is capitalized.]

"Aerobics before Breakfast"

Looking Back: A Chronicle of Growing Up Old in the Sixties [Not a preposition, *up* is part of a phrasal verb.]

Note: In a title capitalize the first word of a hyphenated compound. As a rule, capitalize the word following the hyphen if it is a noun or a proper adjective or if it is equal in importance to the first word.

A Substitute for the H-Bomb [noun]

The Arab-Israeli Dilemma [proper adjective]

"Hit-and-Run Accidents" [parallel words]

Usage varies for the capitalization of words following such prefixes as *anti-, ex-, re-,* and *self-:*

The Anti-Apartheid Movement
OR
The Anti-apartheid Movement

Exception: Titles in an APA-style reference list in a research paper. See Section **34.**

9d
Capitalize the pronoun *I* and the interjection *O* (but not *oh,* except when it begins a sentence).

David sings, "Out of the depths I cry to thee, O Lord."

9e
Capitalize the first word of every sentence (or of any other unit written as a sentence) and of directly quoted speech.

Humorists often describe their zany relatives.

Oh, really! Do such jokes have a point? Not at all.

Women who set a low value on themselves make life hard for all women.   —NELLIE McCLUNG

Bombay, you will be told time and again, is like no other city in India. Indeed, its enthusiasts will point out, it is India's only "real" city.   —SHIVA NAIPAUL

Most first drafts, in fact, can be cut by fifty percent without losing anything organic. (Try it; it's a good exercise.)
—WILLIAM ZINSSER [a parenthetical sentence]

COMPARE: You do this by moving the cursor under the symbol for "carriage return" (it looks like an arrow) and then pressing DELETE.   —WILLIAM ZINSSER [a parenthetical main clause]

One thing is certain: We are still free. [an optional capital after the colon—see also **17d**]

She often replies, "Maybe tomorrow, but not today."

OR "Maybe tomorrow," she often replies, "but not today."

OR "Maybe tomorrow," she often replies. "But not today." [See also **3c**.]

The difference between "Well!" and "Well?" is a difference of tone, hence of meaning.   —J. MITCHELL MORSE

Note: Take care in transcribing poetry. Note whether the poet capitalizes the first letter of every line or not. There is no fixed rule, as the excerpts below illustrate.

Scatter, as from an unextinguished hearth
Ashes and sparks, my words among mankind!
—PERCY BYSSHE SHELLEY

you fit into me
like a hook into an eye

a fish hook
an open eye   —MARGARET ATWOOD

Note: For the treatment of directly quoted written material, see **16a(3)**.

9f
Avoid unnecessary capitals.

If you have a tendency to overuse capitals, review **9a** through **9e**. Also keep in mind this rule: common nouns may be preceded by the indefinite articles (*a, an*) and by such limiting modifiers as *every* or *several.*

> **a** speech course in radio and television writing
> COMPARE   Speech 245: Radio and Television Writing
> **every** university, **several** schools of medicine
> COMPARE   the University of Manitoba School of Medicine

When preceded by *a, an,* or modifiers like *every* or *several,* capitalized nouns name one or many of the members of a class:

> **a** St. Bernard, **an** Angolan, **several** Catholics

Study the following style sheet:

Style Sheet for Capitalization

CAPITALS	NO CAPITALS
Dr. Freda E. Watts	every doctor, my doctor
the War of 1812	a space war in 1999
English, Chinese, French	the language requirement
Harvard University	a university like Harvard
the U.S. Navy	a strong navy
December, Christmas	winter, holiday
the West, Westerners	to fly west, western regions
Canadian Nurses' Association	an association for Canadian nurses
Parkinson's disease	flu, asthma, leukemia
a Chihuahua, Ford trucks	a beagle, pickup trucks
two Liberal candidates	a liberal education
the Charter of Rights	a kind of charter of rights

9f   cap

■ **Exercise 1** Write brief sentences correctly using each of the following pairs of words:

1. college, College
2. south, South
3. cardinals, Cardinals
4. theatre, Theatre
5. professor, Professor
6. nature, Nature
7. hotel, Hotel
8. dickens, Dickens
9. mackintosh, Macintosh
10. street, Street

■ **Exercise 2** Supply capitals wherever needed.

1. last autumn, when I was looking out from signal hill over-looking the harbour, my newfoundland guide told me that st. john's was named for the presumed date of discovery: the feast of st. john the baptist in june 1497.
2. in hopes of raising my grades in both history and political science, I spent most of thanksgiving weekend reading about the way in which the house of commons communicates with the queen, and particularly about the 1981 request for the repatriation of the canadian constitution.
3. At the end of her sermon on god's social justice as set forth in the bible, she said, "we north americans really ought to give more support to the united nations' children's fund."
4. The full title of jonathan swift's essay is "a modest proposal for preventing the children of poor people in ireland, from being a burden to their parents or country; and for making them beneficial to the public."

■ **Exercise 3** Supply capitals wherever needed.

¹in july of the summer of 1890, vincent van gogh completed a portrait of his friend paul gachet, boarded a train to auvers in the south of france, and shot himself in a cornfield. ²*dear theo,*

a book of letters he wrote to his brother in the netherlands, clearly indicates that his chronic poverty was one likely cause of his suicide. ³what a tragic irony! ⁴paintings by the post-impressionist van gogh are now the most expensive in the history of painting. ⁵even casual readers of magazines and newspapers know that van gogh's paintings now routinely sell for enormous amounts at auction houses such as sotheby's in london. ⁶reproductions of his paintings (especially *sunflowers* and *starry night*) show up everywhere: in poster shops and on calendars, textbook covers, the walls of banks, and even coasters for drinks. ⁷tour companies taking clients to amsterdam know they expect to visit not only the Rijks museum to see rembrandt's *the night watch* (renamed *the shooting company of capt. frans banning cocq* after it was cleaned in 1947), but also the van gogh museum to see *wheatfield with crows*. ⁸this, too, is ironic. ⁹the dutch painter who has brought this venice of the north so much renown and so much money was unrecognized and poverty-stricken there. ¹⁰in fact, he lacked any real recognition before he died, although the famous impressionist camille pissarro did offer him some encouragement when they met in paris. ¹¹most ironic may be what happened exactly 100 years after van gogh's death. ¹²*portrait of dr. gachet* was sold at auction at christie's in new york for the sum of $82.5 million to ryoei saito, a japanese papermaker. ¹³that sum still stands as the record sale price for any painting.

■ **Exercise 4** Supply capitals wherever needed.

¹the writer and world-renowned economist john kenneth galbraith was born on october 15, 1908, at iona station in elgin county, ontario. ²many phrases important to economic and social discussions of the last forty years came from his pen: "the affluent society," "the conventional wisdom," "the managerial élite," "the technostructure," "private affluence, public squalor," and "the culture of contentment."
³galbraith graduated in 1931 with a b.a. from ontario agricultural college (now the university of guelph). ⁴he then went west to study at berkeley, where he earned a ph.d. in agricultural economics from the university of california. ⁵he did postdoc-

toral work at cambridge university. [6]there he was much influenced by the theories of the english economist and monetary expert john maynard keynes. [7]these theories, known as keynesian economics, stand as the most influential formulations of the twentieth century. [8]for example, in 1929 keynes advocated a departure from the idea of the free economy. [9]during the great depression he suggested that governments adopt spending programs, such as roosevelt's new deal, and actively intervene in the market. [10]keynes also endorsed a government public works program to promote employment. [11]galbraith's own theories have been shaped by his study of john maynard keynes as well as his training in agricultural economics. [12]galbraith's contribution to economics is similar to keynes's, for it is an alternative to the old concepts of capitalism.

[13]galbraith returned to north america to teach at harvard, enjoying a high public profile for most of his academic and professional life. [14]he was a personal adviser to president franklin roosevelt and to every democratic candidate for the u.s. presidency up to and including lyndon johnson. [15]he has held several u.s. government positions; for example, he served as controller of prices during world war II and u.s. ambassador to india from 1961 to 1963. [16]as a member of americans for democratic action, he took part in anti-vietnam war demonstrations. [17]he produced many books between the fifties and the nineties, the best known being *american capitalism* (1952), *the affluent society* (1958), *the new industrial state* (1967), *the age of uncertainty* (1977), and *a view from the stands: of people, military power, and the arts* (1986). [18]in the eighties he was an outspoken critic of reaganomics and thatcherism, and in his 1991 book, *the culture of contentment,* he looked at the consequences of these economic policies for american society.

[19]galbraith is an american citizen. [20]even though he has lived most of his life away from canada, he has been an adviser and consultant on canadian economics and on arts policies from time to time. [21]he has remarked, "i've always said that one could have a moral and emotional affiliation with any number of countries. [22]i consider myself as much a canadian as an american."

Italics

10

Use underlining to indicate italics in accordance with customary practices. Use italics sparingly for emphasis.

In handwritten or typewritten papers, italics are indicated by underlining. Printers set underlined words in italic type.

TYPEWRITTEN
It was on CBC's
Prime Time.

PRINTED
It was on CBC's
Prime Time.

10a
Titles of separate publications (books, magazines, newspapers, pamphlets, long musical works) and titles of plays, films, radio and television programs, cassettes and software programs, and long poems are underlined (italicized).

As you study the following examples, note that punctuation that is a part of the title is underlined (italicized).

BOOKS   Fitzgerald's *The Great Gatsby,* Blume's
Are You There, God? It's Me, Margaret,
Munro's *Who Do You Think You Are?*

MAGAZINES	*Sports Illustrated, Saturday Night,* the *Atlantic, Maclean's*
NEWSPAPERS	the *Ottawa Citizen* OR the Ottawa *Citizen, Le Devoir*
PLAYS	*Romeo and Juliet,* George Walker's *Tough!*
FILMS	*Malcolm X, The Crying Game, Mon Oncle Antoine*
VIDEOS	*Byron: Mad, Bad and Dangerous to Know, Life Is a Highway*
TV SHOWS	*Murphy Brown, The Nature of Things, 60 Minutes*
RECORDINGS	*Sergeant Pepper's Lonely Hearts Club Band, Cats, Opera for People Who Hate Opera, Shadowland*
MUSICAL COMPOSITIONS	Beethoven's *Moonlight Sonata,* Verdi's *Aida*
PAINTINGS AND SCULPTURE	O'Brien's *Sunrise on the Saguenay,* Cassatt's *Mother and Child,* Michelangelo's *David,* Sorel Etrog's *Sunlife*
COMIC STRIPS	*Peanuts, For Better or For Worse*
SOFTWARE	*WordPerfect for Windows, NetWare, AutoCad 12*

Note: When you mention magazines or daily newspapers in your writing, give the name as it appears on the masthead, but do not underline (italicize) an initial *The,* unless it begins a sentence. (She writes a column for the *Vancouver Sun.*) Depending on whether your audience is likely to know the daily paper you mention, you may wish to include the city name to identify a paper with a common name such as the *Times,* the *Citizen,* the *Gazette,* the *Herald.* Occasionally quotation marks are used for titles of separate publications and of radio and television programs. The usual practice, however, is to reserve quotation marks for titles of the individual parts of longer works (such as short stories, essays, songs, short poems) and for titles of episodes of a radio or television series. See **16b**.

"What Language Do Bears Speak?" is one of the most provocative stories in this anthology, *Canadian Short Fiction*.

Alistair Cooke in his twenty-two years as host of PBS's *Masterpiece Theatre* introduced countless dramatizations of novels, but his introductions to "Upstairs, Downstairs" are the ones that most viewers will remember.

Exceptions: Neither italics nor quotation marks are used in references to the Bible and its parts or to legal documents.

The Bible begins with the Book of Genesis.

How many Canadians have actually read the Charter of Rights and Freedoms?

10b
Foreign words and phrases are usually underlined (italicized) in the context of an English sentence.

The maxim of the French Revolution still echoes in our ears: *liberté, egalité, fraternité.*   —MORTIMER J. ADLER

The beluga whale (*Delphinapterus leucas*) is an endangered species in the St. Lawrence River region.

Je me souviens ("I remember"), the familiar motto appearing on Quebec's coat of arms and on its vehicle plates, alludes to the glory of the *ancien régime.*

Countless words borrowed from other languages are a part of the English vocabulary and are therefore not italicized:

amigo (Spanish)	karate (Japanese)	shalom (Hebrew)
blasé (French)	pizza (Italian)	non sequitur (Latin)

Dictionaries that label certain words and phrases as foreign are fairly dependable guides to the writer in doubt about the use of italics. The labels, however, are not always up to date, and writers must depend on their own judgement after considering current practices.

10c

Names of specific ships, aircraft, satellites, and spacecraft are underlined (italicized).

> H.M.C.S. *Halifax*   the space shuttle *Challenger*
> the satellite *Alouette 1*   the airship *Hindenburg*

Names of trains and names of a general class or a trademark are not italicized: Royal Hudson, a Boeing 767, CF-18s, Anik, ICBMs, a Stealth bomber, a Datsun 240Z.

10d

Words, letters, or figures spoken of as such or used as illustrations are usually underlined (italicized).

> In no other language could a foreigner be tricked into pronouncing *manslaughter* as *man's laughter.*
> —MARIO PEI
>
> The letters *qu* replaced *cw* in such words as *queen, quoth,* and *quick.*   —CHARLES C. FRIES

The *3* and the *0* in the serial number are barely legible.

A boy from Sault Ste. Marie
Said, "Spelling is all Greek to me,
    Till they learn to spell *Soo*
    Without any *u*
Or an *a* or an *l* or a *t*."

—ANONYMOUS

10e
Use underlining (italics) sparingly for emphasis. Do not underline the title of your own paper.

Writers occasionally use italics to show stress, especially in dialogue, or to emphasize the meaning of a word.

> When he sees the child dragging a rotten tomato on a string, Bill Cosby asks, "What *are* you doing?"

> The only real friend of this country is the guy who believes in *excellence,* seeks for it, fights for it, defends it, and tries to produce it.   —MORLEY CALLAGHAN

> I am, in fact, the *only* drama critic in Canada. The rest are reviewers.   —NATHAN COHEN

> No one can imagine a *systematic* conversation.
> —JACQUES BARZUN

Overuse of italics for emphasis (like overuse of the exclamation point) defeats its own purpose. If you overuse italics, study Section **29.** When you are tempted to underline, try substituting a more precise or forceful word.

A title is not italicized when it stands at the head of a book or article. Accordingly, the title at the head of your paper (unless it is the title of a book or it includes the title of a book) should not be underlined.

■ **Exercise 1**   Underline all words in the following sentences that should be italicized.

1. The Canadian Standards Association has published preferred spellings or terms for metric units and prefixes that have several forms, as, for example, litre (not liter), gram (not gramme), and tonne or metric ton (not metric tonne).
2. When The Phantom of the Opera played the Théâtre Maisonneuve in Montreal, the critics declared the production très magnifique.

3. They both sported sweatshirts with printed mottoes; Emily's was "Born to Shop," and Consuelo's was "Caveat Emptor," a Latin phrase that means "let the buyer beware."

4. The generation gap was obvious: her dream holiday began with a trip from New York to Paris on the Concorde, complete with Mumm's Cordon Rouge champagne in an ice bucket; her mother's began with a voyage on the Regal Princess, complete with an assigned deck chair and the sequel to Margaret Mitchell's Gone with the Wind.

5. Bernard Shaw made fun of English spelling conventions when he pointed out that "fish" could be spelled ghoti, in which the gh is like the f sound in "rough" and the ti like the sh sound in "condition."

6. Although the most famous of comic book heroes was only fifty-four years old, DC Comics killed off Superman in 1992 and grabbed the attention of media as diverse as the New York Times, People magazine, and Maclean's.

7. Although he was a many-faceted genius, Leonardo da Vinci is better known for his Mona Lisa in the Louvre Museum and his Madonna of the Rocks than for his work as architect, engineer, or designer.

8. Although population has become the subject of furious arguments among the experts, they all agree that homo sapiens will keep growing in numbers.

9. When he asked where Juan could be found, the woman shrugged, gestured toward the jail, and muttered a few words, including la interrogacion and problema.

10. "Let me say it again," she said. "It is their problem, not yours."

■ **Exercise 2**   Underline all words that should be italicized in the following letter.

Dear Masako:
¹I'm writing this letter to you on my new laptop computer, loaded with WordPerfect 5.1. ²Yahoo! ³My whole family pooled together to get it. ⁴I know I was lucky to share Brad's

IBM PC (even if I did have to learn to use his NotaBene program), but this is really fantastico! ⁵I can take it with me to the library—even to the beach. ⁶It's as easy to carry around as my trusty Roget's Thesaurus of Words and Phrases. (⁷Yes, I still need it. ⁸I'm not a wunderkind like you!) ⁹So, I'm grabbing this half hour to tell you what's up with me this term. (¹⁰By the way, are you still having to read Caesar's Gallic Wars and all that veni, vidi, vici stuff for Roman history? ¹¹Did you ever finish reading War and Peace?)

¹²I have two new assignments. ¹³I spent all Saturday listening to music by Barbara Pentland and R. Murray Schafer and checking the library. ¹⁴I knew nothing—nada! de rien!—about either, not even that they are both Canadian. ¹⁵Schafer's really interested in ecology and landscape, and he worked for years on something that was finally called the World Soundscape Project. ¹⁶Most recently, he's done a song cycle, Gitanjali. ¹⁷It's based on the work of an Indian poet, Tagore. ¹⁸(I'll bet you didn't know he won the Nobel Prize in 1913. Neither did I.) ¹⁹So, I have lots of notes and a stack of tapes already. ²⁰I'm also doing a report on tourism—what drew people back and forth across the Atlantic on ships like the Queen Mary and Andrea Doria. ²¹The New York Times and the London Illustrated News (quite old copies) give me some idea of the ABC's of travel and what was popular. ²²One old copy even has an article on shipboard etiquette, "Minding your P's and Q's on the P&O." ²³Generations of tourists have trooped off to hear Puccini's Madama Butterfly at La Scala (with shouts of bravo! bravo!), visited the Baths of Caracalla in Rome, seen Michelangelo's Pietà, and drunk tankersful of cappuccino on the Piazza San Marco in Venice. ²⁴I'm developing a taste for Italy, I think. ²⁵I'm hoping this will pique your interest. ²⁶If you really want to study Roman history, why not do it in Rome? ²⁷What say we start saving up to go when we graduate?
²⁸Ciao, baby!

Frances
Frances

Abbreviations, Acronyms, and Numbers

11

Use abbreviations only when appropriate; at first use, spell out acronyms, and spell out numbers that can be expressed simply.

Abbreviations and figures are desirable in tables, notes, and bibliographies and in some kinds of special or technical writing. In ordinary writing, however, only certain abbreviations and figures are appropriate. All the principles in this section apply to ordinary writing, which of course includes the kind of writing often required in college.

Abbreviations

11a
In ordinary writing, use *Ms.* (or *Ms*), *Mr., Mrs., Dr.,* and *St.* before a proper name. Use such designations as *Jr., Sr., II,* and *M.D.* after a proper name.

> Ms. Janet Gray   Dr. Bell   St. Boniface
> [Compare "the young doctor," "the early life of the saint."]

> Hal Grant, Sr.   E.R. Ames III   Alice Chow, M.D.

Abbreviations of degrees are often used without a proper name, as in "A *B.A.* in languages."

Caution: Do not use redundant titles: NOT Dr. E.T. Fulton, M.D. BUT Dr. E.T. Fulton OR E.T. Fulton, M.D.

Note: Such abbreviations as *Prof., Sen., 1st Lt.,* or *Capt.* may be used before full names or before initials and last names, but not before last names alone.

Sen. Allan J. MacEachen   Senator MacEachen
Capt. P.T. Gaines   Captain Gaines

11b
Spell out names of provinces, states, countries, continents, months, days of the week, and units of measurement.

On Sunday, October 10, we spent the night in Calgary, Alberta; the next day we flew to South America.
Slightly over a metre tall, Timmy weighs forty-two kilograms.

Exception: The Canadian Standards Association, in cooperation with Metric Commission Canada, has published guidelines for the proper format and presentation of SI units (*Système internationale d'unités*). The standard reference on SI style is the *Canadian Metric Practice Guide* (Rexdale, Ontario: Canadian Standards Association, 1979). According to CSA guidelines, unit *symbols* (they are not referred to as abbreviations) must be used with numerals, and the full name of the unit must be given when numbers are spelled out. SI symbols are never pluralized and are written without a period.

The lake was 8.5 km long but only a few metres deep.

You will find, however, that in newspapers, magazines, and many general-interest books the use of the full name of the unit of measurement with a numeral is still quite common.

An acre is 4047 square metres.

The names of provinces, territories, and districts may be abbreviated when they follow the name of a city, a town, a village, or a prominent geographical feature, such as a mountain or a river.

Chicoutimi, Que. St. John's, Nfld. Cavendish Beach, P.E.I.

The list below shows the abbreviations that are generally used for provinces and territories and the abbreviations that are used for postal codes.

	GENERAL USE	POSTAL CODE USE
Alberta	Alta.	AB
British Columbia	B.C.	BC
Manitoba	Man.	MB
New Brunswick	N.B.	NB
Newfoundland	Nfld.	NF
Northwest Territories	N.W.T.	NT
Nova Scotia	N.S.	NS
Ontario	Ont.	ON
Prince Edward Island	P.E.I.	PE
Quebec	Que. or P.Q.	PQ
Saskatchewan	Sask.	SK
Yukon Territories	Y.T.	YT

The following list gives the U.S. postal abbreviations for states and territories:

Alabama	AL
Alaska	AK
American Samoa	AS
Arizona	AZ

Arkansas	AR
California	CA
Colorado	CO
Connecticut	CT
Delaware	DE
District of Columbia	DC
Florida	FL
Georgia	GA
Guam	GU
Hawaii	HI
Idaho	ID
Illinois	IL
Indiana	IN
Iowa	IA
Kansas	KS
Kentucky	KY
Louisiana	LA
Maine	ME
Maryland	MD
Massachusetts	MA
Michigan	MI
Minnesota	MN
Mississippi	MS
Missouri	MO
Montana	MT
Nebraska	NE
Nevada	NV
New Hampshire	NH
New Jersey	NJ
New Mexico	NM
New York	NY
North Carolina	NC
North Dakota	ND
Ohio	OH
Oklahoma	OK
Oregon	OR

Pennsylvania	PA
Puerto Rico	PR
Rhode Island	RI
South Carolina	SC
South Dakota	SD
Tennessee	TN
Texas	TX
Utah	UT
Vermont	VT
Virginia	VA
Virgin Islands	VI
Washington	WA
West Virginia	WV
Wisconsin	WI
Wyoming	WY

11c

Spell out *Street, Avenue, Road, Park, Mount, River, Company,* and similar words used as an essential part of proper names.

University Avenue is west of Yonge Street.
The Ford Motor Company does not expect a strike soon.

Note: Avoid the use of & (the ampersand) except in copying official titles or names of firms. The abbreviations *Inc.* and *Ltd.* are usually omitted in ordinary writing.

U.S. News & Report	Noranda [NOT Noranda, Inc.]
Alberta & Southern Gas	Brascan [NOT Brascan, Ltd.]

11d

Spell out the words *volume, chapter,* and *page* and the names of courses of study.

The chart is on page 46 of chapter 9.
I registered for physical education and for child psychology.

In addition to the abbreviations listed in **11a,** the following abbreviations and symbols are permissible and usually desirable.

1. *Certain words used with dates or figures:*

   58 B.C.   A.D. 70   8:00 A.M. OR a.m.
   21:31 EST OR E.S.T.   No. 13 OR no. 13 $4.25
   100 km/h   37–C   CF-18s

2. *The names of certain provinces used adjectivally:*

   The P.E.I. potato industry   the B.C. economy

   The District of Columbia and the United States used adjectivally:

   Washington, D.C.'s homeless persons   the U.S. Navy

3. *The names of organizations, agencies, countries, persons, or things usually referred to by their capitalized initials:*

   RCMP   CLC   UBC   CTV   CFL
   U.S.S.R.   JFK   VCRs   IQ   TV

4. *Certain common Latin expressions* (although the English term is usually spelled out in formal writing, as indicated here in brackets):

   cf. [compare]   etc. [and so forth]
   e.g. [for example]   i.e. [that is]
   et al. [and others]   vs. OR v. [versus]

For abbreviations in bibliographies, see pages 520–23.

Acronyms

Acronyms are words formed from the initial letters of other words or from the combination of syllables of other words: *AIDS* (*a*cquired *i*mmune *d*eficiency *s*yndrome), *laser* (*l*ight *a*mplification by *s*timulated *e*mission of *r*adiation).

11e
Spell out the meaning of any acronym that may not be familiar to your reader when you use it for the first time.

> Then there is the Canadian International Development Agency (CIDA). Consider CIDA's budget and mandate.
> OR
> Then there is CIDA (the Canadian International Development Agency).

Your reader will probably be familiar with such terms as *NHL, NATO, sonar,* and *LSAT scores,* but perhaps not with those such as *IMF, CUSO, EURATOM.*

Note: Some clipped forms—such as *info, rep, execs,* or *porn*—are avoided in formal writing. Others—such as *math, lab,* and *Statscan*—are generally acceptable.

■ **Exercise 1**   Strike out any form that is not appropriate in formal writing.

1. Ms. Janet Hogan; a dr. but not a saint
2. 90 km/h; on TV; in Sask. and Man.
3. on Yonge St.; on Yonge Street
4. on Aug. 15; on August 15
5. for Jr.; for John Evans, Jr.
6. before 6 A.M.; before six in the A.M.

Numbers

11f
Although usage varies, writers tend to spell out numbers that can be expressed in one or two words; they regularly use figures for other numbers.

When numbers are used infrequently in a piece of writing, writers tend to spell out those that can be expressed in one or two words and to use figures for the others. Where numbers occur frequently, the general practice is to spell out numbers from one to ten and to use figures for all others. In technical and scientific writing, figures are used for all physical measures, such as distance, length, and area. Very large numbers may be expressed by a combination of words and numbers (e.g., ten million bushels or 10 000 000 or 10 million bushels).

over five inches	BUT	three-quarters of an inch OR 0.75 inches
after twenty-two years	BUT	after 124 years
five thousand voters	BUT	5261 voters
less than three litres	BUT	2.285 litres
about thirty dollars	BUT	$29.99
six million bushels OR 6 million bushels	BUT	6 402 317 bushels

1. *Specific time of day*

   2 A.M. OR 2:00 A.M. OR two o'clock in the morning
   4:30 P.M. OR half-past four in the afternoon

2. *Dates*

   May 7, 1989 OR 7 May 1989 [NOT May 7th, 1989]
   May sixth OR the sixth of May OR May 6 OR May 6th
   the nineties OR the 1990's OR the 1990s
   the twentieth century OR the 20th century
   in 1900 in 1981–1982 OR in 1981–82
   from 1980 to 1985 OR 1980–1985 OR 1980–85
   [NOT from 1980–1985, from 1980–85]

3. *Addresses*

   Apartment 301, 444 Vienna Crescent, North Vancouver, British Columbia V7M 1P2

   [OR Apt. 301, 444 Vienna Cres., North Vancouver, BC V7M 1P2]

Apartment 3C, 8 Redwood Drive, Prescott, Arizona 86301,
   United States of America
[OR Apt. 3C, 8 Redwood Dr., Prescott, AZ 86301, USA]
16 Tenth Street   P.O. Box 247   R.R. 2
350 West 114 Street   OR   350 West 114th Street

4. *Identification numbers*
Channel 13   Highway 99   Henry VIII   Room 10

5. *Pages and divisions of books and plays*
page 30   chapter 6   part 4
in act 3, scene 2   OR   in Act III, Scene ii

6. *Decimals and percentages*
a 2.5 average   12½ percent
0.907 t (*t* is the symbol for *tonne*)

7. *Numbers in series and statistics*
two cows, five pigs, and forty-two chickens
27.5 m long, 15 m wide, and 3.6 m deep
125 feet long, 50 feet wide, and 12 feet deep
scores of 17 to 13 and 42 to 3   OR   scores of 17–13 and
   42–3
The members voted 99 to 23 against the motion.

8. *Large round numbers*
four billion dollars   OR $4 billion   OR   4 000 000 000
   [Figures are used for emphasis only.]
12 500 000   OR   12.5 million

9. *Numbers beginning sentences*
Six percent of the students voted.   [NOT 6 percent of the
   students voted.]

10. *Repeated numbers (in legal or commercial writing)*
The agent's fee will not exceed one hundred (100) dollars.
OR
The agent's fee will not exceed one hundred dollars ($100).

■ **Exercise 2** Using desirable abbreviations and figures, change each item to an acceptable shortened form.

1. on the fifteenth of June
2. Ernest Threadgill, a doctor
3. thirty million dollars
4. Brenda Szeto, a certified public accountant
5. one o'clock in the afternoon
6. by the first of December, 1995
7. at the bottom of the fifteenth page
8. four hundred years before Christ
9. in the second scene of the first act
10. a five-year plan (from 1990 to 1995)

■ **Exercise 3** Edit the following passage to provide abbreviations and numbers appropriate to formal writing.

1. For the last hundred and five years we have known that the *Salmonella* bacteria is a disease-causing agent of the human intestine, active in the spread of typhoid fever, bacterial dysentery, and food poisoning.
2. D.E. Salmon, an American bacteriologist, described it one hundred and nine years ago, noting that there are three main classifications of the bacteria.
3. Two of these classes prefer human hosts, but there are also more than seventeen hundred common microorganisms in the third class with the potential to cause gastroenteritis in humans.
4. In Canada at the present time, *Salmonella* is found in about sixty percent of poultry carcasses and in smoked and processed sausages, cream pies, chocolate confections, and foods prepared with cracked eggs.
5. To prevent salmonellosis, we must prevent contamination and inhibit the growth of bacteria by keeping food cold (four degrees centigrade or lower) or hot (sixty degrees centigrade or more).
6. Of the three classifications of *Salmonella*, the one that troubles humans most has an incubation period of ten to twenty-one days.

7. The bacteria are food-borne and water-borne.

8. Within eight to twenty-four hours of consuming as few as one hundred *Salmonella* organisms, a patient suffers from cramps, diarrhea, nausea, and vomiting.

9. Hospitals from Victoria, British Columbia, to Halifax, Nova Scotia, deal with cases as a matter of routine.

10. Doctor F.C. Blank, MD, formerly at the Hospital for Sick Kids in Toronto, Ontario, advises parents to respond quickly if children become ill.

11. Whereas most adult patients recover in two-and-one-half to five days, young children (as well as the elderly and the weak) can become seriously ill or may even die.

12. Salmonellosis, the illness caused by contact with *Salmonella* bacteria, cost Canadians about a billion dollars from nineteen-ninety-three to nineteen-ninety-four.

13. Medical care alone was estimated to have cost six million, five hundred thousand dollars, for example.

14. We can expect those costs to rise before the year two thousand.

15. Organizations such as the Canadian Medical Association, the United States Food and Drug Administration, and the World Health Organization are working actively to educate those who feed animals, handle food, or work in food-processing plants about the dangers of salmonellosis.

PUNCTUATION

The Comma

12

Learn to apply the basic principles governing comma usage.

Just as pauses and variations in voice pitch help to convey the meaning of spoken sentences, commas help to clarify the meaning of written sentences.

> When the lightning struck, James Harvey fainted.
> When the lightning struck James, Harvey fainted.

Notice how the commas below contribute to ease in reading:

> All ball games feature hitting and socking, chopping and slicing, smashing, slamming, stroking, and whacking, but only in football are these blows diverted from the ball to the opponent. —WRIGHT MORRIS

The use of the comma depends primarily on the structure of the sentence. If you understand sentence structure (see Section **1**) and if you study the rules and examples in this section, you can learn to follow the usual practices of the best modern writers. According to the four basic principles that follow, commas

a) precede co-ordinating conjunctions when they link main clauses;
b) follow introductory adverb clauses and, often, introductory phrases;
c) separate items in a series (including co-ordinate adjectives);
d) set off non-restrictive and other parenthetical elements.

Before Co-ordinating Conjunctions between Main Clauses

12a

A comma ordinarily precedes a co-ordinating conjunction that links main clauses.

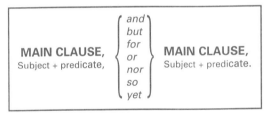

We are here on the planet only once, and we might as well get a feel for the place. —ANNIE DILLARD

The house was dying, but someone had been hastening its death. —JOHN LE CARRÉ

They are hopeless and humble, so he loves them.
—E.M. FORSTER

The rule also applies to co-ordinating conjunctions that link the main clauses of a compound-complex sentence:

Although I do have talent, I have not yet painted a perfect scene, nor do I ever expect to do so, for I can never get on the canvas exactly what I see in my mind. [three main clauses and two subordinate clauses]

Especially when the clauses are short, the comma may be omitted before *and* or *or* (but seldom before *but, for, nor, so, yet*).

> The next night the wind shifted and the thaw began.
>
> —RACHEL CARSON

Sometimes, especially when the second main clause reveals a contrast or when one main clause contains commas, a semicolon is used instead of the usual comma.

> It is one thing to read in a textbook that the footprints of an arctic wolf measure six inches in diameter; but it is quite another thing to see them laid out in all their bald immensity. —FARLEY MOWAT
>
> We do not, most of us, choose to die; nor do we choose the time or conditions of our death. —JOSEPH EPSTEIN
>
> Historically, French Canadians have not really believed in democracy for themselves; and English Canadians have not really wanted it for others. —PIERRE ELLIOTT TRUDEAU

Note: As a rule, do not use a comma before a co-ordinating conjunction that links parts of a compound predicate.

> Colonel Cathcart had courage and never hesitated to volunteer his men for any target available. —JOSEPH HELLER
> [compound predicate—no comma before *and*]

Only occasionally do writers use a comma to emphasize a distinction between the parts of the predicate, as in E.M. Forster's "Artists always seek a new technique, and will continue to do so as long as their work excites them."

■ **Exercise 1** Using the punctuation pattern of **12a,** link the sentences in the following items with an appropriate *and, but, or, nor, for, so,* or *yet*.

EXAMPLE

We cannot win the battle. We cannot afford to lose it.
We cannot win the battle, nor can we afford to lose it.

1. I don't like to have smoke blown in my face, I also dislike eating in smoke-filled restaurants.
2. Customers may return unwanted purchases to the appropriate department. They may choose to return merchandise to the complaints clerk.
3. We decided to visit the west coast of Vancouver Island. We wanted to see the Pacific Ocean.
4. We had arranged to meet them in Halifax. They had still not arrived before we left.
5. One member of the House of Commons attacks another. The Speaker once again intervenes to call for order and demand apologies.
6. He decided to withdraw from the French course. He found he did not have enough time to keep up with the language labs.
7. She slid as she skated into the turn. She recovered quickly and managed to finish in third place.
8. Don't take too long dressing for the concert. You will miss the sensational opening act.
9. He said he won't be able to stay to talk with guests after the lecture. I will just have to be grateful he agreed to talk to our group.
10. She didn't say what had caused the accident. I didn't ask her for any details.

■ **Exercise 2** Follow rule **12a** as you insert commas before connectives linking main clauses in these sentences. (Remember that not all co-ordinating conjunctions link main clauses and that *but, for, so,* and *yet* do not always function as co-ordinating conjunctions.)

1. The students had finished taking the various tests and answering the long questionnaires and they had gone to lunch.
2. There are now special shoes for someone to fill for Jann has resigned and is going to business school.
3. I decided to withdraw from that eight-o'clock class so that I could sleep later but I plan to enrol again for the same class in January.

4. We had seen the stage play and the movie and the University Players' performance was the best of all.
5. Everyone in our group was invited to the party but Gary and Irene decided to go to the hockey game.

After Adverb Clauses and Introductory Phrases

12b

A comma usually follows adverb clauses that precede main clauses. A comma often follows introductory phrases.

(1) Adverb clauses before main clauses

ADVERB CLAUSE, MAIN CLAUSE

When you write, you make a sound in the reader's head.
—RUSSELL BAKER

If thought corrupts language, language can also corrupt thought. —GEORGE ORWELL

While writing his last novel, James recognized and faced his solitude. —LEON EDEL [an elliptical adverb clause—compare "While he was writing. . . ."]

The Meech Lake Accord is a simple document, but if it had been ratified, life in Canada might have become more complicated. [adverb clause preceding the second main clause]

A writer may omit the comma after an introductory adverb clause, especially when the clause is short, if the omission does not make for difficult reading.

When we talk to people we always mean something quite different from what we say. —ANTHONY BURGESS

Note: When the adverb clause follows the main clause, there is usually no need for a comma. Adverb clauses in this position, however, may be preceded by a comma if they are loosely connected with the rest of the sentence.

Henri is now in good health, although he has been an invalid most of his life.

(2) Introductory phrases before subjects of verbs

> **INTRODUCTORY PHRASE,**
> **SUBJECT + PREDICATE**

Prepositional phrases:

> In the next decade, the greenhouse effect will begin to influence the global climate.
> For many feminists, pornography is the theory and rape is the practice.   —CHERIS KRAMARAE AND PAULA TREICHLER

The comma is often omitted after introductory prepositional phrases when no misreading would result:

> In 1980 Terry Fox began his Marathon of Hope. In 1981 he died of cancer.
> After months of listening for some meagre clue he suddenly began to talk in torrents.   —ARTHUR L. KOPIT

In the next two examples the commas are needed to prevent misreading:

> Because of this, beauty differs radically from truth and goodness in one very important aspect.   —MORTIMER J. ADLER
> In a country with a frontier tradition and a deep-rooted enthusiasm for hunting and target shooting, firearms have long been part of the national scene.   —TREVOR ARMBRISTER

Other types of phrases:

> Having attempted nothing, I had no sense of my limitations; having dared nothing, I knew no bounds to my courage.
> —TREVANIAN [participial phrases before both main clauses]
> Even more important, we now have a workable plan. [transitional expression—see the list on page 45]
> All things considered, Third World debt is a serious threat to the global economy. [absolute phrase—see also **12d(3)**]

Note: A comma also follows an introductory interjection or an introductory *yes* or *no:*

> Well, move the ball or move the body.   —ALLEN JACKSON
> Yes, I know that every vote counts. No, I didn't vote.

Caution: Do not use a comma after phrases that begin inverted sentences like these. (See also **29f.**)

> With prosperity came trouble.   —MALACHI MARTIN
> Of far greater concern than censorship of "bad" words is censorship of ideas.   —DONNA WOOLFOLK CROSS
> Only in times of peace can the wastes of capitalism be tolerated.   —F.R. SCOTT

■ **Exercise 3**   Decide whether to use a comma after adverb clauses or after phrases that begin the following sentences. Put a check mark after any sentence in which a comma would be incorrect.

1. If you have been thinking of making a fortune by working for someone else forget it.
2. As far as I know the flight will arrive on schedule.
3. At the same time I recognize that they had good intentions.
4. Before noon the voting lines were two blocks long.
5. Trying to pass three gravel trucks going downhill the driver lost control of his car.
6. Learning to think logically is the concern of almost every university student.
7. With about as much sensitivity as a brick wall the members of the government ignored the petition from the homeless.
8. Under the back seat is an extra heater as well as some storage space.
9. The election far from over the media began to announce the results.
10. When you can help someone less fortunate than yourself.

Between Items in a Series

12c

Commas separate items in a series (including co-ordinate adjectives).

Consisting of three or more items, a series is a succession of parallel elements. See Section **26.** The punctuation of a series depends on its form:

> The air was *raw, dank,* and *grey.* [**a, b,** and **c**—a preferred comma before *and*]
> The air was *raw, dank* and *grey.* [**a, b,** and **c**—an acceptable omission of comma before *and* when there is no danger of misreading]
> The air was *raw, dank, grey.* [**a, b, c**]
> The air was *raw* and *dank* and *grey.* [**a** and **b** and **c**]

(1) Words, phrases, and clauses in a series

> Student reactions were swift and intense: delight, disbelief, fear, horror, anticipation. —ALVIN TOFFLER
> He reported that shoppers fumed, babies wailed, clerks looked flustered, and so on.
> She was a woman of mean understanding, little information, and uncertain temper. —JANE AUSTEN
> He always said percussion clunked, horns went braaaa, violins squeaked, and so on. —ELIZABETH SWADOS
> My famous baked beans are guaranteed to melt the frostiest heart, bring warmth to the palest cheeks, satisfy the most gnawing hunger, and rekindle the spark of hope in the coldest breast. —PIERRE BERTON

Exceptions: If items in a series contain internal commas, the semicolon is used instead of commas for clarity: see **14b.** For special emphasis, commas are sometimes used even when all the items in a series are linked by co-ordinating conjunctions.

> We cannot put it off for a month, or a week, or even a day.

(2) Co-ordinate adjectives

Adjectives are co-ordinate when they modify the same noun (or nominal). Use a comma between co-ordinate adjectives not linked by a co-ordinating conjunction:

> It is a waiting, silent, limp room. —EUDORA WELTY
> [*Waiting, silent,* and *limp* all modify *room.* COMPARE "It is a silent, limp waiting room."]
> They are young, alert social workers. [*Young* and *alert* modify the word group *social workers.* COMPARE "They are young, social, alert workers."]
> It was a solid, red-brick house with an eye-catching, sky-blue door. It stood at the end of a short, quiet street in a sleepy suburb lying in a rich, green valley.

■ **Exercise 4** Using commas as needed, supply co-ordinate adjectives to modify any six of the following ten word groups. Put each of the six word groups and its co-ordinate adjectives into a sentence.

> EXAMPLE
> *metric system*   Most countries use *the familiar, sensible metric system* to measure distances.

1. cinnamon doughnut
2. classical music
3. metal sculpture
4. cheddar cheese
5. software documentation
6. office buildings
7. snowy owl
8. elementary school
9. sports car
10. rhetorical question

With Parenthetical and Miscellaneous Elements

12d
Commas set off non-restrictive and other parenthetical elements as well as contrasted elements, items in dates, and so on.

To set off a word group with commas, use two commas unless the element is placed at the beginning or the end of the sentence.

> "History is a pact," *as Edmund Burke observed,* "between the dead, the living, and the yet unborn."
>
> *As Edmund Burke observed,* "history is a pact between the dead, the living, and the yet unborn."
>
> "History is a pact between the dead, the living, and the yet unborn," *as Edmund Burke observed.*

Caution: When two commas are needed to set off an element, do not forget one of the commas.

> CONFUSING   An experienced driver generally speaking, does not fear the open road.
>
> CLEAR   An experienced driver, generally speaking, does not fear the open road.

(1) Non-restrictive clauses or phrases and non-restrictive appositives are set off by commas. Restrictive elements are not set off.

ADJECTIVE CLAUSES OR PHRASES

Adjective clauses or phrases are non-restrictive when they describe (rather than limit the meaning of) the noun or pronoun they modify: set off by commas, they are non-essential parenthetical elements that may be omitted. Restrictive clauses or phrases are limiting (rather than descriptive) adjectivals: not set off by commas, they identify the noun or pronoun they modify by telling *which one* (or *ones*) and are essential elements that may not be omitted.

As you study the following examples, read each sentence aloud and notice not only meaning but also your pauses and intonation.

NON-RESTRICTIVE	RESTRICTIVE OR ESSENTIAL
Clauses:	
My mother**, who listened to his excuses,** smiled knowingly.	Any mother **who listened to such excuses** would smile knowingly.
We will explore Peggy's Cove**, which is the most photographed spot in Nova Scotia.**	We will explore a cove **that is the most photo-graphed spot in Nova Scotia.**
Phrases:	
In July these mountains**, covered with snow,** seem unreal.	In July mountains **covered with snow** seem unreal.
The old Renault**, glistening in the rain,** looked brand new.	An old car **glistening in the rain** looked brand new.
Such noise**, too loud for human ears,** can cause deafness.	A noise **too loud for human ears** can cause deafness.

Note: Although some writers use *which* at the beginning of restrictive clauses, it is preferable to use *that*.

The party opposed taxes**, which would be a burden to working Canadians.** [*Non-restrictive:* the party opposed levying taxes of any kind, all of which would be a burden to working Canadians.]

The party opposed taxes **that would be a burden to work-ing Canadians.** [*Restrictive:* the party opposed levying taxes of a certain kind.]

Sometimes only the omission or the use of commas indicates whether an adjectival is non-restrictive or restrictive and thus conveys the exact meaning intended by the writer.

She spent months teaching the children**, who were unable to read.** [*Non-restrictive:* she taught all the children to read; they were all unable to do so.]

She spent months teaching the children **who were unable to read.** [*Restrictive:* some of the children were unable to read; she taught only those children.]

APPOSITIVES

Appositives are either non-restrictive (set off by commas) or restrictive (not set off by commas). A non-restrictive appositive supplies additional but non-essential details about the noun or pronoun to which it refers. A restrictive appositive limits the meaning of the noun or pronoun to which it refers by pointing out *which one* (or *ones*).

NON-RESTRICTIVE	RESTRICTIVE OR ESSENTIAL
Even Paul Underhill, **my very best friend,** let me down.	Even my friend **Paul Underhill** let me down.
Voyager photographed Saturn, **the ringed planet.**	*Voyager* photographed the planet **Saturn.**

Abbreviations after names are treated as non-restrictive appositives:

Was the letter from Frances Evans, **Ph.D.,** or from F.H. Evans, **M.D.**?

■ **Exercise 5** Use commas to set off non-restrictive adjective clauses or phrases and non-restrictive appositives in the following sentences. Put a check mark after any sentence that needs no commas.

1. I will interview Mary Smith who manages the bank.
2. I will interview the Mary Smith who manages the bank.
3. Vanessa Berry sitting near the window saw the accident.
4. Coho salmon served with bannock bread is my favourite meal.
5. Few people around here have ever heard of my home town a little place called Marystown.
6. All players who broke the rules had to sit on the bench.
7. The word *malapropism* is derived from the name of a character in Sheridan's *The Rivals* a Mrs. Malaprop.

8. The coach who is chewing gum and clapping his hands is Teddy.
9. The telephone which was invented in 1876 is now a household necessity.
10. Martin Luther King Jr. and Archbishop Desmond Tutu won Nobel peace prizes for their efforts to promote non-violent social change.

(2) Contrasted elements, geographical names, and most items in dates and addresses are set off by commas.

CONTRASTED ELEMENTS

Racing is supposed to be a test of skill, **not a dice game with death.**   —SONNY KLEINFIELD
His phrases dribbled off, **but not his memories.**
—JAMES A. MICHENER
Human beings, **unlike oysters,** frequently reveal their emotions.   —GEORGE F. WILL

Note: Opinion is divided about the placement of a comma before *but* in such constructions as the following:

Other citizens who disagree with me base their disagreement not on facts different from the ones I know, but on a different set of values.   —RENÉ DUBOS
Today the Black Hills are being invaded again, not for gold but for uranium.   —PETER MATTHIESSEN

GEOGRAPHICAL NAMES, ITEMS IN DATES AND ADDRESSES

Geneva, Switzerland, is the site for the next round of disarmament talks.
The letter was addressed to Ms. J.N. Dang, Vancouver, BC V6T 1W5.
Leslie applied for the job in October, 1993, and accepted it on Friday, March 4, 1994.
OR

Leslie applied for the job in October 1993 and accepted it on Friday, 4 March 1994.
[Note that commas may be omitted when the day of the month is not given or when the day of the month precedes rather than follows the month.]

■ **Exercise 6** Insert commas where needed in the following sentences.

1. Those are wolves not dogs.
2. The newspaper's address is 444 Front Street West Toronto Ontario V5V 2S9.
3. On 20 August 1992 Canada's first ministers met in Charlottetown P.E.I. to propose amendments to the Constitution.
4. Norman Bethune was born in Gravenhurst Ontario on March 3 not on March 23.
5. According to the March 1 1993 issue of *Maclean's* the growing squeeze on government spending meant that tuition fees would continue their inexorable rise through-out the 1990s.
6. She said she wanted a thoughtful and considerate room-mate not just someone who washed up her own dishes.

(3) Parenthetical words, phrases, or clauses (inserted expressions), mild interjections, words in direct address, and absolute phrases are set off by commas.

PARENTHETICAL EXPRESSIONS

Language, **then,** sets the tone of our society.
—EDWIN NEWMAN

To be sure, beauty is a form of power.   —SUSAN SONTAG

The company you keep at death is, **of all things,** most dependent on chance.   —KERI HULME

It's healthy to admire, **I suppose,** but destructive to idolize.
—TIM WHITAKER

"The trouble with ministers," **said Mrs. Emerson,** "is that they're not women." —ANNE TYLER [See also **16a(2)**.]

Guard your enthusiasms, **however frail they may be.**
—ARDIS WHITMAN [parenthetical clause]

The Age of Television has dawned in China, **a generation later than in the West.** —LINDA MATHEWS [appended element]

When they cause little or no pause in reading, expressions such as *also, too, of course, perhaps, at least, therefore,* and *likewise* are frequently not set off by commas.

The times **also** have changed in ways that soften the rhetoric.
—HENRY FAIRLIE

In some countries, an author is censored not only for what he says but for how he says it, and an unconventional style is **therefore** a declaration of artistic freedom.
—MARGARET ATWOOD

MILD INTERJECTIONS AND WORDS USED IN DIRECT ADDRESS

Ah, that's my idea of a good meal. [interjection]

Now is the time, **animal lovers,** to protest. [direct address]

ABSOLUTE PHRASES

His temper being what it is, I don't want a confrontation.

He was thumping at a book, **his voice growing louder and louder.** —JOYCE CAROL OATES

12e

Occasionally a comma (although not required by any of the major principles already discussed) may be needed to prevent misreading.

Without commas the following sentences would confuse the reader, if only temporarily.

Still, water must be transported to dry areas.

The day before, I had talked with her on the phone.

In 1986, 19.5 million Canadians were in the work force.

Those who can, pay and forego consumption of other essential goods.   —ERIK P. ECKHOLM

The earth breathes, in a certain sense.   —LEWIS THOMAS

■ **Exercise 7**   Commas have been deleted from the following sentences. Insert commas where they are needed. Prepare to explain the reason for each comma used. Also prepare to point out where optional commas might be placed as a matter of stylistic preference.

1. When I was two we moved to the Gold Coast but by then it was known as Ghana.
2. It was a major uprising not a minor incident; there was civil disobedience anarchy violence.
3. My guess is as the former Soviet Union changes cultural exchange programs will flourish.
4. But alas I do not control airline schedules and that I regret is the story of my life—always delayed never on time.
5. If all laws fail try drafting new ones for situations that defy resolution.
6. To commemorate the bicentennial of the revolution a crowd of people gathered in the streets on the night of July 14 1989.
7. Living in Canada's North is very expensive some families having been known to spend two-thirds of their income on accommodation.
8. The chess player's concentration at the tournament never flagged nor did it disappear at the press conference following his winning match.
9. "I wanted to see the Governor General's residence at Rideau Hall" said the young tourist his eyes shining with genuine interest.
10. Canada and the United States have a long-standing relationship harmonious and friendly much of the time but tense when it comes to negotiating disputes over trade.

■ **Exercise 8** For humorous effect, the writer of the following paragraph deliberately omits commas that can be justified by rules **12a, b,** or **d.** Be prepared for a discussion of the paragraph. Where could commas be inserted to contribute to ease in reading?

The commas are the most useful and usable of all the stops. It is highly important to put them in place as you go along. If you try to come back after doing a paragraph and stick them in the various spots that tempt you you will discover that they tend to swarm like minnows into all sorts of crevices whose existence you hadn't realized and before you know it the whole long sentence becomes immobilized and lashed up squirming in commas. Better to use them sparingly, and with affection, precisely when the need for each one arises, nicely, by itself.

—LEWIS THOMAS, *The Medusa and the Snail*

■ **Exercise 9** Insert commas where they are needed in the following passage. Be prepared to discuss where commas might be considered optional.

¹Community suppers continue to be a feature of life in North America though suppers for the homeless are now more common than fundraising suppers put on by churches social centres youth organizations and service groups. ²Church suppers are still the glue for many prairie communities and one of the chief means of raising money to maintain church buildings. ³Community centres and high schools in small towns put on chili suppers before a hockey or basketball game to raise money for sports equipment and road trips. ⁴Scouts Guides and Explorer groups use suppers to support camping expeditions. ⁵Women's groups which are often allied to cultural organizations put on dinners to fund causes as diverse as aid for refugees hostels for battered women objects for art gallery collections or symphony tickets for children. ⁶The community suppers for homeless and poor people now draw hundreds of thousands each year in Canada.

[7]Served nightly in church halls drop-in centres basements and gymnasiums these modest suppers provided by missions and social agencies feed the hungry. [8]In the past most who turned up for such meals were single men usually middle-aged and older. [9]The image of these men as the norm persists. [10]Now however older women mothers with children of all ages and young people (most in their twenties) are turning up too. [11]In 1993 social agencies across Canada participated in a "snapshot" of their supper guests. [12]The results stunned many. [13]By far the largest proportion of the homeless were people between the ages of eighteen and thirty-six. [14]And for many of these people the modest supper forms the centre of an empty day.

[15]Most of us are unaware of these suppers. [16]In fact the only notice given these community efforts comes in December. [17]At this time TV stations in their attempt to produce human interest or seasonal "feel-good" coverage send their crews out to shelters. [18]What viewers see is the extra effort put into Thanksgiving and Christmas meals the attempts to find a few extras to mark these occasions. [19]But recently these once-a-year broadcasts have shown a change. [20]Business clubs and small independent companies have also begun to join the efforts to organize these suppers. [21]Not only do their men and women raise money to pay for food and table furnishings but they also do the work—they shop prepare the food and serve their guests themselves. [22]Naturally the work of individuals who spend Christmas Day away from home and family has become newsworthy too. [23]The individual participants interviewed all say the same things: that direct action gives them a feeling of connection with the community that can't come from putting a cheque in the mail and that they realize their own good fortune in seeing the misfortune of others.

[24]Across Canada and the United States the spirit of the community supper now finds its expression around the simple trestle tables set up in urban centres rather than around the groaning harvest tables of farm communities.

Superfluous Commas

13

Do not use superfluous commas.

Unnecessary or misplaced commas are false or awkward signals that may confuse the reader. If you tend to use too many commas, remember that although the comma ordinarily signals a pause, not every pause calls for a comma. As you read each sentence in the following paragraph aloud, you may pause naturally at places other than those marked by a period, but no commas are necessary.

> Springboard divers routinely execute manoeuvres in which their body rotates in space. The basic manoeuvres are the somersault and the twist. In the somersault the body rotates head over heels as if the athlete were rotating about an axis extending from his left side to his right side through his waist. In the twist the body spins or pirouettes in midair as if the athlete were rotating about an axis extending from his head to his toes.
> —CLIFF FROHLICH, "The Physics of Somersaulting and Twisting"

To avoid using unnecessary commas, first review Section **12** and then study and observe the following rules.

13a

Do not use a comma to separate the subject from its verb or the verb from its object.

The circled commas should be omitted:

Many nations with low growth rates⟨,⟩ cannot sustain high birth rates. [needless separation of subject and verb]

My instructor said⟨,⟩ that the old laws were antiquated. [needless separation of verb and object (a noun clause)]

13b

Do not misuse a comma before or after a co-ordinating conjunction. See **12a**.

The circled commas should be omitted:

The facts were selected⟨,⟩ and organized with care.

The film captured our attention, but⟨,⟩ others in the audience simply left before the end.

13c

Do not use commas to set off words and short phrases (especially introductory ones) that are not parenthetical or that are very slightly so.

The circled commas should be omitted:

Teresa Stratas made her opera debut⟨,⟩ in La Bohème⟨,⟩ in 1960.

Maybe⟨,⟩ the battery cables need replacing.

13d

Do not use commas to set off restrictive (necessary) clauses, restrictive phrases, and restrictive appositives.

The circled commas should be omitted:

> Everyone⊙ who smokes cigarettes⊙ risks losing about ten years of life. [restrictive clause: see **12d(1)**]
>
> For years she has not eaten anything⊙seasoned with onions or garlic. [restrictive phrase: see **12d(1)**]
>
> The word⊙nope⊙is a colloquial substitute for no. [restrictive appositive: see **12d(1)**]

13e

Do not use a comma before the first item or after the last item of a series (including a series of co-ordinate adjectives).

The circled commas should be omitted:

> Field trips were required in a few courses, such as⊙botany, geology, and sociology.
>
> The company hires talented, smart, ambitious⊙women.

■ **Exercise 1** Study the structure of the following sentence; then answer the question that follows by giving a specific rule number (such as **13a, 13d**) for each item. Be prepared to explain your answers in class.

> Now when you say "newly rich" you picture a middle-aged and corpulent man who has a tendency to remove his collar at formal dinners and is in perpetual hot water with his ambitious wife and her titled friends. —F. SCOTT FITZGERALD

Why is there no comma after (1) *Now*, (2) *say*, (3) *middle-aged*, (4) *man*, (5) *collar*, (6) *dinners*, or (7) *wife*?

■ **Exercise 2**   Change the structure and the punctuation of the following sentences according to the pattern of the examples.

EXAMPLE

A motorcyclist saw our flashing lights, and he stopped to offer aid. [an appropriate comma: see **12a**]

A motorcyclist saw our flashing lights and stopped to offer aid. [second main clause reduced to part of a compound predicate—comma no longer needed]

1. The hail stripped leaves from trees, and it pounded early gardens.
2. Some science fiction presents newly discovered facts, and it predicts the future accurately.
3. Rob likes the work, and he may make a career of it.

EXAMPLE

If any students destroyed public property, they were expelled. [an appropriate comma: see **12b**]

Any students who destroyed public property were expelled. [introductory adverb clause converted to restrictive clause— comma no longer needed]

4. When people lead rather than demand, they often get good results.
5. If a boy is willing to work, he can get a job here.
6. Some people are anxious about their personal safety, and they worry all the time.

■ **Exercise 3**   In the following paragraph some of the commas are needed and some are superfluous. Circle all unnecessary commas. Prepare to explain (see Section **12**) each comma that you allow to stand.

¹Early writers and explorers dismissed Canada as a bleak, forbidding, worthless, land. ²The French philosopher and writer, Voltaire, and the explorer Jacques Cartier, have been much quoted. ³Voltaire's reference to Canada as, "a few acres of snow," actually comes from two phrases about measures for

land, *quelques arpents de neige* ("some acres of snow"), and *quatre arpents de neige* ("four acres of snow"). ⁴The first phrase, which appears in his novel *Candide,* is the one most people recognize. ⁵The second comes from Voltaire's letters, and is in some ways even more dismissive of Canada. ⁶The phrase appears in the following comment: "What a big fuss over a little thing. It's like the war with the English over four acres of snow." ⁷(The French wording for the comparison is, *Cela ressemble à la guerre des Anglais qui commença pour quatre arpents de neige.*) ⁸Voltaire is, elsewhere, reported as saying, "Canada is a few acres of snow and not worth a soldier's bones." ⁹Voltaire's reference to Canada as "a few acres of snow" is rivalled in early French views of Canada, only by Jacques Cartier's phrase on first seeing what is now the Labrador and Quebec shore, in 1534. ¹⁰He described it as, "the land God gave to Cain."

■ **Exercise 4**   In the following paragraph (adapted from *Time*), some of the commas are superfluous. Circle these and be prepared to explain why they should be omitted. Review Section **12** if necessary.

¹Yet, punctuation is something more than a culture's birthmark; it scores the music in our minds, and gets our thoughts moving to the rhythm of our hearts. ²Punctuation, is the notation in the sheet music of our words, telling us when to rest, or when to raise our voices. ³It acknowledges that the meaning of our discourse, as of any symphonic composition, lies, not in the units, but in the pauses, the pacing, and, the phrasing. ⁴Commas adjust things, such as, the tone, the colour, and the volume, till the feeling comes into perfect focus. ⁵A world, which has only periods, is a world without shade. ⁶It has a music without sharps, and flats. ⁷It has a jackboot rhythm. ⁸Words cannot bend, and curve.

The Semicolon

14

Use the semicolon between main clauses not linked by a co-ordinating conjunction and between co-ordinate elements containing commas.

Having the force of a co-ordinator, the semicolon is used chiefly between main clauses that are closely related. Compare the following constructions.

> Some philosophers offer practical wisdom. Others do not. I prefer to study the former. [three simple sentences]
> Some philosophers offer practical wisdom; others do not. I prefer to study the former. [a semicolon linking the more closely related ideas]

If you can distinguish between main and subordinate clauses and between phrases and clauses (see **1d** and **1e**), you should have little trouble using the semicolon. As you study the rules in this section, notice that the semicolon is used only between closely related co-ordinate elements.

14a

Use the semicolon between two main clauses not linked by a co-ordinating conjunction. See also **12a.**

The co-ordinating conjunctions are *and, but, for, or, nor, so, yet.*

MAIN CLAUSE		MAIN CLAUSE
Subject + predicate	;	subject + predicate

No person is born arrogant; arrogance must be taught.
— CLARA M. DOBAY

Small mammals tick fast, burn rapidly, and live for a short time; large mammals live long at a stately pace.
— STEPHEN JAY GOULD

Rule **14a** also applies in compound-complex sentences:

If the new business is a success, I'll take my share of the profits; if it isn't, I think I'll leave the country.

COMPARE If the new business is a success, I'll take my share of the profits. If it isn't, I think I'll leave the country.

Keep in mind that *however, therefore, for example, on the contrary,* and so on (see the list of conjunctive adverbs and transitional expressions on page 45) are not co-ordinating conjunctions. Often appearing at the beginning of a sentence, such adverbials frequently serve as transitional devices between sentences: see **32b(4).** When placed between main clauses, they are preceded by the semicolon: see **3b.**

At the 1988 Olympics, sprinter Ben Johnson won a gold medal; however, he lost it when he failed a drug test.

COMPARE At the 1988 Olympics, sprinter Ben Johnson won a gold medal. However, he lost it when he failed a drug test.

For years he planned to sail around the world; therefore, he worked hard to develop his sailing skills.

COMPARE For years he planned to sail around the world. Therefore, he worked hard to develop his sailing skills.

The comma after a conjunctive adverb or transitional expression is often omitted when the adverbial is not considered parenthetical or when the comma is not needed to prevent misreading.

Glenn Gould was unusual among Canadian musicians; indeed in many ways he was in a class entirely his own.

Sometimes a semicolon (instead of the usual comma) precedes a co-ordinating conjunction when the writer wishes to make a sharp division between the two main clauses. See also **12a,** page 152.

The female bees feed these lazy drones for a while; but they let them starve to death after the mating of the queen bee.

Note: Occasionally, a comma separates short, very closely related main clauses.

We are strengthened by equality, we are weakened by it; we celebrate it, we repudiate it. —THOMAS GRIFFITH [a semicolon used between pairs of main clauses separated by commas]

When the second main clause explains or amplifies the first, a colon may be used between main clauses. See **17d,** page 199.

Caution: Do not overwork the semicolon: see **14c.** Often it is better to revise compound sentences according to the principles of subordination: see Section **24.**

14b   ; /

■ **Exercise 1**   Use semicolons where needed to eliminate errors in punctuation.

1. An engagement is not a marriage a family quarrel is not a broken home.
2. All members of my family save things they will never use, for example, my sister saves old calendars and bent or rusty nails.
3. Many nations now have heterogeneous populations, in Canada for instance, many new citizens come from Asia, Africa, and Europe.
4. He took a course in the art of self-defence, later, during a class demonstration, he broke his wrist.
5. The motor in my car blew up, as a result, I had to take the bus for a month.

14b
Use the semicolon to separate a series of items that themselves contain commas.

> I subscribe to several computer magazines that include reviews of new, better-designed hardware; descriptions of inexpensive, commercial software programs; advice from experts; and actual utility programs that make keeping track of my files easier.

■ **Exercise 2**   Substitute a semicolon for any comma that could result in misreading.

1. Prepared for a lively argument, the three debaters on the stage were Bob White, prominent labour leader, June Callwood, writer and social activist, and Kim Campbell, former prime minister.
2. On the talk shows are entertainers, such as actors or comedians, experts from various fields, such as educators or religious leaders, and authors of bestselling books.
3. His tone was offensive, to her way of thinking, he was unsuited for the job in the personnel office.

4. When the members of Ellen's group arrived, they agreed to sit in the sun at the table, she chose to sit in the shade.
5. It was nearly midnight, when the clouds finally cleared and the hikers could see the stars, they felt the wait had been worthwhile.

14c
Do not use a semicolon between parts of unequal grammatical rank.

Not between a clause and a phrase:

NOT   Along came Gaetan; the dormitory clown.

BUT   Along came Gaetan, the dormitory clown. [appositive phrase]

NOT   We took a detour; the reason being that the bridge was under construction.

BUT   We took a detour, the reason being that the bridge was under construction. [absolute phrase]

NOT   Lucy has three topics of conversation; her courses, her career, and her travels.

BUT   Lucy has three topics of conversation, her courses, her career, and her travels. [noun phrases]

Not between a main clause and a subordinate clause:

NOT   If this report is true; then we should act now.

BUT   If this report is true, then we should act now. [introductory adverb clause]

NOT   We heard about the final decision; which really surprised us.

BUT   We heard about the final decision, which really surprised us. [adjective clause]

NOT   The truck needed repairs; although it would still run.

BUT   The truck needed repairs, although it would still run. [adverb clause]

■ **Exercise 3** Find the semicolons used between parts of unequal rank and substitute a correct mark of punctuation. Do not change properly placed semicolons.

1. Don went jogging one afternoon; never returning; then he was numbered among the tens of thousands who disappear every year.
2. Although the educational TV channel is sometimes a bore; at least tedious commercials do not interrupt the programs.
3. I dislike only two kinds of people; those who tell me what to do and those who don't do anything themselves.
4. Eating hot, cheesy, thick-crust pizza; swooping down a snow-covered mountain; watching old Bogart movies—these are some of my favourite activities.
5. I still play basketball with my old high-school friends on Friday nights; even though I know that we are growing apart.
6. The danger of the situation becoming obvious to all; we returned to the foot of the mountain.
7. If he has done everything he can to make amends; then we must accept his efforts.
8. I want to read *The English Patient;* which has been on the national bestseller list for five months.
9. Many times I've pushed the up button; after I've waited for as long as five minutes; the doors of two elevators roll open at once.
10. The tormented bull lowered his head in readiness for another charge; the one-sided contest not being over yet.

■ **Exercise 4** Compose four sentences to illustrate various uses of the semicolon.

■ **Exercise 5** This is an exercise on the comma and the semicolon. Study the following examples, which illustrate rules in Sections **12** and **14**. Using these examples as guides, punctuate sentences 1–10 on the following page appropriately.

12a Pat poured chlorine into the crucible, for he had not read the warning in his lab manual.

12b Since Pat had not read the warning in his lab manual, he poured chlorine into the crucible.

12c Pat did not read the lab manual, observe the warning, or wait for the solution to cool.

12d Pat did not read his lab manual, which warned against pouring chlorine into a hot crucible.

Pat, a careless young man, poured chlorine into the hot crucible.

First, warnings should be read.

12e A week before, he had glanced at the manual.

14a Pat ignored the warning in the lab manual; he poured chlorine into the hot crucible.

Pat poured chlorine into the hot crucible; thus he caused the explosion.

14b At the hospital Pat said that he had not read the warning; that he had, of course, been careless; and that he would never again, under any circumstances, pour chlorine into a hot crucible.

1. Many patients in the mid-eighties deliberately declined elective surgery for they did not wish to wait months to be admitted to hospital.

2. Dr. Chiang a visiting professor from China says that the Cultural Revolution strengthened the Red Guard but that it did so at a high price.

3. The stalls of the open market along the wharf were filled with tray after tray of glassy-eyed fish slender stalks of pink rhubarb mounds of home-grown tomatoes and jars of bronze honey.

4. Two or three scrawny mangy-looking hounds lay sprawled in the shade of the cabin.

5. While Diana was unpacking the camping gear and Grace was gathering firewood I began to pitch the tent.

6. After attending a preview of the new play the audience left the theatre in utter silence.

7. Still in high school we had to memorize dates and facts such as 1066 the Battle of Hastings 1914–1918 World War I 1939–1945 World War II and 1969 the first moon landing.

8. The dream home that they often talk about is a retreat in the Rockies to tell the truth however they seem perfectly happy in their mobile home on the outskirts of Fredericton.

9. The criminal was asking for mercy his victim was pleading for justice.

10. Chris and I felt that our blustery argument would never end however my weather-watching roommate reminded us that thunderstorms are usually of short duration.

■ **Exercise 6** Provide semicolons and commas for the following paragraph. (You may wish to review Section **12** for uses of the comma before you begin.)

[1]The late eighties and the early nineties have seen a nostalgic almost sentimental interest in country life—a country life that never was. [2]This fondness shows up in a variety of ways: the popularity of "country home" as a decorating style (attested to by the appearance of numerous magazines devoted to this topic) the adulation given to country and western stars like Dolly Parton and k.d. lang Kenny Rogers and Billy Ray Cyrus (adulation formerly given almost exclusively to Hollywood and rock stars) an interest in country fairs and country crafts (evident even in the upscale gift shops of major urban hotels) the fashion for four-wheel drive trucks and pickups (now driven by yuppies who rarely drive anywhere but to the office) and the renewed interest in "home style" or "down home" cooking (served in expensive, handmade dishes). [3]It is not only the cocooning couples in the suburbs who want comfort food hopeful first-time restaurateurs want to recreate for their patrons the Normal Rockwell image of a family gathered around the Sunday dinner table. [4]Social historians think this interest in the country lifestyle is consumer-driven specifically, urban dwellers want to create a comfort zone in an increasingly more violent pressured and socially complex environment.

The Apostrophe

15

**Use the apostrophe to indicate the posses-
sive case (except for personal pronouns),
to mark omissions in contractions, and to
form certain plurals.**

15a
**Use the apostrophe to indicate the possessive case
of nouns (including acronyms) and indefinite
pronouns.**

The possessive (or genitive) case shows ownership or a
comparable relationship: *Kelsey's* car, two *weeks'* pay. The
possessive case of nouns and of indefinite pronouns may
be indicated by the use of 's or by the apostrophe alone.

> everybody's friend   the students' laughter

Occasionally, the idea of the possessive is indicated by the
use of both an *of* phrase and 's:

> that tie **of** Al's [often called a double possessive]

COMPARE   this description of Al [Al is described.]
this description of Al's [Al did the describing.]

A possessive may follow the word it modifies:

Is that old broken-down baby buggy **Frank**'s or **Jane**'s?
[Compare "Frank**'s** or Jane**'s** baby buggy."]

(1) **For singular nouns (including acronyms) and indefinite pronouns, add the apostrophe and *s*.**

Sue's idea   a day's work   OPEC's aim   anyone's guess

Option: Adding an apostrophe and *s* is never wrong, but an apostrophe without an *s* may be added to a singular word ending in *s* when another *s* would make the word difficult to pronounce: *Sue Rogers's essay* OR *Sue Rogers' essay; Moses's deliberations* OR *Moses' deliberations.*

(2) **For plural nouns ending in *s*, add only the apostrophe. For plurals not ending in *s*, add the apostrophe and *s*.**

her sons' room   ten dollars' worth   the Ameses's home
BUT
men's watches   women's names   children's rights

(3) **For compounds, add the apostrophe and *s* only to the last word.**

my sister-in-law's shop   someone else's turn
the minister of trade's idea   George Heming, Jr.'s reply
[Notice that no comma follows *Jr.'s* although *Jr.* is normally set off by commas.]

(4) **To indicate individual ownership, add the apostrophe and *s* to each name.**

the doctor's and the dentist's offices
Al's and Sue's cars [Note that *cars* is plural.]

Option: To indicate joint ownership, add the apostrophe and *s* only to the last name or to each name.

Al and Sue's car OR Al's and Sue's car

Note: Proper names (organizations, geographical locations, and so on) sometimes do not have the apostrophe or the apostrophe and *s*.

Devil's Island   Devils Tower   Devil Mountain

■ **Exercise 1**   Change the modifier after the noun to a possessive form before the noun, following the pattern of the examples.

EXAMPLES
the laughter of the crowd   *the crowd's laughter*
suggestions made by James   *James's suggestions*
                                    OR *James' suggestions*

1. the acreage belonging to John L. Field III
2. the boat bought by the Weinsteins
3. the voices of Tess and Mary
4. the efforts of the editor-in-chief
5. the strategy that Doris uses
6. worth a quarter
7. ideas of somebody else
8. stories by Dickens
9. shoes for women
10. a song written by Robyn and Pavola

15b

Use the apostrophe to mark omissions in contracted words and numbers.

> didn't he'll they're there's she'd class of '91
> o'clock [contraction of "of the clock"]
> "Well, Curley's pretty handy," the swamper said skeptically.
> "Never did seem right to me. S'pose Curley jumps a big guy
> an' licks him. Ever'body says what a game guy Curley is."
>
> —JOHN STEINBECK [See also **19b.**]

15c

Use the apostrophe and *s* to form certain plurals.

Use the apostrophe and *s* for the plural forms of lower-case letters and of abbreviations followed by periods.

> his *e*'s and *o*'s   no more *ibid.*'s   two V.P.'s [The 's
> following an italicized letter or word is not italicized
> (underlined). See also **10d.**]

When needed to prevent confusion, the 's is used for the plural of capital letters and of words referred to as words.

> too many *I*'s   several *A*'s   two *the*'s   the *ha ha*'s

Options:

the 1900's OR the 1900s	his 7's OR his 7s
two *B*'s OR two *B*s	the &'s OR the &s
her *and*'s OR her *ands*	the MLA's OR the MLAs

15d

Do not use the apostrophe with the pronouns *his, hers, its, ours, yours, theirs,* **or** *whose* **or with plural nouns not in the possessive case.**

A friend of **theirs** knows a cousin of **yours.**
Some **architects** design **offices** for **lawyers.**

Caution: Do not confuse *its* with *it's* or *whose* with *who's:*

Its motor is small.   **It's** [It is] a small motor.
Whose responsibility is it?   **Who's** [Who is] responsible?

■ **Exercise 2**   Insert apostrophes where needed.

1. Many students attitudes changed at the end of the 1980s.
2. Two of Mr. Hughes students won awards for their essays.
3. Those newsstands sell Marian Rosss homemade candy.
4. Theyre not interested in hockey; its roughness repels them.
5. Snapshots of the class of 94 cover Jerrys bulletin board.
6. "Its just one C.P.A.s opinion, isnt it?" Sean commented.
7. There are four *is* and four *ss* in *Mississippi.*
8. Theres a difference between her attitude and theirs.
9. OPECs decision took a few economic analysts by surprise.
10. The computer confused my account with somebody elses.

■ **Exercise 3**   Revise each of the following sentences, replacing the italicized phrase with a possessive noun or pronoun. Add any other apostrophes where needed.

EXAMPLE

The two students have rented an apartment together, and the *sister of the younger one* is going to be the guest *of both of them* at Christmas.

The two students have rented an apartment together, and younger one's sister is going to be their guest at Christmas.

1. The praise *of Ira Dilworth* for the writing *of Emily Carr* finally drew the attention *of the Canadian reading public.*

2. The clowning *of Silly Sally* is much in demand for the parties *of children,* and its a rare child who doesn't love the tricks *of her dogs.*

3. Whats remarkable is the way the group staged all kinds of activities to attract the attention *of the media* to its activities and its goals.

4. Tomás said that the problems are *her problems,* not the problems *of Henry and Liz Jones,* and that she should have paid for the assessment *of an inspector* instead of asking for the opinion *of her brother-in-law.*

5. The stories *of Jamaica Kincaid* and *of John Updike* often appear in the fiction pages *of the New Yorker.*

6. Its too early to tell if its somebody elses fault, but she will have the answer *of the arbitrator* quite soon.

7. He told her, "Youre mad to think that the house or the car *of the aunt of Tom* could be worth less than a million dollars."

8. Its everyones hope that things will work out for the friends *of Francis* and that they will not have to pay the medical expenses *of the last two years.*

9. She flatly refused to give presents for the A's and the B's *on the work of their term* until she received the school reports *of her sons.*

10. The customers *of the business* decided to start a lawsuit to recover the costs *of them.*

Quotation Marks

16

Use quotation marks for direct quotations (other than those set off from the text), for some titles, and for words used in a special sense. Place other marks of punctuation in proper relation to quotation marks.

Quotation marks (like scissors) are always used in pairs. The first mark indicates a beginning (meaning *quote*) and the second an ending (*unquote*). Do not carelessly omit or misplace the second quotation mark.

16a
Use quotation marks for direct quotations and in all dialogue. Set off long quotations by indention.

(1) Use double quotation marks for direct quotations. Use single quotation marks to enclose a quotation (or a minor title—see also 16b) within a quotation.

Double quotation marks:

> "If we believe absurdities," said Voltaire, "we shall commit atrocities." [Quotation marks enclose only the quotation, not expressions like *she said* or *he replied*. Quotation

marks are not used for indirect quotations: Voltaire said that believers in absurdities commit atrocities.]

According to Disraeli, Gladstone was a person who did not have "a single redeeming defect." [The quoted phrase is an integral part of the sentence.]

Disraeli once said, "He [Gladstone] has not a single redeeming defect." [Not a part of the direct quotation, the information inserted in brackets contributes to clarity.]

Single quotation marks:

"Earl keeps calling my idea 'the impossible dream,' " she said. [a quotation within a quotation]

"Roch Carrier's 'The Hockey Sweater' is one of the funniest short stories I've ever read!" Tony exclaimed. [a title within a quotation]

(2) Use quotation marks for dialogue (directly quoted conversation).

In dialogue the standard practice is to write what each person says, no matter how short, as a separate paragraph. Expressions such as *he said,* as well as closely related bits of narrative, are included in the paragraph along with the direct quotations.

Alec Monkman stood, smacking his hard palms together, laughing. "I believe I just saw a fight to the death between two dust-devils," he declared.

"We were polka-ing," explained Daniel.

"You don't need to tell me," said his grandfather. "I know them all. When I was young I used to be a dancing fool."

"I think I got the hang of that one," confided Daniel, "but that waltzing is something else."

"Nothing nicer than a waltz," stated his grandfather.

"It's easier than rolling out of bed. Let me give you a few tips." He made a perfunctory, mocking bow to Vera. "May I have the honour, daughter?"

Vera didn't answer. She looked doubtful.

"We're well matched," her father cajoled. "You're winded and I'm old."

"All right," she said.

—GUY VANDERHAEGHE, *Homesick*

(3) Set off long quotations of prose and poetry by indention.

PROSE

When you quote one paragraph or less, all lines of a long quotation (generally more than four lines) are indented ten spaces from the left margin and are double-spaced. When you quote two or more paragraphs, indent the first line of each complete paragraph thirteen spaces rather than the usual ten. Quotation marks are used only if they appear in the original.

Metal coins replaced bartering. Then paper money became more convenient to use than metal coins not only because it is easy to handle but also because it has other advantages. As Cetron and O'Toole say in Encounters with the Future,

> Printing more zeros is all it takes on a bill to increase its value. Careful engraving makes it easy to recognize and difficult to counterfeit. The fact that private individuals cannot create it at will keeps it scarce. Karl Marx once said that paper money was valued "only insofar as it represents gold" but that may never have been true. (188)

Today, cheques and credit cards are even more convenient than paper money.

An omission within a quotation is indicated by the use of ellipsis points: see **17i**.

For the proper documentation of sources in a research paper, see Section **34**.

POETRY

Except for a very special emphasis a quotation of three (or fewer) lines of poetry is handled like other short quotations—run in with the text and enclosed in quotation marks. A slash indicates the divisions between lines: see **17h**. Passages of more than three lines are set off from the text—double-spaced and indented ten spaces from the left margin. (Within the quotation the pattern of indention in the original should be followed as closely as possible.) Quotation marks are used only if they appear in the original. (Numbers in parentheses are often used to indicate the line numbers of the poem.)

```
Wordsworth deeply reveres nature. In "My Heart

Leaps Up," he expresses a hope that his rever-

ence for its beauty will not diminish as he

grows older:

     My heart leaps up when I behold
          A rainbow in the sky;
     So was it when my life began,
     So is it now I am a man,
     So be it when I shall grow old
          Or let me die! (1-6)
```

■ **Exercise 1** Change each indirect quotation to a direct quotation and each direct quotation to an indirect one.

1. Dolores said that she had a theory about me.
2. He says that he has read David Baltimore's "The Brain of a Cell."
3. A Weight Watcher, Eileen explained that she could eat as much as she wanted—of vegetables like spinach, eggplant, and zucchini.

4. Lucie asked, "Will you go to the opera with me?"
5. Last night Paolo said that he thought that Amanda's favourite expression was "Tell me about it!"

16b
Use quotation marks for minor titles (short stories, essays, short poems, songs, episodes of a radio or television series, articles in periodicals) and subdivisions of books.

> The "*Regina* vs. *Truscott*" episode of CBC's *Scales of Justice* suggested that Stephen Truscott's conviction was based on circumstantial evidence.
> On the subway, I scanned Adrian Forsyth's "The Golden Alphabet" in an old issue of *Equinox.*
> Margaret Laurence's *Heart of a Stranger* contains the essays "Down East" and "Where the World Began."

Use double quotation marks to enclose a minor title appearing in a longer italicized (underlined) title, and single marks for one within a longer title that is enclosed in double quotation marks.

> *Modern Interpretations of* "*My Last Duchess*"
> "An Introduction to 'My Last Duchess' "

Note: Quotation marks are sometimes used to enclose titles of books, periodicals, and newspapers, but italics are generally preferred: see **10a.**

16c
Used sparingly, quotation marks may enclose words intended in a special or ironic sense.

> His "castle" was a cozy little rat-trap.
> OR
> His so-called castle was a cozy little rat-trap. [The use of *so-called* eliminates the need for quotation marks.]

And I do mean good and evil, not "adjustment and deviance," the gutless language that so often characterizes modern discussions of psychological topics.

—CAROL TAVRIS

Note: Either quotation marks or italics may be used in definitions such as the following. See also **10d**.

"Ploy" means "a strategy used to gain an advantage."
Ploy means "a strategy used to gain an advantage."
Ploy means *a strategy used to gain an advantage.*

16d
Do not overuse quotation marks.

In general, do not enclose in quotation marks common nicknames, bits of humour, technical terms, or trite or well-known expressions (see **20c**). Instead of using slang and colloquialisms within quotation marks, try to use more formal English. Avoid the use of quotation marks for emphasis, for a *yes* or *no* in indirect discourse, or for diction that you may consider questionable.

REVISE   A "wimp" can't say "no" to anyone.
TO   A wimp can't say no to anyone.

Do not use quotation marks around the titles that head your own compositions.

■ **Exercise 2**   Insert quotation marks where needed in the following sentences.

1. In a short story entitled Cloning, scientists turn one Einstein into three Einsteins.
2. Here, bushed means suffering from cabin fever.
3. David enjoyed reading the short story The Progress of Love.

4. *The Great Cat Massacre* opens with a chapter entitled Peasants Tell Tales: The Meaning of Mother Goose.
5. Theresa said, My grandmother often said, When poverty comes in the door, love goes out the window.

16e
When using various marks of punctuation with quoted words, phrases, or sentences, follow the conventions of North American printers.

(1) **Place the period and the comma within the quotation marks.**

"Jenny," he said, "let's have lunch."
She replied, "OK, but first I want to finish 'The Machine Stops.' "

Exception:
The author states: "Time alone reveals the just" (471).
[The period follows the parenthetical reference to the source of the quotation.]

(2) **Place the colon and the semicolon outside the quotation marks.**

She spoke of "the protagonists"; yet I remembered only one in "The Tell-Tale Heart": the mad murderer.

(3) **Place the question mark, the exclamation point, and the dash within the quotation marks when they apply only to the quoted matter. Place them outside when they do not.**

Within the quotation marks:

Pilate asked, "What is truth?"
Gordon replied, "No way!"

"Achievement—success!—," states Heather Evans, "has become a national obsession."

Why do children keep asking "Why?" [a question within a question—one question mark inside the quotation marks]

Outside the quotation marks:

What is the meaning of the term "half-truth"?

Stop whistling "All I Do Is Dream of You"!

The boss exclaimed, "No one should work for the profit motive!"—no exceptions, I suppose.

■ **Exercise 3**   Insert quotation marks where they are needed.

1. Were you humming the song from the musical *Oliver!* called Where is Love?
2. Get aholt, instead of get a hold, is still used in that region.
3. Have you read Judy Syfers' essay Why I Want a Wife?
4. Last spring I discovered Frost's poem The Road Not Taken.
5. No, Peg said, I didn't agree to do that. I may be a softie, but I haven't gone bananas yet!
6. Whitney Houston's love song I Will Always Love You is on its way to becoming an American classic.
7. Helen Mirren starred in Prime Suspect, part of the Mystery! series on PBS.
8. His favourite story is James Thurber's The Catbird Seat and mine is Alice Munro's Spelling.
9. Why cry over spilled milk? my grandmother used to ask. Be glad you have the milk to spill.
10. Catherine said, Do the townspeople ever say to me You're a born leader? Yes, lots of times, and when they do, I just tell them my motto is Lead, follow, or get the heck out of the way!

The Period
and Other Marks

17

Use the period, question mark, exclamation point, colon, dash, parentheses, brackets, slash, and ellipsis points appropriately. For the use of the hyphen, see **18f**.

Notice how the marks in colour below signal meaning and intonation.

> The days are dark. Why worry? The sun never stops shining!

> In *Lady Windermere's Fan* (1892) is this famous line: "I [Lord Darlington] can resist everything except temptation."

> According to *Consumer Reports*, "The electronic radio/clock . . . is extremely complicated—enough so to require five pages of instructions in the owner's manual."

The Period

17a

Use the period as an end mark and with some abbreviations.

(1) **Use the period to mark the end of a declarative sentence and a mildly imperative sentence.**

Everyone should drive defensively. [declarative]
Learn how to drive defensively. [mild imperative]

She asks how drivers can cross the city without driving offensively. [declarative sentence containing an indirect question]

"How can drivers cross the city without driving offensively?" she asked. [declarative sentence containing a direct question]

"Don't do it!" he hollered. [declarative sentence containing an exclamation]

(2) Use periods after some abbreviations.

Mrs., Jr.   A.D., B.C.   A.M., P.M.   vs., etc., et al.

Periods are not used with most abbreviations in ordinary writing (for example, *SSW, MVP, FM, km/h*—see also page 143). The period is not used after clipped or shortened forms (*premed, lab, 12th*) or after modern postal abbreviations of provinces (*AB, ON, SK*) and states (*NJ, TX, KY*). (See also page 642.)

When in doubt about punctuating an abbreviation, consult a good college dictionary. Dictionaries often list options, such as *USA* or *U.S.A., DST* or *D.S.T.*

Caution: When an abbreviation ending in a period appears last in the sentence, do not add a second period:

Someday I hope to be an R.N.

The Question Mark

17b

Use the question mark after direct (but not indirect) questions.

Who started the rumour? [direct question]
BUT She asked who had started the rumour. [indirect question]
Did you hear her ask, "Are you accusing me of starting the rumour?" [a direct question within a direct question—followed by one question mark inside the quotation marks]

Declarative sentences may contain direct questions:

> "Who started the rumour?" he asked. [No comma follows the question mark.]
>
> He asked, "Who started the rumour?" [No period follows the question mark.]
>
> She told me—did I hear her correctly?—who started the rumour. [interpolated question]

Questions are sometimes used between parts of a series:

> Did they clean the attic? the basement? the whole house?
>
> COMPARE Did they clean the attic? The basement? The whole house?

Note: A question mark within parentheses is used to express the writer's uncertainty as to the correctness of the preceding word, figure, or date:

> Chaucer was born in 1340 (?) and died in 1400.

The Exclamation Point

17c

Use the exclamation point after an emphatic interjection and after other expressions to show strong emotion, such as surprise or disbelief.

> Boo!   What a game!   Look at that windshield!

Use the exclamation point sparingly. Use a comma after mild interjections; use a period after mildly exclamatory expressions and mild imperatives.

> Oh, look at that windshield.   How quiet the lake was.

Caution: Do not use a comma or a period after an exclamation point.

> "Watch out!" he yelled.   Mi exclaimed, "It's snowing!"

■ **Exercise 1** Illustrate the chief uses of the period, the question mark, and the exclamation point by composing and correctly punctuating brief sentences of the types specified.

1. a direct question
2. a mild imperative
3. a declarative sentence containing a quoted exclamation
4. a declarative sentence containing an indirect question
5. a declarative sentence containing an interpolated question

The Colon

17d

Use the colon as a formal introducer to call attention to what follows and as a mark of separation in scriptural and time references and in certain titles.

(1) The colon may direct attention to an explanation or summary, a series, or a quotation.

> The government wanted a tax increase, but of a certain type: a "value-added tax," to be tacked on to every item and service, from food to haircuts.
>
> So this was her kingdom: an octagonal house, a roomful of books, and a bear. —MARIAN ENGEL

> I had worn four hoods: childhood, girlhood, womanhood, and motherhood. Now there were two more waiting: widowhood and selfhood. —DOROTHY LIVESAY

> Of all the distinctions between man and animal, the characteristic gift which makes us human is the power to work with symbolic images: the gift of imagination.
>
> —JACOB BRONOWSKI

> David Suzuki points to a dangerous modern assumption: "It is a delusion to think that we know enough to control, manipulate and manage nature." [Note that the first letter after a colon need not be capitalized unless it begins a quoted sentence.]

The colon may separate two main clauses when the second clause explains or amplifies the first:

Fashion is architecture: it is a matter of proportions.
—COCO CHANEL

The first rule in opera is the first rule in life: see to everything yourself.   —NELLIE MELBA

Few tasks are more like the torture of Sisyphus than housework, with its endless repetition: the clean becomes soiled, the soiled is made clean, over and over, day after day.
—SIMONE DE BEAUVOIR

Similarly, a colon is occasionally used after one sentence to introduce the next sentence. (Capitalization of the first letter following the colon is optional.)

The electorate was volatile: In two consecutive polls, the results were contradictory.

There are no dangerous thoughts: thinking itself is dangerous.
—HANNAH ARENDT

(2) Use the colon between figures in scriptural and time references and between titles and subtitles.

Then he quoted John 3:16.
At 13:35 the factory whistle blew.
at 2:15 A.M. the phone rang.
Read *Metamorphosis: Stages in a Life.*

Note that MLA practice now recommends periods instead of colons in biblical references: John 3.16, Genesis 2.5 (rather than John 3:16, Genesis 2:5).

Note: The colon is also used after the salutation of a business letter and in bibliographical data: see **35a(1)** and **34e(2)**.

(3) Do not use superfluous colons.

Be especially careful not to use an unnecessary colon between a verb and its complement or object, between a preposition and its object, or after *such as*.

NOT The winners were: Pat, Lydia, and Jack.
BUT The winners were Pat, Lydia, and Jack.
　OR There were three winners: Pat, Lydia, and Jack.
　OR The winners were as follows: Pat, Lydia, Jack.
NOT Many vegetarians do not eat dairy products, such as: butter, cheese, yogurt, or ice cream.
BUT Many vegetarians do not eat dairy products, such as butter, cheese, yogurt, or ice cream.

■ **Exercise 2** Punctuate the following sentences by adding colons. Put a check mark after any sentence that needs no change.

1. At 1530, he began the class with his favourite quotation "Mind without heart is nothing."
2. The downtown streets are narrow, rough, and dirty.
3. Three scientists noted for their engaging writing are these Stephen Jay Gould, Jay Ingram, and Lewis Thomas.
4. During our tour of the library, our guide recommended that we find one of the following periodicals *Canadian Forum, Commentary,* or *Queen's Quarterly.*
5. All their thoughts were centred on equal pay for equal work.

■ **Exercise 3** Decide whether to use a colon or a semicolon between the main clauses of the following sentences. See also **14a**.

1. These laws all have the same purpose they protect us from ourselves.
2. Some of these laws have an obvious purpose others seem senseless.
3. Few things are certain perhaps we could count them on one hand.
4. One thing is certain the future looks bright.

The Dash

17e
Use the dash to mark a break in thought, to set off a parenthetical element for emphasis or clarity, and to set off an introductory series.

On the typewriter, the dash is indicated by two hyphens without spacing before, between or after. In handwriting, the dash is an unbroken line about the length of two hyphens.

(1) **Use the dash to mark a sudden break in thought, an abrupt change in tone, or faltering speech.**

A hypocrite is a person who——but who isn't?
—DON MARQUIS

When I was six I made my mother a little hat——out of her new blouse.   —LILY DACHÉ

Aunt Esther replied, "I put the key on the——in the——no, under the doormat, I think."

(2) **Use the dash to set off a parenthetical element for emphasis or (if it contains commas) for clarity.**

Lightning is an electrical discharge——an enormous spark.
—RICHARD E. ORVILLE

Recently, there has been a great deal of news in the press about the consequences——all bad——of high cholesterol levels.

Sentiments that human shyness will not always allow one to convey in conversation——sentiments of gratitude, of apology, of love——can often be more easily conveyed in a letter.
—ARISTIDES

(3) Use the dash after an introductory list or series.

Notice that in the main part of each of the following sentences a word like *all, that, such,* or *none* points to or sums up the meaning of the introductory list.

> Keen, calculating, perspicacious, acute and astute——I was all of these. —MAX SHULMAN
>
> Muddy, messy, muddled——that is a brief description of life in the trenches during World War I.

Caution: Use the dash carefully in formal writing. Do not use dashes as awkward substitutes for commas, semicolons, or end marks.

Parentheses

17f

Use parentheses to set off parenthetical, supplementary, or illustrative matter and to enclose figures or letters when used for enumeration.

> They call this illness Seasonal Affective Disorder (SAD).
> —LOWELL PONTE [a first-time use of an acronym in an article—see **11e**]

> In less than a week I became an outsider because I refused to conform and blindly nod my head in agreement to what my elders (which happened to be everybody else in the company) said. —SUN-KYUN YI [The explanatory comment for *elders* clarifies the nature of the writer's difficulty.]

> In contrast, a judgment is subject to doubt if there is any possibility at all (1) of its being challenged in the light of additional or more accurate observations or (2) of its being criticized on the basis of more cogent or more comprehensive reasoning. —MORTIMER J. ADLER [In long sentences especially, the enumeration contributes to clarity.]

Notice in the next examples that the writer may choose between a parenthetical main clause and a parenthetical sentence. See also **9e**.

More stray cows come up to my lane (cows do like to get together as much as possible). —LEO SIMPSON

Strangely, he didn't seem to know much about cows. (That was when he told me that cows could not run downhill, and neither could bears.) —LEO SIMPSON

Dashes, parentheses, commas—all are used to set off parenthetical matter. Dashes set off parenthetical elements sharply and usually emphasize them:

Man's mind is indeed—as Luther said—a factory busy with making idols. —HARVEY COX

Parentheses usually de-emphasize the elements they enclose:

The human mind is indeed (as Luther said) a factory busy with making idols.

Commas are the most frequently used separators:

The human mind is indeed, as Luther said, a factory busy with making idols.

Note: Use parentheses sparingly, and remember that the elements they enclose should read smoothly within the sentence as a whole.

Brackets

17g
Use brackets to set off interpolations in quoted matter and to replace parentheses within parentheses.

The *Home Herald* printed the beginning of the mayor's speech: "My dear fiends [sic] and fellow citizens." [A bracketed *sic*—meaning "thus"—tells the reader that the error appears in the original.]

Mozart once said, "Some day he [Beethoven] will make quite a noise in the world."

Some of Marshall McLuhan's writings should be required reading for prospective teachers. (See, for example, *City as Classroom* [Agincourt: The Book Society of Canada, 1977].)

The Slash

17h

Use the slash between terms to indicate that either term is applicable and to mark line divisions of quoted poetry. See also 16a(3).

Note that the slash is used unspaced between terms, but with a space before and after it between lines of poetry.

Today's visions of the checkless/cashless society are not quite as popular as they used to be.   —KATHRYN H. HUMES

Equally rare is a first-rate adventure story designed for those who enjoy a smartly told tale that isn't steeped in blood and/or sex.   —JUDITH CRIST

When in "Mr. Flood's Party" the hero sets down his jug at his feet, "as a mother lays her sleeping child / Down tenderly, fearing it may awake," one feels Robinson's heart to be quite simply on his sleeve.   —WILLIAM H. PITCHARD

Note: Extensive use of the slash to indicate that either of two terms is applicable (*he/she, and/or*) can make writing choppy.

■ **Exercise 4**   Correctly punctuate each of the following sentences by supplying commas, dashes, parentheses, brackets, or the slash. Prepare to explain the reason for all marks you add, especially those you choose for setting off parenthetical matter.

1. Gordon Gibbs or is it his twin brother? plays the drums.
2. Joseph who is Gordon's brother is a lifeguard at English Bay.
3. "I admit that I" he began, but his voice broke; he could say no more.
4. This organization needs more of everything more money, brains, initiative.

5. Some of my courses for example, French and biology demand a great deal of work outside the classroom.
6. During his life, René Lévesque 1922–1987 worked as a journalist, a broadcaster, and a politician.
7. This ridiculous sentence appeared in the school paper: "Because of a personal fool sic the Cougars failed to cross the goal line during the last seconds of the game."
8. Body language a wink or yawn nose-rubbing or ear-pulling folded arms or crossed legs can often speak much louder than words.
9. Gently rolling hills, rich valleys, beautiful lakes these things impress the tourist in New Zealand.
10. Some innovations for example the pass fail system did not contribute to grade inflation.

■ **Exercise 5** Prepare for class discussion of the paragraphs below. Explain why the authors have chosen to use the commas, question marks, exclamation points, colons, dashes, and parentheses as they have done.

(a) [1]*Feng-shui* combined an intricate set of related variables that reflected the three great religions of China—Taoism, Buddhism, and Confucianism. [2]First were the Taoist principles of yang and yin—male and female. [3]The five Buddhist planets corresponded to the five elements, the five directions (north, south, west, east, and centre), and the five seasons (the usual four and midsummer) [4]*Feng-shui* employed the sixty-four hexagrams of the *I-Ching,* a classic manual of divination popularized by Confucius, and also made use of the astrological signs: the constellations were divided into four groups: the Azure Dragon (east), the Black Tortoise (north), the White Tiger (west), and the Red Bird (south).

—WITOLD RYBCZYNSKI

(b) [1]I feel a bit like you: nothing nice happens, or ever will happen. [2]I dreamed I was made head of a school somewhere, I think, in Canada. [3]I felt so queer about it: such a vivid dream—that I half wonder if it is my destiny! [4]A job!—[5]But I manage to make a living still.   —D.H. LAWRENCE [*from his letters*]

(c) [1]Indeed, in the ideally good-looking man a small imperfection or blemish is considered positively desirable. [2]According to one movie critic (a woman) who is a declared Robert

Redford fan, it is having that cluster of skin-colored moles on one cheek that saves Redford from being merely a "pretty face." ³Think of the depreciation of women—as well as of beauty—that is implied in that judgment. —SUSAN SONTAG

(d) ¹So let us replace the yuppies' cruel and empty slogan—"Go for it!"—with the cry that lies deep in every true worker's heart: "Gimme a break!" ²What this nation needs is not the work ethic, but a job ethic: if it needs doing—highways repaired, babies changed, fields plowed—let's get it done. ³Otherwise, take five. —BARBARA EHRENREICH

(e) ¹Ask who reigns as the king of the talk show in the United States, and no one will pause: Johnny Carson. ²Ask who holds the same title in Canada, and the pause may be longer, but the consensus will be just as strong: Peter Gzowski. ³Carson and Gzowski, Gzowski and Carson—somehow even the names sound dissonant, the one pure white-bread, the other a dark loaf of consonants. But let's stop and examine. ⁴If the Meech debate was just another (albeit intense) chapter in our interrogative saga—aren't we always wondering Whither Canada? Why Canada? Who Canada?—perhaps a comparative peek at these media icons may offer us a small identifying clue. ⁶This, then, is not just a story of two talk *meisters,* it's a tale of two countries. —RICK GROEN

Ellipsis Points

17i

Use ellipsis points (three spaced periods) to mark an omission from a quoted passage and to mark a reflective pause or hesitation.

(1) Use ellipsis points to indicate an omission within a quoted passage.

Original:

> If—or is it when?—these computers are permitted to talk to one another, when they are interlinked, they can spew out a roomful of data on each of us that will leave us naked before whoever gains access to the information. (From Walter Cronkite, Foreword, *The Rise of the Computer State* by David Burnham [New York: Random, 1983], viii.)

OMISSION WITHIN A QUOTED SENTENCE

As Walter Cronkite has observed, "If . . . these computers are permitted to talk to one another . . . , they can spew out a roomful of data on each of us that will leave us naked before whoever gains access to the information." [The comma after the second group of ellipsis points could be omitted, but it marks the end of an introductory adverb clause and contributes to the grammatical integrity of the sentence.]

OMISSION AT THE END OF A QUOTED SENTENCE

If an omission at the end of the quoted sentence coincides with the end of your sentence, use a period before the three ellipsis points, leaving no space before the period. If a parenthetical reference is cited, however, place the period after the second parenthesis.

According to Walter Cronkite, "If—or is it when?—these computers are permitted to talk to one another, when they are interlinked, they can spew out a roomful of data on each of us. . . . " [OR "each of us . . . " (viii) .]

OMISSION OF A SENTENCE OR MORE

Original:

There's an uncertainty in our minds about the engineering principles of an elevator. We've all had little glimpses into the dirty, dark elevator shaft and seen the greasy cables passing each other. They never look totally safe. The idea of being trapped in a small box going up and down on strings induces a kind of phobia in all of us. (From Andrew A. Rooney, *Pieces of My Mind* [New York: Atheneum, 1984], 121.)

Use a period before ellipsis points to mark the omission of a sentence or more (even a paragraph or more) within a quoted passage.

Andrew A. Rooney writes about everyday experiences—for example, riding an elevator: "There's an uncertainty in our minds about the engineering principles of an elevator. . . . The idea of being trapped in a small box going up and down induces a kind of phobia in all of us." [A sentence comes both before and after the period and ellipsis points.]

To indicate the omission of a full line or more in quoted poetry, use spaced periods covering a whole line.

> All I can say is—I saw it!
> . . . .
> Impossible! Only—I saw it!   —ROBERT BROWNING

(2) Use ellipsis points to mark a reflective pause or hesitation.

> Love, like other emotions, has . . . causes and consequences.
> —LAWRENCE CASLER
> It's a bird . . . it's a plane . . . well, it's the Gossamer Penguin, a 68-pound flying machine fueled only by the sun.
> —CATHLEEN McGUIGAN
> "It's well for you . . . " began Lucille. She bit the remark off.
> —ELIZABETH BOWEN [a deliberately unfinished statement]

Ellipsis points to show a pause may also come after the period at the end of a sentence:

> All channels are open. The meditation is about to begin. . . .
> —TOM ROBBINS

■ **Exercise 6**   Beginning with *According to John Donne,* or with *As John Donne has written,* quote the following passage, omitting the words placed in brackets. Use three or four periods as needed to indicate omissions.

> No man is an island [entire of itself;] every man is a piece of the continent, a part of the main. [If a clod be washed away by the sea, Europe is the less, as well as if a promontory were, as well as if a manor of thy friend's or of thine own were.] Any man's death diminishes me because I am involved in mankind [and therefore never send to know for whom the bell tolls; it tolls for thee].   —JOHN DONNE

■ **Exercise 7**   First, observing differences in meaning and emphasis, use ellipsis points in place of the dash, commas, and italicized words in the following sentences. Then write two sentences of your own to illustrate the use of ellipsis points to mark a pause or hesitation.

1. The journey had ended—*and, I wondered,* what would happen to us?
2. Our lives would have been different if *the journey had not ended.*

■ **Exercise 8** Punctuate the following sentences by supplying appropriate end marks, commas, colons, dashes, and parentheses. Do not use unnecessary punctuation. Be prepared to explain the reason for each mark you add, especially when you have a choice of correct marks (for example, commas, dashes, or parentheses).

1. For once he had done something to please only himself and not his parents register in a drama class
2. Freeways throughout North America are all the same aluminum guardrails green signs white lettering
3. "Was he was he wearing a helmet" was the first thing his brother asked
4. He repeated once again "Revenge is a kind of wild justice" but he failed to acknowledge the author of the phrase Sir Francis Bacon
5. The students were outraged by the rise in fees and matters weren't made easier by the following error "An increase in tuition fees by $3000 per year isn't beyond the means of most students"
6. "Tanya" she exclaimed "Tanya is going to represent Canada in the finals" She had meant to tell only Daniel but the letter had caught her by surprise now the whole table knew
7. Despite their remarkably different backgrounds Rajinder and Jeanne-Marie have one thing in common a passion for scuba diving
8. I believe that the proposed high school curriculum will not satisfy the educators either radicals or conservatives who demanded a review and changes
9. As one woman put it "Office politics party politics and international politics are all gutter politics to me"
10. "User friendly" means "easy to operate" "This software is user friendly" and "a fresh pot of tea" means that the tea not the pot is fresh

■ **Exercise 9** Punctuate the following paragraph by supplying appropriate question marks, exclamation points, colons, dashes, parentheses, slashes, and ellipsis points. When you have a choice of correct marks (for example, commas, dashes, or parentheses), be prepared to explain the reason for each mark you supply.

¹Bernal Diaz was a foot soldier under the command of Cortés when the Conquistadors in 1519 sailed into a small coastal settlement in the New World ²The site is in modern-day Yucatán ³Although he experienced firsthand the events leading to the fateful clash of the Spaniards and the Aztecs Diaz did not write about them until some years after ⁴He recorded the arrival of eleven ships in all or according to other sources ten or twelve ⁵He noted the friendly greeting of the Aztecs who rowed out to the fleet with gifts ⁶Although the Spaniards were supposedly intent on trade and exploration their ships were laden with the necessaries of war heavy cannons light cannons muskets gunpowder gunshot crossbows and swords ⁷The ships carried over 100 sailors but the vessels also carried soldiers over 550 of them and horses ⁸When the Spaniards engaged the Aztecs in battle in 1519 1520 they found themselves greatly outnumbered ⁹Even so they enjoyed some remarkable advantages that ensured certain victory their weapons of hard metal easily repulsed the stone and wood of the Aztec implements of war their mounted soldiers overran the Aztecs fighting on foot their armour withstood the fiercest assaults and the noise and effect of gunpowder wholly unnerved their enemy ¹⁰We know surprising details remarkable details in fact about the Spaniards' preparation ¹¹And an enduring image of Cortés's soldiers has come down to us through the writing of Diaz long lines of men winding across the country many on horseback and all suited in armour flashing in the sun ¹²Who would have thought that students of history could owe so much to a common foot soldier

SPELLING AND DICTION

Spelling and Hyphenation

18

Spell every word according to established usage as shown by your dictionary. Hyphenate words in accordance with current usage.

Spelling

Because problems with spelling are usually highly individual, one of the best ways to improve your spelling is to keep, for study and reference, a record of those words (correctly spelled) that you have misspelled: see **8f**.

Always proofread to detect misspellings, many of which are slips of the pen or errors in typing. If you have access to a computer that singles out such mistakes for you to correct, use it as a time-saving tool, but be aware of its limitations—for example, its inability to recognize a misspelling that spells some other word, such as *bread* for *beard*.

If you have any doubt about a correct spelling, consult your dictionary. Check the meaning to be sure you have found the word you have in mind. Be mindful of restrictive labels such as *British* or *Chiefly British* in American dictionaries (for example, *The Random House College Dictionary*) and *U.S.* or *Chiefly U.S.* in British dictionaries (for example, *The Concise Oxford Dictionary*).

BRITISH	connexion	humour	centre	offence	realise
AMERICAN	connection	humor	center	offense	realize

Canadian writers should note that Canadian spelling patterns are the product of both British and American practices. It is not uncommon, for example, to find writers in this country using such British spellings as *traveller's cheques* and *catalogue centre* as well as such American spellings as *connection, program,* and *plow.* At present, neither practice dominates completely, but at least one expert has suggested that the simplified and usually phonetic American spellings have begun to edge out the formerly more prevalent British forms.

Dictionaries designed to meet the needs of the Canadian market (see page 233) will list variant and preferred spellings. Unless otherwise directed, you should use the preferred spelling (listed first in an entry) and maintain consistency within classes of words.

In ordinary writing, do not use spellings or words labelled *obsolete* or *archaic* (*compleat* for *complete*); *dialectal* or *regional* (*heighth* for *height, boughten* for *bought*); or *nonstandard* or *slang* (*weirdo*). Words and spellings labelled *informal* or *colloquial* (*kind of, kids*) are acceptable in informal writing.

If your dictionary lists two unlabelled spellings, either form is correct—for example, *fulfil* or *fulfill, symbolic* or *symbolical, tornadoes* or *tornados, likeable* or *likable.*

18a
Do not allow mispronunciation to cause you to misspell a word.

Although pronunciation is often not a dependable guide to spelling, mispronunciation does frequently lead to misspelling. In the following words, trouble spots are in boldface.

ath**l**ete	drown**ed**	mod**ern**	repre**s**ent
barb**ar**ous	every**one**	**per**spire	sur**p**rise
can**d**idate	gratitude	quan**t**ity	umb**r**ella

As you check pronunciations in the dictionary, give special attention to / ə /, the symbol for a neutral vowel sound in unaccented syllables, usually an indistinct *uh* sound (as in *confidence*). Be especially careful not to omit letters representing / ə /. (The term *schwa* is used to refer to this vowel sound or to its phonetic symbol.)

A word that is difficult to spell may have alternate pronunciations. Of these, one may be a better guide to spelling. Here are examples of such words:

arc**t**ic	govern**m**ent	lit**era**ture	vet**era**n
Feb**r**uary	inte**r**est	soph**o**more	w**h**ere

Do not misspell words like *and* or *than* because they are not stressed in speech.

We had ham and [NOT *an*] eggs.
The movie is even more exciting than [NOT *then*] the book.

18b

Distinguish between words of similar sound and spelling; use the spelling required by the meaning.

Words such as *forth* and *fourth* or *sole* and *soul* sound alike but have vastly different meanings. Be sure to choose the right word for your context.

A number of frequently confused spellings may be studied in groups:

Contractions and possessive pronouns:

It's best to wait.	The team did **its** best.
You're required to attend.	**Your** attendance is required.
There's a change in plans.	**Theirs** have changed.

Single words and two-word phrases:

It's an **everyday** event.	It happens nearly **every day.**
Maybe that is true.	That **may be** true.
I ran **into** trouble.	I ran **in to** get it.
Nobody cared.	The ghost had **no body.**

*Singular nouns ending in **nce** and plural nouns ending in **nts**:*

not much **assistance**	too many **assistants**
for **instance**	just **instants** ago
even less **patience** with	several **patients**

As you study the following list, use your dictionary to check the meaning of words that are not thoroughly familiar to you. You may find it helpful to devise examples of usage such as these:

breath—a deep breath	**breathe**—to breathe deeply
passed—had passed	**past**—in the past

Words Frequently Confused

You may find it helpful to study the following list in units of ten or twenty words at a time. Consult your dictionary for the exact meanings of any words you are not sure of.

accept, except
access, excess
adapt, adopt
advice, advise
affect, effect
aisles, isles
alley, ally
allude, elude
allusion, illusion
10 already, all ready
altar, alter
altogether, all together
always, all ways
angel, angle
ascent, assent
assistance, assistants
baring, barring, bearing
birth, berth
board, bored
20 born, borne
break, brake
breath, breathe
buy, by
canvas, canvass
capital, capitol

censor, censure, sensor
choose, chose
cite, site, sight
clothes, cloths
30 coarse, course
complement, compliment
conscience, conscious
council, counsel
credible, creditable
cursor, curser
dairy, diary
decent, descent, dissent
desert, dessert
detract, distract
40 device, devise
dominant, dominate
dual, duel
dyeing, dying
elicit, illicit
envelop, envelope
fair, fare
faze, phase
formerly, formally
forth, fourth
50 forward, foreword

gorilla, guerrilla
hear, here
heard, herd
heroin, heroine
hole, whole
holy, wholly
horse, hoarse
human, humane
instance, instants
60 its, it's
later, latter
led, lead
lesson, lessen
licence, license
lightning, lightening
lose, loose
maybe, may be
minor, miner
moral, morale
70 of, off
passed, past
patience, patients
peace, piece
persecute, prosecute
perspective, prospective
personal, personnel
plain, plane
practice, practise
pray, prey
80 precede, proceed

predominant, predominate
presence, presents
principle, principal
prophecy, prophesy
purpose, propose
quiet, quite
respectfully, respectively
right, rite, write
road, rode
90 sense, since
shown, shone
stationary, stationery
statue, stature, statute
straight, strait
taut, taunt
than, then
their, there, they're
through, thorough
to, too, two
100 tract, track
waist, waste
weak, week
weather, whether
were, where
who's, whose
your, you're

18c
Distinguish between the prefix and the root.

The root is the base to which prefixes and suffixes are added. Notice in the following examples that no letter is added or dropped when the prefix is added to the root.

dis-	disagree, disappear	**mis-**	misspent, misspell
im-	immortal, immoral	**re-**	reelect [OR re-elect]
un-	unnecessary, unnoticed	**ir-**	irrational, irregular

18d
Apply the rules for adding suffixes.

(1) Dropping or retaining a final unpronounced *e*

Drop the *e* before a suffix beginning with a vowel:

engage	engaging
desire	desirable
scarce	scarcity
fame	famous

Retain the *e* before a suffix beginning with a consonant:

care	careful
mere	merely
safe	safety
manage	management

Options: *judgment* or *judgement, likable* or *likeable*

Some exceptions: *acreage, mileage, argument, ninth, truly, wholly*

To keep the sound /s/ of *-ce* or /j/ of *-ge,* do not drop the final *e* before *-able* or *-ous:*

noticeable   changeable   outrageous   courageous

Similarly, keep the *e* before *-ance* in *vengeance*.

■ **Exercise 1** Practise adding suffixes to words ending in an unpronounced *e*.

EXAMPLES
-ing: rise, lose, guide   *rising, losing, guiding*
-ly, -er, -ness: late   *lately, later, lateness*

1. *-ly:* like, safe, sure
2. *-able, -ing, -ment:* excite
3. *-ing:* come, notice, hope
4. *-ing, -less:* use
5. *-ous:* continue, courage
6. *-ful:* care, hope, use
7. *-ing, -ment, -able:* argue
8. *-ly, -ing:* complete
9. *-able:* desire, notice
10. *-ing, -ment:* manage

(2) Doubling a final consonant before a suffix

Double a final consonant before a suffix beginning with a vowel if both (a) the consonant ends a stressed syllable or a one-syllable word and (b) the consonant is preceded by a single vowel.

One-syllable words:
drag	dragged
hid	hidden
shop	shoppers
stun	stunning
wet	wettest

Words stressed on last syllable:
abhor	abhorrent
begin	beginning
occur	occurrence
regret	regrettable
unwrap	unwrapped

Compare benefited, reference [stressed on first syllable]

■ **Exception:** Following British practice, accepted Canadian usage doubles the consonant *l* in words stressed on the first syllable:

counsellor   travelled   labelling   marvellous

■ **Exercise 2**   Write the present participle (-*ing* form) and the past tense of each verb:

EXAMPLE: *rob, robbing, robbed*

1. audit
2. conceal
3. drag
4. drop
5. grip

6. hope
7. job
8. permit
9. plan
10. rebel

(3) Changing or retaining a final *y* before a suffix

Change the -*y* to *i* before suffixes—except -*ing*.

apply → applies, applied, appliance   BUT   applying
study → studies, studied   BUT   studying
happy → happily, happiness, happier, happiest

Exceptions: Verbs ending in *y* preceded by a vowel do not change the *y* before -*s* or -*ed*: *stay, stays, stayed*. Following the same pattern of spelling, nouns like *joys* or *days* have *y* before *s*. The following irregularities in spelling are especially troublesome:

lays, laid   pays, paid [*Compare* says, said.]

(4) Retaining a final *l* before -*ly*

Do not drop a final *l* when you add -*ly:*

real—really
cool—coolly

usual—usually
formal—formally

■ **Exercise 3** Add the designated suffixes to the following words.

1. *-able:* vary, ply
2. *-er:* funny, carry
3. *-ous:* vary, luxury
4. *-ly:* easy, final
5. *-ed:* supply, stay
6. *-ing:* study, worry
7. *-d:* pay, lay
8. *-hood:* lively, likely
9. *-ness:* friendly, lonely
10. *-ly:* usual, cool

(5) Adding *-s* or *-es* to form the plural of nouns

Form the plural of most nouns by adding *-s* to the singular:

two boy**s**   many nation**s**   a few scientist**s**
several safe**s**   three cupful**s**   all the radio**s**
both sister**s**-in-law [chief word pluralized]
the Dudley**s** and the Ito**s** [proper names]

Note: To form the plural of some nouns ending in *f* or *fe,* change the ending to *ve* before adding the *s: a thief, two thieves; one life, our lives.*

Add *-es* to singular nouns ending in *s, ch, sh,* or *x:*

many loss**es**   these mailbox**es**   the Rogers**es**
two approach**es**   a lot of ash**es**   two Doris**es**

Add *-es* to singular nouns ending in *y* preceded by a consonant, after changing the *y* to *i:*

company—compan**ies**   industry—industr**ies**
ninety-nine**ties**   party—par**ties**

Note: Although *-es* is often added to a singular noun ending in *o* preceded by a consonant, usage varies:

echo**es**   hero**es**   potato**es**   veto**es** [*-es* only]
autos   memos   pimentos   pros [*-s* only]
nos/no**es**   mottos/motto**es**   zeros/zero**es** [*-s* or *-es*]

Exceptions: Irregular plurals (including retained foreign spellings) are not formed by adding *s* or *es*. Irregular plurals based on older forms of English may have forms with an internal change (*man/men*) or an *-en* ending.

SINGULAR	PLURAL
brother	brethren*
child	children
deer	deer
foot	feet
goose	geese
mouse	mice
man	men
tooth	teeth
woman	women
ox	oxen
alga	algae
alumna (f)	alumnae (f)
alumnus (m)	alumni (m)
analysis	analyses
criterion	criteria
datum	data
matrix	matrices
plateau	plateaux
species	species

*Brother has two plurals: the regularly formed *brothers*, and *brethren*, which is used chiefly in religious contexts.

■ **Exercise 4** Supply plural forms (including any optional spelling) for the following words, applying rule **18d(5)**. (If a word is not covered by the rule, use your dictionary.)

1. belief
2. theory
3. church
4. genius
5. Kelly
6. bath
7. hero
8. story

9. wish
10. forty
11. radius
12. scarf
13. wife
14. speech
15. tomato
16. phenomenon
17. halo
18. child
19. handful
20. video

18e

Apply the rules to avoid confusion of *ei* and *ie*.

When the sound is /ē/ *(ee)*, write *ie* (except after *c*, in which case write *ei*).

chief, grief, pierce, wield, field, niece, relief, yield
BUT, after *c*:
ceiling, deceive, conceit, perceive

When the sound is other than /ē/ *(ee)*, usually write *ei*.

counterfeit, foreign, heifer, heir, sleigh, vein, forfeit, freight, height, neighbour, stein, weigh

Exceptions: friend, mischief, seize, sheik

■ **Exercise 5** Fill in the blanks in the following words with the appropriate letters, *ei* or *ie*.

1. p____ce
2. ach____ve
3. rec____ve
4. n____gh
5. fr____ght
6. ap____ce
7. bel____f
8. conc____ve
9. th____r
10. dec____t
11. n____ce
12. sh____ld
13. w____rd
14. shr____k
15. pr____st

Words Frequently Misspelled

You may find it helpful to study the following list in units of ten or twenty words at a time. Consult your dictionary for the exact meanings of any words you are not sure of.

absence
acceptable
accessible
accidentally
accommodate
accompanied
accomplish
accumulate
accuracy
10 achievement

acquaintance
acquire
acquitted
across
actually
address
admission
adolescent
advice
20 advised

affected
affectionately
aggravate
aggressive
alcohol
allotted
all right
a lot of
always
30 amateur

among
analysis
analyze
annihilate
announcement
annual
anxiety
anywhere
apartment
40 apiece

apology
apparent
appearance
appoint
appreciate
appropriate
approximately
arguing
argument
50 arrangement

arrest
article
aspirin
assassination
associate
athlete
athletics
attacked
attendance
60 attendant

authentic
average
awkward
bachelor
balance
bargain
basically
beginning
belief
70 believed

beneficial
benefited
biscuit
boundaries
breath
breathe
brilliant
bulletin
bureaucracy
80 burglar

business
busy
cafeteria
calendar
candidate
career
category
ceiling
cemetery
90 certain

challenge
changeable
changing
characteristic
chief
children
chocolate
choice
choose
100 chosen

coarsely
column
coming
commercial
commission
commitment
committed
committee
comparative
110 compelled

competence
competition
completely
conceited
conceivable
concentrate
condemn
confidence
conscience
120 conscientious

conscious
consensus
consistency
consistent
contradict
control
controlled
controlling
controversial
130 convenience

convenient
coolly
correlate
counterfeit
courteous
criticism
criticize
cruelty
curiosity
140 curious

dealt
deceive
decided
decision
defence
defensible
define
definitely
definition
150 descend

describe
description
desirable
despair
desperate
destroy
develop
dictionary
difference
160 different

dilemma
dining
disagree
disappearance
disappoint
disapprove
disastrous
discipline
discussion
170 disease

dispensable
disturbance
divide
divine
dormitory
ecstatic
effect
efficiency
eighth
180 elaborately

eligible
eliminate
embarrass
emphasis
emphasize
empty
enemy
entirely
environment
190 equipment

equipped
escape
especially
everything
evidently
exaggerate
exceed
excellence
excellent
200 except

exercise
exhaust
existence
exonerate
expense
experience
explanation
extraordinary
extremely
210 familiar

fascinate
favourite
February
finally
financially
forehead
foreign
foreword
forfeit
220 forty

forward
friend
gauge
generally
government
governor
grammar
grammatically
grief
230 guaranteed

guard
guerrilla
guidance
happened
harass
height
hero
heroes
hindrance
240 humour

hypocrisy
hypocrite
idiosyncrasy
ignorant
illogical
imaginary
imagine
imitate
immediately
250 immense

incalculable
incidentally
incredible
independent
indispensable
inevitable
infinite
influential
initiative
260 innocence

innocuous
innumerable
inoculate
intellectual
intelligence
intelligent
interest
interpret
interrupt
270 introduce

irrelevant
irresistible
irritated
jewellery
knowledge
laboratory
legitimate
leisure
liable
280 library

licence
license
lightning
literature
lively
loneliness
lonely
lose
lying
290 magazine

maintenance
manageable
manoeuvre
manual
manufacture
marriage
material
mathematics
meant
300 medicine

mere
messenger
miniature
minutes
mischievous
missile
morning
mortgage
muscles
310 mysterious

naturally
necessary
nickel
niece
ninety
ninth
noticeable
noticing
nuclear
320 nuisance

occasionally
occur
occurred
occurrence
omission
omitted
opinion
opponent
opportunity
330 opposite

optimism
organize
origin
original
paid
pamphlet
parallel
particular
pastime
340 peculiar

performance
perhaps
permanent
permissible
personal
phase
physical
physician
pigeon
350 planned

pleasant
poison
possess
possession
possible
possibly
practically
prairie
precede
360 preferred

prejudiced	receipt	secede
preparation	receive	secretary
prepare	receiving	seize
presence	recognize	separate
prevalent	recommend	sergeant
privilege	reference	severely
probably	referred	sheriff
procedure	referring	shining
proceed	regular	similar
370 profession	400 rehearsal	430 simply
professor	relieve	since
prominent	religious	sincerely
pronunciation	remembrance	skiing
propaganda	reminisce	sophomore
prophecy	repetition	specimen
prophesy	representative	speech
psychology	reproduce	sponsor
publicly	resemblance	strength
pumpkin	resistance	strenuous
380 purpose	410 resources	440 strict
pursue	restaurant	stubbornness
pursuit	rhythm	studying
quandary	ridiculous	subtlety
quantity	roommate	succeed
questionnaire	sacrifice	successful
quiet	safety	succession
quite	salary	sufficient
quizzes	scarcity	suicide
realize	scenery	summary
390 really	420 schedule	450 superintendent

supersede
suppose
suppress
surely
surprise
surround
susceptible
suspicious
swimming
460 symbol

sympathize
technique
temperament
temperature
tendency
tenet
than
their
themselves
470 then

therefore
thorough
thought
through
till
tobacco
together
tomorrow
tournament
480 traffic

trafficked
tragedy
transferred
tremendous
tried
tries
trouble
truly
twelfth
490 tyranny

unanimous
unconscious
undoubtedly
unmistakably
unnecessary
until
usage
useful
useless
500 using

usually
vacuum
valuable
varies
various
vegetable
vengeance
venomous
vice
510 view

vigilance
villain
violence
visible
vitamins
waive
warrant
warring
weather
520 Wednesday

weird
where
wherever
whether
whichever
wholly
whose
wield
wintry
530 withdrawal

woman
women
worshipped
wreck
write
writing
written
yacht
yield
540 zephyr

Frequently Misspelled Words   229

Hyphenation

18f

Hyphenate words to express the idea of a unit and to avoid ambiguity. For the division of words at the end of a line, see **8d.**

Notice in the following examples that the hyphen links (or makes a compound of) two or more words that function as a single word.

> We planted forget–me–nots and Johnny–jump–ups. [nouns]
> He hand–fed them. I double–parked. Hard–boil an egg. [verbs]
> Was it a head–to–head confrontation? [adjectival]

Consult a good recent dictionary when you are not sure of the form of compounds, since some are connected with hyphens (*eye-opener, cross-examine*), some are written separately (*eye chart, cross street*), and others are written as one word (*eyewitness, crossbreed*).

Note: Different dictionaries may treat these words differently. For example, the *Gage Canadian Dictionary* gives *eye-opener,* but *Funk & Wagnalls Canadian College Dictionary* gives *eye opener.*

(1) Use the hyphen to join two or more words serving as a single adjective before a noun.

> A well–known surgeon
> BUT a surgeon who is well known
> chocolate–covered peanuts
> BUT peanuts covered with chocolate
> a ten–year–old plane
> BUT a plane that is ten years old
> "I reject get–it–done, make–it–happen thinking," he says.
> —THE ATLANTIC MONTHLY

In a series, hyphens are carried over:
> second–, third–, or fourth–class mail

Note: The hyphen is omitted after an adverb ending in *-ly:*

a brand–new product	BUT	a completely new product
soft–spoken words	BUT	softly spoken words

■ **Exercise 6** Convert the following word groups according to the pattern of the examples.

EXAMPLES

a training period lasting two months	*a two-month training period*
ideas that boggle the mind	*mind-boggling ideas*
notes stained with coffee	*coffee-stained notes*

1. a garage for two cars
2. a textbook costing fifty dollars
3. a freeway with eight lanes
4. a conference that lasts a week
5. a shopper conscious of costs
6. a dictionary with a thumb-index
7. pipes covered with rust
8. parents who solve problems
9. cheese that is two years old
10. a club for cat lovers

(2) **Use the hyphen with spelled-out compound numbers from twenty-one to ninety-nine (or twenty-first to ninety-ninth).**

forty-sixth, fifty-eighth   BUT   three hundred twenty

Note: Usage varies regarding the hyphenation of spelled-out fractions. They hyphen is required, however, only when the fraction functions as a compound modifier.

almost one-half full	BUT	eating only one half of it
a two-thirds vote	BUT	two thirds of the voters

(3) **Use the hyphen to avoid ambiguity or an awkward combination of letters or syllables between prefix and root or suffix and root.**

a dirty movie-theatre [Compare "a dirty-movie theatre."]
to re-sign a petition [Compare "to resign a position."]
semi-independent, shell-like BUT   semifluid, childlike

(4) **Use the hyphen with the prefixes *ex-* ("former"), *self-, all-;* with the suffix *-elect;* and between a prefix and a capitalized word.**

ex-wife   self-help   all-inclusive   mayor-elect
mid-September   pre-Renaissance   anti-American

Note: The hyphen is also used with figures or letters such as *mid-1980s* or *T-shirt,* as well as with codes having more than five numbers: ISBN 0-03-921811-3.

■ **Exercise 7**   Refer to **18f** and to your dictionary as you convert each phrase (or words within each phrase) to a compound or to a word with a prefix. Use hyphens when needed.

EXAMPLES
glasses used for water   *water glasses* OR *waterglasses*
not combustible   *noncombustible*
not Christian   *non-Christian*
a job that pays $45 000 a year   *a $45 000-a-year job*

1. people who don't smoke cigarettes
2. a light used at night
3. in the shape of a *U*
4. knowledge of oneself
5. ham smoked with hickory
6. a brush for all purposes
7. trees covered with ice
8. flights from London to Rome
9. a weekend lasting three days
10. a computer that is five years old

Good Usage and Glossary

19

Use a good dictionary to help you select the words that express your ideas exactly.

You can find valuable information about words in a good concise or college dictionary, such as one of the following:

The Concise Oxford Dictionary
Funk & Wagnalls Canadian College Dictionary
Gage Canadian Dictionary
The Random House College Dictionary
Webster's Ninth New Collegiate Dictionary
Webster's New World Dictionary

Several other texts may also be helpful to you because of their special features. For example, *The Oxford Advanced Learner's Dictionary of Current English* and *The Collins Cobuild English Language Dictionary* offer useful information to students studying English as an additional language.

When buying a dictionary, you should keep in mind that only a Canadian dictionary or a Canadian edition of a dictionary will provide detailed information about Canadian words, weights and measures, and preferred spellings.

Occasionally you may need to refer to an unabridged dictionary or to some other special dictionary: see the two lists on pages 482–83.

19a
Use a good dictionary intelligently.

Examine the introductory matter as well as the arrangement and presentation of material in your dictionary so that you can easily find the information you need. Note meanings of any special abbreviations your dictionary uses.

Two sample dictionary entries, from *The Random House College Dictionary,* follow. Note the definitions of *empty* as an adjective, as a transitive verb, as an intransitive verb, as a noun, and as part of an idiomatic phrase (with *of*). Observe the examples of usage. Note that the second entry defines a hyphenated compound form, *empty-handed.* Finally, note the various other kinds of information (labelled in colour) that the dictionary provides.

Pronunciation Forms as adjective (with spelling) Forms as verb (with spelling)

Syllabication

Spelling

emp•ty (emp′tē), *adj.,* **-ti•er, -ti•est,** *v.,* **-tied, -ty•ing,** *n., pl.* **-ties.—***adj.* **1.** containing nothing; void of the usual or appropriate contents: *an empty bottle.* **2.** vacant; unoccupied: *an empty house.* **3.** without burden or load. **4.** destitute of people or human activity: *empty streets.* **5.** destitute of some quality or qualities; devoid (usually fol. by *of*): *a life empty of happiness.* **6.** without force, effect, or significance; hollow; meaningless: *empty compliments; empty pleasures.* **7.** hungry. **8.** without knowledge or sense; frivolous; foolish: *an empty head.* **9.** completely spent of emotion.—*v.t.* **10.** to make empty; discharge the contents of. **11.** to discharge (contents): *to empty the water out of a bucket.*—*v. i.* **12.** to become empty. **13.** to discharge contents, as a river.—*n.* **14.** something that is empty, as a box, bottle, can, etc. [ME (with intrusive *-p-*); OE *æm(et)-tig* (*æmett(a)* leisure + *-ig-*Y¹)]—**emp′ti•a•ble,** *adj.*—**emp′-ti•er,** *n.*—**emp′ti•ly,** *adv.*—**emp′ti•ness,** *n.*

Etymology

—**Syn. 1.** vacuous. EMPTY, VACANT, BLANK denote absence of content or contents. EMPTY means without appropriate or accustomed contents: *empty barrel; The house is empty* (has no furnishings). VACANT is usually applied to that which is temporarily unoccupied: *vacant chair; vacant* (uninhabited) *house.* BLANK applies to surfaces free from any marks or lacking appropriate markings, openings, etc.:

blank paper; a blank wall. **6.** delusive, vain. **10.** unload.— **Ant. 1.** full. ⸺ Antonym

emp•ty-hand•ed (emp′tē han′did), *adj., adv.* **1.** having nothing in the hands, as in doing no work. **2.** having gained nothing: *to come back from fishing empty-handed.*

(1) Spelling, syllabication, and pronunciation

Your dictionary describes both written and spoken language: you can check spelling and word division as well as pronunciation of unfamiliar words. Notice in the sample dictionary entries the way words are divided into syllables (syllabication) by the use of dots or sometimes accent marks. (For end-of-line division of words, see **8d.**) A key to the sound symbols is provided at the bottom of the entry pages as well as in the front of the dictionary. A primary stress (′) normally follows the syllable that is most heavily accented. Secondary stress marks follow lightly accented syllables.

■ **Exercise 1** With the aid of your dictionary, write out the words below using sound symbols and stress marks to show the correct pronunciation (or a correct one if options are given).

1. advertisement
2. catalogue
3. chalet
4. harass
5. linear
6. lymphatic
7. minutia
8. Mozart
9. perfunctory
10. reciprocation
11. schedule
12. uniformity

(2) Parts of speech and inflected forms

Your dictionary labels the possible uses of words in sentences—for instance, *adj.* (adjective), *adv.* (adverb), *v.t.* (verb, transitive). It also lists ways that nouns, verbs, and modifiers change form to indicate number, tense, or comparison or to serve as other parts of speech (for example, under *repress, v.t.,* you may also find *repressible, adj.*).

■ **Exercise 2** With the aid of your dictionary, classify each of the following words as a verb (transitive or intransitive), a noun, an adjective, an adverb, a preposition, or a conjunction. Give the principal parts of each verb, the plural (or plurals) of each noun, and the comparative and superlative of each adjective and adverb. (Note that some words are used as two or more parts of speech.)

1. angry	7. fine
2. combat	8. for
3. crisis	9. futile
4. deadly	10. sweet-talk
5. early	11. take
6. easy	12. tattoo

(3) Definitions and examples of usage

Observe whether your dictionary gives the most common meaning of a word first or arranges the definitions in historical order. Notice also that examples of a word used in phrases or sentences are often given to clarify each definition.

■ **Exercise 3** Study the definitions of any five of the following pairs of words, paying special attention to any examples of usage in your dictionary; then write sentences to illustrate the shades of difference in meaning.

1. brutal—cruel	7. lethargy—lassitude
2. contradict—deny	8. mercy—clemency
3. display—flaunt	9. pity—sympathy
4. draw—draft	10. rash—impudent
5. insolent—rude	11. rot—putrefy
6. inspire—motivate	12. sensual—sensuous

(4) Synonyms and antonyms

Lists and discussions of synonyms in dictionaries often help to clarify the meaning of closely related words. Studying denotations and connotations of words with similar meanings will help you choose words more exactly and convey more subtle shades of meaning. Lists of antonyms are also helpful because they provide words that mean the opposite of a word.

Note: For more complete lists of synonyms, antonyms, and related and contrasted words, refer to a special dictionary or a thesaurus. A sample thesaurus entry, from *The Random House Thesaurus,* follows.

> **empty** *adj.* **1** *Our voices echoed in the empty house:* vacant, unoccupied, uninhabited, bare, void. **2** *He didn't want to retire and lead an empty life:* aimless, meaningless, without substance, vacuous, insignificant, worthless, purposeless, futile, unfulfilled, idle, hollow; shallow, banal, trivial, inane, insipid, frivolous—*v.* **3** *Empty the glass before putting it in the dishwasher. The Mississippi empties into the Gulf of Mexico:* pour out, drain, dump, void, evacuate; discharge, flow, debouch. *Ant.* **1** full, stuffed, crammed, packed, jammed; occupied, inhabited. **2** meaningful, significant, substantial, useful, valuable, worthwhile, purposeful, fulfilled, busy, full, rich, vital, interesting, serious. **3** fill, pack, put in, stuff, cram, jam; receive.

Before choosing a synonym or closely related word from such a list, look it up in the dictionary to make sure that it expresses your meaning exactly. Although *void, idle,* and *inane* are all listed as synonyms of *empty,* they have different meanings.

■ **Exercise 4**   With the aid of your dictionary or thesaurus, list two synonyms and one antonym for each of the following words.

1. ugly
2. pleasure
3. defy
4. support
5. stingy

(5) Origin: development of the language

In college dictionaries the origin of a word—also called its *derivation* or *etymology*—is shown in square brackets. For example, after *expel* you might find this information:

[<L *expellere* <*ex-* out + *pellere* to drive, thrust]

This means that *expel* is derived from (<) the Latin (L) word *expellere,* which is made up of *ex-,* meaning "out," and *pellere,* meaning "to drive or thrust." Breaking up a word, when possible, into *prefix—root—suffix* will often help to get at the basic meaning of a word.

	prefix		*root*		*suffix*
interruption	**inter-**	+	**rupt**	+	**-ion**
	between		to break		act of
transference	**trans-**	+	**fer**	+	**-ence**
	across		to carry		state of

The bracketed information given by a good dictionary is especially rich in meaning when considered in relation to the historical development of our language.

The parenthetical abbreviations for language here and on the next few pages are those commonly used in bracketed derivations in dictionaries. English is one of the Indo-European (IE) languages, a group of languages apparently derived from a common source. Within this group of languages, many of the more familiar words are remarkably alike. Our word *mother,* for example, is *mater* in Latin (L), *meter* in Greek (Gk.), and *matar* in ancient Persian and in the Sanskrit (Skt.) of India. Such words, descended from or borrowed from the same form in a common parent language, are called *cognates.* The large number of cognates and the many correspondences in sound and structure in most of the languages of Europe and some languages of Asia indicate that they are derived from the common language that linguists call Indo-European, which it is believed was spoken in parts of Europe about six thousand years ago. By the opening of the Christian Era the speakers of this language had spread over most of Europe and as far east as India, and the original Indo-European had developed into eight or nine language families. Of these, the chief ones that influenced English were the Hellenic (Greek) group on the eastern Mediterranean, the Italic (Latin) on the central and western Mediterranean, and the Germanic in northwestern Europe. English is descended from the Germanic.

Two thousand years ago the Hellenic, the Italic, and the Germanic branches of Indo-European each comprised a more or less unified language group. After the fall of the Roman Empire in the fifth century, the several Latin-speaking divisions developed independently into the modern Romance languages, chief of which are Italian, French, and Spanish. Long before the fall of Rome the Germanic group was breaking up into three families: (1) East Germanic, represented by the Goths, who were to play a large part in the history of the last century of the Roman Empire before losing themselves in its ruins; (2) North Germanic, or Old Norse (ON), from which modern Danish (Dan.), Swedish (Sw.), Norwegian (Norw.), and Icelandic (Icel.) derive; and (3) West Germanic, the direct ancestor of English, Dutch (Du.), and German (Ger.).

The English language may be said to have begun about the middle of the fifth century, when the West Germanic Angles, Saxons, and Jutes began the conquest of what is now England and either absorbed or drove out the Celtic-speaking inhabitants. (Celtic—from which Scots Gaelic, Irish Gaelic, Welsh, and other languages later developed—is another member of the Indo-European family.) The next six or seven hundred years are known as the Old English (OE) or Anglo-Saxon (AS) period of the English language. The fifty or sixty thousand words then in the language were chiefly Anglo-Saxon, with a small mixture of Old

Norse words as a result of the Danish (Viking) conquests of England beginning in the eighth century. But the Old Norse words were so much like the Anglo-Saxon that they cannot always be distinguished.

The transitional period from Old English to Modern English—about 1100 to 1500—is known as Middle English (ME). The Norman Conquest began in 1066. The Normans, or "Northmen," had settled in northern France during the Viking invasions and had adopted Old French (OF) in place of their native Old Norse. Then, crossing over to England by the thousands, they made French the language of the king's court in London and of the ruling classes—both French and English—throughout the land, while the masses continued to speak English. Only toward the end of the fifteenth century did English become once more the common language of all classes. But the language that emerged at that time had lost most of its Anglo-Saxon inflections and had taken on thousands of French words (derived originally from Latin). Nonetheless, it was still basically English, not French, in its structure.

The kinds of changes that occurred during the development of the English language (until it was partly stabilized by printing, introduced in London in 1476) are suggested by the following passages, two from Old English and two from Middle English.

Hē ǣrest gescēop   eorðan bearnum
He first created   *for earth's children*
heofon tō hrōfe,   hālig Scyppend.
heaven as a roof,   *holy creator.*
                          From the "Hymn of Caedmon"
                          about eighth century

Ǣlc þāra þe þās mīn word gehīerþ, and þā wyrcþ, biþ gelīc
Thus each who hears these my words, and does them, is like

þǣm wīsan were, sē his hūs ofer stān getimbrode. Þā cōm þǣr
a wise man, who builds his house on a stone. Then there came

regen and micel flōd, and þǣr blēowon windas, and āhruron on
rain and a great flood, and blowing winds, and a roaring in

þǣt hūs, and hit nā ne fēoll: sōþlīce hit wǣs ofer stān getimbrod.
that house, and it did not fall: truly it was built on stone.

Matthew 7:24–25
tenth century

Therefor ech man that herith these my wordis, and doith
hem, shall be maad lijk to a wise man, that hath bildid his
hous on a stoon. And reyn felde doun, and flodis camen, and
wyndis blewen, and russchiden into that hous; and it felde
not doun, for it was foundun on a stoon.

Matthew 7:24–25
fourteenth century

A knight ther was, and that a worthy man,
That fro the tyme that he first bigan
To ryden out, he loved chivalrye,
Trouthe and honour, fredom and curteisye.

From Chaucer's Prologue
to the *Canterbury Tales,* about 1385

A striking feature of Modern English (that is, English
since 1500) is its immense vocabulary. As already noted,
Old English used some fifty or sixty thousand words, very
largely native Anglo-Saxon; Middle English used perhaps
a hundred thousand words, many taken through the French
from Latin and others taken directly from Latin; and
unabridged dictionaries today list over four times as many.
To make up this tremendous word hoard, we have borrowed
most heavily from Latin, but we have drawn some words
from almost every known language. English writers of the
sixteenth century were especially eager to interlace their
works with words from Latin authors. And, as the English
pushed out to colonize and to trade in many parts of the
globe, they brought home new words as well as goods.
Modern science and technology have drawn heavily from the
Greek. As a result of all this borrowing, English has become
one of the richest and most cosmopolitan of languages.

In the process of enlarging our vocabulary we have lost most of our original Anglo-Saxon words. But those that are left make up the most familiar, most useful part of our vocabulary. Practically all of our simple verbs and our articles, conjunctions, prepositions, and pronouns are native Anglo-Saxon; and so are many of our familiar nouns, adjectives, and adverbs. Every speaker and writer uses these native words over and over, much more frequently than the borrowed words. Indeed, if every word is counted every time it is used, the percentage of native words runs very high—usually between 70 and 90 percent. Milton's percentage was 81, Tennyson's 88, Shakespeare's about 90, and that of the King James Bible about 94. English has been enriched by its extensive borrowings without losing its individuality; it is still fundamentally the *English* language.

■ **Exercise 5** With the aid of your dictionary, give the etymology of each of the following words:

1. aspirin	7. OK
2. dysfunctional	8. quasar
3. hallmark	9. radar
4. ketchup	10. tariff
5. laughter	11. veal
6. lunatic	12. Velcro

(6) Special usage labels

In your dictionary, you will find special usage labels for words or particular definitions of words that differ from general (or unlabelled) usage. Here is a sampling of labels frequently used, each of them found in two or more college dictionaries:

unalienable	*Archaic, Obsolete*	inalienable
lift	*Informal, Colloquial*	plagiarize
codder	*Non-Standard, Dialect, Colloquial*	a boat used for cod fishing
Spud Island	*Slang*	Prince Edward Island

The classification of usage is often difficult and controversial because our language is constantly changing. Good writers try to choose the words, whatever their labels, that exactly fit the audience and the occasion, informal or formal.

■ **Exercise 6** Classify the following words and phrases according to the usage labels in your dictionary. If a word has no special usage label, classify it as *General*. If a given definition of a word has a usage label, give the meaning after the label.

EXAMPLES
job—general
murther—dialectal for *murder*
nutty—informal for *silly,* slang for *insane*

1. ain't
2. caitiff
3. gofer
4. holler
5. lout
6. mukluk
7. rink rat
8. schmooze
9. screech
10. sleazy
11. smog
12. snigger

19b
Use informal words only when appropriate to the audience.

Words or expressions labelled *Informal* or *Colloquial* (meaning "characteristic of speech") in college dictionaries are standard English and are used by writers every day, particularly in informal writing, especially dialogue. On occasion, informal words can be used effectively in formal writing, but they are usually inappropriate. Unless an informal expression is specifically called for, use the general English vocabulary, the unlabelled words in your dictionary.

| INFORMAL | dopey | gypped | belly button |
| FORMAL | stupid | swindled | navel |

Contractions are common in informal English, especially in dialogue: see the examples on page 184. But contracted forms (like *won't* or *there's*) are usually written out (*will not, there is*) in a formal composition—which is not as casual or spontaneous as conversational English.

■ **Exercise 7**   Make a list of ten words or phrases you would consider informal. Then check your dictionary to see how (or if) each definition you have in mind is labelled.

19c
Use newly coined words and slang only when appropriate to the audience.

Newly coined words are usually fresh and interesting but may be unfamiliar to your reader since they are often regional. A few years ago no one had ever heard of a *docudrama,* and current words such as *geriphobia* and *advertorial* are still unfamiliar to many. If you are unsure whether your reader will understand the new word you use, define it or find another one.

Slang words, including certain coinages and figures of speech, are variously considered breezy, racy, extremely informal, non-standard, facetious, taboo, offbeat, or vigorous. On occasion, slang can be used effectively, even in formal writing. Below is an example of the effective use of the word *spiel,* still labelled by dictionaries as *Slang:*

> Here comes another Question Period. Here come the backbenchers, the frontbenchers, the barbs, the spiels, the catcalls, the hoopla. Here comes another difficult day for the Speaker of the House.

A few years ago the word *hoopla* was also generally considered slang, but now dictionaries disagree: one classifies this word as *Standard* (unlabelled); another as *Colloquial (Informal);* still another as *Slang.* Like *hoopla,* words such as *spiel, spiffy, uptight, raunchy, schlep,* and *party pooper* have a particularly vivid quality; they soon may join former slang words such as *sham* and *mob* as part of the general English vocabulary. Conversely, they may also disappear from common usage.

Slang can easily become dated—which is a good reason to be cautious about using it in writing. Also, much slang is trite, tasteless, and inexact. For instance, when used to describe almost anything disapproved of, *gross* becomes inexact, flat.

Caution: As you avoid the use of ineffective slang in your writing, remember that many of the most vivid short words in our language are general, standard words. Certain long words can be as inexact and as drab as trite slang. For examples of the ineffective use of big words, see Exercise 9, page 248.

■ **Exercise 8**   Replace the italicized words in the following sentences with more exact words or specific phrases.

1. He was so *bagged* that he had to *crash* for a couple of hours.
2. Amanda told her that Ted was a real *flake.*
3. She has been feeling really *crummy* for over a week now.
4. Their new concert CD is *awesome.*
5. That *wisecrack ticked* him *off.*
6. I thought I *had it made* after my interview.
7. It wasn't his experience that got him the job: it was his political *pull.*
8. I'm not going to waste any time on that *dork.*
9. That movie was the biggest *snore* of the year.
10. She sent him on a real *guilt trip* after he showed up without the book.

19d
Use regional words only when appropriate to the audience.

Regional or dialectal usages (also called *localisms* or *provincialisms*) should normally be avoided in writing outside the region where they are current. Speakers and writers may, however, safely use regional words known to the audience they are addressing. *Salt chuck,* for example, is widely used by both Canadians and Americans in the Pacific Northwest to refer to the sea.

> REGIONAL   He slung the **nunny bag** over his shoulder.
> GENERAL   He slung the **knapsack** over his shoulder.

19e
Avoid non-standard words and usages.

Words and expressions labelled by dictionaries as *Non-standard* or *Illiterate* should be avoided in most writing—for example, "He don't know how" for "He doesn't know how." Many expressions of this kind are not listed in college dictionaries.

19f
Avoid archaic and obsolete words.

All dictionaries list words (and meanings for words) that have long since passed out of general use. Such words as *ort* (fragment of food) and *yestreen* (last evening) are still found in some dictionaries because these words, once the standard vocabulary of great authors, occur in our older literature and must be defined for the modern reader.

A number of obsolete or archaic words—such as *worser* (for *worse*) or *holp* (for *helped*)—are still in use but are now non-standard.

19g
Use technical words and jargon only when appropriate to the audience.

When writing for the general reader, avoid all unnecessary technical language. The careful writer will not refer to an organized way of finding a subject for writing as a *heuristic* or a need for bifocals as *presbyopia.* (Of course, the greater precision of technical language makes it desirable when the audience can understand it, as when one physician writes to another.)

Jargon is technical slang that is tailored specifically for a particular occupation. It can be an efficient shortcut for specialized concepts, but you should use jargon only when you can be sure that all your readers understand it.

19h
Avoid overwriting, an ornate or flowery style, or distracting combinations of sounds.

Overwriting, as well as distracting combinations of sounds, calls attention to words rather than to ideas. Such writing makes for slow, difficult reading.

ORNATE	The majority believes that the approbation of society derives primarily from diligent pursuit of allocated tasks.
BETTER	Most people believe success results from hard work.
DISTRACTING	The use of catalytic converters is just one contribution to the solution of the problem of air pollution.
BETTER	The use of catalytic converters is just one way to help solve the problem of air pollution.
PRETENTIOUS	The investigators reprehended their resorting to a lachrymator.
BETTER	The investigators denounced their use of tear gas.

Also avoid the overuse of alliteration (repetition of the same consonant sound), as in "**S**ome people **sh**un the **sea**shore."

■ **Exercise 9**   Using simple, formal, straightforward English, rewrite the following sentences (cited by Edwin Newman in *A Civil Tongue*).

1. We have exceptional game plan capabilities together with strict concerns for programming successful situations.
2. In order to improve security, we request that, effective immediately, no employees use the above subject doors for ingress and egress to the building.
3. We will also strategize with the client on ways to optimize usage of the spots by broadcast management.
4. Muzak helps human communities because it is a non-verbal symbolism for the common stuff of everyday living in the global village.
5. These precautions appeared to be quite successful in dissuading potential individuals with larcenous intent.

■ **Exercise 10**   Rewrite the following passage to eliminate inflated diction and bureaucratic jargon. Write clear sentences using simple, formal, straightforward English.

¹At the present time, we are cognizant of the fact that many patients eligible for financial assistance for their dental expenses are unaware of their entitlement to seek partial reimbursement for expenditures incurred in consequence of referral to a specialist. ²What the council has in mind to propose, if the agency sees such a proceeding as efficacious, is an augmentation of publicity and a simplification of procedures. ³The board must be mindful of the unfortunate prodigality in time usage with respect to the activities of those clerical staff members appointed to serve at the reception desk. ⁴We believe we should give consideration to the possible implementation of a process to clarify the information required on the forms so that the necessity for clients to request clerical assistance in the completion of applications

can be addressed. [5]Staff in managerial positions have made observations to the effect that the confidential nature of the financial information that must be provided by the clients must be observed since the need for privacy ought to preclude clerical assistance. [6]We urge, therefore, that the board act as expeditiously as possible to implement these changes.

19i
Avoid sexist and biased words.

Language reflects attitudes. Without meaning to be hurtful or to suggest prejudices toward a particular group of people, you may use a word that offends. Certain words can suggest bias against persons and can stereotype people according to gender, sexual orientation, race, ethnic group, appearance, or age. For example, gender-biased or sexist language conveys assumptions about the roles and occupations of women and men and assigns characteristics according to gender or sexual orientation. Writers who are careless of their language may present themselves as thoughtless or unfeeling. Whereas statements such as "She's a real dish," "I think he's a hunk," "He's as queer as a three-dollar bill," "Sikhs are pushing their way into the RCMP," or "She's a typical little old lady" are overtly offensive, some statements may offend in more subtle fashion. Consider, for example, the comment that thinking about overpopulation evokes for some people "the desire to put fences on our borders and **stop the most wretched from breeding.**" This phrase appeared in an article in the *Atlantic Monthly* (February 1993), a journal that strives for fair treatment. The author might have been attributing such views to others, but the phrasing implies that poverty-stricken persons who contribute to overpopulation are less than human, becoming *the wretched;* that it is those from other nations (those beyond *our borders*) who are the *most wretched;* and that bearing children is for them nothing more than *breeding—*

a term we usually associate with animal, not human, reproduction. The writer might have meant to be ironic in separating his views from those of less tolerant Americans, but the language is hurtful, demeaning, and nationalist.

Avoid language that demeans, stereotypes, patronizes, or excludes any group. The following examples illustrate ways to overcome sexism.

SEXIST	The **babes** in my class are **opinionated and surprisingly brainy.**
REVISED	The women in my class are articulate and intelligent.
SEXIST	A **nurse's** contract should provide for leave after **she bears** a child. And this should apply for any **male nurse,** too.
REVISED	Nurses' contracts should provide for leave after the birth of a child.
SEXIST	A **stewardess** and a **policeman** have at least one thing in common in their work: they both have to remain cool under pressure.
REVISED	Both flight attendants and police officers must have the ability to remain cool under pressure.
SEXIST	President Clinton was proud of **Hillary's** commitment to education.
REVISED	President Clinton was proud of Hillary Clinton's commitment to education.
REVISED	President Clinton was proud of Mrs. Clinton's commitment. (*This solution is workable but not as good, since Hillary Clinton is known for her work on education reform and has a separate identity as a lawyer.*)
SEXIST	A **man** who wants to entertain **his** audience will use humour.
REVISED	A person who wants to entertain an audience will use humour.
REVISED	Speakers who want to entertain their audiences will use humour.

Note: See **6b** for ways to avoid using *he* and *his* as generic pronouns.

■ **Exercise 11**   Revise the following sentences to eliminate sexist and biased language.

1. The actor Denzel Washington, a black who is a devoted father and husband, is outstanding in character roles.
2. Ellen thought he behaved like a real gentleman.
3. Since the French Embassy people had been invited, she expected a wine and cheese reception. She also decided to dress with extra care since she imagined the Consul and his wife would be present.
4. His admiration for the weaker sex was unbounded, and he was especially proud of his mother's activities as a suffragette in the march on Parliament.
5. Charlotte Ross, a woman doctor and the first to practise in Quebec, was nicknamed "Iron Rose."
6. The Irish Catholic James Joyce and Mrs. Virginia Woolf have both influenced prose style in this century.
7. He told the lawyers they were welcome to bring their wives.
8. I was pleased to meet Kelvin Wong, who is going to give the opening remarks at lunch tomorrow, and to learn that his English is perfect.
9. Sylvia Plath, the celebrated American poetess, was married to Ted Hughes before he became British Poet Laureate.
10. Fall is the time that an author may be expected to tour the country to promote his books and sign autographs.

19j
Consult a glossary of usage.

Consider your purpose and your audience as you consult the following glossary to determine appropriate usage. This short glossary covers only the most common usage problems. See **18b** for a supplementary list of frequently confused words.

The entries in this glossary are authoritative only to the extent that they describe current usage. The usage labels included do not duplicate the description in any one dictionary, but justification for each label can usually be found in at least two of the leading dictionaries. For a discussion of the restrictive labels used in dictionaries, see **19a(6)**.

As you study the descriptions of usage in this glossary, keep in mind the following categories:

GENERAL	Words or expressions in the Standard English vocabulary—listed in dictionaries without special usage labels.
INFORMAL	Words or expressions that dictionaries label *Informal* or *Colloquial*—used in speech and in informal writing.
STANDARD	All general and informal words or expressions.
NON-STANDARD	Words or expressions labelled in dictionaries as *Archaic, Illiterate, Non-standard, Obsolete, Slang,* or *Substandard*—words not considered a part of the standard English vocabulary.

a, an   Use *a* before the sound of a consonant; **a** yard, **a** U-turn, **a** one-base hit. Use *an* before a vowel sound: **an** empty can, **an** M.D. **an** axe, **an** X ray, **an** hour, **an** NHL game.

above   Acceptable as a modifier or as a noun in such references as "in the paragraph above" or "none of the above." Some writers, however, avoid "the above."

accidently, accidentally   *Accidentally* is the correct form.

ad, advertisement   Use the full word in your formal writing.

adverse, averse   *Adverse* describes something as "hostile, antagonistic": **adverse** criticism. *Averse* means "having feelings of hostility against or repugnance for": He is **averse** to criticism.

advise   Non-standard as a substitute for the noun *advice:* the doctor's **advice** [NOT advise].

affect, effect   The verb *affect* means "to influence, attack" or "to touch the emotions." The noun *effect* means "result of a cause."

Smoking **affects** the heart.	His tears **affected** her deeply.
Drugs have side **effects.**	The **effect** on sales was good.

When used as a verb, *effect* means "to produce as an effect": The medicine **effected** a complete cure.

aggravate   Widely used for *annoy* or *irritate*. Many writers, however, restrict the meaning of *aggravate* to "intensify, make worse": Noises **aggravate** a headache.

a half a   Omit one of the *a*'s: half a loaf, a half loaf.

ahold of   Informal for "a hold of, a grasp on something," as in "to get ahold of a rope."

ain't   A non-standard contraction generally avoided in writing, unless used in dialogue or for humorous effect.

alibi   Appropriate in a legal context but informal when used in place of "to give an excuse" or for the noun *excuse*.

allusion, illusion   An *allusion* is a casual or indirect reference. An *illusion* is a false idea or an unreal image.

> The author's **allusion** to a heaven on earth amused me.
> The author's concept of a heaven on earth is an **illusion.**

a lot   Sometimes misspelled as *alot*.

already, all ready   *Already* means "before or by the time specified." *All ready* means "completely prepared."

> The theatre was **already** full by seven o'clock.
> The cast was **all ready** for the curtain call.

alright   Not yet a generally accepted spelling of *all right*.

altogether, all together   *Altogether* means "wholly, thoroughly." *All together* means "in a group."

> That law is **altogether** unnecessary.
> They were **all together** in the lobby.

A.M., P.M. (OR **a.m., p.m.**) Use only with figures.

> NOT   The wedding begins at ten-thirty in the **a.m.**
> BUT   The wedding begins at 10:30 **A.M.** [OR at ten-thirty in the morning]

among, between   Prepositions with plural objects (including collective nouns). As a rule, use *among* with objects denoting three or more (a group), and use *between* with those denoting only two (or twos).

> walked **among** the crowd, quarrelling **among** themselves
> a choice **between** war and peace, reading **between** the lines

Note: Do not use this guideline unthinkingly for *between*. *Between* is also used to express the relations of a thing to many things severally or individually.

> Switzerland is located **between** [NOT among] France, Germany, Austria, and Italy.
> Parliament debated the free trade agreement **between** [NOT among] Canada, Mexico, and the United States.

amount of, number of   *Amount of* is followed by singular nouns; *number of,* by plural nouns.

> an **amount of** money, light, work, or postage [singular]
> a **number of** coins, lights, jobs, or stamps [plural]

See also **a number, the number.**

an   See **a, an.**

and etc.   *Etc.* is an abbreviation of *et* ("and") *cetera* ("other things"). Omit the redundant *and*. See also **etc.**

and/or   Now acceptable in general writing. Some writers, however, avoid the form because they consider it distracting.

and which, and who   Do not use *and* before only one *which* or *who* clause. The *and* may be used to link two subordinate clauses.

> They are competent volunteers **who** [NOT and who] work overtime.
> OR They are volunteers *who are competent* **and** *who work overtime.*
> [two subordinate clauses]

a number, the number   As a subject, *a number* is generally plural and *the number* is singular. Make sure that the verb agrees with the subject.

> **A number** of options **are** available.
> **The number** of options **is** limited.

anyone, any one; everyone, every one   Distinguish between each one-word and two-word compound. *Anyone* means "any person at all"; *any one* refers to one of a group. Similarly, *everyone* means "all," and *every one* refers to each one in a group.

> Was **anyone** hurt? Was **any one** of us prepared?
> **Everyone** should attend. **Every one** of them should attend.

anyways   Non-standard for *anyway*.

as   (1) Do not use *as* instead of the preposition *like* in making a comparison: Natalie, **like** [NOT as] her mother, is a shrewd judge of character.

(2) In your formal writing, do not use *as* instead of *if, that,* or *whether* after such verbs as *feel, know, say,* or *see:* I do not know **if** [NOT as] my adviser is right.

(3) To avoid even a slight chance of ambiguity, many writers prefer not to use *as* for *because, since,* or *while.*

PREFERRED   **While** [NOT As] it was raining, we watched TV.
OR **Because** [NOT As] it was raining. . . .

as far as   Not acceptable as a substitute for the phrasal preposition *as for:* **As for** fasting [NOT As far as fasting], many doctors discourage it for weight loss.

at   Redundant after *where.* See **where . . . at, where . . . to.**

awful   Overworked for *ugly, shocking,* or *very.*

awhile, a while   *Awhile,* an adverb, is not used as the object of a preposition: We rested **awhile.** COMPARE We rested for **a while.**

back of   Informal for *behind* or *in back of.*

backwards   Use *backward* [NOT backwards] as an adjective: a **backward** motion.

bad, badly   The adverb *badly* is preferred after most verbs. But either *bad* or *badly* is now standard in the sense of "ill" or "sorry," and some writers now prefer *bad* after such verbs as *feel* or *look.*

The organist plays **badly.** Charles feels **bad.**

because   See **reason . . . because.**

beef, bellyache   Slang for *complain* or *grumble.*

being as, being that   Unacceptable for *since, because.*

beside, besides   Always a preposition, *beside* usually means "next to," sometimes "apart from." As a preposition meaning "in addition to" or "other than," *besides* is now more common in writing than *beside.* When used adverbially, *besides* means "also" or "moreover."

Martin was sitting **beside** Jenny.
Besides countless toys, these children have their own TV set.
The burglars stole our silver—and my stereo **besides.**

better, had better   Do not omit the *had* in your formal writing.

> We **had** better consider history as we plan for our future.

between   See **among, between.**

bias, prejudice   Synonyms in the sense of "a preconceived opinion" or "a distortion of judgement." But a bias may be in favour of or may be against, whereas a prejudice is against. Many writers do not use *bias* for *discrimination* because they consider the usage bureaucratic jargon.

borrow off, borrow from   Use *borrow from* in your writing.

bottom line   An overworked term for "outcome, upshot," or "the final result."

brass   Slang for "high-ranking officials" and informal for "insolence, impudence."

bug   Slang as a verb for *annoy* or *spy on* and as a noun for *fanatic* or *hidden microphone.*

bunch   Informal if used to refer to a group of people.

burger, hamburger   In your formal writing, use the full word.

bursted   Archaic for *burst.*

but what   Informal after *no* or *not* following such expressions as "no doubt" or "did not know."

> INFORMAL   There was no doubt but what they would win.
> GENERAL   There was no doubt **that** they would win.

but which, but who   Do not use *but* before one *which, that,* or *who* clause. *But* may be used to link two subordinate clauses.

> It is a needed change that [NOT but that] will not be accepted.
> OR It is a change *that is needed* but *that will not be accepted.* [two
> subordinate clauses]

can, may   Interchangeable when permission is sought. But formal English distinguishes between *can* referring to ability and *may* referring to permission in such sentences as these:

> **Can** student nurses give injections? [Are they able to?]
> **May** student nurses give interjections? [Are they permitted to?]

can't hardly, can't scarcely   Use *can hardly, can scarcely.*

cause of . . . on account of, due to   Redundant. Omit the *on account of* or *due to;* or recast to avoid wordiness.

> WORDY   One cause of misunderstandings is on account of lack of communication.
>
> BETTER   One cause of misunderstandings is lack of communication.
>
> CONCISE   Lack of communication causes misunderstandings.

centre about, centre around   Informal for "to be focussed on or at" or for "centre on."

compare to, compare with   Formal English prefers *compare to* for the meaning "regard as similar" and *compare with* for the meaning "examine to discover similarities or differences."

> The speaker **compared** the earth **to** a lopsided baseball.
>
> Putting one under the other, the expert **compared** the forged signature **with** the authentic one.

complementary, complimentary   *Complementary* means "completing" or "supplying needs." *Complimentary* means "expressing praise" or "given free."

> His talents and hers are **complementary.**
>
> Admiring the performance, he made several **complimentary** remarks.

conscious, conscience   An adjective, *conscious* means "aware, able to feel and think." A noun, *conscience* means "the sense of right and wrong."

> When I became **conscious** of my guilt, my **conscience** started bothering me.

consensus of opinion   Redundant. Omit the *of opinion.*

could of   Non-standard for *could have.* See **of.**

couple, couple of   Informal for *two* or for *several* in such phrases as "a couple aspirin," "a couple more litres of paint," or "in just a couple of seconds."

different from   In formal English the preferred preposition after *different* is *from.* But the less formal *different than* is accepted by many writers if the expression is followed by a clause.

> The Stoic philosophy is **different from** the Epicurean.
>
> The outcome was **different from** what I expected.
>
> OR The outcome was **different than** I had expected [it to be].

differ from, differ with *Differ from* means "to be unlike." *Differ with* means "to disagree."

disinterested *Disinterested* means "impartial" or "lacking prejudice": a **disinterested** referee; *uninterested* means "indifferent, lacking in interest."

don't Unacceptable when used for *doesn't:* He **doesn't** [NOT don't] agree.

due to *Due to* means "the result of," and it follows the verb *to be:*

> The smoke was **due to** fire. [The smoke was **the result of** fire.]
> The spread of cholera was **due to** the contamination of the water supply.

Due to in place of *because of* or *on account of* is not acceptable in formal writing.

Because of [NOT Due to] holiday traffic, we arrived an hour late.

> The cholera spread **because of** the contamination of the water supply.

each other Not used as the subject of a verb in formal writing.

> NOT We hoped each other would keep in touch.
> BUT Each of us hoped the other [OR others] would keep in touch.

effect See **affect, effect.**

emigrate from, immigrate to The prefix *e-* (a variant of *ex-*) means "out of"; *im-* (a variant of *in-*) means "into." To *emigrate* is to go out of one's own country to settle in another. To *immigrate* is to come into a different country to settle there. The corresponding adjective or noun forms are *emigrant* and *immigrant*. (Compare *export, import.*)

> Many families **emigrated from** Hong Kong. The number of **emigrants** increased during the 1990s.
> Many Hong Kong Chinese **immigrated** to Canada. These **immigrants** contributed to the growth of our economy.

eminent, imminent *Eminent* means "distinguished." *Imminent* means "about to happen, threatening."

> Carlotta is an **eminent** scientist.
> Bankruptcy seemed **imminent.**

enthuse   Informal for "to show enthusiasm."

etc.   Appropriate informally but use sparingly in formal writing. Many writers prefer to substitute *and so on* or *and so forth.* (Since *etc.* means "and other things," *and etc.* is redundant.)

> NEEDLESS   Ordinary games like Monopoly, backgammon, etc., did not interest these electronics hobbyists.
>
> REVISED   Ordinary games like Monopoly and backgammon did not interest these electronics hobbyists.

ever so often, every so often   *Ever so often* means "very often, frequently." *Every so often* means "every now and then, occasionally."

everyone, every one   See **anyone, any one; everyone, every one.**

except, accept   To *except* is to exclude or make an exception of. To *accept* is to approve or receive.

> These laws **except** [exclude] juveniles.
> These schools **accept** [admit] juveniles.

expect   Informal for *suppose, surmise,* or *presume.*

explicit, implicit   *Explicit* means "expressed directly or precisely." *Implicit* means "implied or expressed indirectly."

> The advertisement was **explicit:** "All sales final."
> Reading between the lines, I understood the **implicit** message.

fantastic   Informal—overworked for "extraordinarily good" or "wonderful, remarkable."

farther, further   Used interchangeably. Some writers, however, prefer *farther* in references to geographic distance: six kilometres **farther.** *Further* is used as a synonym for *additional* in more abstract references: **further** delay, **further** proof.

fewer, less   Formally, *fewer* (used with plural nouns) refers to *how many,* and *less* (used with singular nouns) to *how much.*

> **fewer** noises, **fewer** hours, **fewer** children
> **less** noise, **less** time

figure   Informal for *believe, think, conclude,* or *predict.*

flunk   Informal for *fail,* as in an examination or test.

folks   Informal for *parents, relatives.*

former Refers to the first named of two. If three or more items are named, use *first* and *last* instead of *former* and *latter*.

> Manawaka and Deptford are two fictional settings: Margaret Laurence created **the former,** and Robertson Davies created the latter.

fun Informal if used adjectivally, as in "a fun person," "a fun car."

further See **farther, further.**

get Useful in numerous idioms but not appropriate formally in such expressions as "get with the times," "always gets in with his instructors," and "a stubborn attitude that gets me."

go, goes Informal for *say, says.*

> INFORMAL I go, "Hello there!" Then he goes, "Glad to see you!"
>
> GENERAL I say, "Hello there!" Then he **says,** "Glad to see you!"

good In your formal writing, do not use *good* as an adverb.

> Watson played **well** [NOT good] under pressure.

great Overworked informally for *skilful, good, clever, enthusiastic,* or *very well,* as in "really great at guessing the answers" or "with everything going great for us."

guy(s) Informal for *any person(s).*

had of, had have Non-standard for *had.*

> NOT I wish I had of [OR had have] said that.
>
> BUT I wish I **had** said that.

had ought, hadn't ought Use *ought, ought not,* or *oughtn't.*

half a, a half, a half a Use *half a* or *a half* in your writing.

hang Useful in numerous idioms but slang in such expressions as "a hang-up about sex" and "to hang out in video arcades."

hanged, hung Informally interchangeable in the sense of "put to death by hanging." Formally, it is *hanged* (often used figuratively nowadays) that refers to such an act, never *hung.*

> When my parents supplied enough rope, I usually **hanged** myself— but not always.

hardly, scarcely Words with negative force, usually considered non-standard if used with an unnecessary negative like *not, nothing,* or *without.*

> I **could hardly** quit then. [NOT couldn't hardly]
> **Hardly anything** went right today. [NOT hardly nothing]
> The motion passed **with scarcely** a protest. [NOT without scarcely]

hisself   Non-standard for *himself.*

hooked on   Slang for *addicted to* or *obsessed with.*

hopefully   Still questionable for *I hope* or *it is hoped.*

how come   Informally used as a substitute for *why.*

illusion   See **allusion, illusion.**

immigrate   See **emigrate from, immigrate to.**

implicit   See **explicit, implicit.**

imply, infer   Most writers carefully distinguish between *infer* (meaning "draw a conclusion based on evidence") and *imply* ("suggest without actually stating").

> His attitude **implies** that money is no problem.
> I **infer** from his attitude that money is no problem.

incidently, incidentally   *Incidentally* is the correct form.

include   When precisely used, *include (includes, included)* precedes an incomplete rather than a complete list.

> Precipitation **includes** sleet and hail. COMPARE Precipitation has four forms: rain, snow, sleet, and hail.

inferior than   Use *inferior to* or *worse than.*

ingenious, ingenuous   *Ingenious* means "clever, resourceful"; *ingenuous* means "open, frank; artless."

> This electric can opener is an **ingenious** device.
> Don's **ingenuous** smile disarms the critics.

input   Useful as a computer term but questionable in the sense of "a voice in" or "an active role," as in "Students had no input in these decisions."

in regards to, with regards to   Non-standard for *in regard to, with regard to,* or *as regards.*

into   Informal for "interested in" or "involved with," as in "We are into computers now."

irregardless   Non-standard for *regardless.*

its, it's *Its* is a possessive pronoun ("for *its* beauty"). *It's* is a contraction of *it is* ("*It's* beautiful!") or of *it has* ("*It's* been a beautiful day!").

kick Slang or very informal in such expressions as "to kick in my share," "just for kicks," "on another kick," "just kicking around town."

kind, sort Singular forms, which may be modified by *this* or *that*. The use of *these* or *those* is increasingly common but is still questionable.

QUESTIONABLE These kind of arguments are deceptive.
CORRECT **These kinds** of arguments are deceptive.
OR **This kind** of argument is deceptive.
This sort of hat is best.

kind of, sort of Informal when used adverbially in the sense of "to a degree, somewhat, a bit" or "in a way" (as in "kind of silly," "sort of hesitated," or "kind of enjoying it").

kind of a, sort of a Omit the *a* in your formal writing: NOT "this kind of a tour" BUT "this *kind of* tour."

later, latter Comparative forms of *late* often confused in writing. In modern English, *later* (like *sooner*) refers to time; *latter* (like *former*) refers to one of two—to the second one (but not to the last of several).

We set a **later** date. They arrived **later** than usual.
She wrote a song and a play. The **latter** won a prize.

See also **former.**

lay (laid, laying) Use *lay (laid, laying)* in the sense of "put," "place"; José *laid* the book on the desk. Use *lie (lay, lain, lying)* in the sense of "to rest or recline."

I should **lie** down [NOT lay]. Had he **lain** down [NOT laid]?
The truck **was lying** [NOT laying] on its side.

learn Unacceptable for *teach, instruct, inform.*

leave Unacceptable for *let* except when followed by an object and *alone*, as in "*Leave* [OR let] them alone."

Let sleeping dogs lie.   **Let** her go.   **Let** the baby be.

less See **fewer, less.**

let's us Redundant. Use *let's* or *let us.*

liable to Informally used in place of *likely to* in reference to mere probability. Formally, *liable to* not only denotes likelihood or possibility but also suggests the idea of harm or danger.

> INFORMAL   It's liable to be cooler soon. [mere likelihood]
> GENERAL   The roof is **liable** to collapse. [likelihood + danger]

lie (lay, lain, lying) Non-standard for *lay (laid, laying)* in the sense of "put, place."

> Onion slices are then **laid** [NOT lain] on the fillet.
> Last night I **laid** [NOT lay] my homework aside.

like Widely used as a conjunction (in place of *as, as if,* or *as though*) in conversation and in public speaking. Formal English, however, still rejects the use of *like* as a conjunction.

> FORMAL   He drives **as** [NOT like] I did before my accident.
>   OR He drives **the way** I did before my accident.
> FORMAL   They acted **as though** [NOT like] they owned the town.

lose, loose *Lose* is a verb: did **lose,** will **lose.** *Loose* is chiefly an adjective: a **loose** belt.

may be, maybe Do not confuse the verb phrase *may be* with the adverb *maybe.*

> The story **may be** [OR might be] true.
> **Maybe** [OR Perhaps] the story is true.

me and Non-standard as part of a compound subject.

> NON-STANDARD   Me and Jeanne took an early flight.
> STANDARD   Jeanne and I took an early flight.

mighty Informal for *very* or *extremely* (as in "mighty fine" or "mighty big").

militate, mitigate *Militate* means "to act, work, or operate *against* (rarely, *in favour of*) something." *Mitigate* means "to make less unpleasant, serious, or painful; to soften or moderate."

> Excessive noise can **militate** against learning.
> A good doctor tries to **mitigate** a patient's suffering.

morale, moral   *Morale* (a noun) refers to mood or spirit. *Moral* (chiefly an adjective) refers to right conduct or ethical character.

> the **morale** of our team, affecting **morale,** low **morale**
> a **moral** person, **moral** judgements, an im**moral** act

most   Informal if used instead of *almost,* as in "most everyone."

Ms. (OR **Ms**)   Correctly used before a woman's name but not before her husband's name: **Ms.** Martha Jamison OR **Ms.** Jamison [NOT Ms. Philip Jamison].

much   Use *many* [NOT much] to modify plural nouns: **many** children, too **many** facts. See also **fewer, less.**

myself   Not acceptable formally and still questionable informally as a replacement for the subjective form *I* or the objective *me.*

> My sister and **I** [NOT myself] prefer soccer.
> He confided in Hayden as well as **me** [NOT myself].

nauseous   Generally avoided in writing as a substitute for *nauseated.*

no . . . nor   Use *no . . . or* in compound phrases: "they had **no** water **or** food." BUT "They had **neither** water **nor** food."

not . . . no/none/nothing   The double negative is unacceptable. See **4e.**

> NOT   We **didn't** have **no** fun.
>   We could **not** do **nothing** about it.
> BUT   We **didn't** have any fun.
>   We could do **nothing** about it.

number   See **amount of, number of; a number, the number.**

of   Do not write *of* for an unstressed *have.*

> COMPARE   I could have it done. [stressed]
>   I could have done it. [unstressed]
> NON-STANDARD   I might of [may of, could of, would of, must of, should of, ought to of] said that.
> STANDARD   I might **have** [may *have,* could *have,* would *have,* must *have,* should *have,* ought to *have*] said that. [auxiliary plus *have*]

off of   In formal writing, omit the *of* after *off* in such phrases as "fell off of the ladder."

OK, O.K., okay   All three are acceptable spellings. However, a more specific word usually replaces *OK* in a formal context.

parameter   Informal for *boundary* or *perimeter.*

party   Unacceptable in general writing when used for *person.*

per   Used especially in commercial writing. Many authors prefer to use *per* only in Latinisms ("per capita," "per se," or "per cent/percent").

plenty   Informal when used adverbially to mean *quite* or *sufficiently* (as in "plenty good enough").

plus   Many writers do not use or accept *plus* as a substitute for *and* between main clauses (see **12a**)—or for conjunctive adverbs like *moreover, besides,* or *in addition* placed between main clauses or sentences.

P.M.   See **A.M., P.M.**

prep   Informal for *prepare, preparation,* or *preparatory.* Use the full word in your formal writing.

principal, principle   Distinguish between *principal,* an adjective or noun meaning "chief" or "chief official," and the noun *principle,* meaning "fundamental truth."

> A **principal** factor in his decision was his belief in the **principle** that men and women are born equal.

raise, rise   *Raise (raised, raising)* means "to lift or cause to move upward, to bring up or increase." *Rise (rose, risen, rising)* means "to get up, to move or extend upward, ascend." *Raise* (a transitive verb) takes an object; *rise* (an intransitive verb) does not.

> Retailers **raised** prices.   Retail prices **rose** sharply.

rarely ever   In formal writing, either omit the *ever* or use *hardly* instead of *rarely.*

> He **rarely** mentions money. OR He **hardly ever** mentions it.

real   In non-standard and some informal use, an adverb meaning *very,* as in "real tired."

reason . . . is because   Formal usage prefers *that* instead of *because.*

> The reason he missed the test was that he overslept.
>
> OR He missed the test because he overslept.

reckon   Informal for *guess, think.*

relate to   Overworked in the sense of "be sympathetic with, understand" or "respond to in a favourable manner," as in "I don't relate to algebra."

respectively, respectfully   *Respectively* means "in the order designated." *Respectfully* means "showing respect."

> I considered becoming a farmer, a landscape artist, and a florist, **respectively.**
> They considered the rabbi's suggestion **respectfully.**

rise   See **raise, rise.**

says   Avoid the use of *says* for *said* after a past-tense verb: stood up and **said** [NOT says].

scarcely   See **hardly, scarcely.**

seldom ever   Omit the *ever* in your formal writing.

sit   Occasionally misused for *set* (put, place): to **set** something [NOT to sit something].

so, so that   *So that* is preferred in formal writing when there is even a remote possibility of ambiguity.

> AMBIGUOUS   We stay with Uncle Ed so we can help him out.
> [Does *so* mean *therefore* or *so that?*]
> PREFERRED   We stay with Uncle Ed **so that** we can help him out.

someone, some one   See **anyone, any one; everyone, everyone.**

sort   See **kind, sort.**

sort of a   Omit the *a* in your formal writing.

stationary, stationery   *Stationary* means "in a fixed position"; *stationery* means "writing paper and envelopes."

subsequently   Do not confuse with *consequently. Subsequently* means "afterward, occurring later." *Consequently* means "as a result, therefore."

> The last three pages of the novel are missing; **consequently** [NOT subsequently], I do not know the ending.

suppose to, supposed to   Be sure to add the *-d:* was **supposed** to do that.

sure Informal for *surely* or *certainly.*

their, there, they're *Their* is the possessive form of *they; there* is ordinarily an adverb or an expletive; *they're* is a contraction of *they are.*

> **There** is no explanation for **their** refusal.
> **They're** installing a traffic light **there.**

theirself, theirselves Non-standard for *themselves.*

them Non-standard when used adjectivally: **those** apples OR **these** apples [NOT them apples].

then Sometimes incorrectly used for **than.** Unlike **then, than** does not relate to time.

> Last summer, we paid more **than** that. [Compare "We paid more *then.*"]
> Other **than** a pension cheque, they had no income.

these kind, these sort, those sort See **kind, sort.**

this here, that there, these here, them there Non-standard expressions. Use *this, that, these, those.*

thusly Grammatically redundant. Write *thus* (already an adverb without the *-ly*).

to Redundant after *where.* See **where . . . at, where . . . to.**

to, too Distinguish the preposition *to* from the adverb *too.*

> If it isn't **too** cold Saturday, let's go **to** the fair.

try and Informal for *try to.* Use *try to* in writing.

type Informal for *type of* (as in "that type program").

use to, used to Be sure to add the *-d* to *use* unless the auxiliary is accompanied by *did* in questions or in negative constructions.

> He **used** to sail.   We **used** to argue about trifles.
> Did he **use** to sail?   We didn't **use** to argue about trifles.

very Omit when superfluous (as in "very unique" or "very terrified"). If you tend to overuse *very* as an intensifier, try using more exact words; in place of "very strange," for example, try *outlandish, grotesque,* or *bizarre.*

want in, want out Informal for "want to enter, want to leave."

ways Informal for *way* when referring to distance, as in "It's a long ways to Halifax."

where   Informal for *that* in such sentences as "I saw in the paper where the strike had been settled."

where . . . at, where . . . to   Omit the superfluous *at, to.*

> NOT   Where is she at? Where is she going to?
> BUT   Where is she? Where is she going?

which   Use *who* or *that* to refer to persons.

-wise   An overused adverb-forming suffix. Such recent coinages as *computerwise, advertisingwise,* or *cost-benefit-analysiswise* are generally unacceptable in college writing.

with regards to   Use *with regard to* or *as regards.*

would of   Non-standard for *would have.* See **of.**

your, you're   *Your* is the possessive of *you:* on **your** desk. *You're* is a contraction of *you are:* **You're** a winner.

zap   Slang for *destroy, jolt.*

Exactness

20

Choose words that are exact, idiomatic, and fresh.

Strive to choose words that express your ideas and feelings exactly. If you can make effective use of the words you already know, you need not have a huge vocabulary and you need not resort to a thesaurus in the hope of making your writing appear more sophisticated. Good writing often consists of short, familiar words:

> You can't teach your children anything important. You can teach them the sounds of consonants, how to tie shoelaces, the rules of chess or the manual gearshift. You can give them your recipe for date squares, your dentist's phone number and your barber's name and preference in Christmas gifts. You can enroll them in the schools you went to, introduce them to your best teachers, give them subscriptions to your favourite magazines and keep them up late at night playing excerpts from your cherished collection of records. But no matter how great your efforts and how profound your love, they will learn nothing from what you *try* to teach them. They will, of course, *assimilate* from you—your mannerisms, your gestures, your laugh, your bad habits. They will walk like you and you will see parts of

yourself, and hear echoes, every time you are with them, but
which parts those are, and which echoes—which they have
chosen and which they have rejected—will be irrelevant to
those you have tried to impart.

—PETER GZOWSKI, *The Morningside Papers*

Adding to your vocabulary, however, will help you
become a better writer. When you discover a valuable new
word, make it your own by mastering its spelling, meaning, and exact use.

20a
Select the word that expresses your idea exactly.

**(1) Choose words to denote precisely what you mean.
Avoid wrong, inexact, or ambiguous usage.**

WRONG	A loud radio does not detract me when I am reading a good novel. [*Detract* means "to subtract a part of" or "to remove something desirable."]
RIGHT	A loud radio does not **distract** me when I am reading a good novel. [*Distract* means "to draw attention away."]
WRONG	They acted out of prejudism. [non-standard]
RIGHT	They acted out of **prejudice.**
WRONG	She never reverts to herself as an expert. [*Revert* means "to go or turn back to a former place or position."]
RIGHT	She never **refers** to herself as an expert.
	OR
	She never **reminds** anyone that she is an expert.
INEXACT	Patrice felt ill, and she went home early. [*And* adds or continues.]
EXACT	Patrice felt ill, **so** she went home early. [*So* states results.]
	OR
	Because Patrice felt ill, she went home early. [*Because* explains Patrice's action.]

AMBIGUOUS   I knew enough German to understand I would
have to drive ten kilometres—but no more.
[Confusion involves whether "no more" refers
to the number of kilometres to drive or the ade-
quacy of the writer's German.]

CLEAR   I **knew only enough German** to understand I
would have to drive ten kilometres.

OR

I knew enough German to understand I would
have to **drive only** ten kilometres.

■ **Exercise 1** The italicized words in the following sentences
are wrong or inexact. Correct the errors and replace inexact
words with exact ones.

1. Sunera thought that the new lighting in the library carrels
   would have a good *affect* on study habits.
2. The listless cat was entirely *disinterested* in the new toy.
3. We must persuade club members to *adapt* a policy to
   end smoking.
4. Elinor is forever *flauting* her wealth by talking about her
   family's vacation homes in Spain and Hawaii.
5. He was willing to coach the soccer teams, *and* he didn't
   have the time.
6. Monsoons are *seasonable,* and people in tropical countries become *customized* to them.
7. Among the items at the auction was an *antiquated* desk,
   said to have belonged to John A. Macdonald.
8. The stage designer of the Bastion Theatre received rave
   reviews for his *craftiness.*
9. Emile has not yet learned to express himself clearly, *and
   only one conclusion can be drawn.*
10. They had the afternoon to decide whether to support
    Helen in her next year of college, *but not any longer.*

■ **Exercise 2** Underline the inexact, wrong, and ambiguous
words in the following paragraph, and then make all necessary
corrections. (Some sentences have more than one error.)

¹The co-ordinators of the Drafting for Engineering Program met to discuss how they could affect a policy change. ²They wanted to encourage more women to apply. ³Mr. Collins offered his view that more women wouldn't apply unless the admittance committee were to decline the mathematics scores required. ⁴Mr. Wang said his assumption that women couldn't "make the cut" was incredulous. ⁵He didn't say directly that he feared future graduates wouldn't be as good, but he intimidated it. ⁶Mr. Wang asked Mr. Collins straight out, "Are you inferring that all women score badly in math and that's why we have less women than we need? ⁷Do you really think admitting more women will effect standards?" ⁸Mr. Collins said, "I'm not saying that. ⁹I don't want to aggravate you, but I think the general moral of the school will change." ¹⁰Ms. Carter jumped in to support Mr. Collins with her view that the college should adapt a new entrance requirement: a minimum performance rate in mathematics quite separate from an overall average. ¹¹Mr. Wang combatted the idea, arguing that some students—men as well as women—might be only mediocre in their comprehensiveness of mathematics, but they would be able to overcome this. ¹²He reminded them that one set of scores in tests might not reliably foretell future performance. ¹³He tried to light up the tone of the meeting by saying that the imminent physicist Albert Einstein would be rejected on the base of his high school math scores. ¹⁴They all agreed at the end they would not alternate their entry requirements but would instead recruit women students in two ways. ¹⁵They would make a conscience effort in the coming year to visit every high school, and they would use the media of radio to develop ads directed at young women going on to collegiate.

■ **Exercise 3** With the aid of your dictionary, give the exact meaning of each italicized word in the quotation below. (Italics have been added.)

1. Ignorance of *history* is dangerous. —JEFFREY RECORD

   Those who cannot remember *the past* are condemned to repeat it. —GEORGE SANTAYANA

2. The ideal of happiness has always taken material form in the *house,* whether cottage or castle; it stands for permanence and separation from the world.

—SIMONE DE BEAUVOIR

Home is the place where, when you have to go there,
They have to take you in.

—ROBERT FROST, "The Death of the Hired Man"

3. Travel is no cure for melancholia; space-ships and time machines are no *escape* from the human condition.

—ARTHUR KOESTLER

Well, Columbus was probably regarded as an *escapist* when he set forth for the New World.

—ARTHUR C. CLARKE

4. Reading is to the mind what *exercise* is to the body.

—RICHARD STEELE

There's a hell of a distance between wisecracking and wit. Wit has truth in it; wisecracking is simply *calisthenics* with words. —DOROTHY PARKER

5. We had a *permissive* father. He *permitted* us to work.

—SAM LEVENSON

(2) Choose the word with the connotation, as well as the denotation, appropriate to the idea you wish to express.

The *denotation* of a word is what the word actually refers to in the physical world. According to the dictionary, the word *beach* denotes "the shore of a body of water, especially when sandy or pebbly." The *connotation* of a word is what the word suggests or implies. *Beach,* for instance, may connote natural beauty, warmth, surf, water sports, fun, sunburn, crowds, or even gritty sandwiches.

A word may be right in one situation, wrong in another. *Female parent,* for instance, is a proper expression in a biology laboratory, but it would be inappropriate to say "John wept because of the death of his female parent."

Female parent used in this sense is literally correct, but the connotation is wrong. The more appropriate word, *mother,* conveys not only the meaning denoted by *female parent* but also the reason why John wept. The first expression simply implies a biological relationship; the second includes emotional suggestions.

■ **Exercise 4** Give one denotation and one connotation for each of the following words.

1. aerobics
2. computer
3. golden
4. justice
5. liberal
6. rat
7. star
8. triumph
9. valley
10. Yukon

■ **Exercise 5** Prepare for a class discussion of word choice. After the first quotation below are several series of words that the author might have used but did not select. Note the differences in meaning when an italicized word is substituted for the related word at the head of each series. Be prepared to supply your own alternatives for each of the words that follow the other four quotations.

1. Creeping gloom hits us all. The symptoms are usually the same: not wanting to get out of bed to start the day, failing to smile at ironies, failing to laugh at oneself.

—CHRISTOPHER BUCKLEY

   a. gloom: *sadness, depression, melancholy*
   b. hits: *strikes, assaults, infects, zaps*
   c. usually: *often, frequently, consistently, as a rule*
   d. failing: *too blue, unable, neglecting, too far gone*

2. Our plane rocked in a rain squall, bobbed about, then slipped into a patch of sun.   —THEODORE H. WHITE
   a. rocked   b. bobbed   c. slipped   d. patch

3. It's hard not to feel menaced in a subway car that resembles a moving coal bin, where the few working lights flicker wanly, and every possible surface (including emergency exit instructions) is a black smear of illiterate spray-painted scrawl.   —MICHELE LANDSBERG

a. menaced   b. flicker   c. wanly   d. smear

4. Stereotypes economize on our mental effort by covering up the blooming, buzzing confusion with big recognizable cut-outs. —ROBERT L. HEILBRONER

a. economize   b. effort   c. blooming   d. recognizable
e. cut-outs

5. No emotion is so corrosive of the system and the soul as acute envy. —HARRY STEIN

a. corrosive   b. system   c. soul   d. acute   e. envy

(3) Choose the specific and concrete word rather than the general and abstract one.

A *general* word is all-inclusive, indefinite, sweeping in scope. A *specific* word is precise, definite, limited in scope.

GENERAL	SPECIFIC	MORE SPECIFIC/CONCRETE
food	fast food	pizza
prose	fiction	short stories
place	city	Edmonton

An *abstract* word deals with concepts, with ideas, with what cannot be touched, heard, or seen. A *concrete* word has to do with particular objects, with the practical, with what can be touched, heard, or seen.

ABSTRACT WORDS	democracy, loyal, evil, hate, charity
CONCRETE WORDS	mosquito, spotted, crunch, wedding

Often, writers tend to use too many abstract or general words, making their writing drab and lifeless. As you select words to fit your context, be as specific and concrete as you can. For example, instead of the word *bad,* consider using a more precise adjective.

bad planks:	rotten, warped, scorched, knotty, termite-eaten
bad children:	rowdy, rude, ungrateful, selfish, perverse
bad meat:	tough, tainted, overcooked, contaminated

To test whether or not a word is specific, ask one or more of these questions about what you want to say: Exactly who? Exactly what? Exactly when? Exactly where? Exactly how? As you study the following examples, notice what a difference specific, concrete words can make in the expression of an idea. Notice, too, how specific details can be used to expand or develop ideas.

VAGUE   I always think of a good museum as one that is very big.

SPECIFIC   I always think of a good museum as one I get lost in. —EDWARD PARKS

VAGUE   The discontented people debated the matter and finally found a suitable leader in William Lyon Mackenzie.

SPECIFIC   The malcontents argued on the platforms and in the end they found a leader to their hearts in William Lyon Mackenzie, a Scot, arrived in 1820, editing the *Colonial Advocate,* as honest as daylight, and as uncompromising as the Westminster Catechism. —STEPHEN LEACOCK

VAGUE   I remember my pleasure at discovering new things about language.

SPECIFIC   I remember my real joy at discovering for the first time how language worked, at discovering, for example, that the central line of Joseph Conrad's *Heart of Darkness* was in parentheses.

—JOAN DIDION

Notice in the sentence below how specific details can be used to develop an idea.

He closes up the clinic, where all the paperwork has weights of various kinds—stones, inkpots, a toy truck his son no longer plays with—to keep it from blowing away by the fan.

—MICHAEL ONDAATJE

All writers use abstract words and generalizations when these are vital to the communication of ideas, as in the following sentence:

He is immortal, not because he alone among all creatures has an inexhaustible voice, but because he has a soul, a spirit capable of compassion and sacrifice and endurance.

—WILLIAM FAULKNER

To be effective, however, the use of these words must be based on clearly understood and well-thought-out ideas.

■ **Exercise 6** Replace the general words and phrases in italics with specific ones.

1. I always think of an airport as *very busy.*
2. They were pleased with *a variety of changes* made during the renovation.
3. He expressed irritation with *the way the children play* on the playground.
4. Living on campus *has numerous advantages.*
5. Jennifer told her parents that she *was experiencing some difficulties* in adjusting to university life.
6. The shop *offered an amazing range* of health foods.
7. The dog *walked over* to its *food.*
8. My friend looked at my history essay and said *what I least expected to hear.*
9. *Various aspects of the movie* were criticized *in the article.*
10. *A lot of people* are threatened by *pollution.*

(4) Use figurative language appropriately.

Figurative language uses words in an imaginative rather than a literal sense. Figures of speech are commonly found in nonfiction prose as well as in fiction, poetry, and drama. And, of course, they are a part of everyday speech and language. Sports reporters, for example, conventionally use figurative language when they say one team has *beaten, scuttled,* or *whipped* another, or that one team was *skunked, routed,* or *buried* by another. *Simile* and *metaphor* are the chief figures of speech. A simile is the comparison of dissimilar things using *like* or *as.* A metaphor is an implied comparison of dissimilar things, without using words of comparison such as *like* or *as*.

SIMILES

Writers who choose domicile in a foreign place, for whatever reason, usually treat their native language like a delicate timepiece, making certain it runs exactly and that no dust gets inside. —MAVIS GALLANT

His death was like the flash of his gun, sudden, accurate and—since one must die—merciful. —GEORGE WOODCOCK

The whole place is silent as an empty classroom, like a house suddenly without children. —W.P. KINSELLA

The two men passed through the crowd as easily as the Israelites through the Red Sea. —WILLIAM X. KIENZLE

He was like a piece of rare and delicate china which was always being saved from breaking and which finally fell.

—ALICE WALKER

METAPHORS

Dress is language. —LANCE MORROW

Successful living is a journey toward simplicity and a triumph over confusion. —MARTIN E. MARTY

A North American supermarket is market place, temple, palace, and parade all rolled into one. —MARGARET VISSER

We are born princes and the civilizing process turns us into frogs. —ERIC BERNE

Wolf pups make a frothy ribbon of sound like fat bubbling.
—EDWARD HOAGLAND [a metaphor and a simile]

Single words are often used metaphorically:

These roses must be **planted** in good soil. [literal]
A man's feet must be **planted** in his country, but his eyes should survey the world.

—GEORGE SANTAYANA [metaphorical]

We always **sweep** the leaves out of the garage. [literal]
She was letting her imagination **sweep** unchecked round every rock and cranny of the world that lies submerged in the depths of our unconscious being.

—VIRGINIA WOOLF [metaphorical]

Writers do, of course, use metaphors and similes within single sentences as well.

> Time is the continuous loop, the snakeskin with scales endlessly overlapping without beginning, or time is an ascending spiral if you will, like a child's toy Slinky.
> —MARGARET ATWOOD

> Inside the house I found a wilderness of bottles and glasses and a maze of unmade beds, undusted furniture, and piled-up cardboard boxes. —TIMOTHY FINDLEY

Similes and metaphors are especially valuable when they are concrete and point up essential relationships that cannot otherwise be communicated. (For faulty metaphors, see **23c.**) Similes and metaphors can also be extended throughout a paragraph of comparison. See **32d(10).**

There are many other common figures of speech. *Personification* is the attribution to the nonhuman (objects, animals, ideas) of characteristics possessed only by the human.

> Time talks. It speaks more plainly than words. . . . It can shout the truth where words lie. —EDWARD T. HALL

Paradox is a seemingly contradictory statement that actually makes sense when thoughtfully considered.

Only where love and need are one
And the work is play for mortal stakes. . . . —ROBERT FROST

Overstatement (also called *hyperbole*) and *understatement* are complementary figures of speech often used for ironic or humorous effect.

> I, for one, don't expect till I die to be so good a man as I am at this minute, for just now I'm fifty thousand feet high—a tower with all the trumpets shouting.
> —G.K. CHESTERTON [overstatement]

> You have a small problem; your employer has gone bankrupt. [understatement]

Irony involves a deliberate incongruity between what is stated and what is meant (or what the reader expects). In verbal irony, words are used to express the opposite of what they literally mean; for example, in Shakespeare's *Julius Caesar,* Marc Antony stirs a mob to anger against Brutus by repeatedly stating, "Brutus is an honorable man." An *allusion* is a brief reference to a work or a person, place, event, or thing (real or imaginary) that serves as a kind of shorthand to convey a great deal of meaning compactly. The administration of President John F. Kennedy was often referred to as "Camelot," an allusion to the domain of the legendary King Arthur. An *image* represents a sensory impression in words; for example, Tennyson describes the sea as seen from the point of view of an eagle as "wrinkled."

■ **Exercise 7**   Write sentences containing the specified figure of speech.

1. Metaphor
2. Simile
3. Personification
4. Overstatement or understatement
5. Allusion

■ **Exercise 8**   Complete each sentence with an effective simile, metaphor, hyperbole, or personification.

> EXAMPLES
> The grass rolls out to the bleachers like a *freshly brushed billiard table.*   —JAY WRIGHT
> The sentence is a *bridge* we build and cross to reach one another.   —ROBIN ENDRES

1. Sightseers flocked around the TV crew like _____.
2. Viewed from outer space, the earth is _____.
3. The mosquitoes in those weeds _____.
4. The third hurricane of the season slashed through Jamaican towns _____.
5. Death in a hovel or in a penthouse is _____.

6. Like _____, the class sat speechless.
7. The lecture was as _____.
8. Her eyes looked like _____.
9. Surging forward, the crowd _____.
10. Constant bickering is as _____.
11. She was as self-confident as _____.
12. The alarm sounded like _____.

20b
Choose expressions that are idiomatic.

Be careful to use idiomatic English, not unidiomatic approximations. *She talked down to him* is idiomatic. *She talked under to him* is not. Occasionally the idiomatic use of prepositions may prove difficult. If you are uncertain which prepositions to use with a given word, check the word in the dictionary. For instance, *agree* may be followed by *about, on, to,* or *with.* The choice depends on the context. Writers often have trouble with expressions such as these:

> according **to** the plan [NOT with]
> accuse **of** perjury [NOT with]
> comply **with** rules [NOT to]
> conform **to/with** standards [NOT in]
> die **of** cancer [NOT with]
> in accordance **with** policy [NOT to]
> independent **of** her family [NOT from]
> inferior **to** ours [NOT than]
> jealous **of** others [NOT for]

Many idioms—such as *all the same, put up a fight,* and *to mean well*—defy literal interpretation. That is, their meanings cannot be understood from the individual meanings of their elements. As you encounter idioms that are new to you, master their meanings just as you would any new word.

■ **Exercise 9** Write sentences using each of the following idioms correctly. Use your dictionary as necessary.

1. agree with, agree to, agree on
2. differ from, differ with, differ about
3. wait on, wait for
4. necessity for, necessity of
5. part from, part with
6. pick on, pick out, pick up
7. put on, put off, put by
8. on the go, on the spot

20c
Choose fresh expressions instead of trite, worn-out ones.

Such expressions as *to the bitter end, lazy as the day is long,* and *dead as a doornail* were once striking and effective. Excessive use, however, has drained them of their original force and made them clichés. Some euphemisms (pleasant-sounding substitutions for more explicit but possibly offensive words) are not only trite but wordy—for example, *laid to rest* for *buried* or *pecuniary difficulties* for *debt.* Many political slogans and the catchy phraseology of advertisements soon become hackneyed. Faddish or trendy expressions like *interface, impacted, viable, input,* or *be into* (as in "I am into dieting") are so overused that they quickly lose their force.

Nearly every writer uses clichés from time to time because they are so much a part of the language, especially of spoken English, and do contribute to the clear expression of ideas in written English.

> We feel free when we escape—even if it be but **from the frying pan into the fire.**   —ERIC HOFFER

It is often possible to give a fresh twist to an old saying or a well-known literary passage.

If a thing is worth doing, it is worth doing badly.
—G.K. CHESTERTON

She calls a spade a delving instrument. —RITA MAE BROWN

Into each life a little sun must fall. —L.E. SISSMAN

Washington is Thunder City—full of the sound and fury signifying power. —TOM BETHELL [Compare Shakespeare's "full of sound and fury, / Signifying nothing."—*Macbeth*]

Proverbs and familiar expressions from literature or the Bible, many of which have become a part of everyday language, can often be used effectively in your own writing.

Our lives are empty of belief. They are **lives of quiet desperation.** —ARTHUR M. SCHLESINGER, JR. [Compare Thoreau's *Walden:* "The mass of men lead lives of quiet desperation."]

A man's reach must exceed his grasp, or what's a metaphor? —MARSHALL McLUHAN [Compare Browning's "Ah, but a man's reach should exceed his grasp, / Or what's a Heaven for?"]

Slowly but steadily, in the following years, a new vision began gradually to replace the dream of political power—a powerful movement, the rise of another ideal to guide the unguided, another **pillar of fire by night** after a clouded day. —W.E.B. DU BOIS [Compare Exodus 13:21: "And the Lord went before them . . . by night in a pillar of fire, to give them light."]

Good writers, however, do not rely too heavily on the words of others; they choose their own words to communicate their own ideas.

■ **Exercise 10**   From the following list of trite expressions—only a sampling of the many in current use—select ten that you often use or hear, and replace them with carefully chosen words or phrases.

EXAMPLES
a bolt from the blue   *a shock*
beyond the shadow of a doubt   *undoubtedly*

1. a crying shame
2. after all is said and done
3. as cold as ice
4. at the crack of dawn
5. bored to tears/death
6. to make a long story short
7. drop a bombshell
8. get in a rut
9. hoping against hope
10. horse of a different colour
11. in the last analysis
12. in this day and age
13. launch a campaign
14. over and done with
15. sea of red ink
16. shun like the plague
17. sleep like a log
18. smell a rat
19. stick to your guns
20. the depths of despair
21. the powers that be
22. the spitting image of
23. throw in the towel
24. with a ten-foot pole

■ **Exercise 11** Choose five of the ten items below as the basis for five original sentences. Use language that is exact, idiomatic, and fresh.

EXAMPLES

the appearance of her hair
Her hair poked through a broken net like stunted antlers.
—J.F. POWERS

OR *Her dark hair was gathered up in a coil like a crown on her head.* —D.H. LAWRENCE

1. the sound of his voice
2. her response to deadlines
3. the first day of classes
4. the way she walks
5. the start of fall
6. the noises of the city
7. the appearance of the room
8. the scene of the accident
9. the final minutes of play
10. the approaching storm

■ **Exercise 12** Read the two passages that follow in preparation for a class discussion of the authors' choice of words, their use of concrete, specific language, and their use of figurative language.

¹The days were short, and often sombre, but we kept a good fire going in the house, we ate pumpkin pie, we sorted walnuts and corn. ²We also set tomatoes to ripen on the window sills, and on certain days the whole house was permeated with the odour of pickles cooking over a gentle fire in large pans. ³The saw could be heard singing in the yard; its

two-toned song, first clear, then deeper and heavier as it bit into the wood, seemed to me to promise us joyfully, "I'm cutting you fine logs, fine logs for the whole winter." [4]All this time the house, like a ship ready to weigh anchor or a city about to undergo a siege, was being filled with provisions—sauerkraut, maple syrup from Quebec, red apples from British Columbia, plums from Ontario. [5]Soon also we began to receive from our uncles in the country fat geese and turkeys, dozens of chickens, hams and salt bacon, cases of fresh eggs and farm butter. [6]To help ourselves we had only to go into our summer kitchen, now transformed into a storehouse, where the frost preserved our stock. [7]Such were the joys of autumn, based upon abundance and a feeling of security that I think I appreciated even then.   —GABRIELLE ROY

[1]They say, too, that nature did its best to co-operate. [2]A wind came up from somewhere, bending trees, shaking the house. [3]You could hear the screech of giant trunks grinding against each other. [4]You could hear the squeal of nails wrenched in the lumbered walls and the cedar roof above you. [5]The water in the strait was churned up into waves that smashed against the cliff, and leapt upwards high enough to spray the windows and toss driftwood like sticks across the yard. [6]A door flew open in the wind, crashed against the wall, and was forced shut again by someone whose face was streaming with rain and salt water and strips of kelp. [7]Sticks and bits of limbs were flying across the floor. [8]Dead pine needles clotted like hairballs in the corner. [9]Keneally's voice rose above the tumult to include it. . . . [10]He would be transformed, Keneally said, his voice suddenly heavy with importance. [11]He would be transformed from flesh into spirit this night. [12]He would, in fact, be dead. [13]The organ music spiralled upward into a final impossible note that lay across the sudden silence like a clear metallic lid, though frightened Kathleen's feet kept pumping madly still and her forehead pressed against the elaborately carved wood of the instrument like a cyclist against the wind. [14]Logs crashed on the verandah; men whimpered; bladders weakened; a light in the ceiling dimmed.
—JACK HODGINS

Wordiness and Needless Repetition

21

Avoid wordiness. Repeat a word or phrase only when it is needed for emphasis or clarity.

Wordiness is the use of more words than necessary to express an idea.

WORDY	In the early part of the month of January, a blizzard was moving threateningly toward St. John's.
REVISED	In early January, a blizzard was threatening St. John's.

Needless repetition of words or phrases distracts the reader and blurs meaning.

REPETITIOUS	This **interesting** instructor knows how to make an un**interesting** subject **interesting.**
REVISED	This instructor knows how to make a dull subject interesting.

For the effective use of repetition in parallel structures, for emphasis, and as a transitional device, see **26b, 29e,** and **32b(3),** respectively.

Wordiness

21a
Make every word count; omit words or phrases that add nothing to the meaning.

(1) **Avoid tautology (the use of different words that say the same thing).**

WORDY	Commuters going back and forth to work or school formed carpools.
CONCISE	Commuters formed carpools.
WORDY	Each writer has a distinctive style, and he or she uses this in his or her own works.
CONCISE	Each writer has a distinctive style.

Notice the useless words in brackets below:

yellow [in colour]	circular [in shape]
at 21:45 [that night]	return [back]
[basic] essentials	rich [and wealthy] nations
bitter [-tasting] salad	small [-size] potatoes
but [though]	to apply [or utilize] rules
connect [up together]	[true] facts

Avoid grammatical redundancy—such as a double subject (subject + subjective pronoun), double comparison, or double negative.

my sister [she] is	[more] easier than	could[n't] hardly

(2) **Do not use many words when a few will express the idea well. Omit unnecessary words.**

WORDY	**In the event that** the grading system is changed, expect complaints **on the part** of the students.
CONCISE	**If** the grading system is changed, expect complaints **from** the students. [Two words take the place of eight.]

WORDY **As far as sexism is concerned, it seems to me that** a woman can be as guilty of sexism as a man.

CONCISE A woman can be as guilty of sexism as a man. [Unnecessary words are deleted.]

One or two words can replace expressions such as these:

at this point in time	**now**
has the capability of working	**can work**
made contact by personal visits	**visited**
on account of the fact that	**because**
somewhere in the neighbourhood of $2500	**about $2500**

One exact word can say as much as many. (See also **20a.**)

spoke in a low and hard-to-hear voice	**mumbled**
persons who really know their particular field	**experts**

Notice below that the words in brackets are not necessary.

because [of the fact that]	was [more or less] hinting
[really and truly] fearless	by [virtue of] his authority
fans [who were] watching TV	the oil [that exists] in shale

■ **Exercise 1** Revise each sentence to eliminate tautology.

1. The exact date has not been set and is not known to us.
2. During the last two innings, many senseless mistakes occurred without any apparent reason for them.
3. Starving refugees in need of food lined up for supplies given out by the Red Cross volunteer people.
4. Perhaps maybe the chief cause or reason for obesity in people who are overweight is lack of exercise.
5. The tall skyscraper buildings form a dark silhouette against the evening sky.

■ **Exercise 2** Substitute one or two words for each item.

1. in this day and age
2. has the ability to sing
3. was of the opinion that
4. in a serious manner
5. prior to the time that
6. did put in an appearance
7. located in the vicinity of
8. has a tendency to break
9. during the same time that
10. involving too much expense

■ **Exercise 3**   Delete unnecessary words below.

1. As far as she was concerned, the politician had no national identity that could be recognized by Canadians across the country.
2. It was apparent to me that the solution was obvious.
3. It seemed to him that the public opinion polls asking people to express their views about the candidates in the next election to be held in the spring would, in effect, influence the vote.
4. Because of the fact that Larry was there, the party was lively.
5. Other things being equal, it is my opinion that all of these oil slicks, whether they are massive or not so big, do damage to the environment to a greater or lesser degree.
6. As for the nature of biased newscasts, I can only say that I realize that reporters have to do some editing, though they may not use the finest type of judgement when they are underscoring, as it were, some of the stories and downplaying others.

21b
Eliminate needless words by combining sentences or by simplifying phrases and clauses.

Note differences in emphasis as you study the following examples.

WORDY   The grass was like a carpet. It covered the whole playground. The colour of the grass was blue-green.

CONCISE   A carpet of blue-green grass covered the whole playground.

WORDY   A few of the listeners who had become angry called in so that they would have the opportunity of refuting the arguments set forth by the host.

CONCISE   A few angry listeners called in to refute the host's arguments.

■ **Exercise 4**   Condense the following sentences based on the patterns of the examples provided.

EXAMPLE

These were theories that were, in essence, concerned with politics.

These were political theories.

1. These are pitfalls that do, of course, pose a real danger.
2. This is an act that, in truth, partakes of the nature of aggression.

EXAMPLE

It was a house built with cheap materials.

It was a cheaply built house.

3. It was a garden planned with a great deal of care.
4. It was a speech delivered with a lot of passion.

EXAMPLE

The stories written by Alice Munro are different from those composed by Jack Hodgins.

Alice Munro's stories are different from Jack Hodgins'.

5. The dishes prepared by her husband are not as good as those fixed by her father.
6. The ideas shared by the students were different from those promoted by the advertiser.

EXAMPLE

It is unfortunate. A few come to college so that they can avoid work.

Unfortunately, a few come to college to avoid work.

7. It is inevitable. Corporations produce goods so that they can make a profit.
8. It is predictable. Before an election legislators reduce taxation so that they can win the approval of voters.

EXAMPLE

The forces that were against censorship ran an advertisement that covered two pages.

The anti-censorship forces ran a two-page advertisement.

9. A group that is in favour of labour wants contracts that last twelve months.

10. One editorial supporting day care stressed the need for centres that are government funded.

■ **Exercise 5** Restructure or combine sentences to reduce the number of words.

1. These hazards are not visible, and they cause accidents, many of which are fatal ones.
2. The countryside was being invaded. What I mean by that is a takeover of land. Urban developers were buying up farms.
3. In spite of the fact that my parents did not approve of it, I was married to Evelyn last June.
4. The fire chief made the recommendation saying that wooden shingles should not be used on homes now being built or in the future.
5. Crows are very numerous all across North America. They are also very active. And are monochromatic. All of which makes it difficult to distinguish one crow from another.

Needless Repetition

21c

Avoid needless repetition.

NEEDLESS	His uncle is not like her uncle. Her uncle takes more chances.
REVISED	His uncle is not like hers. Hers takes more chances.
NEEDLESS	I think that he knows that that woman is not the one for him to marry.
REVISED	I think he knows he should not marry that woman.

Note: Avoid the distracting repetition of a word (or part of a word) used in different senses.

CARELESS	Even at the graveside services, the brothers kept quarrelling. It was a grave situation.
BETTER	. . . It was a **serious** situation.

Do not unintentionally use jingles like "compared the fare there." A repetition of sounds can be distracting: see **19h**.

21d
Eliminate needless repetition by using pronouns and elliptical constructions.

Use a pronoun instead of needlessly repeating a noun or substituting a clumsy synonym. If the reference is clear, several pronouns may refer to the same antecedent.

> NEEDLESS   The hall outside these offices was empty. The hall had dirty floors, and the walls of this corridor were full of gaudy portraits.
>
> REVISED   The hall outside these offices was empty. It had dirty floors, and its walls were full of gaudy portraits.

The writer of the following sentence uses an elliptical construction. The omitted words (shown here in brackets) will be understood by the reader without being repeated.

> Prosperity is the goal for some people, fame [is the goal] for others, and complete independence [is the goal] for still others. . . . —RENÉ DUBOS

Sometimes, as an aid to clarity, commas are used to mark omissions that avoid repetition.

> Family life in my parents' home was based upon a cosmic order: Papa was the sun; Mamma, the moon; and we kids, minor satellites. —SAM LEVENSON

For effective use of the repetition of words or phrases, see **29e**.

■ **Exercise 6**   Revise each sentence to eliminate wordiness and needless repetition.

1. The manager returned the application back because of illegible handwriting that could not be read.
2. In this day and time, it is difficult today to find in the field of science a physicist who shows as much insight into the field of space and time as Stephen Hawking shows.

3. From time to time during one's life, one needs to remember that one who is learning to walk has to put one foot before the other one.

4. When the fans in the stadium shout and yell, the shouting and yelling are deafening, and so the total effect of all this is that it is a contributing factor in decisions to stay home and watch the games on TV.

5. A distant hurricane or a seaquake can cause a tidal wave. This wave can form when either occurs.

6. A comedy of intrigue (or a situation comedy) is a comedy that relies on action instead of characterization for its comedy.

7. In my family, schoolwork came first, chores came second, fun and games came next, and discussions came last.

8. Numerous products can be made from corn. The oil from this plant is used in soap. A starch extracted from corn helps make gravy without lumps.

■ **Exercise 7** Rewrite the following passage to cut down on wordiness and needless repetition. Delete unnecessary words and redundancies, combine sentences, simplify phrases, and use pronouns and elliptical constructions wherever appropriate. Your revision should be about half the length of the original.

[1]Works of art depicting sports may have different appeals for the many people who collect them. [2]These works of art don't necessarily carry the same value for all collectors. [3]Not all collectors collect for the same reasons. [4]Some collect because the art work interests them as an object. [5]Others collect because the art object has some historical importance. [6]They are interested in the work as a social or historical record.

[7]Paintings of athletes and sports figures are understandably popular with sports fans, but most such works are not treated as serious art by art collectors. [8]One indicator of this lack of valuing is purely commercial. [9]That is, in market terms, the reproductions or prints of such paintings are reproduced in such numbers that there is relatively little likelihood that they will appreciate, that is to say, increase, in marketplace value.

[10]Some painters, however, control the numbers of their works. [11]Thus, limited-edition prints of paintings of hockey stars by James Lumber, for example, begin to gain value from the moment they go on sale. [12]And, of course, some painters who are highly respected in the larger art world may paint athletes or sports scenes because they capture their interest. [13]Two mainstream painters known for such works are Alex Colville and Ken Danby. [14]Colville has painted a mysterious bicycle, and Ken Danby has painted hockey players in such characteristic scenes as lacing up their skates.

[15]One of the most famous paintings on the subject of hockey was painted by Ken Danby. [16]This painting is titled *At the Crease* and it shows a goalkeeper crouched in front of the net in the marked area of the ice called "the crease." [17]Ken Danby painted *At the Crease* in 1972. [18]A work in the style of painting called "magic realism," it shows every minute detail in a very distinct way. [19]*At the Crease* records an important moment of real significance in hockey. [20]The painting portrays a goalie wearing a flat, armour-like mask with narrow slits for eyes. [21]The mask gives a mysterious power to the goalie, suggesting something like the unknown knight in armour. [22]The power is a bit sinister.

[23]Hockey fans and art collectors value the painting for different reasons. [24]First, hockey fans value it as an artistic record of the putting on of the first protective mask by a player in professional hockey, for up to this time, no goalie ever wore a mask at any time. [25]Second, many fans may believe the player in the goalie mask is Jacques Plante, so they like to have a print of this particular hockey star. [26]Plante was the first National Hockey League player to wear such a mask. [27]Since Plante's action it is now commonplace for goalies to wear masks, and the masks have become more and more distinctive. [28]Whereas some still have the look of armour, others look more like primitive tribal masks donned in war. [29]Finally, the art enthusiast sees something else. [30]One who is really interested in the painting as a work of art might want to collect an example of magic realism. [31]Or one who is interested in Danby in particular may want an example of Danby's painting style or subjects from this particular period of his works. [32]Whatever their reasons, these collectors see the print as valuable.

Omission of Necessary Words

22

Do not omit a word or phrase necessary to the meaning of the sentence.

If you omit necessary words in your compositions, your mind may be racing ahead of your pen, or your writing may reflect omissions in your spoken English.

> The analyst talked about the tax dollar goes. [The writer thought "talked about where" but did not write *where*.]
> You better be there on time! [When speaking, the writer omits *had* before *better*.]

To avoid omitting necessary words, proofread your compositions carefully and study **22a–c**.

22a
Do not omit a necessary article, pronoun, conjunction, or preposition. See also **26b**.

(1) Omitted article or pronoun

> INCOMPLETE   The first meeting was held on other campus.
> COMPLETE   The first meeting was held on **the** other campus.

| INCOMPLETE | I know a man had a horse like that. |
| COMPLETE | I know a man **who** had a horse like that. |

It is often necessary to repeat a pronoun or an article before the second part of a compound to avoid ambiguity.

AMBIGUOUS	A friend and helper stood nearby. [One person or two?]
CLEAR	A friend and **a** helper stood nearby. [two persons clearly indicated by repetition of *a*]
ALSO CLEAR	My mother and father were there. [clearly two persons—repetition of *my* before *father* not necessary]

(2) Omitted conjunction or preposition

CONFUSING	Fran noticed the passenger who was sleeping soundly had dropped his wallet in the aisle. [The reader may be momentarily confused by "noticed the passenger."]
BETTER	Fran noticed **that** the passenger who was sleeping soundly had dropped his wallet in the aisle.
INFORMAL	I had never seen that type movie before.
FORMAL	I had never seen that type **of** movie before.

When two verbs requiring different prepositions are used together, do not omit the first preposition. See also **20b**.

| INCOMPLETE | Such comments neither contribute nor detract from his reputation. |
| COMPLETE | Such comments neither contribute **to** nor detract from his reputation. |

In sentences such as the following, if you omit the conjunction, use a semicolon in its place.

They put all of the large pieces of furniture into the van; then they filled the remaining space with boxes. [Compare "into the van and then they filled the remaining space."]

You will note, however, that it is now becoming common practice to use a comma instead of a semicolon. A comma is correct in the following sentence.

The fact is, very few people in this society make a habit of thinking in ethical terms.
—HARRY STEIN [Compare "The fact is *that* very few people. . . . "]

■ **Exercise 1**   Insert needed words below.

1. Lars reminded Sheila Richard might not approve.
2. What kind course to take is the big question.
3. Winter and spring breaks the campus is dead.
4. She lent me a dollar then decided to take it back.
5. The trouble was my good pair shoes got stolen.
6. Don will not ask or listen to any advice.
7. Fires had burned for weeks were still not out.
8. The book which he referred was not in our library.
9. It is the exception proves the rule.
10. The recipe calls for a variety spices.

22b
Avoid awkward omission of verbs and auxiliaries.

AWKWARD	Scott has never and cannot be wholly honest with himself.
BETTER	Scott has never **been** and cannot be wholly honest with himself.
INCOMPLETE	Since I been in college, some of my values have changed.
COMPLETE	Since I **have** been in college, some of my values have changed.

INCOMPLETE	This problem easy to solve.
COMPLETE	This problem **is** easy to solve.
INCOMPLETE	As far as the speed limit, many drivers think they have to drive that fast.
COMPLETE	As far as the speed limit **is concerned,** many drivers think they have to drive that fast.
LESS WORDY	**As for** the speed limit, many drivers think they have to drive that fast.

Option: In sentences such as the following, the omission or inclusion of the second verb is optional.

The sounds were angry, the manner violent.
—A.E. VAN VOGT [omission of second verb]

The sounds were angry, the manner **was** violent. [inclusion of second verb]

22c
Do not omit words needed to complete comparisons.

INCOMPLETE	Broken bottles around a swimming area are more dangerous than picnic tables.
COMPLETE	Broken bottles around a swimming area are more dangerous than **around** picnic tables.
INCOMPLETE	Snow here is as scarce as Fiji.
COMPLETE	Snow here is as scarce as **it is in** Fiji.
INCOMPLETE	After I started believing in myself, the world offered me more challenges.
COMPLETE	After I started believing in myself, the world offered me more challenges **than before.**
INCOMPLETE	Students in small schools may achieve higher test scores.
COMPLETE	Students in small schools may achieve higher test scores **than those in large schools do.**

INCOMPLETE	The amateur's performance was as good, possibly even better than, the professional's.
COMPLETE	The amateur's performance was as good **as,** possibly even better than, the professional's.
CONFUSING	Sometimes counsellors help an alcoholic less than the rest of the family.
CLEAR	Sometimes counsellors help an alcoholic less than **they do** the rest of the family.
	OR
	Sometimes counsellors help an alcoholic less than the rest of the family **does.**

In a comparison such as the following, the word *other* may indicate a difference in meaning:

O'Brien runs faster than any player on the team. [O'Brien is apparently not on the team. In context, however, this may be an informal sentence meaning that O'Brien is the fastest of the players on the team.]

O'Brien runs faster than any **other** player on the team. [*Other* clearly indicates that O'Brien is on the team.]

■ **Exercise 2** Supply needed words in verb phrases and in comparisons.

1. They been trying to make small cars safe.
2. The consumers better listen to these warnings.
3. Ed's income is less than his wife.
4. Bruce admires Cathy more than Aline.
5. Fiberglass roofs are better.
6. The scenery here is as beautiful as any place.
7. I always have and always will like to read the comics.
8. One argument was as bad, maybe even worse than, the other.
9. The ordinance never has and never will be enforced.
10. The crusty old man irritates his roommate more than the cranky young nurse.

22d

When used as intensifiers in informal writing, *so,* *such,* and *too* are generally (but not always) followed by a completing phrase or clause.

The line was **so** long that we decided to skip lunch.
Guillaume has **such** a hearty laugh that it is contagious.
Laura was **too** angry to think straight.

■ **Exercise 3**   Insert words where needed.

1. I had my senior year a strange type virus.
2. As far as Victoria, I could see the people were proud of their history.
3. The group was opposed and angered by these attempts to amend the Constitution by referendum.
4. It is good to talk with a person has a similar problem.
5. In our province the taxes are as high as Quebec.
6. They thought the water bomber scenes in the movie were so exciting.
7. Here is the hole which the rabbit escaped.
9. If Jack gets a job that he is not trained, he will fail.
10. The stadium was already filled with people and still coming.

EFFECTIVE SENTENCES

Sentence Unity

23

Write unified sentences.

Good writing is unified: it sticks to its purpose. Whether in sentences (covered in this section), paragraphs (Section **32**), or whole compositions (Section **33**), unity is achieved when all the parts contribute to fulfilling the writer's aim. A sentence may lack unity because it combines unrelated ideas or may have excessive details or may contain mixed metaphors, mixed constructions, or faulty predication. Clear, precise definitions often depend on careful attention to sentence unity.

23a
Make the relationship of ideas in a sentence imme-diately clear to the reader.

UNRELATED   The St. Elias Range has majestic glaciers, but most Canadians must travel great distances. [unity thwarted by a gap in the thought]

RELATED   The St. Elias Range has majestic glaciers, but to see them most Canadians must travel great distances.

■ **Exercise 1** All the sentences below contain ideas that are apparently unrelated. Adding words when necessary, rewrite each of the sentences to clearly indicate a relationship between ideas. If you cannot establish a close relationship, put the ideas in separate sentences.

1. There are many irritating commercials on AM radio, but I prefer to listen to the CBC.
2. A politician devoted to the needs of his or her constituents can prove a good representative, and poor representation can be found at all levels of government.
3. Marissa was directed to see a faculty adviser immediately, but her many commitments to extracurricular activities kept her grades low.
4. Canada is not the only country to experience constitutional problems, and Professor Boisvin, for example, likes to draw parallels between modern leaders and constitutional crises.
5. Birds migrate to the warmer countries in the fall and in the summer get food by eating worms and insects that are pests to the farmer.

23b

Do not allow excessive detail to obscure the central thought of a sentence.

EXCESSIVE DETAIL In 1789, when Sir Alexander Mackenzie set out to chart the major river that ran out of Great Slave Lake and when he discovered it flowed to the Arctic instead, he was a partner in the fur firm of Gregory, McLeod and Company and second in command to Peter Pond, a famous explorer in his own right who believed the river flowed to the Pacific Ocean.

ADEQUATE DETAIL In 1789, when Sir Alexander Mackenzie charted the course of the river running out of Great Slave Lake, he found that it led to the Arctic Ocean, not the Pacific as the explorer Peter Pond had theorized.

As you strive to eliminate excessive detail, remember that length alone does not make a sentence ineffective. Your purpose sometimes requires a long, detailed sentence. Even a sentence of paragraph length can be unified by parallel structure, balance, rhythm, effectively repeated connectives, and careful punctuation. Consider this sentence about a Newfoundland outport kitchen and its furnishings.

> [The kitchen] always contains at least one "day bed" (a combination of sofa and single bed) which provides a place for the man to stretch out for a few minutes before his meal; a place for the woman to sit with the children beside her as she knits, sews, or spins; a place for a gaggle of neighbours' children to perch in owl-eyed silence; a place for a grandfather or an aging aunt to rest and reminisce; a place where young lovers come together when the rest of the house lies sleeping.   —FARLEY MOWAT, *This Rock within the Sea*

■ **Exercise 2** Revise the following paragraph to eliminate excessive detail.

¹Our visit to Toronto, which we had been planning since the beginning of summer and which we had been looking forward to for some time, was an eventful one. ²This city located on the shores of Lake Ontario, which we had never visited before, was very different from our own city of Vancouver, located on the shores of Burrard Inlet. ³We saw many sights during our stay, which lasted some two weeks and three days. ⁴We spent time at Harbourfront, at Kensington Market, at the Beaches, and at the University of Toronto, located near the Ontario Legislature, which we did not have time to visit. ⁵We capped our visit with a tour of the CN Tower, which is a very tall building, and an afternoon at Skydome, where the Toronto Blue Jays lost to the Milwaukee Brewers, who were in the city to play a three-game series over the Victoria Day Weekend, which celebrates the birthday of the Queen.

23c

Avoid mixed metaphors and mixed constructions.

(1) Do not mix metaphors. See also **20a(4)**.

MIXED	Playing with fire can get you into deep water.
BETTER	Playing with fire can result in burned fingers.
MIXED	Her climb up the ladder of success was nipped in the bud.
BETTER	Her climb up the ladder of success was soon halted.
	OR
	Her promising career was nipped in the bud.

(2) Do not mix constructions.

MIXED	When Howard plays the martyr taxes his wife's patience. [adverb clause + predicate]
REVISED	When Howard plays the martyr, he taxes his wife's patience. [adverb clause, main clause]
	OR
	Howard's playing the martyr taxes his wife's patience. [subject + predicate]
MIXED	It was an old, ramshackle house but which was quite livable.
REVISED	It was an old, ramshackle house, but it was quite livable.
	OR
	It was an old, ramshackle house that was quite livable. [noun + adjective clause]

Note: Sometimes a sentence is flawed by the use of a singular noun instead of a plural one: "Hundreds who attended the convention drove their own **cars** [NOT car]."

23d

Avoid faulty predication.

Faulty predication occurs when the subject and predicate do not fit each other logically.

FAULTY	One book I read believes in eliminating subsidies. [A person, not a thing, believes.]
REVISED	The author of one book I read believes in eliminating subsidies.
	OR
	One book I read says that subsidies should be eliminated.
FAULTY	An example of discrimination is an apartment owner, especially after he has refused to rent to people with children. [The refusal, not the owner, is an example of discrimination.]
REVISED	An example of discrimination is an apartment owner's refusal to rent to people with children.

■ **Exercise 3** Revise each sentence to eliminate faulty predication, a mixed construction, or a mixed metaphor.

1. Another famous story from Canadian history is Laura Secord.
2. One example of a rip-off would be a butcher, because he could weigh his heavy thumb with the steak.
3. When people avoid saying or doing something tactless shows they have good manners.
4. Like a bat guided by radar, Judy was always surefooted in her business dealings.
5. Could anyone be certain why George resigned or where did he find a better job?
6. For Kenji money does grow on trees, and it also goes down the drain quickly.
7. Because his feet are not the same size explains the difficulty he has finding shoes that fit.
8. I felt like a grain of sand crying out in the wilderness.
9. When children need glasses causes them to make mistakes in reading and writing.
10. The forecast of subnormal temperatures in late March was predicted by Environment Canada.

23e
Avoid awkward definitions. Define a word or an expression clearly and precisely. See also **32d(7)**.

(1) Avoid faulty is-when or is-where definitions.

FAULTY Banishing a man is where he is driven out of his country. [Banishing is an act, not a place.]

REVISED Banishing a man is driving him out of his country.

FAULTY Unlike a fact, a value judgement is when you express personal opinions or preferences.

REVISED Unlike a fact, a value judgement is a personal opinion or preference.

(2) Write clear, precise definitions.

A short dictionary definition may be adequate when you need to define a term or a special meaning of a word that may be unfamiliar to your reader.

Here *galvanic* means "produced as if by electric shock." [See also the note on page 192.]

Giving a synonym or two may clarify the meaning of a term. Often such synonyms are used as appositives.

An enigma is a puzzle, a mystery.

Lotus Land, otherwise known as British Columbia, is the fastest-growing province in Canada.

If you press your forefinger gently against your closed eyelid for a minute or less, you will probably start to see phosphenes: shapes and colors that march and swirl across your darkened field of view.

—JEARL WALKER [word substitutions with restrictive details]

Writers frequently show—rather than tell—what a word means by giving examples.

Many homophones (*be* and *bee, in* and *inn, see* and *sea*) are not spelling problems.

A "formal definition" first states the term to be defined and puts it into a class; then differentiates the term from other members of its class.

A phosphene [term] is a luminous visual image [class] that results from applying pressure to the eyeball [differentiation].

You may formulate your own definitions of the concept you wish to clarify.

Questions are windows to the mind.   —GERARD I. NIERENBERG
[use of a metaphor—see also **20a(4)**]
Clichés are sometimes thought of as wisdom gone stale.
—JOSEPH EPSTEIN

■ **Exercise 4**   Define any two of the following terms.

1. éclair
2. uncanny
3. hatred
4. racist
5. quixotic

6. Dutch oven
7. corrupt
8. Francophone
9. pragmatism
10. integrity

Subordination and Co-ordination

24

Use subordination to relate ideas concisely and effectively. Use co-ordination to give ideas equal emphasis.

One of the marks of mature writing is the ability to relate ideas effectively using subordination and co-ordination.

Subordinate means "being of lower structural rank." In the following sentence, the italicized subordinate elements are grammatically dependent on the sentence base (subject + compound predicate) in boldface.

> *Although Canada entered the war a unified and confident nation,* **the demands and emotions of war exacerbated the ethnic, class, and regional tensions** *that had been simmering during the pre-war years.* —RAMSAY COOK

As this example shows, grammatically subordinate structures may contain very important ideas.

Co-ordinate means "being of equal structural rank." Co-ordination gives equal grammatical emphasis to two or more ideas. In the following sentence, each main clause (subject + predicate) is a co-ordinate element.

> **These are mysteries performed before our very eyes; we
> can see every detail, and yet they are still mysteries.**
>
> —ANNIE DILLARD

Co-ordination gives equal emphasis not only to two or
more clauses but also to two or more words, phrases, or
sentences. See also Section **26**.

> *tactless, abrasive* language   [co-ordinate adjectives]
> *on the roof* or *in the attic*   [compound prepositional phrases]
> *I have not gone on a diet.* Nor *do I intend to.*   [sentences
>   linked by co-ordinating conjunction]

A study of this section should help you to use subordination effectively when you revise a series of short,
choppy simple sentences or stringy compound ones. It
should also help you use co-ordination to secure the grammatical emphasis you want and to eliminate faulty subordination. If you cannot distinguish between phrases and
clauses and between subordinate and main clauses, see **1d**
and **1e**.

24a
**Use subordination to combine a series of related
short sentences into longer, more effective units.**

CHOPPY
: The hill was not very high. It was steep. Both Vera
and Daniel found themselves leaning into it. Their
eyes were on their feet and the fine, floury dust.
This dust rose about their ankles with the impact of
each plodding footfall.

BETTER
: Although the hill was not very high, it was steep,
and both Vera and Daniel found themselves leaning into it, their eyes on their feet and the fine,
floury dust which rose about their ankles with the
impact of each plodding footfall.

—GUY VANDERHAEGHE

When combining a series of related sentences, first choose a sentence base (subject + predicate); then use subordinate elements to relate the other ideas to the base. (Co-ordination is also used to combine short sentences, but inexperienced writers tend to use too much of it: see **24b**.)

(1) **Use adjectives and adjective phrases**.

CHOPPY   The limbs were covered with ice. They sparkled in the sunlight. They made a breathtaking sight.

BETTER   *Sparkling in the sunlight,* the *ice-covered* limbs made a breathtaking sight. [participial phrase and hyphenated adjectival]

(2) **Use adverbs or adverb phrases**.

CHOPPY   Season the chicken livers with garlic. Use a lot of it. Fry them in butter. Use a very low heat.

BETTER   Season the chicken livers *heavily* with garlic, and *slowly* fry them in butter. [Note the use of both subordination and co-ordination.]
OR
After seasoning the chicken livers heavily with garlic, slowly fry them in butter.

CHOPPY   The lecture halls were filled with young children. So were the laboratories and the cafeterias. The university looked a bit like a kindergarten on that spring day.

BETTER   *Its lecture halls, laboratories, and cafeterias filled with young children,* the university looked a bit like a kindergarten on that spring day. [first two sentences combined in an absolute phrase]

(3) **Use appositives and contrasting elements**.

CHOPPY   These kindnesses were acts of love. They were noticed. But they were not appreciated.

BETTER   These kindnesses—*acts of love*—were noticed *but not appreciated.*

(4) Use subordinate clauses.

Subordinate clauses are linked and related to main clauses by such markers as *who, that, when,* and *if.* See the lists of these markers (subordinating conjunctions and relative pronouns) on page 20.

CHOPPY   The blizzard ended. Then helicopters headed for the mountaintop. It looked dark and forbidding.

BETTER   *As soon as the blizzard ended,* helicopters headed for the mountaintop, *which looked dark and forbidding.* [adverb clause and adjective clause]

Caution: Do not use *but* or *and* before *which, who,* or *whom* when introducing a single adjective clause, as in "Irene is a music major who can play several instruments [NOT and who]." See also **23c(2).**

■ **Exercise 1**   Combine the following short sentences into longer sentences by using effective subordination and co-ordination. (If you wish, keep a short sentence or two for emphasis: see **29h.**)

¹I have just read "The Idea of a University" by John Henry Newman. ²I am especially interested in his views regarding knowledge. ³He says that knowledge is its own reward. ⁴It is not just a means to an end. ⁵Newman says knowledge is a treasure in itself. ⁶I had looked upon knowledge only in terms of practical results. ⁷One result would be financial security. ⁸But that was before I read this essay. ⁹Now I accept Newman's definition of knowledge. ¹⁰Such knowledge is worth pursuing for its own sake.

24b
Do not string main clauses together when some ideas should be subordinated. Use co-ordination to give ideas equal emphasis.

Do not overwork co-ordinating connectives like *and, then, and then, so, and so, but, however, therefore.* For ways to revise stringy or loose compound sentences, see **30c**. Methods of subordination that apply to combining two or more sentences also apply to revising faulty or excessive co-ordination in a single sentence: see **24a**.

(1) Do not blur your emphasis with stringy compound sentences; subordinate some ideas to others.

AWKWARD	I wanted to go to college, so I built and painted houses all summer, and that way I could earn my tuition.
BETTER	*Because I wanted to go to college,* I built and painted houses all summer *to earn my tuition.*
AWKWARD	Peters lost, and it was a decisive vote, but she was determined to succeed in politics.
BETTER	Peters, *who was determined to succeed in politics,* lost by a decisive vote.
	OR
	Determined to succeed in politics, Peters lost by a decisive vote.

(2) Use co-ordination to give ideas equal emphasis.

The offer was tempting, but I didn't accept it. [equal grammatical stress on the offer and the refusal]

COMPARE	Although the offer was tempting, I didn't accept it. [stress on the refusal]
	Although I didn't accept it, the offer was tempting. [stress on the offer]

■ **Exercise 2**   Revise each sentence by using effective subordination and co-ordination.

1. First she selected a topic and narrowed it to a focus, and then she listed and arranged her main arguments and wrote the first draft.

2. Yesterday, I was working on a lab report, so I did not read the paper, but I heard from a friend that the Prime Minister had called an election.
3. Two ambulances tore by, and an oncoming bus crowded a truckload of labourers off the road, but nobody got hurt.
4. Jean Henri Dunant was a citizen of Switzerland, and he felt sorry for Austrian soldiers wounded in the Napoleonic Wars; therefore, he started an organization, and it was later named the Red Cross.
5. The administrators stressed career education, and not only did they require back-to-basics courses, but they also kept students informed about job opportunities.

24c
Avoid faulty or excessive subordination.

FAULTY   I have never before known a person like Annie, who is ready to help anybody who is in trouble that involves finances.

BETTER   I have never before known a person like Annie, who is ready to help anybody in financial trouble. [one subordinate clause reduced to a phrase, another reduced to an adjective]

■ **Exercise 3**   Observing differences in emphasis, convert each pair of sentences to (a) a simple sentence, (b) a compound sentence consisting of two main clauses, and (c) a complex sentence with one main clause and one subordinate clause.

EXAMPLE
Canada's farmers sometimes face disastrous crop failures. These farmers must struggle to save their farms even in the best of times.

a. *Struggling to save their farms even in the best of times, Canada's farmers sometimes face disastrous crop failures.*

b. *Canada's farmers sometimes face disastrous crop fail-
    ures; these farmers must struggle to save their farms
    even in the best of times.*
c. *Although Canada's farmers must struggle to save their
    farms even in the best of times, they sometimes face dis-
    astrous crop failures.*

1. The couple smuggled drugs into Turkey. They were sen-
    tenced to life in prison.
2. The city council first condemned the property. Then it
    ordered the owner's eviction.
3. Elinor applied for a patent on her invention. She learned
    of three hundred such devices already on the market.
4. The border guards delayed every tourist. They carefully
    examined passports and luggage.

■ **Exercise 4**   Prepare for a discussion of the subordination and
the co-ordination of ideas in the paragraph below.

¹Going by canoe is often the best—and sometimes the
only—way to go. ²Some difficult country can't be reached any
other way, and once you arrive, the aches of paddling and sitting unsupported on a canoe seat seem a small price to pay
for being there. ³One such place is the Boundary Waters area
along the border of northeastern Minnesota and Ontario. ⁴The
terrain is rolling and pocked by thousands of glacier lakes.
⁵Some are no more than bowls of rock that hold the accumu-
lated clear green water; others are spring-fed and dark. ⁶The
maze of lakes, islands, and portage trails is inhabited by all
sorts of wildlife: beaver, otter, loons, and bear. ⁷It is a landscape suited to the canoe and has in fact been canoe country
since the time of the fur-trading voyageurs—hard Frenchmen
whose freighters were up to twenty-five feet long and
required eight paddlers.   —GEOFFREY NORMAN, "Rapid Transit"

Misplaced Parts, Dangling Modifiers

25

Avoid needless separation of related parts of the sentence. Avoid dangling modifiers.

25a
Avoid needless separation of related parts of the sentence.

As a rule, place modifiers near the words they modify. Note how the meaning of the following sentences changes according to the position of modifiers:

> Hal **just** left with the clothes on his back.
> Hal left with **just** the clothes on his back.
> **Just** Hal left with the clothes on his back.

> The woman **who drowned** had tried to help the child.
> The woman had tried to help the child **who drowned.**

(1) **In formal English, modifiers such as *almost, only, just, even, hardly, nearly,* and *merely* are regularly placed immediately before the words they modify.**

> The truck costs **only** $850. [NOT only costs]
> She works **even** during her vacation. [NOT even works]

■ **Exercise 1** Circle each misplaced modifier; draw an arrow to show its proper position.

1. The earthquake only killed one person.
2. The blouse nearly cost fifty dollars.
3. On Thanksgiving Day the guests almost ate all the turkey.
4. Compulsive talkers hardly show any interest in what other people may have to say.

(2) **The position of a modifying prepositional phrase should clearly indicate what the phrase modifies.**

MISPLACED   A garish poster attracts the visitor's eye **on the east wall.**

BETTER   A garish poster **on the east wall** attracts the visitor's eye.

MISPLACED   One student said that such heated discussion was not rational debate but civil war **in class.**

BETTER   **In class** one student **said** that such heated discussion was not rational debate but civil war.

OR

One student **said in class** that such heated discussion was not rational debate but civil war.

■ **Exercise 2** Circle each misplaced prepositional phrase below; draw an arrow to show its proper position.

1. Newspapers carried the story of the companies' merging in every part of the country.
2. Lucille bakes date muffins just for her friends with pecans in them.
3. At the picnic Sharon and Michael served sundaes to hungry guests in paper cups.
4. The professor made it clear why plagiarism is wrong on Monday.

(3) **Adjective clauses should be placed near the words they modify.**

MISPLACED   We bought gasoline in Manitoba at a small country store **which cost $20.25.**

BETTER   At a small country store in Manitoba, we bought gasoline **which cost $20.25.**

(4) **Avoid "squinting" constructions—modifiers that may refer to either a preceding or a following word.**

SQUINTING   Jogging **often** relaxes her.
BETTER   **Often,** jogging relaxes her.
            OR
            It relaxes her to jog **often.**

(5) **Avoid the awkward separation of the sentence base and the awkward splitting of an infinitive.**

AWKWARD   The citizens' **coalition protested** at the provincial legislature and at public rallies the government's **decision** to introduce user fees for health care. [awkward separation of a verb from its object]

BETTER   At the provincial legislature and at public rallies, the citizens' **coalition protested** the government's **decision** to introduce user fees for health care.

AWKWARD   Longpré is the person **to,** if we can, **nominate** for councillor. [awkward splitting of an infinitive]

BETTER   Longpré is the person **to nominate** for councillor if we can.

Splitting an infinitive is often not only natural but desirable.

For her to **never** complain seems unreal.
I wished to **properly** understand programming.

■ **Exercise 3**   Revise the sentences to eliminate squinting modifiers or needless separation of related sentence parts.

1. The flight attendant asked the passenger not to carry a suitcase onto the flight that wouldn't fit into the overhead bin.
2. Selby said in the evening he would go.
3. Kuniko wanted to, because she was winning, finish the game.
4. Darren promised when he was on his way home to stop at the library.

5. The car advertised in last night's paper which is only two
   years old is in excellent condition.

25b
Avoid dangling modifiers.

Although any misplaced word, phrase, or clause can be
said to dangle, the term *dangling* is applied primarily to
verbal phrases that do not refer clearly and logically to
another word or phrase in the sentence.

To correct a dangling modifier, rearrange the words in
the sentence to make the modifier clearly refer to the right
word, or add words to make the meaning clear and logical.

(1) Avoid dangling participial phrases.

DANGLING   **Encouraged by high grades,** taking another
           course seemed to make sense.

REVISED   **Because I was encouraged by high grades,** tak-
           ing another course seemed to make sense.
           OR
           Encouraged by high grades, I thought taking
           another course made sense.

Placed after the sentence base, the participial phrase in the
revision below refers to the subject.

DANGLING   The evening passed very pleasantly, **playing
           backgammon and swapping jokes.**

REVISED   **They** passed the evening very pleasantly, **play-
           ing backgammon and swapping jokes.**

**(2) Avoid dangling phrases containing gerunds or
infinitives.**

DANGLING   **Instead of watching the late show,** a novel was
           read.

REVISED   **Instead of watching the late show,** Hilary read
           a novel.

DANGLING **Not able to swim that far,** a lifeguard came to my rescue.

REVISED **I was not able to swim that far,** so a lifeguard came to my rescue.

OR

Because I was not able to swim that far, a lifeguard came to my rescue.

(3) Avoid dangling elliptical adverb clauses.

Elliptical clauses have words that are implied rather than stated.

DANGLING **When confronted with these facts,** not one word was said.

REVISED **When confronted with these facts, nobody** said a word.

OR

When they were confronted with these facts, not one word was said.

DANGLING **Although only a member of the chorus,** the director expected me to rehearse until I dropped.

REVISED **Although I was only a member of the chorus,** the director expected me to rehearse until I dropped.

Note: Sentence modifiers (see page 678) are considered standard usage, not danglers.

To judge from reports, all must be going well.
His health is fairly good, **considering his age.**

■ **Exercise 4**   Revise the following sentences to eliminate dangling modifiers. Put a check mark after any sentence that needs no revision.

1   While whispering in the darkened theatre, the popcorn fell to the floor.
2. By summarizing the main points, the lecture came to an end.

3. Once updated, you should print out the document.
4. Prepare to make an incision in the abdomen as soon as completely anesthetized.
5. After sitting there awhile, it began to snow, and we went indoors.
6. Darkness having fallen, we stopped for the night.
7. Having taken his seat, we began to question the witness.
8. Ready to pitch camp, the windstorm hit.
9. The prisoners did not yield, thinking they could attract the support of the press.
10. Reduced to helpless laughter, the curtain fell and the audience sat silent.

■ **Exercise 5**   Combine the two sentences in each item below into a single sentence. Use an appropriately placed verbal phrase or elliptical clause as an introductory parenthetical element.

EXAMPLES

We were in a hurry to leave Banff. The dented fender was not noticed.

Being in a hurry to leave Banff, we did not notice the dented fender.

Students may sometimes be confused. At such times they ought to ask questions.

When confused, students ought to ask questions.

1. The statue has a broken arm and nose. I think it is an interesting antique.
2. James sometimes worried about the famine in Africa. At such times working for OXFAM seemed to him a good idea.
3. I read the first three questions on the test. The test covered material that I had not studied.
4. Ravi was only twelve years old. His teachers noticed his inventive abilities.
5. I turned on the flashers and lifted the hood. A passing motorist, I thought, might see my predicament, slow down, and offer me a ride.

Parallelism

26

Use parallel structure to express matching ideas.

Parallel (grammatically equal) sentence elements regularly appear in lists or series, in compound structures, in comparisons using *than* or *as,* and in contrasted elements. As the examples below illustrate, parallelism contributes to clarity, rhythm, memorability, and ease in reading.

> Music expresses, at different moments, **serenity or exuberance, regret or triumph, fury or delight.** —AARON COPLAND
> **Listening** is as much a persuasive technique as **speaking.** —GERARD I. NIERENBERG [a comparison with *as . . . as*]

Many parallel elements are linked by a co-ordinating conjunction (such as *and, or, but*) or by correlatives (such as *neither . . . nor, whether . . . or*). Others are not. In the following examples, verbals used as subjects and complements are parallel in form.

> **To define** flora is **to define** climate. —NATIONAL GEOGRAPHIC
> **Seeing** is **deceiving.** It's **eating** that's **believing.**
> —JAMES THURBER

Parallel structures are also used in topic outlines: see **33f**, pages 434–35.

Faulty parallelism disrupts the balance of co-ordinate elements:

FAULTY We are not so much **what we eat** but **the thoughts we think.** [The co-ordinate elements differ in grammatical form.]

REVISED We are not so much **what we eat** but **what we think.**

OR

We are not so much **the food we eat** but **the thoughts we think.**

If you cannot readily distinguish between parts of speech and between types of phrases and clauses, study Section **1**.

26a

For parallel structure, balance nouns with nouns, prepositional phrases with prepositional phrases, main clauses with main clauses, and so on.

As you study the parallel words, phrases, clauses, and sentences that follow, notice that repetition can be used to emphasize the balanced structure.

(1) Parallel words and phrases

We like the human condition as long as it is
seen as ‖ **personal**
and ‖ **individual.** —MARGARET ATWOOD

Freedom is ‖ **the right to be wrong,**
not ‖ **the right to do wrong.** —JOHN G. DIEFENBAKER

She had ‖ **no time to be human,**
‖ **no time to be happy** —SEAN O'FAOLAIN

(2) Parallel clauses

Almost all of us want things ‖ **that we do not need**
and fail to want things ‖ **that we do need.**

—MORTIMER J. ADLER

‖ **Let us be English** or
‖ **let us be French,** but above all
‖ **let us be Canadians.**   —SIR JOHN A. MACDONALD

(3) Parallel sentences

‖ **There's no story so fantastic that I cannot imagine
myself the hero.** And
‖ **there's no story so evil that I cannot imagine myself
the villain.**   —LEONARD COHEN

‖ **The emphasis was helped by the speaker's mouth,
which was wide, thin, and hard set.**
‖ **The emphasis was helped by the speaker's voice,
which was inflexible, dry, and dictatorial.**

—CHARLES DICKENS

■ **Exercise 1**   Underline the parallel structures. Then write sentences containing parallel (1) words, (2) phrases, (3) clauses, and (4) sentences.

1. From time to time it seems we are running out of fuel, out of water, out of housing, out of wilderness, out of ozone, out of all the stuff we need to make more rubbish.
—BRIAN HAYES

2. Through a squeaky, hinged gate you could pass from vicarage garden to churchyard, from overgrown, shady green to sunny, close-clipped graves.   —EMILY CARR

3. We are all sick, all lonely, all in need of love. —JEAN VANIER

4. Style in writing, as in painting, is the author's thumbprint, his mark.   —MAVIS GALLANT

5. Reading through *The Origin* is like eating Cracker Jacks and finding an I O U note at the bottom of the box.
—JOHN FLUDAS

6. The smallest, St. Lawrence Islands National Park, is no bigger than a large shopping mall, while the largest,

Wood Buffalo National Park, occupies a slice of boreal forest the size of Denmark. —ANDREW NIKIFORUK

7. There might be some people in the world who do not need flowers, who cannot be surprised by joy, but I haven't met them. —GLORIA EMERSON

8. Top soil, once blown away, can never be returned; virgin prairie, once plowed, can never be reclaimed.

—MARILYN COFFEY

9. Think before you speak. Read before you think.

—FRAN LEBOWITZ

26b

To make the parallel clear, repeat a preposition, an article, the *to* of the infinitive, or the introductory word of a phrase or clause.

The reward rests not ‖ **in** the task
but ‖ **in** the pay. —JOHN K. GALBRAITH

Life is ‖ **a** mystery
and ‖ **an** adventure
which he shares with all living things. —JOSEPH WOOD KRUTCH

It is easier ‖ **to love humanity as a whole**
than ‖ **to love one's neighbor.** —ERIC HOFFER

It is all the things we think we know—
‖ **because** they are so elementary
or ‖ **because** they surround us—
that often present the greatest difficulties when we are actually challenged to explain them. —STEPHEN JAY GOULD

■ **Exercise 2** Insert words needed to bring out the parallel structure in the following paragraph.

¹My grandfather was a true music lover. ²He could listen to music for an hour or entire day without ever getting bored or restless. ³Seated quietly beside his old gramophone, he would seem to drift off and find peace amid the sounds of Bach, Beethoven, and Mozart. ⁴When I was a little girl, he used to tell me that music took him away from the noise of

this world and he could almost imagine the great musicians of the past living and breathing again in their notes. ⁵He taught me that a person can learn to enjoy music and life more by listening than speaking. ⁶Looking back, I realize that he was my first music teacher; he taught me to love the classical before I learned to love modern.

26c

Use parallel structures with correlatives (*both . . . and; either . . . or; neither . . . nor; not only . . . but also; whether . . . or*).

FAULTY	Either they obey the manager or get fired.
PARALLEL	Either ‖ **they obey the manager** or ‖ **they get fired.**
PARALLEL	They either ‖ **obey the manager** or ‖ **get fired.**
FAULTY	Whether employed or when he was unemployed, he resolved to pay his bills on time.
PARALLEL	Whether ‖ **employed** or ‖ **unemployed,** he resolved to pay his bills on time.
FAULTY	Laura not only jogs at 6:00 A.M. during the week, but she also works out on Sunday afternoons.
PARALLEL	Laura not only ‖ **jogs at 6:00 A.M. during the week** but also ‖ **works out on Sunday afternoons.** OR Not only does Laura jog at 6:00 A.M. during the week, but she also works out on Sunday afternoons. [The *also* may be omitted.]

■ **Exercise 3** Revise each sentence by using parallel structure to express parallel ideas.

1. Shirley not only likes to play tennis but watching basketball.

2. Our personalities are shaped by both heredity and what type of environment we have.
3. My friend asked me whether the trip would be delayed or to be ready to start on Friday as planned.
4. He was quiet and in a serious mood after the lecture.
5. Clauses fall quite clearly into two classes: the independent and those which depend on other clauses.

■ **Exercise 4**   Study the parallelism in the following sentences. Then, using any three of the sentences as models, write sentences of your own, each of which imitates the structure of the original.

EXAMPLE
The hotel was *silent and empty and black.* —P.K. PAGE
The children seemed *curious and bright and exuberant.*
—imitation

1. In countries like India and Nigeria, English is used at all levels of society: in local English-language newspapers and broadcasting, in public administration, in university administration, in university education, in the major industries, the court and the civil service.
           —ROBERT MCCRUM, WILLIAM CRAN, AND ROBERT MACNEIL
2. What is true of coral and of all other forms of marine life is also true of whales.   —JACQUES-YVES COUSTEAU
3. We have seen that the capacity to be alone is a valuable resource. It enables men and women to get in touch with their deepest feelings; to come to terms with loss; to sort out their ideas; to change attitudes.   —ANTHONY STORR
4. Calm, relaxed people get ulcers as often as hard-pressed, competitive people do, and lower-status workers get ulcers as often as higher-status ones.   —CAROL TAVRIS
5. People build bridges and cities and roads; they write music and novels and constitutions; they have ideas.
                                                        —ANNIE DILLARD
6. But it is the human mind that can summon up the power to resist, that can imagine a better world than the one before it, that can retain memory and courage in the face of unspeakable suffering.   —MARGARET ATWOOD

Shifts

27

Avoid needless shifts in grammatical structures, in tone or style, and in viewpoint.

Abrupt, unnecessary shifts—for example, from past to present, from singular to plural, from formal diction to slang, from one perspective to another—obscure meaning and make for difficult reading.

27a
Avoid needless or incorrect shifts in tense, mood, and voice. See also **Section 7.**

SHIFT   During the meeting Claire **argued** against the status quo while her classmates **discuss** the dangers of radical reform. [shift from past to present tense]

BETTER   During the meeting Claire **argued** against the status quo while her classmates **discussed** the dangers of radical reform. [both verbs in the past tense]

SHIFT   If I **were** older and if I **was** more experienced, I would have less trouble finding a job. [shift from subjunctive to indicative mood]

BETTER   If I **were** older and if I **were** more experienced, I would have less trouble finding a job. [verbs in the subjunctive mood]

SHIFT	The homeless man finally **had to enter** a shelter, but it **was** not **liked** by him. [The voice shifts from active to passive.]
BETTER	The homeless man finally **had to enter** a shelter, but he **did** not **like** it. [Both verbs are active.]

When using the literary present, as in summarizing plots of novels and plays, avoid slipping from the present into the past tense.

> Romeo and Juliet fall in love at first sight, marry secretly, and die [NOT *died*] together in the tomb within the same hour.

27b

Avoid needless shifts in person and in number. See also **6b**.

SHIFT	**One** reads for pleasure during **our** spare time. [shift from third person to first person]
BETTER	**We** read for pleasure during **our** spare time. [first person]
	OR
	You read for pleasure during **your** spare time. [second person]
	OR
	People read for pleasure during **their** spare time. [third person]
SHIFT	The drama class **is** planning to ask six faculty members to **their** spring production. [shift in number]
BETTER	The drama class **is** planning to ask six faculty members to **its** spring production.

■ **Exercise 1** Correct all needless shifts in tense, mood, voice, person, and number.

1. After their easy victory, Kurt and Marla strutted over to me and challenges me to a rematch.

2. McDougall recommended that capital gains taxes be raised and spend revitalizing the economy.

3. Kevin added green peppers to the frozen pizza, and then it was baked fifteen minutes by him.

4. Every bystander was suspect, so they were taken away for questioning.

5. I was told that hundreds of fans would want tickets for the concert and that you should plan to camp out overnight to be at the head of the line.

27c

Avoid needless shifts from indirect to direct discourse. See also **26a**.

SHIFT	The Gordons wonder **how the thieves got the CD player out** and **why didn't they steal the CDs?** [shift from indirect to direct discourse]
BETTER	The Gordons wonder **how the thieves got the CD player out** and **why they didn't steal the CDs.** [two indirect questions]
	OR
	The Gordons asked, **"How did the thieves get the CD player out? Why didn't they steal the CDs?"**
SHIFT	The secretary said **that he was sick** and **would I please read the minutes.** [shift from indirect to direct discourse]
BETTER	The secretary said **that he was sick** and **asked me to read the minutes.** [indirect discourse]

27d
Avoid needless shifts in tone or style.

INAPPROPRIATE	Critics who contend that the inefficiency of our courts will lead to the total elimination of the jury system are **nuts.** [Replace *nuts* (slang) with a word like *wrong* or *uninformed.*]

INAPPROPRIATE The darkness of the auditorium, the monotony of the ballet, and the strains of music drifting sleepily from the orchestra aroused in me a desire to **zone out.** [Replace *zone out* (slang) with a word like *doze* or *sleep*.]

27e
Avoid needless shifts in perspective or viewpoint.

FAULTY PERSPECTIVE The underwater scene was dark and mysterious; the willows lining the shore dipped gracefully into the water. [The perspective abruptly shifts from beneath the surface of the water to above it.]

BETTER The underwater scene was dark and mysterious; **above,** the willows lining the shore dipped gracefully into the water.

■ **Exercise 2** Correct all needless shifts. Put a check mark after any sentence that needs no revision.

1. A woman stepped forward, approaches the microphone, clears her throat, and asked her question.
2. A vacation is enjoyed by everyone because it refreshes the mind and body.
3. Hilda spent her summers in Ontario but flew to Florida for the winters.
4. Jim wondered whether Jack had left and did he say when he would return?
5. Every cook has their own recipes for making chili.
6. She told them that there is somebody in the room.
7. If Tarek really likes someone, he would make any sacrifice for them.
8. Take your raincoat. They will be needed.
9. The outside of the building looks like a fortress; the comfortable furnishings seem out of place.
10. The instructor asked me why I missed class and will I take the make-up quiz on Tuesday?

■ **Exercise 3** Revise the following paragraph to eliminate all needless shifts.

¹She was a serious scholar, or so it had always seemed to me. ²She engages in extensive research, which takes her to several national libraries, and spent long hours interviewing experts in her field of interest. ³When questioned about her methods, she up and says, "I'm methodical enough to have some success in my work." ⁴Not one mistake was made by her; moreover, her reluctance to discuss the obstacles in her path is evident. ⁵Take these observations for what they are worth; they may help one in understanding this woman's modesty and competence.

Reference of Pronouns

28

Make a pronoun refer unmistakably to its antecedent. See also **6b.**

Each boldfaced pronoun below clearly refers to its italicized antecedent, a single word or a word group:

> *Languages* are not invented; **they** grow with our need for expression. —SUSANNE K. LANGER
> There is no *country* in the world **whose** population is stationary. —KENNETH BOULDING
> Thus, *being busy* is more than merely a national passion; **it** is a national excuse. —NORMAN COUSINS

Without any loss of clarity, a pronoun can often refer to a noun that follows:

> With **its** gaping grin and sinister teeth, the *ichthyosaur* has long sent shudders down human spines. —VIRGINIA MORELL

As you edit your compositions, check to see that the meaning of each pronoun is immediately obvious. If there is any chance of confusion, repeat the antecedent, use a synonym for it, or recast your sentence.

28a
Avoid an ambiguous reference.

When a pronoun could refer to either of two possible
antecedents, the ambiguity confuses, or at least inconve-
niences, your reader. (A pronoun, of course, may clearly
refer to two or more antecedents: *My sister* and *brother-in-
law* will soon celebrate *their* wedding anniversary.)

> AMBIGUOUS   Lisa wrote to Jennifer every week when she
> was in Germany.
>
> CLEAR   When Lisa was in Germany, she wrote to
> Jennifer every week.
> OR
> When Jennifer was in Germany, Lisa wrote to
> her every week.
>
> AMBIGUOUS   After listening to Ray's proposal and to
> Avram's objections, I liked his ideas better.
>
> CLEAR   I agreed with Avram after listening to his
> objections to Ray's proposal.

28b
Avoid a remote or an awkward reference.

Placing a pronoun too far away from its antecedent may
force your reader to backtrack to get your meaning.
Making a pronoun refer to a modifying phrase or clause
can obscure your meaning.

> REMOTE   A first-year student found herself the unanimously
> elected president of a group of animal lovers, **who**
> was not a joiner of organizations. [*Who* is too far
> removed from the antecedent *student*. See also
> **25a(3)**.]
>
> BETTER   A first year student **who** was not a joiner of orga-
> nizations found herself the unanimously elected
> president of a group of animal lovers.

OBSCURE   Before Ellen could get to the jewellery store, **it** was all sold. [The reference to *jewellery,* which modifies the noun *store,* is unclear.]

BETTER   Before Ellen could get to the jewellery store, all the **jewellery** was sold.

Note: As a rule, writers avoid using a pronoun like *it, this,* or *he* to refer to the title of a composition or to a word in the title.

Title: Justice with Mercy

AWKWARD FIRST SENTENCE   How can this ever be?

BETTER   How can justice be merciful?

■ **Exercise 1**   Revise each sentence below to eliminate ambiguous, remote, or obscure pronoun reference.

1. The children's respect for their parents did not disappear until they told them about their decision to divorce.
2. On the keyboard, the various function and tab keys often confuse the user that move one through this program.
3. In Beckett's play, he presents two tramps who wait for someone who never arrives.
4. The lake is peaceful. Near the shore, water lilies grow in profusion, spreading out their green leaves and sending up white blossoms. It is well stocked with fish.
5. The Queen spoke to the Princess as she waved to the crowd.

28c
Use broad or implied reference only with discretion.

Pronouns such as *it, this, that, which,* and *such* may refer to a specific word or phrase or to the sense of a whole clause, sentence, or paragraph.

SPECIFIC REFERENCE   The concept of fun is elusive and resists easy definition, but it is an undisputed element—perhaps *the* element—of play.
—WITOLD RYBCZYNSKI [*It* refers to *fun.*]

28d ref

BROAD REFERENCE
BROAD REFERENCE   Have you ever noticed that when you're tired and there's silence in your brain, you begin to sing? That's good health taking over. —TIMOTHY FINDLEY [The pronoun *that* refers to the entire idea expressed in the first sentence.]

When used carelessly, however, broad reference can interfere with clear communication.

(1) Avoid broad reference to an expressed idea.

VAGUE   Although the story referred to James, Henry misapplied it to himself, which is true in real life.

CLEAR   Although the story referred to James, Henry misapplied it to himself. Such mistakes occur in real life.

(2) As a rule, do not refer to a word or an idea not expressed but merely implied.

VAGUE   Yuki said that she would stay in Rome for at least a year. This suggests that she is happy there. [*This* has no expressed antecedent.]

CLEAR   Yuko said that she would stay in Rome for at least a year. This remark suggests that she is happy there.

VAGUE   The people of China suffered tremendously both during and after World War II. It was plain to see. [*It* has no expressed antecedent.]

CLEAR   The people of China suffered tremendously both during and after World War II. That suffering was plain to see.

28d
Avoid the awkward use of *you* or *it*.

AWKWARD   When one cannot swim, you fear deep, stormy waters. [The pronoun *you* (second person) refers to *one* (third person). See also **27b**.]

REVISED   The person who cannot swim fears deep, stormy waters.

| AWKWARD | In the book **it** says that many mushrooms are edible. [The pronoun *it* clumsily refers to *book*.] |
| REVISED | The book says that many mushrooms are edible. |

In some contexts, the use of the impersonal, or indefinite, *you* is both natural and acceptable. Notice in the following example that *you* is equivalent in meaning to "people in general" or "the reader."

> The study of dreams has become a significant and respectable scientific exploration, one that can directly benefit **you.**
> —PATRICIA GARFIELD

Some writers, however, prefer not to use *you* in a formal or academic context.

Note: Avoid the awkward placement of *it* near another *it* with a different meaning.

AWKWARD	Although it was very hot on the beach, it was a beautiful place. [The first *it* is the indefinite or unspecified *it*. The second *it* refers to *beach*.]
REVISED	Although it was very hot on the beach, the place was beautiful.
AWKWARD	It would be unwise to buy the new model now, but it is a superior machine. [The first *it* is an expletive. The second *it* refers to *model*.]
REVISED	Buying the new model now would be unwise, but it is a superior machine.

■ **Exercise 2**   Revise the following sentences as necessary to correct faults in reference. Put a check mark after any sentence that needs no revision.

1. At the Chinese restaurant, the Meltons had a hard time eating with chopsticks, but that is their favourite food.

2. Apparently the dishwasher was out of order; it leaked all over the kitchen floor.

3. Copiers and other fine modern office machines enable business executives to accomplish more work because their assistants can manage them easily and quickly.

4. In the article it states that Sable Island in Nova Scotia is the only breeding site of the rare Ipswich sparrow.

5. Our language is rich in connectives that express fine distinctions of meaning.

6. I did not even buy a season ticket, which was very disloyal to my school.

7. Mary told Ann that she had to read *Pride and Prejudice.*

8. When building roads the Romans tried to detour around valleys as much as possible for fear that flood waters might cover them and make them useless.

9. The extra fees surprised many students that seemed unreasonably high.

10. In Frank's suitcase he packs only wash-and-wear clothes.

■ **Exercise 3**   Revise the following paragraph as necessary to correct faults in reference.

[1]Recently, our poetry class has been focussing on Canadian poets and their work who have been writing for most of this century. [2]This has introduced me to the poems of Earle Birney and Al Purdy, and I have come to appreciate them. [3]Birney has written poems about this country and about those he has travelled to during his long and energetic life. [4]Al Purdy has written about these too, and you can see it in many poems that he is interested in Canada's past and in how that fits into the present.

Emphasis

29

Write sentences that will give emphasis to important ideas.

You may emphasize ideas by using exact diction (see Section **20**), concise language (Section **21**), and appropriate subordination and co-ordination (Section **24**). This section presents other ways to gain emphasis.

29a

Gain emphasis by placing important words at the beginning or end of the sentence—especially at the end.

UNEMPHATIC   They claim to believe in the free market. They, however, do support government subsidies to agriculture. [Parenthetical elements in an important position weaken the sentence.]

EMPHATIC   They claim to believe in the free market. However, they do support government subsidies to agriculture.

OR

They claim to believe in the free market. They do support government subsidies to agriculture, however.

UNEMPHATIC	There was an underground blast that rocked the whole area. [Unemphatic words begin the sentence.]
EMPHATIC	An underground blast rocked the whole area.

Since the semicolon, sometimes called a weak period, is a strong punctuation mark when used between main clauses, the words placed immediately before and after a semicolon tend to receive emphasis.

The colon and the dash often precede an emphatic ending.

> I would like to point out to these people a type of labour from which they are certain to profit: an expedition by canoe.   —PIERRE TRUDEAU
> *The Coast* meant only one thing—British Columbia.
> —MARGARET LAURENCE

■ **Exercise 1** Giving special attention to the placement of important words, revise the following sentences to improve emphasis.

1. Music has the power to hypnotize, so they say.
2. In fact, only one person could have written all these articles because of their same editorial slant, I am convinced.
3. There is one stunt woman who earns five thousand dollars for two hours of work.
4. It had never before entered her mind to resent her co-worker's complacent ignorance or to ignore his unreasonable demands, however.

29b

Gain emphasis by occasionally changing loose sentences into periodic sentences.

In a *loose* sentence, the main idea (grammatically a main clause or sentence base) comes first; less important ideas or details follow. In a *periodic* sentence, however, the main idea comes last, just before the period.

LOOSE Such pallid adjectives do not adequately describe the view from atop Grouse Mountain—for example, adjectives like *nice, interesting, worthwhile,* or *pleasant.*

PERIODIC Such pallid adjectives as *nice, interesting, worthwhile,* or *pleasant* do not adequately describe the view from atop Grouse Mountain.

LOOSE Hair has always been a statement for men, variously representing strength (Samson), fashionable virtue (King Charles I of England, whose wigs were long-locked and elaborate), bravado (General Custer), and genius (Einstein).
—OWEN EDWARDS [The main idea comes first.]

PERIODIC When you die, when you get a divorce, when you buy a house, when you have an auto accident, not to mention the hundreds of times during your lifetime when you are fleeced in your role as a consumer, a lawyer either must or should be involved. —DAVID HAPGOOD [The main idea comes last.]

Both types of sentences can be effective. The loose sentence is, and should be, the more commonly used. Although the periodic sentence is often the more emphatic, you should take care in your writing not to overuse it.

■ **Exercise 2** Convert loose sentences to periodic sentences, and the periodic to loose. Notice how your revisions make for varying emphasis.

1. Italy remains cheerful, despite everything.
—AUBERON WAUGH
2. Even where people want better relations, old habits and reflexes persist. —HEDRICK SMITH
3. The Milky Way Galaxy is entirely unremarkable, one of billions of other galaxies strewn through the vastness of space. —CARL SAGAN

4. Many pacifist feminists and pacifists changed their philosophy in the 1930s, when the rise of fascism seemed to many to call for military action rather than peaceful solution. —BONNIE ANDERSON AND JUDITH ZINSSER

5. By the time the production studios moved from New York to Hollywood, the movie Mountie was a fixture on the screens of the nation. —PIERRE BERTON

29c

Gain emphasis by arranging ideas in the order of climax.

Notice in the following examples that the ideas are arranged in an order that places the writer's most dramatic or important idea last.

Urban life is unhealthy, morally corrupt, and fundamentally inhuman. —RENÉ DUBOS [adjectives in the series arranged in climactic order]

The island of Chiloe is celebrated for its black storms and black soil, its thickets of fuschia and bamboo, its Jesuit churches and the golden hands of its woodcarvers.
—BRUCE CHATWIN [nouns in the series arranged in climactic order]

In the language of screen comedians four of the main grades of laugh are the titter, the yowl, the belly laugh and the boffo. The titter is just a titter. The yowl is a runaway titter. Anyone who has ever had the pleasure knows all about a belly laugh. The boffo is the laugh that kills. —JAMES AGEE [First, words are placed in climactic order, then sentences.]

Note: Anticlimax—an unexpected shift from the dignified to the trivial or from the serious to the comic or ironic—is sometimes used for special effect.

John Crosbie was the gold medallist when he graduated from Queen's University. He was the gold medallist when he graduated from Dalhousie Law School, the top law student in Canada and winner of a scholarship to the London School of Economics. Unfortunately, he did not receive a degree in common sense.   —ALLAN FOTHERINGHAM

■ **Exercise 3**   Arrange the ideas in the following sentences in what you consider to be the order of climax.

1. The playwright used the tree as a symbol of nature, vitality, and hope.
2. Among the images in the poem are sun-drenched orchards, diamond-eyed children, and golden-flecked birds.
3. He left the city because his health was failing, his taxes were going up, and his pet dog was tired of the leash.
4. Something must be done at once. Unless we act now, the city will be bankrupt in five years. The council is faced with a deficit.
5. The would-be prime minister attended a community church supper, spoke at a rally, promised new jobs, and visited homes for senior citizens.

29d
Gain emphasis by using the active voice and by using verbs more forceful than *have* or *be*.

(1) Use the active voice instead of the passive voice.

UNEMPHATIC	Little attention is being paid to changing economic conditions by the average political candidate.
EMPHATIC	The average political candidate is paying little attention to changing economic conditions.

Exception: If the receiver of the action is more important than the doer, the passive voice is more effective.

There in the tin factory, in the first moment of the atomic age, a human being was crushed by books.   —JOHN HERSEY
Freedom can be squashed by the tyrant or suffocated by the bureaucrat.   —WILLIAM F. RICKENBACKER

(2) Use an action verb or a linking verb more forceful than a form of *have* or *be*.

UNEMPHATIC	Our debating team is always the winner of this competition.
EMPHATIC	Our debating team always wins this competition.
UNEMPHATIC	The chowder has a bitter taste.
EMPHATIC	The chowder tastes bitter.

■ **Exercise 4** Make each sentence more emphatic by substituting the active for the passive voice or by substituting a more forceful verb for a form of *have* or *be*.

1. Pennies are often thrown into the fountain by tourists.
2. My brother is a manipulator of other people.
3. Every Saturday, TV is being watched by easily influenced children.
4. Bad pizza has a taste like cardboard.
5. It is greatly feared by the citizens that the judge will have too harsh a sentence for the defendant.

■ **Exercise 5** Make the following paragraph more emphatic by substituting the active for the passive voice or by substituting a more forceful verb for a form of *have* or *be*.

[1]The essay was originally given its name in the sixteenth century by the French writer Michel de Montaigne. [2]The name was derived from the French word *essayer*, which is "to attempt." [3]In the seventeenth century, the essay often had the look of a sermon and was published not individually but in collections of writings. [4]In the eighteenth century, individual essays were often found by readers in periodicals, whereas in the nineteenth century, the essay had a more personal tone for many writers. [5]Finally, in this century, the essay has had many forms and purposes, but one thing is certain: the essay is here to stay.

29e
Gain emphasis by repeating important words.

Note the repetitions in the following excerpt, in which Hugh MacLennan recalls his conversation with an editor who asked him to write about Canada using certain stereotypical images.

[He] explained that this would be what he called a "duty piece." His magazine sold several hundred thousand copies in Canada every month, and occasionally the management felt it a duty to print some Canadian material. I must have made a comment about there being no Eskimos, trappers, or husky dogs within fifteen hundred miles of where we were sitting, for he cut me short with a gesture.

"No, they're imperative. In an African duty-piece you stress the heat and the jungle. In an English duty-piece you stress how old everything is. A French duty-piece has got to be romantic, but at the same time we like an angle showing the French are also practical and getting themselves orientated to the up-to-date. But in a Canadian duty-piece you simply have to go heavy on the snow and the cold." —HUGH MACLENNAN, "On Living in a Cold Country"

■ **Exercise 6** First make each sentence below more emphatic by substituting repetition for the use of synonyms; then write two sentences of your own using repetition for emphasis.

1. Sometimes we lie to avoid hurting someone's feelings; occasionally we prevaricate to make another person like us.
2. He gripes all the time: he complains about the weather, fusses in heavy traffic, grumbles about high prices, and is critical of his meals.

29f
Gain emphasis by occasionally inverting the word order of a sentence. See also **30b**.

At the feet of the tallest and plushiest offices lie the crummiest slums.   —E.B. WHITE [Compare "The crummiest slums lie at the feet of the tallest and plushiest offices."]

Only with great difficulty can the history of clowns and fools be distinguished from legend.   —LOUISA JONES

Caution: This method of gaining emphasis, if overused, will make the style distinctly artificial.

29g
Gain emphasis by using balanced sentence construction.

A sentence is balanced when grammatically equal structures—usually main clauses with parallel elements—are used to express contrasted (or similar) ideas: see Section **26**. A balanced sentence emphasizes the contrast (or similarity) between parts of equal length and movement.

Nonviolence is the first article of my faith. It is also the last article of my creed.   —MOHANDAS GANDHI
I can remember the day I learned to read; I can remember the room in which I did so.   —SALLY BEAUMAN
Reading was my first solitary vice (and led to all the others). I read while I ate, I read in the loo, I read in the bath.
—GERMAINE GREER
Love is positive; tolerance negative. Love involves passion; tolerance is humdrum and dull.   —E.M. FORSTER
A compliment is a statement of an agreeable truth; flattery is the statement of an agreeable untruth.
—SIR JOHN A. MACDONALD

■ **Exercise 7** Write emphatic sentences using balanced construction to show the contrast between the following:

1. summer and winter
2. youth and age
3. teachers and students
4. hypocrisy and candour

29h
Gain emphasis by abruptly changing sentence length.

The head steward kept you waiting a moment until he led you to a table of four, a snowy tablecloth with white table napkins folded like wigwams presiding over the population—those knives, forks, three kinds of spoons, the jug of ice water, silver-and-cream bowls, balls of butter on ice, and that most fascinating basket containing crisp round rolls and soda biscuits. You did not have to feel hungry. —DOROTHY LIVESAY [The short sentence, which abruptly follows a much longer one, is emphatic.]

I suppose each painter has his own way of launching into the adventure in shape, colour, texture and space that we call painting. I mostly fall into them.   —DAVID MILNE

■ **Exercise 8**   Write a short, emphatic sentence to follow each of the two long sentences. Then write another pair of sentences—one long and one short—of your own.

1. According to some minor prophets of doom, the next century will be a push-button era, a computer-controlled and robot-dominated one with life dependent on the movement of a forefinger.
2. In sequined costumes the skaters glide into the huge arena, smile at the applauding spectators, strike a brief pose, and then race into a series of intricate leaps and spins, their feet perfectly balanced on thin wedges of shining steel.

■ **Exercise 9**   Prepare for a class discussion of emphasis in the following passages.

1. Refugees from every country, immigrants of every race, peoples of all faiths, and persons seeking political asylum have all found their place in Canadian life. It is our good fortune not to be of one common descent, not to speak one language only. We are not cursed with a triumphant ideology; we are not given to mindless patriotism.
   —THOMAS BERGER

2. In fantasy, the timid can be bold and aggressive, the weak are strong, the clumsy are full of grace, the tongue-tied discover vast verbal resources. In the privacy of the mind, we can all rise up in righteous wrath, and vengeance is ours. —ADELAIDE BRY

3. Contained within the Arctic lands of Canada is the vast inland sea of Hudson Bay, in which the British Isles could be sunk without a trace. —FARLEY MOWAT

■ **Exercise 10**   Revise each sentence for emphasis.

1. I think that replacing human organs with animal organs should stop, even if it might extend a person's life.
2. Such jokes are offensive to many people because they have references to minorities or to religion.
3. Fields of alpine flowers were all around us.
4. Fools talk about each other; ideas fill the conversations of the wise.
5. In any event, the opening ceremony began when the young girl sang the national anthem of her country *a capella*.
6. The storm broke in all its fury at the close of a hot day.
7. A rink-wide pass was made by Sandstrom to Gretzky, and a goal was scored by him before the whistle was blown by the referee.
8. I asked her to marry me, two years ago, in a shop on Tremont Street, late in the fall.
9. The theatrical production of the students was rough in spots, but a great deal of energy was displayed by all of them.
10. I can identify the guilty person in every Agatha Christie novel by the simple device of choosing the least likely suspect whose alibi is airtight.

Variety

30

Vary the structure and the length of your sentences.

Inexperienced writers tend to rely too heavily—regardless of content or purpose—on a few comfortable, familiar structures. Seek variety in your sentences.

Compare the two paragraphs below. Both express the same ideas in virtually the same words; both use acceptable sentence patterns. The variety in sentence structure and length makes the difference.

NOT VARIED
Most Canadians highly value their freedom to do this or that. They value their ability to own this or that. Freedom to them means the right to become something or other. But I have a different point of view. I prize most the freedom not to do, not to have, and not to become. I can, as a Canadian, choose not to vote, and I don't have to buy. Moreover, I can also choose not to be ambitious; I don't have to be successful. I can pursue my own kind of happiness. I prize this freedom the most. [nine sentences, seven simple and two compound—all except two beginning with the subject]

VARIED

To do this or that, to own this or that, to become something or other—these freedoms are what most Canadians value highly. But I have a different point of view. What I prize most is the freedom not to do, not to have, not to become. As a Canadian, I can choose not to vote, and I can choose not to buy. Although I am free to be ambitious and success- ful, I can choose not to be either. To pursue happiness—as I define it—is the freedom I prize most. [six sentences: four complex, one compound, and one simple—two beginning with the subject]

Note: If you have difficulty distinguishing various types of structures, review the fundamentals of the sentence treated in Section **1,** especially **1d.**

30a

As a rule, avoid a series of short simple sentences. Vary the length. See also **29h.**

Rather than present your ideas in a series of choppy, inef- fective sentences, learn how to relate your ideas precisely in a longer sentence. See Section **24.**

CHOPPY | In some ways the Gulf Islands and Cape Breton look very much alike. The houses by the sea, however, are different. It's a matter of architec- tural style.

EFFECTIVE | Although the Gulf Islands and Cape Breton look very much alike in some ways, the architectural styles of the houses by the sea are different. [use of subordination to combine sentences]

CHOPPY | Some people simply put coffee in an enamel saucepan. Next, they pour very hot water over it. Then they wait until the flavour develops. Finally, they add eggshell or a small amount of cold water. The idea is to get the floating grounds to settle to the bottom.

EFFECTIVE Some people simply put coffee in an enamel saucepan, pour very hot water over it, wait until flavour develops, and get the floating grounds to settle to the bottom by adding eggshell or a small amount of cold water. [use of co-ordination to combine sentences]

Note: Occasionally, as the example below illustrates, a series of brief, subject-first sentences may be used for special effect:

He stumbled, recovered, picked up his pace. Now he was running. He broke out of the ring. People were throwing things at him. An egg hurtled past his head. A tomato hit someone nearby and splattered onto his suit.
—GERRY NADEL [The short sentences suggest staccato action.]

■ **Exercise 1** Study the structure of the sentences below, giving special attention to the variety of sentence lengths.

As she picked her way toward the garden chairs beside the front porch, she poured out a customary torrent of complaint. Her eyesight was failing. She found herself swatting raisins on the kitchen table, thinking they were flies, and bringing her stick down on spiders that turned out to be scurrying tufts of lint. Her hearing was going, and she suffered from head noises. She imagined she heard drums beating.
—PETER DE VRIES

■ **Exercise 2** Convert each of the following series of short simple sentences into one long sentence in which ideas are carefully related.

1. There were three minutes left in the movie. The chase scene was becoming more exciting by the minute, and the audience held its breath. The scene ended with a massive explosion.
2. Her statistical study had tremendous significance. Children in northern settlements were dropping out of school in

large numbers. They were committing suicide at alarming rates. The government had a responsibility to act.

3. Bennett's Comet appeared in 1969. It disappeared again in 1970. It will not be visible again for thousands of years.

4. Ellen Dolan did not buy a second car. She bought a Piper. It is a small airplane. It flies at just under two hundred kilometres an hour.

5. Paula Blanchard is the author of *The Life of Emily Carr.* In her book Blanchard describes Carr's struggles to record the Native art of the West Coast. Carr worked in isolation. She travelled to remote Native villages. She did this even the year she turned sixty.

30b

Avoid a long series of sentences beginning with the subject. Vary the beginnings.

Most writers begin about half their sentences with the subject—far more than the number of sentences begun in any other one way. But overuse of the subject-first beginning results in monotonous writing.

(1) Begin with an adverb or an adverb clause.

> **Outside,** auto rickshaws—three wheelers—were parked along the station in a long line.   —ROHINTON MISTRY [adverb]
> **But as we advanced,** the ridge became more and more narrow and eventually we emerged on to a perfect knife edge.
> —ERIC NEWBY [adverb clause]

(2) Begin with a prepositional phrase or a verbal phrase.

> **For the writer,** the wild dream is the first step to reality.
> —NORMAN COUSINS [prepositional phrase]
> **To produce small boys quicker than you can say "kite,"** fly one.   —P.K. PAGE [infinitive phrase]

Travelling on a special train of war brides from Halifax as a young and ignorant reporter, I kept asking them to comment on what they saw.

—MAVIS GALLANT [participial phrase]

(3) **Begin with a sentence connective—a co-ordinating conjunction, a conjunctive adverb, or a transitional expression.**

Notice how each sentence connective relates the ideas in each set of sentences. See also **32b(4)**.

Transitory popularity is not proof of genius. **But** permanent popularity is. —STEPHEN LEACOCK [The co-ordinating conjunction *but* marks a contrast.]

All human cultures seek to realize and protect their identity. **And** identity is definable only by reference to former times.

—HUGH BRODY

Boat scrubbed and tidied, sleeping bags out in the sun—everybody had their jobs. **Then** we collected our clothes for washing, piled into the dinghy and rowed across to the landslide. —M. WYLIE BLANCHET [conjunctive adverb]

In the past decade more than a few doubts have been raised about the magnitude, distribution and location of the earth's water supply. **Before long,** such questions may play a role in geology somewhat like the one played in astrophysics by the mystery of the missing mass.

—RAYMOND JEANLOZ [transitional phrase]

(4) **Begin with an appositive, an absolute phrase, or an introductory series.**

A city of ancient origins, Varna lies on the Black Sea coast.
—COLIN RENFREW [appositive referring to the subject]
His eyebrows raised high in resignation, he began to examine his hand. —LIONEL TRILLING [absolute phrase]

> **Logging, sawmilling, mixed farming, commercial fishing, and sport fishing**—these are the bases of Bella Coola's economy. [See also **17e(3)**.]

Note: An occasional declarative sentence with inverted word order can contribute to sentence variety. See **29f**.

■ **Exercise 3**   Prepare for a class discussion of the types of sentence beginnings in the following paragraph.

¹We can be proud of Canadian cities because, being so much slower than our American friends, we missed sacrificing our core housing to commercial development as happened down south. ²Housing in the core maintains the healthy mix that is characteristic of every great city in the world, and avoids the segregated zoning that blighted American cities, leaving them with deserted, unsafe streets. ³In Vancouver the downtown core is isolated by geography and will eventually be ringed with housing. ⁴Because of the insular form, downtown housing faces water, open sea or parkland in over eighty per cent of its circumference and those broad vistas should be factored into the floor space ratio to allow a greater density than is acceptable for land-locked development. ⁵An indigenous response to these circumstances originated here in the sixties—the very slender high rise apartments which answered the need for outlook and view—though the slender tower has only lately been recognized by officialdom and incorporated into the zoning regulations of the city. ⁶Vancouver became a city preoccupied with view, sacrificing inward-looking streets and neighbourhoods. ⁷With everyone straining to look out, the "no there there" of Gertrude Stein came to pervade the inner city. ⁸Even so, at the residential centre of the peninsula where the view is not important some successful inward-looking neighbourhoods have grown in.   —ARTHUR ERICKSON

■ **Exercise 4**   Recast each sentence twice to vary the beginning.

EXAMPLE
Two businesspeople dropped by the dean's office and discussed the co-operative education program.
  a. *Dropping by the dean's office, two businesspeople discussed the co-operative education program.*
  b. *In the dean's office, two businesspeople discussed the co-operative education program.*

1. Reporters cornered the newly appointed Minister of External Affairs and asked her some very tricky questions about world affairs.
2. Some consultants are concerned about the cost of post-secondary education but not about the quality of instruction.
3. Jesse enjoyed the course in science-fiction literature most of all.
4. The green fireballs travelled at great speed and fascinated sky watchers throughout the Maritimes.

30c
Avoid loose, stringy compound sentences. See also **24b.**

To revise an ineffective compound sentence, try one of the following methods.

(1) Make a compound sentence complex.

COMPOUND The Mississippi River is one of the longest rivers in the world, and in the springtime it often overflows its banks, and the lives of many people are endangered.

COMPLEX The Mississippi River, which is one of the longest rivers in the world, often overflows its banks in the springtime, endangering the lives of many people.

(2) Use a compound predicate in a simple sentence.

COMPOUND   He put on his coat, and next he picked up his keys, and then he dashed out of the house.

SIMPLE   He put on his coat, picked up his keys, and dashed out of the house.

(3) Use an appositive in a simple sentence.

COMPOUND   Emma Lake is north of Prince Albert in Saskatchewan, and it is a summer camp, and it is the site of an influential artists' workshop.

SIMPLE   A summer camp north of Prince Albert in Saskatchewan, Emma Lake is the site of an influential artists' workshop.

COMPOUND   Her ability to listen is an acquired skill, and it attracts many friends.

SIMPLE   Her ability to listen, an acquired skill, attracts many friends.

(4) Use a prepositional or verbal phrase in a simple sentence.

COMPOUND   The streets were icy, and we could not drive the car.

SIMPLE   Because of the icy streets, we could not drive the car.

COMPOUND   He arrived in Calgary at 1:30 A.M., and then he made the toll-free call.

SIMPLE   After arriving in Calgary at 1:30 A.M., he made the toll-free call.

COMPOUND   The town was north of the Red River, and a tornado struck it, and it was practically demolished.

SIMPLE   The town, located north of the Red River, was struck by a tornado and practically demolished.

■ **Exercise 5** Using the methods illustrated in **30c,** revise the loose, stringy compound sentences below.

1. The tall player dominates the team, and she is easily the top scorer, but she is not generous with her teammates.
2. The Séguins grew tired of ocean views and sand in their shoes, so they vacationed in Paris, but they ran out of travellers' cheques and French phrases, so they came home early.
3. The young Canadian at first struggled to be a model soldier, and then he began to question his commander's orders, and finally he defied an order to attack a small, unprotected village.
4. My classmate kept complaining about the tone of Canadian literature, and she mentioned such things as the gloominess of plots and the passivity of characters, but she did not offer any evidence or name any specific works.

30d
Vary the conventional subject-verb sequence by occasionally separating subject and verb with words or phrases.

Each subject and verb below is in boldface.

SUBJECT-VERB	**The auditorium is** across from the park, and **it is** a gift of the alumni. [compound sentence]
VARIED	**The auditorium,** across from the park, **is** a gift of the alumni. [simple sentence]
SUBJECT-VERB	**The crowd sympathized** with the visitors **and applauded** every good play.
VARIED	**The crowd,** sympathizing with the visitors, **applauded** every good play.

■ **Exercise 6** Using the methods illustrated in **30d,** vary the conventional subject-verb sequence.

1. This magazine is like a newspaper; it is produced on newsprint, and its articles are brief and quite bland.
2. St. John's is the capital of Newfoundland, and it lies over 900 km east of Halifax and lies about 1900 km east of New York.
3. My parents value perseverance and encourage us to keep trying until we succeed.
4. Margaret was racing back to the library to avoid getting wet, and she fell broadside into a big puddle of water.
5. Niagara-on-the-Lake is now recognized as an architectural and historical treasure house, but it was a forgotten town until the early sixties.

■ **Exercise 7** Using the methods illustrated in **30d,** rewrite the following paragraph.

¹Many children led difficult lives in Victorian England. ²Some of them worked twelve- or fourteen-hour days in factories. ³They were assigned the dangerous job of repairing heavy machinery because they were small enough to crawl inside and around broken mechanisms. ⁴Other children worked in coal mines, travelling through small, airless shafts on tiny coal trucks. ⁵Other children worked as chimney sweeps, and when they were sometimes trapped in a smokestack, their cruel employers would light fires underneath them in an attempt to force them to free themselves. ⁶The exploitation of children in these ways finally prompted Britain to enact child labour laws that still influence the workplace today.

30e
Occasionally, instead of the usual declarative sentence, use a question, an exclamation, or a command.

When is a chair not a chair? When it is a work of art. That, at least, is the assumption of a growing number of collectors, critics, museum curators, gallery owners, and furniture makers who form the vanguard of the growing studio-furniture movement. —WITOLD RYBCZYNSKI [Here a question is followed by a deliberate fragment-answer and the usual declarative statement.]

Now I stare and stare at people, shamelessly. Stare. It's the way to educate your eye. —WALKER EVANS [A one-word imperative sentence provides variety.]

■ **Exercise 8** Prepare for a class discussion of sentence variety in the following paragraph.

¹How does a lump of lead that draws a creditable line evolve into a modern pencil? ²How does a rounded rock turn into a wheel? ³How does a dream become a flying machine? ⁴The process by which ideas and artifacts come into being and mature is essentially what is now known as the engineering method, and the method, like engineering itself, is really as old as *Homo sapiens*—or at least *Homo faber*—and the process is about as hard to pin down and as idiosyncratic in each of its peculiar applications as is the individual of the species. ⁵But while each invention and artifact has its unique aspects, there is also a certain sameness about the evolutionary way in which a stylus develops into a pencil, a sketch into a palace, or an arrow into a rocket. ⁶And this observation itself is as old as Ecclesiastes, who may have been the first to record, but probably was not the first to observe, that "what has been is what will be, and has been done is what will be done; and there is nothing new under the sun."
—HENRY PETROSKI, *The Pencil: A History of Design and Circumstance*

LARGER ELEMENTS

Logical Thinking

31

Base your writing on logical thinking. Avoid common fallacies.

Logical thinking involves the natural reasoning processes of induction and deduction. As you study **31a** and **31b,** keep in mind that both kinds of reasoning help you win your reader's confidence. One kind of reasoning often leads to the other. The most important thing is to ensure that your reader confidently follows your thinking.

31a
Learn how to use inductive reasoning in your writing.

Whenever you interpret evidence, you reason inductively. Every time you flick the light switch, the lights come on, and so you conclude that they will do so the next time you flick the switch. But inductive reasoning can never lead to absolute certainty. The next time you flick the switch, the lights may not come on. Induction is the basic method of science: a phenomenon is observed so often that scientists feel confident in reaching a conclusion.

Inductive reasoning is useful not only for arriving at conclusions but for persuading others to accept conclusions you have already reached. An inductive argument is built on facts; as evidence mounts, your reader arrives at the conclusion you intend. It is crucial that the amount of evidence be sufficient (see Hasty Generalization, page 366). You also need to be sure that the conclusions you draw fit the fact (see *Post Hoc, Ergo Propter Hoc,* page 367). Be sure that you have not inadvertently ignored evidence that might invalidate your conclusion ("neglected aspect"). Also resist the temptation to present only the evidence that supports a predetermined conclusion ("slanting").

When you use induction in your writing, the organizational strategy can vary with the situation. You may wish to state the logical conclusion first and then present the evidence on which it is based. Conversely, you may wish to present the evidence first and let your reader draw the conclusion. This strategy works well when your conclusion is one your reader may resist.

31b
Learn how to use deductive reasoning in your writing.

Although the terminology may be new to you, you are already familiar with deductive reasoning. For example, you know that the only prerequisite for enrolling in honours history is a B+ average. You have a B+ average. Therefore, you can conclude, with certainty, that you are eligible for honours history. This kind of reasoning is based on a logical structure called a syllogism. A syllogism has three terms: a major premise (usually a generalization), a minor premise (a specific fact), and a conclusion that fits both the major premise and the minor premise.

When the major premise and the minor premise are correctly related to form a conclusion, the syllogism is valid. Even if it is valid, however, the conclusion may be false if one of the premises is false. In the example just given, if your assumption that the honours history requirement is a B+ were not true, or if you had miscalculated your own average, your conclusion might be false even though your reasoning was valid. But when both premises are true and the syllogism is valid, then the conclusion must be true.

Deductive reasoning can be a powerful tool in argumentative papers. However, when you argue deductively, you must think about your premises very carefully to be sure your argument is sound—both true and valid (see Non Sequitur, page 366; Either . . . or Fallacy, page 367; Circular Reasoning, page 366; and Equivocation, page 367).

When you write a deductive argument, you should frame a premise that you consider to be true and that your reader is likely to accept as both valid and true. For instance, if you want to convince a reader that vivisection should be outlawed, you might think of a premise such as this:

> Anything that inflicts pain on living creatures should be outlawed.

But on further consideration it may occur to you that this premise might be difficult for your reader to accept. After all, sometimes pain is inflicted on living creatures for a benefit; if you have appendicitis, you willingly submit to the pain of surgery to have your appendix removed. So the premise needs to be qualified:

> Anything that *needlessly* inflicts pain on living creatures should be outlawed.
> Vivisection *needlessly* inflicts pain on living creatures.
> Vivisection should be outlawed.

In other situations you may decide to limit your objectives. You may be able to succeed in getting a reader to agree that anything that needlessly inflicts pain on living creatures is morally wrong, but not necessarily to agree that a law should be enacted to prohibit every moral wrong. You could alter your premise like this:

> Anything that needlessly inflicts pain on living creatures *is morally wrong.*
> Vivisection needlessly inflicts pain on living creatures.
> Vivisection is morally wrong.

Although you always need to think carefully about both of your premises and you should be able to state them correctly for yourself, you do not always have to express both of them in your writing.

> Because vivisection needlessly inflicts pain on living creatures, it is morally wrong. [major premise unstated]

■ **Exercise 1**   Prepare for a class discussion of the premises and conclusions in the following items.

1. First, many situations in real life have unhappy endings; therefore, if fiction is to illuminate life, it must present defeat as well as triumph.   —LAURENCE PERRINE
2. Universities must stop using students as an important part of the process of evaluating teachers. Evaluation of teaching performance should be done by peers who know what good teaching is and who can separate good teaching from mere entertainment.
   —DAVID BERCUSON, ROBERT BOTHWELL, AND J.L. GRANATSTEIN,
   The Great Brain Robbery: Canada's Universities on the Road to Ruin

31c
Avoid fallacies.

Fallacies are faults in reasoning. They may result from misusing or misrepresenting evidence, from relying on faulty premises or omitting a needed premise, or from distorting the issues.

31c log

(1) **Non Sequitur:**   A statement that does not follow logically from what has just been said—a conclusion that does not follow from the premises.

   FAULTY   Victoria is tall; therefore she must work as a model. [Many tall people do not work as models.]

(2) **Hasty Generalization:**   A generalization based on too little evidence or on exceptional or biased evidence.

   FAULTY   Teenagers are reckless drivers. [Many teenagers are careful drivers.]

(3) *Ad Hominen:*   Attacking the person who presents an issue rather than dealing logically with the issue itself.

   FAULTY   Her proposed child-care legislation would be more credible if she were married with children. [The woman's marital status and her childlessness need not invalidate her legislation.]

(4) **Bandwagon:** An argument saying, in effect, "Everyone's doing or saying or thinking this, so you should too."

   FAULTY   Everyone in this neighbourhood shops across the border, so why shouldn't you? [The majority is not always right.]

(5) **Circular Reasoning:**   An assertion that restates the point just made. Such an assertion "begs the question" by drawing as a conclusion a point stated in the premise.

   FAULTY   They are lazy because they just don't like to work. [Being lazy and not liking to work mean essentially the same thing.]

(6) **Red Herring**: Dodging the real issue by drawing attention to an irrelevant issue.

FAULTY Why worry about a few terrorists when we ought to be doing something about the hole in the ozone layer? [The hole in the ozone layer has nothing to do with the actions of terrorists.]

(7) ***Post Hoc, Ergo Propter Hoc:*** "After this, so because of this"—the mistake of assuming that because one event follows another, the first must be the cause of the second.

FAULTY The film critic for the *Globe and Mail* recommended the new movie about Norman Bethune, and it drew large crowds at theatres in Regina. [The assumption is that having the critic's endorsement caused the large crowds in Regina, an assumption unlikely to be true.]

(8) **Either . . . or Fallacy**: Stating that only two alternatives exist when in fact there are more than two.

FAULTY We have only two choices: create new jobs or protect the environment. [In fact, other possibilities exist.]

(9) **False Analogy**: The assumption that because two things are alike in some ways, they must be alike in other ways.

FAULTY Since the two restaurants serve Thai food and feature dishes in the same price range, one is probably as good as another. [The menu and prices of the restaurants cannot predict whether one is as good as the other.]

(10) **Equivocation**: An assertion that falsely relies on the use of a term in two different senses.

FAULTY You have a right to vote, so do what is right and vote. [The word *right* means both "a just claim" and "correct."]

31c log

■ Exercise 2 Prepare for a class discussion of the faulty logic in the following sentences.

1. A person who comes from Western Canada should not become prime minister.
2. True, many citizens cheat on their income tax, but you should consider how much good they do for the economy by spending the money that they saved.
3. If you walk self-confidently, with your head high, you won't be attacked.
4. Our prisons are full because our laws are too severe.
5. I will not vote for him as my representative because he was not born in Canada.
6. Women just can't handle corporate politics; men just can't manage a household.
7. Everybody likes Jacqueline, so she will be a good class president.
8. I've never met a Newfoundlander who didn't like cod; all Newfoundlanders do.
9. Todd missed class twice last week; he must have been skiing.
10. These electric razors give the smoothest shave; all successful executives use them.
11. After that oil spill, the fish I caught tasted greasy. Those fish are contaminated.
12. There are only two kinds of politicians: those interested in their own welfare and those interested in the welfare of the people.

The Paragraph

32

Write paragraphs that are unified, coherent, and adequately developed.

An essential unit of thought in writing, the paragraph usually consists of a group of related sentences, though occasionally no more than one sentence. The first line of a paragraph is indented, about 2.5 cm when handwritten and five spaces when typewritten.

Good paragraphs are unified, coherent, and well developed. As you read the following paragraph, observe the unity—how all of the sentences in the paragraph relate to a single main idea. Notice also the easy, natural progression of ideas from sentence to sentence (coherence), and the use of plenty of specific information, appropriately arranged to support the main idea (development). (For easy reference, the paragraphs in this section are numbered—except for those in need of revision.)

1   The modern typewriter keyboard was deliberately designed to be as inconvenient as possible. On earlier models of the typewriter, the keyboard was arranged so that the most common letters in the English language were located in the middle row. Typists soon become so quick that they

continually jammed the primitive machines. The inventor solved the problem by scrambling the letters on the keyboard and creating a deliberately inconvenient arrangement. This slowed down the typists and thus prevented them from accidentally jamming the typewriter. Although modern typewriters are virtually jam-proof, they still have the deliberately inefficient keyboard arrangement designed for the first primitive typing machines.

—PAUL STIRLING HAGERMAN,
The Odd, Mad World of Paul Stirling Hagerman

2   Starting school in Banff began as a cultural nightmare. I am no sculptor; plasticine bored me. I was handed babybooks that insulted my soul. A disciplinary problem, I was happily kicked upstairs to Grade Three and there by great luck exposed to some quite recent Canadian fiction. Miss Dykeman, our young teacher, who had come all the way from Musquodobit, N.S., on the Atlantic Ocean (no one knew why), liked to read us stories of "her country" (as we thought of it). So I was introduced to L.M. Montgomery's *Anne of Green Gables* and *Anne of Avonlea,* and G.S. Porter's *Girl of the Limberlost.* "Popular sentimental fiction," the *Literary History of Canada* labels them now. And so they were, and far too concerned with girls, but I liked them anyway. I had red hair too, and lived in Canadian woods. I liked *Mooswa* even more, and the other all-too-humanized animals of Ernest Thompson Seton and Charles G.D. Roberts. What Jay Macpherson calls "their fuzzy natural religion" I must have found better than Presbyterianism, if I noticed it at all, and I was excited by hearing stories about wildernesses, even if they were Atlantic ones. I needed those authors then as much as my grandchildren need Farley Mowat now. Farley, indeed, would have been better for us, but he wasn't there yet. And I benefited from them even more because there was then nothing literary Canadian at all in the official school curriculum.

—EARLE BIRNEY, "Spring Plowing, 1904–26"

Paragraphs have no set length. Typically, they range from 50 to 250 words, averaging perhaps 100 words. Paragraphs intended for books are on average longer than those written for the narrow columns of newspapers and magazines. The shortest paragraphs generally occur in dialogue (see also **16a[2]**).

Note: Modern writers generally avoid extremely long paragraphs, especially those that belabour one point or combine too many points.

32a
Construct unified paragraphs.

In a unified paragraph each sentence contributes to developing a certain thought. Stating the central thought in a topic sentence will help you achieve unity.

(1) Make sure each sentence is related to the central thought.

Hold to the main idea; eliminate information that is unrelated or only vaguely related to it. Suppose, for instance, the main idea of one of your paragraphs is this: "Computers help students organize their time." In such a paragraph, if you include sentences about other benefits of computers, you will disrupt the unity. Every statement should pertain to the usefulness of the computer for organizing time. Notice in paragraph 3 how each sentence helps to show exactly what the writer means by the curious experiences referred to in the first sentence.

3   A number of curious experiences occur at the onset of sleep. A person just about to go to sleep may experience an electric shock, a flash of light, or a crash of thunder—but the most common sensation is that of floating or falling, which is why "falling asleep" is a scientifically valid description. A nearly universal occurrence at the beginning of sleep (although not everyone recalls it) is a sudden, uncoordinated jerk of the head, the limbs, or even the entire body. Most people tend to think of going to sleep as a slow slippage into oblivion, but the onset of sleep is not gradual at all. It happens in an instant. One moment the individual is awake, the next moment not.   —PETER FARB, *Humankind*

As you check your paragraphs for unity, if any information does not relate to your main idea, eliminate this irrelevant material. If any material is related to the main idea but not clearly so, revise to make the relationship clear. Sometimes, the problem is that the main idea itself needs to be more clearly formulated. (See also **32a[2]**.) Or there may be too many major ideas in a single paragraph. If so, the chances are that you should develop each in a separate paragraph. Occasionally, however, the best strategy is to formulate a new "umbrella" sentence, one expressing an idea that all the others will support.

■ **Exercise 1**   Revise the following faulty paragraph to improve unity. Be prepared to give the reasons for your revisions.

When I visited Vancouver Island's west coast last summer, I noticed that it looked very much like the coast of Oregon. It was very cold and rainy at Long Beach, and we had to wear coats even though it was late July. The Island's coastline is rocky, and in many places evergreens march straight to the water. In other places, bluffs lined with evergreens overlook the sea. One day we saw a large sailboat driving hard toward some half-submerged rocks. In Oregon, pine-rimmed bluffs usually overlook the ocean, but sometimes the trees extend to a partially submerged rocky ledge or a pebble beach. Small islands, called sea stacks, dot this coastline much as the wooded islands lie offshore in Barkley Sound. Lighthouses can be found here and there along both coastlines.

(2) State the main idea of the paragraph in a clearly constructed topic sentence.

A topic sentence embodies the central thought of a paragraph. Notice how the topic sentence of paragraph 4 (the first sentence) announces the idea of the playful quality of sign language; it also suggests the approach of the paragraph by establishing an expectation that the writer will go on to provide examples and explanations.

4   One has only to watch two people signing to see that signing has a playful quality, a style, quite different from that of speech. Signers tend to improvise, to play with signs, to bring all their humor, their imaginativeness, their personality, into their signing, so that signing is not just the manipulation of symbols according to grammatical rules, but, irreducibly, the voice of the signer—a voice given a special force, because it utters itself, so immediately, with the body. One can have or imagine disembodied speech, but one cannot have disembodied Sign. The body and soul of the signer, his unique human identity, are continually expressed in the act of signing.

     —OLIVER SACKS, *Seeing Voices: A Journey into the World of the Deaf*

Notice in paragraph 5 how the phrase "two Canadian authors" in the topic sentence introduces the writer's approach.

5   In the turn-of-the-century period, two Canadian authors had great success with domestic fiction that was both sentimental and informed with Christian uplift (like some English books in the Edwardian period). *Glengarry schooldays* (1902) by Ralph Connor (Charles William Gordon) was written for adults, but its youthful characters, schoolhouse scenes, and descriptions of pioneer activities in which chil-

dren were involved quickly captured the interest of the young. Connor's sentimental look backwards to pioneer days in Glengarry County, Ontario, gave him ample opportunity for some gentle proselytizing, but this never quite detracts from the force of his narrative skill or his ability to arouse emotion. *Glengarry schooldays* remains in print and can still be read with pleasure. This cannot be said of Nellie McClung's *Sowing seeds in Danny* (1908), whose heroine, twelve-year-old Pearlie Watson, is closely related to the pious and sacrificial Elsie Dinsmore. Yet McClung shared with Connor an ability to write vividly about a particular setting, in this case the small-town and farm life of Manitoba.

—SHEILA EGOFF, *The Oxford Companion to Canadian Literature*

The main idea of a paragraph is most often stated at or near the beginning, as in examples 4 and 5, although it may appear anywhere in the paragraph. When the main idea is stated early, it is sometimes also restated at the end, to point up its importance.

6   Ever-palpable in Ottawa even now is the immensity of the landscape all around—one of the most monotonous landscapes on earth, but one of the most challenging too. Bears sometimes turn up in Ottawa suburbs, beavers impertinently demolish National Capital Commission trees, the air is pellucid, and from any vantage point you can still see the open country. Only half an hour away are the wooded tracks and lakes of the Gatineau Hills, where the log jams *do* still lie in the Gatineau River; on the very edge of town begin the farmlands of the Ottawa Valley, whose produce you can buy any morning in the Byward Market, just a couple of blocks from the prime minister's office. At least in my fancy the hush of the back country penetrates Ottawa even now: sometimes in the very centre of the city I seem to enter an abrupt inexplicable silence, broken not by the thrum of traffic but only by the swish of forest winds.

—JAN MORRIS, *City to City*

Occasionally, as in paragraph 7, the topic sentence is the last sentence, especially when the writer progresses from particulars to a generalization.

7   In 1938, on the occasion of the addition of Konrad Gesner's book to the exhibit on the history of the recorded word, *The New York Times* editorialized about the evolution of the pencil since Gesner's first reference to one. The typewriter, it was feared, was driving out "writing with one's own hand," in both pen and pencil, which the editor clearly preferred, and he concluded with the concern that "libraries of a century or two hence may be searching for the last reference to pencils." Almost half a century later it was the computer that was going to be the end of the pencil, but that too is not likely to come to be. Pencils are being manufactured worldwide at the rate of about fourteen billion per year, and reports of the pencil's impending passing have been so greatly exaggerated that its staying power has come to be a subject of amusement.

—HENRY PETROSKI, *The Pencil:*
A History of Design and Circumstance

A single topic sentence (such as the first sentence below) may serve for a sequence of two or more paragraphs.

8   No two places in the continent are less alike than Montreal, where I grew up, and Santa Barbara, where I live. Montreal is big and dirty, with the worst weather of almost any city on the continent, Winnipeg the possible exception. Hockey has been a civic passion since the 1850s, long before Wayne Gretzky tied on a skate. Local history means the struggle between the French and English. There's a Notre Dame de Grâce Kosher Meat Market, a museum operated by French-speaking midgets, a Portuguese/Central American neighborhood called St-Louis de Mile End. Taxi drivers are Haitian and almost all pizza places are owned by Greeks, some of whom emigrated from Egypt. French-Canadian politicians have names like Johnson, Ryan, O'Neill.

9   In Santa Barbara almost everyone is either Hispanic or white/Anglo. There's perfect weather and zero interest in hockey. I don't know who drives the taxis because I've never taken one; who takes taxis in southern California? It makes sense to own a convertible. Rents are two to three times more expensive than in Montreal; gas, booze, and cigarettes much cheaper. Winter, a short, brisk season, makes everyone feel especially healthy. There's plenty of local history, but except for the destruction of the native American Chumash culture, it's history done in soft pastels. Chapters that can't be peddled to tourists are readily forgotten.

—PETER BEHRENS, "Refugee Dreams"

Occasionally, no topic sentence is needed because the details unmistakably imply the central idea.

10   Tennis has become more than the national sport; it is a rigorous discipline, a form of collective physiotherapy. Jogging is done by swarms of people, out onto the streets each day in underpants, moving in a stolid sort of rapid trudge, hoping by this to stay alive. Bicycles are cures. Meditation may be good for the soul but it is even better for the blood pressure.

—LEWIS THOMAS, *The Medusa and the Snail*

■ **Exercise 2** Write a paragraph with a topic sentence at the beginning, another with the topic sentence at the end, and a two-paragraph sequence containing a single topic sentence. Here are a few possible approaches.

1. Two kinds of . . .
2. Reasons for travelling . . .
3. The things that happen when . . .
4. Examples of . . .

32b

Make paragraphs coherent by arranging ideas in a clear, logical order and providing appropriate transitions.

A paragraph has coherence when the relationship among ideas is clear and the progression from one sentence to the next is easy and natural for the reader to follow. To achieve coherence, arrange ideas in a clear, logical order. Also provide transitions between sentences (not only within the paragraph but between paragraphs) by the effective use of pronoun reference, repetition of key words and ideas, appropriate conjunctions and other transitional expressions, and parallel structure.

ARRANGEMENT OF IDEAS

There are many common, logical ways to order ideas in a paragraph. The choice depends on the context and on the writer's purpose. One of the simplest orders is **time order.**

11   In the early afternoon several children and I walk for an hour along the beach—from the foot of the garden at Uswetakeiyawa, past the wrecks, to the Pegasus Reef Hotel. After twenty minutes, with sun burning just the right side of our faces and bodies, climbing up and down the dunes, we are exhausted, feel drunk. One of my children talking about some dream she had before leaving Canada. Spray breaking and blazing white. Mad dog heat. On our left the cool dark of village trees. Crabs veer away from our naked steps. I keep counting the children, keep feeling that one is missing. We look down, away from the sun. So that we all suddenly stumble across the body.

—MICHAEL ONDAATJE, *Running in the Family*

Descriptive passages are often arranged in **space order,** moving from east to west, from near to distant, from left to right, and so on. In paragraph 12, Thomas Merton presents details in a near-far perspective, enabling the reader to share the experience of approaching the monastery that was to become his home.

12   I had looked at the rolling country, and at the pale ribbon of road in front of us, stretching out as grey as lead in the light of the moon. Then suddenly I saw a steeple that shone like silver in the moonlight, growing into sight from behind a rounded knoll. The tires sang on the empty road, and, breathless, I looked at the monastery that was revealed before me as we came over the rise. At the end of an avenue of trees was a big rectangular block of buildings, all dark, with a church crowned by a tower and a steeple and a cross: and the steeple was as bright as platinum and the whole place was as quiet as midnight and lost in the all-absorbing silence and solitude of the fields. Behind the monastery was a dark curtain of woods, and over to the west was a wooded valley, and beyond that a rampart of wooded hills, a barrier and a defense against the world.   —THOMAS MERTON, *The Seven Storey Mountain*

Another useful arrangement of ideas is that of **order of importance,** from most important to least or from least to most. (See also **29c.**) In paragraph 13, Miller focusses on a series of social and economic conditions facing Native people, moving from the problems of everyday life to the possibility of early death.

13   The social and economic conditions in which natives in Canada live—or, more accurately, exist—are a national disgrace. Indian children are more likely than the general population to be born outside a stable nuclear family, are far less likely to complete enough schooling to obtain a job and become self-sustaining, are much more highly represented in the figures of unemployed and incarcerated people than the rest of the population, and have shorter life expectancy

than most others in the country. What is worse is the fact that these conditions have existed for close to a century, and have been known by governments and churches to exist for most of that time. Ottawa and the missionaries have tried unsuccessfully to impose their programs of economic development on Indians, Métis, and Inuit.

—J.R. MILLER, *Skyscrapers Hide the Heavens:*
A History of Indian-White Relations in Canada

Sometimes the movement within the paragraph is from **general to specific,** or from **specific to general.** A paragraph may begin with a general statement or idea, which is then supported by particular details (as in paragraph 14). Reversing the order, it may begin with a striking detail or series of details and conclude with a summarizing statement (as in paragraph 15).

14   The *conventions* of a period are the inherited, invented, and prescribed formulas that the people who formed its culture generally understood. The traditional arrangement of areas and rooms in a temple or dwelling, the larger-than-life representations and rigid postures of gods and rulers, the appearance of a masked deity or hero to pronounce the prologue and epilogue of a Greek drama, the required fourteen lines of a sonnet, the repeated rhythmic patterns of dances, the way characters speak in rhymed meters in poetic drama and sing their lines in opera—all are conveniences that became conventions through their acceptance by a representative number of people whose commonly held values and attitudes formed a culture.   —WILLIAM FLEMING, *Arts and Ideas*

15   If you have a morbid fear of peanut butter sticking to the roof of your mouth, there is a word for it: *arachibutyrophobia.* . . . And there's a word for describing a sudden breaking off of thought: *aposiopesis.* If you harbor an urge to look through the windows of the homes you pass, there is a word for the condition: *crytoscopophilia.* When you are just dropping off to sleep and you experience that sudden sensation

of falling, there is a word for it: it's a *myoclonic jerk*. If you want to say that a word has a circumflex on its penultimate syllable, without saying flat out that it has a circumflex there, there is a word for it: *properispomenon*. There is even a word for a figure of speech in which two connotative words linked by a conjunction express a complex notion that would normally be conveyed by an adjective and a substantive working together. It is a *hendiadys*. (But of course.) In English, in short, there are words for almost everything.

—BILL BRYSON, *Mother Tongue: English & How It Got That Way*

One common form of the general-specific pattern is **topic-restriction-illustration.** In this pattern, the writer announces the topic, restricts or qualifies it, and illustrates the restriction in the remaining sentences of the paragraph.

16   History reveals that every technology, however, beneficial, has costs. And almost always those costs cannot be anticipated or predicted. For example, one of the great scientific discoveries was penicillin. I vividly remember what a wonder drug it was when I caught pneumonia in the early 1950s. I was terribly sick and my father didn't think I would pull through, so he squandered the family savings to buy me a watch before I died. Then the doctor came and gave me a shot of penicillin, and overnight I was up and around. (I kept the watch.)

—DAVID SUZUKI, "Nuclear Menus (Or, Eating in the Nuclear Age)"

In paragraph 16 the general topic "technology and its unexpected costs" is introduced in the first two sentences. The next sentence restricts the topic to "the discovery of penicillin," and the remaining sentences illustrate its unexpected costs with the story of David Suzuki's bout of pneumonia.

In the **problem-solution** pattern the first sentence states a problem, and the solution follows:

17   Dinner is at eight, and so is your favorite television show. Solution? Tape the show on your video cassette recorder.

18   Two must-see shows are scheduled for the same hour? Watch one on your TV while taping the other on your VCR.

19   Want to see "Casablanca" tomorrow night? Rent a copy from your local video store, and pop it into your VCR.

—CONSUMER REPORTS

The topic sentences in the **question-answer** pattern asks a question and the supporting sentences answer it, as in paragraph 20.

20   What does he do, this business mogul, this multimillionaire, this comfortable man? He thinks up ways for people to dress. Fifty years ago he might have been a tailor or a dressmaker; if he had lived in France he would have been called a couturier. But to call Ralph Lauren a tailor is like calling the Bechtel Corporation a builder. The word does not convey the sheer size or the international scale of the operation. A tailor makes clothes; Lauren's corporation franchises manufacturers on four continents who turn out products that are sold in more than three hundred shops carrying his name, as well as in specialty boutiques in department stores in the United States, Canada, England, Italy, Switzerland, Scandinavia, Mexico, and Hong Kong. As it has grown, his business has also diversified. It started modestly, with neckties, but soon expanded to men's wear, then clothes for women, lately a special line for children. Now perfumes, soaps, cosmetics, shoes, luggage, belts, wallets, and eyeglasses all bear his imprimatur. Lauren's is that most modern of professions: he is the total fashion designer.

—WITOLD RYBCZYNSKI, *Home: A Short History of an Idea*

Paragraphs 11 through 20 illustrate seven of many possible types of clear arrangement within the paragraph. Any order, or any combination of orders, is satisfactory as long as it makes the sequence of thought clear.

■ **Exercise 3** Prepare to discuss how paragraphs with various arrangements of ideas might be developed by using (or building on) the information provided below.

COCKROACH

Description: An urban grasshopper, cynical, corrupt, dissatisfied, dangerous.

Habitat: Any city with more than a 50,000 population, and swank resort hotels in the tropics.

Habits: Defiance and survival. Likes to pop up from time to time to run across the tablecloths at really expensive restaurants.

Foods: Likes ethnic fare but will eat greedily anything that isn't tightly covered. Will take an occasional after-dinner cigar.

Comments: Cockroaches are perhaps the most unsung social force of all time. They were directly responsible for the great human migration to the suburbs in the 1950s and early 1960s, and thus they can be blamed for a wide variety of social ills.

—CHARLES A. MONAGAN, *The Reluctant Naturalist*

TRANSITIONS BETWEEN SENTENCES

The linking of sentences by transitional devices such as pronoun reference, repeated key words or ideas, appropriate conjunctions and other transitional expressions, and parallel structure helps create a coherent paragraph. Usually, several of these aids to coherence are found in a single paragraph:

Baby turtles in a turtle bowl are a puzzle in geometrics. They're as decorative as pansy petals, but they are also self-directed building blocks, propping themselves on one another in different arrangements, before upending the tower. The timid individuals turn fearless, or vice versa. If one gets a bit arrogant he will push the others off the rock and afterwards climb down into the water and cling to the back of one of those he has bullied, tickling him with his hind feet until he bucks like a bronco. On the other hand, when this same milder-mannered fellow isn't exerting himself, he will stare right into the face of the sun for hours. What could be more lionlike? And he's at home in or out of the water and does lots of metaphysical tilting. He sinks and rises, with an infinity of levels to choose from; or, elongating himself, he climbs out on the land again to perambulate, sits boxed in his box, and finally slides back in the water, submerging into dreams.

—EDWARD HOAGLAND, "The Courage of Turtles"

transitional expression

transitional expression

transitional expression

[Words and phrases relating to *turtles* are circled; those relating to *puzzles in geometrics* are placed in boxes. Pronouns are underlined.]

(1) Link sentences by using pronouns.

In paragraph 22 the writer links sentences by using the pronouns *their* and *they*. Although these same two pronouns are used repeatedly, their referent, "the native people," is always clear.

22   Now the industrial system beckons to the native people. But it does not merely beckon: it has intruded into their culture, economy and society, now pulling, now pushing them towards another, and in many ways an alien, way of life. In the North today, the native people are being urged to give up their life on the land; they are being told that their days and their lives should become partitioned like our own. We have often urged that their commitment to the industrial system be entire and complete. Native people have even been told that they cannot compromise: they must become industrial workers, or go naked back to the bush.

—THOMAS BERGER, *Northern Frontier, Northern Homeland*

(2) Link sentences by repeating key words or ideas.

In paragraph 23, the repetition of the key words "sick and tired" links the sentences. (The repetition also provides emphasis: see **29e**.)

23   I was sick and tired of January, and sick and tired of February following January year after year like famine and pestilence following war. I was sick and tired of football, and sick and tired of football being followed by ice hockey and basketball as pestilentially as February followed January. I was especially sick and tired of people interrupting my grouch with commands to smile and cheer up. I was sick and tired of everything except being sick and tired of it all, which I enjoyed immensely.

—RUSSELL BAKER, "Confessions of a Three-Day Grouch"

(3) **Link sentences by using conjunctions and other transitional expressions.**

Here is a list of some frequently used transitional connectives arranged according to the kinds of relationships they establish.

1. *Alternative and addition:* or, nor, and, and then, moreover, further, furthermore, besides, likewise, also, too, again, in addition, even more important, next, first, second, third, in the first place, in the second place, finally, last.

2. *Comparison:* similarly, likewise, in like manner.

3. *Contrast:* but, yet, or, and yet, however, still, nevertheless, on the other hand *(to be used together with "on the one hand"),* on the contrary, conversely, even so, notwithstanding, for all that, in contrast, at the same time, although this may be true, otherwise, nonetheless.

4. *Place:* here, beyond, nearby, opposite to, adjacent to, on the opposite side.

5. *Purpose:* to this end, for this purpose, with this object.

6. *Cause, result:* so, for, hence, therefore, accordingly, consequently, thus, thereupon, as a result, then.

7. *Summary, repetition, exemplification, intensification:* to sum up, in brief, on the whole, in sum, in short, as I have said, in other words, that is, to be sure, as has been noted, for example, for instance, in fact, indeed, to tell the truth, in any event.

8. *Time:* meanwhile, at length, soon, after a few days, in the meantime, afterward, later, now, then, in the past.

(4) Link sentences by means of parallel structure.

Parellelism is the repetition of the sentence pattern or of other grammatical structures. See also Section **26**.

In paragraph 24, the author uses parallel constructions in almost every sentence. This, combined with repetition of the phrase "I have seen," strengthens the impression of repeated, first-hand experience and prepares the reader for the summing up in the final sentence.

24   On the Old Crow Flats, in the Mackenzie Delta, and along the Beaufort Sea coast I have seen the immense flocks of birds that migrate in their thousands to this arctic area each summer. I have seen the white whales swimming in the shallow coastal waters of the Beaufort Sea around the Mackenzie Delta. I have seen the Porcupine caribou herd in early summer at its calving grounds in the Northern Yukon, and the Bathurst herd at its wintering grounds north of Great Slave Lake. And in every native village I have seen the meat and fish, the fur and hides that the people have harvested from the land and water.

—THOMAS BERGER, *Northern Frontier, Northern Homeland*

■ **Exercise 4**   Prepare for a class discussion of the specific linking devices (pronouns, transitional words, repetition, parallelism) used in the following paragraph.

25   By about the beginning of the sixteenth century, table manners began to move in the direction of today's standards. The importance attached to them is indicated by the phenomenal success of a treatise, *On Civility in Children,* by the philosopher Erasmus, which appeared in 1530; reprinted more than thirty times in the next six years, it also appeared in numerous translations. Erasmus' idea of good table manners was far from modern, but it did represent an advance. He believed, for example, that an upper-class diner was distinguished by putting only three fingers of one hand into the bowl, instead of the entire hand in the manner of the lower

class. Wait a few moments after being seated before you dip
into it, he advises. Do not poke around in your dish, but take
the first piece you touch. Do not put chewed food from the
mouth back on your plate; instead, throw it under the table
or behind your chair.

—PETER FARB AND GEORGE ARMELAGOS,
Consuming Passions: The Anthropology of Eating

■ **Exercise 5** Revise the sentences in the following paragraph
so that the thought flows smoothly from one sentence to the
next.

   Cable television sounds like a good deal at first. All available local channels can be piped in to a television set for a relatively low cost per month. The reception is clear—a real
bonus in fringe and rural areas—and in addition several channels for news and local access are in the basic monthly fee. A
cable connection to a second or third TV set costs extra. In
most places subscribers have to pay as much as thirty dollars
a month extra to get the desirable channels like CNN,
Newsworld, Arts & Entertainment and the Sports Network.
Although the movies change each month, the pay-TV movie
channels run the same films over and over during a month's
time. Many of the films offered each month are box office
flops or reruns of old movies that can be viewed on regular
channels. Cable television isn't really a bargain.

(5) **Provide clear transitions between paragraphs**.

Clear writing depends on clear transitions between paragraphs as well as between sentences.
   For example, read paragraph 26, in which the economist
Galbraith introduces Karl Marx's criticisms of capitalist
theory. Then observe the types of transitional devices used
in the first sentences of subsequent paragraphs that summarize Marx's views.

26

> The vulnerable points in the capitalist system and its interpretation were, as he saw them, first, the distribution of power—which had been effectively and almost universally ignored by the classical economists.
>
> Second, there was the highly unequal distribution of income. . . .
>
> Third, there was the susceptibility of the economic system to crises and unemployment—in modern terms, to depression. . . .
>
> Finally, there was monopoly, a flaw that was conceded by the classical tradition. But for Marx this was not an isolated phenomenon; it reflected a basic tendency, one that would be decisive in the final fate of capitalism.
>
> —JOHN KENNETH GALBRAITH,
> *Economics in Perspective*

transitional expressions and parallel constructions

repetition of words/ideas

The closely related words in each of the groups that follow are often placed at or near the beginnings of sentences to link ideas in separate paragraphs (as illustrated in paragraph 26) or within a paragraph.

1. First. . . . Second. . . . Third. . . .
2. First. . . . Then. . . . Next. . . . Finally. . . .

3. Then. . . . Now. . . . Soon. . . . Later. . . .

4. One. . . . Another. . . . Still another. . . .

5. Some. . . . Others. . . . Still others. . . .

6. A few. . . . Many. . . . More. . . . Most. . . .

7. Just as significant. . . . More important. . . .
   Most important of all. . . .

Sometimes a transitional paragraph serves as a bridge between two paragraphs. Ordinarily, such a paragraph is short (often consisting of only one sentence) because the writer intends it to be merely a signpost. Notice below that the first noun phrase in the transitional paragraph 28 echoes the preceding key idea and that the second noun phrase points to a fact to be explained next.

27   Indeed, instead of seeing evolution as a smooth process, many of today's life scientists and archeologists are studying the "theory of catastrophes" to explain "gaps" and "jumps" in the multiple branches of the evolutionary record. Others are studying small changes that may have been amplified through feedback into sudden structural transformations. Heated controversies divide the scientific community over every one of these issues.

28   **But all such controversies are dwarfed by a single history-changing fact.**

29   One day in 1953 at Cambridge in England a young biologist, James Watson, was sitting in the Eagle pub when his colleague, Francis Crick, ran excitedly in and announced to "everyone within hearing distance that we had found the secret of life." They had. Watson and Crick had unraveled the structure of DNA.

—ALVIN TOFFLER, *The Third Wave*

32c
Develop the paragraph adequately.

Many short paragraphs are adequately developed. A one-sentence paragraph such as the following supplies enough information to satisfy the reader.

30   The village contains a railway station which hasn't been used since 1965 when the CNR discontinued passenger service in that part of northwestern New Brunswick, a one-room school that was closed five years ago when the government began using buses to carry local children to the regional school in Cumberland Centre, a general store and two churches: St. Edward's Anglican, which used to be attended by the station agent, the teacher and the store-keeper, and the Fire-Baptized Tabernacle of the Living God, attended by practically everyone else in Indian River.

—ALDEN NOWLAN, *Miracle at Indian River*

Sometimes, however, short paragraphs (especially a series of them) are a sign of inadequate development of the idea. Sometimes the solution is to combine the paragraphs if they deal with the same idea. If not, each paragraph should be expanded so that the thought is adequately developed.

PARAGRAPHS THAT SHOULD BE COMBINED

    The line of demarcation between capitalism and socialism is sharp and clear.

    Capitalism is that form of organization in which the means of production—and by that is meant the machine and the funds required to use the machine—are controlled by private individuals or by privately owned organizations.

    Under a socialist regime the control of the means of production, the control of capital—for even socialists concede the need for capital—is by the group. Under capitalism the profits accrue to the private individual; under socialism, to the group.

Taken separately, these three paragraphs are short and choppy; if combined, they would form a paragraph adequately developing an idea stated in the first sentence and clarified in the last.

The following paragraphs (from different compositions) stop before supplying enough information to satisfy an interested reader.

PARAGRAPHS THAT SHOULD BE EXPANDED

Many adoptees searching for their natural parents have similar experiences. A few of the stories they tell, however, are unique. [Which kinds of experiences are similar? Which kinds unique?]

Forestry work is healthful, educational, and financially rewarding. For example, a forester soon learns how to prevent and to fight forest fires. [The reader expects to find out about three aspects of forestry work, but the writer comments briefly on only the educational benefit. How is the work healthful? What else does a forester learn? What are the financial rewards?]

If the paragraphs in your compositions tend to be inadequately developed, study the methods of paragraph development described and illustrated in **32d**.

32d
Learn to use various methods of paragraph development.

You can learn to write good paragraphs by studying the various techniques professional writers use to develop ideas. All the strategies for developing paragraphs discussed in the following pages are equally useful for developing whole compositions. (See also Section **33**.)

The more you read, the more you will find that paragraphs are rarely developed by a single method; a combination of methods is more common. No one method, or no one combination, is better than another except insofar as it better suits the writer's purpose in a given paragraph. As you study the following illustrations of good paragraphs, notice how each main idea is worked out.

(1) Develop the main idea by supplying relevant specific details.

The main idea of a paragraph often brings specific details to mind. Consider, for example, "Another person's mind is the most engrossing of all the puzzles in the world." This statement raises such questions as "How is the mind a puzzle?" and "For whom is it a puzzle?" and "What is puzzling about it?" By answering these questions, and choosing details with care (omitting irrelevant details, no matter how interesting they are in themselves), the writer can develop the main idea effectively—as in the following paragraph.

31   Another person's mind is the most engrossing of all the puzzles in the world. This is what first catches the attention of children from the moment speech begins to take hold. Earlier in infancy the mind seems totally preoccupied by the most personal needs: food, warmth, comfort, the mother. But with speech at hand the child begins paying close attention to the world around, which means people, all needing to explain themselves. Tell me why, the child says with his first words—not why any particular phenomenon but why everything? Why you? Why the world? What are you thinking? Tell me the world.

    —LEWIS THOMAS, *Et Cetera, Et Cetera: Notes of a Word-Watcher*

(2) Illustrate a generalization using several closely related examples or one striking example.

Examples are especially useful for illustrating a generalization that a reader might question or might not understand. A paragraph developed by examples begins with a statement that is followed by one or more examples to illustrate it.

32   The modern corporation has deep historical roots. One goes back to the Middle Ages and before, ever since substantial trade in goods has been carried out over a distance. This is the merchant caravan or, at sea, the convoy. In a caravan, merchants gained the strength of numbers and organization against predators such as highwaymen, toll collectors, locally entrenched business competitors, monopolistic suppliers, and tax-hungry politicians. The Silk Route from China to Damascus was traversed by such caravans, and so were the routes to leading market cities in Europe. In Renaissance Europe, the famous East India companies organized by the British, Dutch, and French provided merchant ventures with strength in oceangoing ventures.
                —ARTHUR FLEISCHER, GEOFFREY C. HAZARD,
                        and MIRIAM Z. KLIPPER, *Board Games*
[Numerous examples illustrate the generalization.]

33   He was one of the greatest scientists the world has ever known, yet if I had to convey the essence of Albert Einstein in a single word, I would choose *simplicity*. Perhaps an anecdote will help. Once, caught in a downpour, he took off his hat and held it under his coat. Asked why, he explained, with admirable logic, that the rain would damage the hat, but his hair would be none the worse for its wetting. This knack for going instinctively to the heart of the matter was the secret of his major scientific discoveries—this and his extraordinary feeling for beauty.
                —BANESH HOFFMAN, "My Friend, Albert Einstein"
[A single example, an anecdote, illustrates Einstein's simplicity.]

(3) Narrate a series of events.

Narrative paragraphs present a series of events, normally in the order in which they occur. (Longer narratives often begin in the middle of a sequence of events and contain flashbacks to earlier events.)

In paragraph 34, O.B. Hardison uses a narrative to illustrate his point about the convergence of human beings and their machines, and the anxiety arising from that convergence.

34   In one of Rod Serling's "Twilight Zone" episodes, a man is injured in an automobile accident. His arm is badly cut. He opens the folds of the cut. Inside his arm are transistors and wires. He is stunned. He had always assumed he was human. Now he must acknowledge that he is an android. Should he tell his family? Are there any human beings left? At some time in the future that question may become unanswerable, but by that time it will not make any difference.

—O.B. HARDISON, JR., *Disappearing through the Skylight: Culture and Technology in the Twentieth Century*

(4) Explain a process.

Process paragraphs explain how something is done or made. For this reason, they often have a temporal element that makes a step-by-step chronological arrangement both possible and natural, as in paragraph 35.

35   The best of all scientific tricks with an egg is the well-known one in which air pressure forces a peeled hard-boiled egg into a glass milk bottle and then forces it out again undamaged. The mouth of the bottle must be only slightly smaller than the egg, and so you must be careful not to use too large an egg or too small a bottle. To get the egg through the mouth you must heat the air in the bottle. That is best done by standing the bottle in boiling water for a few minutes. Put the

egg upright on the mouth and take the bottle off the stove. As the air in the bottle cools it contracts, creating a partial vacuum that draws the peeled egg inside. To get the egg out again invert the bottle so that the egg falls into the neck. Place the opening of the bottle against your mouth and blow vigorously. This will compress the air in the bottle. When you stop blowing, the air expands, pushing the egg through the neck of the bottle and into your waiting hands.

—MARTIN GARDNER, "Mathematical Games"

(5) Show cause and effect.

A paragraph developed by causal analysis must not only raise the question *why* (directly or indirectly) but answer it to the satisfaction of the reader. The cause or causes must satisfactorily explain the result.

Paragraph 36 shows how the constraint of writing in Chinese and the exclusion of Japanese women from higher studies accounted for the effect named in the opening sentence.

36   For one brief and shining moment in world literature, writing "in feminine" gave women an edge in creative expression. Japanese nobility during the tenth-century Heian period believed the Chinese language was superior to their own. They reserved Chinese for higher study barred to women, and they attempted to write their serious work in Chinese as well, in much the same manner that Western scholars used Latin and Greek. While they struggled to master the square, formal characters of a foreign language, women of the court were free to use *kana,* a simplified, phonetic script, to set down the language they actually spoke. Permitted a fluidity and a native idiom that men denied themselves, Murasaki Shikibu (Lady Murasaki), author of *The Tale of Genji,* and Sei Shonagon, author of *The Pillow Book,* produced the lasting masterworks of their age.

—SUSAN BROWNMILLER, *Femininity*

(6) Use classification to relate ideas.

To classify is to group things in categories. Classification is a method for understanding or explaining a large or diverse subject and discovering the relationships within it. For example, of a variety of trees, black oak, sycamore, and cottonwood may be classified as deciduous; cedar, fir, and pine as evergreen. In paragraph 37, White classifies three views of New York.

37   There are roughly three New Yorks. There is, first, the New York of the man or woman who was born there, who takes the city for granted and accepts its size and its turbulence as natural and inevitable. Second, there is the New York of the commuter—the city that is devoured by locusts each day and spat out each night. Third, there is the New York of the person who was born somewhere else and came to New York in quest of something. Of these three trembling cities the greatest is the last—the city of final destination, the city that is a goal. It is this third city that accounts for New York's high-strung disposition, its poetical deportment, its dedication to the arts, and its incomparable achievements. Commuters give the city its tidal restlessness, natives give it solidity and continuity, but the settlers give it passion. And whether it is a farmer arriving from Italy to set up a small grocery store in a slum, or a young girl arriving from a small town in Mississippi to escape the indignity of being observed by her neighbors, or a boy arriving from the Corn Belt with a manuscript in his suitcase and a pain in his heart, it makes no difference: each embraces New York with the fresh eyes of an adventurer, each generates heat and light to dwarf the Consolidated Edison Company.

—E.B. WHITE, "Here Is New York"

(7) Formulate a definition.

Paragraphs of definition explain. As in the following paragraph, a *formal* definition explains a thing (viruses) by putting it in a class (infectious agents) and then by distinguishing it from other members of that class (small size, simple composition, and so on).

38   Viruses are a unique group of infectious agents that are characterized by their small size, simple composition, and the need to grow in an animal, plant, or bacterial cell. In general, viruses are much smaller than bacteria, ranging in size from 20 to 400 nanometres (nm) in diameter (1 nanometre = 10^{-9} metre). They are composed of a core of nucleic acid, a coat of protein, and in some cases, lipid (fatty) and carbohydrate material. Viruses vary in their detailed morphology (form and structure) and in their specificity for different types of host cells.

—WILLIAM COFIELD SUMMERS,
"Viruses," *Britannica Macropaedia,* 15th Edition, 1987

An *informal* definition differs from a formal definition in that it does not rely on the formula of class and differentiation. It defines by describing, narrating, comparing, or providing examples or synonyms. Paragraph 39 illustrates an informal definition that relies on description and narration.

39   In the 1970s, leading academics and educators began demonstrating that a "whole language" program might be the most effective method of teaching children to read and write. Under such an approach, children initially experience a story—not a text created by a textbook writer, but a real story not intended to "teach" anything—by reading it themselves or by having it read to them by their teacher. After this initial reading, students are directed through activities designed to prompt them to respond to the ideas, the sentences, the words, and other components of the story they have just experienced. A whole language program operates on the premise that children learn to read if they are interested in what they are reading. Thus, the stories used in a whole language reading program must be high-quality

literary works that are likely to appeal to a child's interests and imagination. The activities accompanying each story are often discussion-centred, drama-based, and thought-provoking, designed to retain interest while teaching language arts skills.   —DAVID BOOTH, *Censorship Goes to School*

(8) Describe by presenting an orderly sequence of sensory details.

An effective description presents carefully chosen details in some clear order, for instance, from near to far, from general to particular, from right to left, from top to bottom. Moving in such a way, it provides an orderly scheme so that the reader can visualize what you are describing.

In paragraph 40, Peter Newman presents the details of the dress of the voyageurs, moving from footwear to headgear.

40   They [the Voyageurs] kept their hair long so that a shake of the head would help drive away the marauding summer insects. Short and bulky like Belgian workhorses, they took the pride of dandies in their simple but distinctive dress code. They wore deer- or moose-skin moccasins with no socks, corduroy trousers and sky blue *capots* (hooded frock coats with brass buttons) over red-and-black flannel shirts. The pants were tied at the knees with beadwork garters and held at the waist with crimson handwoven sashes—the famous *ceintures fléchées*. One variation was an embroidered buckskin coat, its seams decorated with bear hair; when caught by the wind after a rainstorm, the garment would make a strange and desolate sound like the ground drumming of a grouse. Choice of hats expressed at least a touch of individuality. Some wore high, scarlet-tasselled night bonnets, others coarse blue cloth caps with peaks, or toques or colourful handkerchiefs wound into turbans. The Northmen proclaimed their vanity by sticking what they called "ostrich plumes" into their headgear, though these were usually dyed chicken feathers—and, sometimes, fox tails.   —PETER C. NEWMAN, *Caesars of the Wilderness*

(9) Analyze the parts of a subject.

Analysis breaks an object or idea into its elements and examines the relationships among them. In paragraph 41 the author analyzes the parts of a factory trawler.

41   Common to all factory trawlers are four essential elements that set them apart from the generations of fishing vessels that preceded them. These are a stern ramp or slipway for the rapid recovery of nets from astern (rather than over the side), a sheltered belowdecks factory section with assembly-line machines to gut and fillet fish (as opposed to cleaning by hand on an exposed main deck), an ammonia or freon refrigerating plant for the quick freezing and frozen storage of fish (in place of heavy and space-consuming chopped ice), and equipment to make fishmeal (to utilize both the factory leavings and trash or nonmarketable fish).

—WILLIAM W. WARNER,
Distant Water: The Fate of the North American Fisherman

(10) Compare or contrast to develop a main idea.

A comparison points out similarities; a contrast points out differences. A comparison or contrast may be organized in either of two ways (or a combination of them), the choice depending on the writer's purpose. Paragraph 42 illustrates a part-by-part organization: it first identifies the two items being compared or contrasted (beggars and "respectable people"), and then it alternates between them as it considers various characteristics.

42   Yet if one looks closely one sees that there is no *essential* difference between a beggar's livelihood and that of numberless respectable people. Beggars do not work, it is said; but then, what is *work?* A navvy works by swinging a pick. An accountant works by adding up figures. A beggar works by standing out of doors in all weathers and getting

varicose veins, chronic bronchitis, etc. It is a trade like any other; quite useless, of course—but, then, many reputable trades are quite useless. And as a social type a beggar compares well with scores of others. He is honest compared with the sellers of most patent medicines, high-minded compared with a Sunday newspaper proprietor, amiable compared with a hire-purchase tout—in short, a parasite, but a fairly harmless parasite. He seldom extracts more than a bare living from the community, and, what should justify him according to our ethical ideas, he pays for it over and over in suffering. I do not think there is anything about a beggar that sets him in a different class from other people, or gives most modern men the right to despise him.

—GEORGE ORWELL, *Down and Out in Paris and London*

Paragraph 43 illustrates a whole-by-whole organization, which treats all the pertinent qualities of one item being compared or contrasted (men's faces) before going on to treat the corresponding qualities in the next item (women's faces).

43   Women do not simply have faces, as men do; they are identified with their faces. Men have a naturalistic relation to their faces. Certainly they care whether they are good-looking or not. They suffer over acne, protruding ears, tiny eyes; they hate getting bald. But there is a much wider latitude in what is esthetically acceptable in a man's face than what is in a woman's. A man's face is defined as something he basically doesn't need to tamper with; all he has to do is keep it clean. He can avail himself of the options for ornament supplied by nature: a beard, a mustache, longer or shorter hair. But he is not supposed to disguise himself. What he is "really" like is supposed to show. A man lives through his face; it records the progressive stages of his life. And since he doesn't tamper with his face, it is not separate from but is completed by his body—which is judged attractive by the impression it gives of virility and energy. By contrast, a woman's face is potentially separate from her

body. She does not treat it naturalistically. A woman's face is the canvas upon which she paints a revised, corrected portrait of herself. One of the rules of this creation is that the face *not* show what she doesn't want it to show. Her face is an emblem, an icon, a flag. How she arranges her hair, the type of make-up she uses, the quality of her complexion—all these are signs, not of what she is "really" like, but of how she asks to be treated by others, especially men. They establish her status as an "object."

—SUSAN SONTAG, "The Double Standard of Aging"

Sometimes a concept can be vividly conveyed by an analogy, a kind of comparison in which one thing is explained by its similarities to something more familiar. (See also **20a[4]**.) Notice in the next paragraph how Roger Shattuck compares literature and wine.

44   Literature has two advantages over wine. A good book ages forever; and you can read it as often as you wish without diminishing its substance. The devoted reader is like a wine lover whose dream has come true. His stock will never spoil or be consumed. He can sample, enjoy, and share his cellar without fear of depleting his reserve; it will grow as he grows. He never need go thirsty.

—ROGER SHATTUCK, "How to Rescue Literature"

(11) Use a combination of methods to develop the main idea.

Many good paragraphs are developed not by one specific method but by a combination of methods. Some good paragraphs almost defy analysis. The important consideration is not that a specific method is used to develop the paragraph but that the development is clear, complete, and appropriate. Notice the combination of methods in each of the following paragraphs.

45   "Trifles make the sum of life," said David Copperfield; and novelists and essayists share that principle. A book is chambered like a beehive, and prose is like comb honey—honey sweeter (to its devotees) because it has its wax still on. Going the other way, from fifteen years of essay writing to doing a novel again, can be exhilarating, as I later found, because one is inventing, not simply recording, the world. I could myth-make a little, draw things a bit differently from how they were, grab for the brass ring, go larger than life, escape the nitty-gritty of reality for a while. Novelists want the site of their drama to be ground zero, but most of us do not live at ground zero. Most of us live like stand-up comedians on a vaudeville stage—the way an essayist does—by our humble wits, messing up, swallowing an aspirin, knowing Hollywood won't call, thinking no one we love will die today, just another day of sunshine and rain.

—EDWARD HOAGLAND, "To the Point: Truths Only Essays Can Tell"
[The first sentence announces the topic, which is then developed by comparison, analogy, and specific details.]

46   The ideal ballet body is long limbed with a small compact torso. This makes for beauty of line; the longer the arms and legs the more exciting the body line. The ideal ballet foot has a high taut instep and a wide stretch in the Achilles' tendon. This tendon is the spring on which a dancer pushes for his jump, the hinge on which he takes the shock of landing. If there is one tendon in a dancer's body more important than any other, it is this tendon. It is, I should say, the prerequisite for all great technique. When the heel does not stretch easily and softly like a cat's, as mine did not, almost to the point of malformation, the shock of running or jumping must be taken somewhere in the spine by sticking out behind, for instance, in a sitting posture after every jump. I seemed to be all rusty wire and safety pins. My torso was long with unusually broad hips, my legs and arms abnormally short, my hands and feet broad and short. I was besides fat. What I did not know was that I was constructed for endurance and that I developed through effort alone a capacity for outperforming far, far better technicians. Because I was built like a mustang, stocky, mettlesome and sturdy, I became a good jumper, growing special compensating muscles up the front of my shins for the lack of a helpful heel. But the long, cool, serene classic line was forever denied me.

—AGNES DE MILLE, *Dance to the Piper*

[The paragraph is developed by definition, description, and cause and effect.]

■ **Exercise 6**   Prepare for a class discussion of the following paragraphs. Bear in mind unity, organization, coherence, and development.

47   In studies of perception, subjects were fitted with goggles that turned their visual image upside down. The goggles were worn constantly, the subjects having to adjust to an upside-down world as best they could. After several days, however, the visual process suddenly *righted* that upside-down vision of the world. After a time the goggles were removed. And immediately the world was seen *upside down* again. After about the same period of adjustment time, however, the inordinately complex relationship between eye-brain-mind again reversed the reversal, and turned that world view back upright.

—JOSEPH CHILTON PEARCE, *Exploring the Crack in the Cosmic Egg*

48   There are two basic kinds of literature. One helps you to understand, the other helps you to forget; the first helps you to be a free person and a free citizen, the other helps people to manipulate you. One is like astronomy, the other is like astrology.

—STEPHEN VIZINCZEY, *Truth and Lies in Literature*

49   *The West,* of course, meant us, that is, the three prairie provinces, especially Manitoba and Saskatchewan. Alberta just barely qualified—it was a little too close to those mountains for our entire trust. We sometimes suspected that Albertans had more in common with *The Coast* than they did with us. *The Coast* meant only one thing—British Columbia. As far as we were concerned, there was only one coast. The eastern coast, presumably, was so distant as to be beyond our ken. *The Coast* was a kind of Lotus Land which

we half scorned and half envied. All prairie people, as was well known, wanted to retire there. Think of it—a land with no winter, semi-tropical beaches, breezes which were invariably balmy; a land where the apricots and apples virtually dropped into your mouth. Jerusalem the Golden, with milk and honey blest—that was how we thought of it. At the same time we considered in our puritanical hearts that our climate was healthier, as we sneezed our way through the desperate winter and thawed our white-frozen ears and knees gently, not too close to the stove, as we had been taught.   —MARGARET LAURENCE, *Heart of a Stranger*

50   Tall, gangling, black curls flopping about his neck, a bantering, deprecating smile on his full lips, he looked more like a provincial theatrical manager than a statesman. He was blest with that rarest of political talents: a sense of humour. An American senator's wife once found herself chatting with a thin backwoodsy fellow who offered that he was from Canada. She remarked that she had heard about "a smart man up there," one John A. Macdonald, but that he was a "regular rascal." Her acquaintance solemnly agreed. "Why do the Canadians keep such a man in power?" the woman asked, "They say he's a real scalawag." "Well," came the answer, "they can't seem to get on without him." At this point the Senator came up and introduced his wife formally to Macdonald. The Prime Minister laughed and soothed the lady's confusion. "Don't apologize," he said. "All you have said is perfectly true and well known at home."   —W.L. MORTON and L.F. HANNON, *This Land, These People*

51   Quotation marks should be used honestly and sparingly, when there is a genuine quotation at hand, and it is necessary to be very rigorous about the words enclosed by the marks. If something is to be quoted, the *exact* words must be used. If part of it must be left out because of space limitations, it is good manners to insert three dots to indicate the omission, but it is unethical to do so if this means connecting two thoughts which the original author did not intend to have tied together. Above all, quotation marks should not be used for ideas that you'd like to disown, things in the air so to speak.

Nor should they be put in place around clichés; if you want to use a cliché you must take full responsibility for it yourself and not try to fob it off on anon., or on society. The most objectionable misuse of quotation marks, but one which illustrates the dangers of misuse in ordinary prose, is seen in advertising, especially in advertisements for small restaurants, for example "just around the corner," or "a good place to eat." No single, identifiable, citable person ever really said, for the record, "just around the corner," much less "a good place to eat," least likely of all for restaurants of the type that use this type of prose.

—LEWIS THOMAS, "Notes on Punctuation"

52   Many researchers say that violent TV and movie images lead to increased violence in society. They also point out that children witness an enormous amount of violence on television. Gregory Fouts, a psychology professor at the University of Calgary who has studied the effect of television on the behavior of children, says that there are, on average, 25 to 27 acts of violence an hour in children's programming, which is made up largely of cartoons. Brian Bontekoe, who teaches media literacy at the Kingston Collegiate and Vocational Institute in Ontario, said that television producers rely on visually jarring and noisy scenes, or "jolts per minute," to hold the attention of their viewers.

—D'ARCY JENISH, "Prime-Time Violence"

53   I feel . . . that there is a close connection among three aspects of langauge in our society. First is the associative squirrel-chatter that one hears on streets, and even in college halls, jerking along apologetically or defiantly in a series of unshaped phrases, using slang or vogue words for emphasis and punctuation. Second is the poetic illiteracy which regards anything in a verse as a verbal puzzle, not even a puzzle to be worked out, but a disdainful and inscrutable puzzle without an answer. Third is the dead, senseless, sentenceless, written pseudo-prose that surrounds us like a boa constrictor, which is said to cover its victims with slime before strangling them. This last, under the names of jargon,

gobbledygook, and the like, has often enough been recognized as a disease of contemporary language and ridiculed or deplored as such.   —NORTHROP FRYE, *The Well-Tempered Critic*

54   I thought of the country as a retreat, a quiet place, where life would be simple and pleasant and cheap, and where I could cut down on the need I have felt most of my adult life to make as much money as I could just to stay even. Well, quiet and simple and pleasant it has been, I assure you, but cheap? I might as well have bought a racehorse. I pay rent on my mailbox and tax on my trees. Fertilizer costs money so the grass will grow long, and the local university student charges me to keep it, occasionally, short. The tomatoes I have tried to grow have been more expensive—if better— than those I could buy in a city supermarket, and I have not been able to put up the capital to buy equipment to do my own preserves. Even my daily newspaper, which I have to use gasoline to go to buy, costs me more than it would have cost in the city. At times I have looked at my city friends the way the have provinces have looked at the have-nots in a federal conference, as if I were subsidizing them and they didn't realize it.   —PETER GZOWSKI, *The Morningside Papers*

55   Some of the eagles and ravens which topped the totem poles were really magnificent. Certain carvers projected the upper part of the great black eye-pupil of their birds to give the impression that the creature was looking earthward. Bird eyes were humanly shaped and deep-set. They were frequently overhung by a heavy eyebrow painted black. The eyeball was shown in an oblong of white such as the human eye has. These crest birds, endowed with supernatural powers, were supposed to see more, hear more, know more than ordinary birds. Ravens and eagles were provided with huge square ears, one on either side of the top of the head. Birds that had wings wide spread were crudely braced from the back to prevent the wind from tearing the wings away. Cumbersome, heavy as was the build of these wooden birds, you felt the lift and sweep of the carved wings amazingly.

—EMILY CARR, *The Heart of a Peacock*

The Whole Composition

33

Learn to plan, draft, and revise your compositions effectively.

Whenever you write you develop, for some purpose, an appropriate subject for a certain audience. Focussing the subject and shaping a thesis statement will help you choose the information you will include, plan an appropriate arrangement, and draft your essay. You will probably revise several drafts before preparing a final version.

This process of planning, drafting, and revision is seldom as neat and straightforward as inexperienced writers may suppose. As you move through the process, you may need to engage in any of the activities several times. For example, you may need to go back and collect more ideas. Or you may write a draft only to discover that you have strayed from your main idea (or thesis). Such a discovery is not the catastrophe it may seem at first: writing is one of the best ways of clarifying your own views and gaining new insights. You may want to go back and change your thesis, or even throw it out and start with a new one. Whatever repetition of the steps in the process is necessary, the effort will be worthwhile if the result is a clear, coherent, unified essay.

As you read the following composition, observe how effectively Richard Preston marshals an abundance of sharply observed details to communicate his experience and knowledge of a commonplace subject—ice.

Ice

1   A pond sits in the middle of the woods on a windless night. The moon has set. A few leaves hang on emptied branches. Winter constellations gleam in the water. Molecules of water dance with each other. On the brink of becoming crystals, they break up, gather again. As the liquid skin of the pond cools below the freezing point, the pond's surface expands slightly. The surface becomes a wobbly lattice of water molecules, a kind of "flowing crystal." It is tensing itself. Now, in silence from rocks at the water's edge, needles of ice begin to grow. Pure water cannot freeze; it must build on a solid object. Ice can grow from a floating leaf, a root, the wing of a dead moth, a microscopic speck. Even a stray snowflake can start ice. If the snowflake happens to be a needle, it will send a spear shooting in a single direction; if the snowflake is a hexagonal star, it will throw a radiance of blades from all six points.

2   A trellis of ribs is growing toward the center of the pond. Sometimes the ice hisses as it moves. Meanwhile, crystals of ice that look like upside-down Christmas trees reach their way downward under the water. By morning, fish observe the sun as though through a cathedral window.

3   If the weather holds, the pond will soon reverberate with the whisk and click of skates. Why is ice so slippery? At normal temperatures, ice has a layer of water a few hundred molecules thick on its surface. Anything rubbed across it enlarges that liquid layer through frictional heating. A skate's blade *floats* on water.

4   Scientists like to speak of the "habits" of ice, as if ice were a creature. Nearly all substances, when they cool from liquid to solid, become denser, heavier. They form into a few predictable crystal shapes. Not water. It becomes lighter, emptier, 9 per cent bigger by volume, able

to float on itself. Water assumes a frenzy of solid forms. In addition to eighty known types of snow crystal, it becomes hoar, rime, silver thaw, depth hoar, subsoil lenses, bergs, mushrooms on the sea floor, glaciers that ooze like tar, arctic clouds 50 miles high that glow after midnight, and the labyrinth of frost on a windowpane. Two hundred billion balls of ice circle the sun outside the orbit of Pluto. The largest ice crystals on Earth are under Siberia, 2 feet in diameter and as old as the pyramids.

5 It is a lucky thing that ice floats. Otherwise, the oceanic abysses might gradually fill with sunken ice until the planet froze. But ice is an excellent insulator. It keeps lakes warm and fish alive. Ten million crystals in a cubic foot of snow trap dead air like goose down; a quilt wraps the earth in winter. Underneath a layer of fluffy snow, the ground temperature can be 50 degrees higher than the air above. Pheasants, grouse, rabbits, bears, meadow mice, spring peepers, beetle larvae, and many dormant plants depend on the snow's protection for survival.

6 According to its habits, ice plays with light. Arctic explorers have reported flashes in the darkness when sea ice moves. Plates of ice floating in water give off blue light when they snap. Nobody knows why. Hexagonal prisms in the upper air cleave light from the sun and moon into spots, pillars, arcs, and rings of iridescence. They portend snow.

7 To the Apollo astronauts Earth was a blue-and-white disk. The blue was water; the white was clouds and the polar caps—and many of those clouds were ice. Earth could be considered a fairly icy planet. Ice covers one quarter of the globe every year, including land and sea. Eighty per cent of the earth's fresh water is locked up in cold storage at the poles. It would melt into 8 billion *billion* gallons of water.

8 A melting pond adds only a drop to the planet's fresh water. As spring comes and sun warms the ice, water molecules spin away from their crystalline bonds. The pond's ice vanishes in a day. But it is still there, lurking hidden in the structure of water, as molecules dance with each other, waiting for the cold nights of next year. Ice keeps to its own habits.   —RICHARD M. PRESTON

Essays like Preston's, seemingly so natural and effortless, are the result of hard work. Experienced writers wrestle with the same writing activities inexperienced writers do: planning, drafting, and especially revising. For almost everyone, writing is a process of returning again and again to the various writing tasks, adjusting and fine-tuning until the result is a unified, coherent, and well-developed composition.

33a
Consider the purpose of your composition.

Writing is never done in a vacuum; the writer is always in a particular situation that involves some purpose—some reason for writing. The clearer the purpose is in the writer's mind, the more successful the writing is likely to be. The purposes of non-fiction writing are often classified as expressive, informative, and persuasive. Although these purposes are usually combined in an extended piece of writing, one of them almost always predominates.

Expressive writing emphasizes the writer's feelings and reactions to the world—to people, objects, events, and ideas. Some examples of expressive writing are journals and diaries, reminiscences, and, frequently, personal letters. The following example is drawn from a writer's notebook.

> All at once, a pony-sized figure appeared on the hillside. Pure white and nervous, it emerged from the darkness of the woods and stood, taking in the view.
>
> I ran and got the glasses. Through the binoculars, clearly what I was watching was a small white horse—but its features and shadows made it look exactly like a unicorn. Two or three days later—having spent a good deal of time per-

suading it to trust me—I had it eating out of my hand. It has blue eyes and milk-white hooves. It is altogether the most extraordinary likeness of a unicorn I can imagine. It even has a pale red blaze in the shape of a horn that reaches down between its eyes from under its forelock. I fed it apples every day that year until we left.

—TIMOTHY FINDLEY, *Inside Memory: Pages from a Writer's Workbook*

Informative writing focusses the reader's attention on the objective world, the objects, the events, and the ideas themselves rather than on the writer's feelings or attitudes about them. Some examples of informative writing are news accounts, encyclopedia articles, laboratory and scientific reports, textbooks, and, usually, articles in professional journals and other publications directed to specialized audiences. Notice that in the following account the writer presents facts objectively.

For most of the Earth's egg layers, proximity to water is a critical constraint on life. Fish, frogs and salamanders, for instance, must deposit their eggs in completely humid environments and often directly in water, which provides moisture for embryonic development and a buoyant medium that prevents the embryo from flattening and collapsing. But birds and reptiles have slipped the aqueous bonds of their ancestors by evolving an egg with a rigid shell and an amniotic membrane. Relatively watertight, the shell prevents the embryo in its water-filled amniotic sac from drying out. And the two structures offer the developing bird a spatially stable environment in which to take shape. Crack a hen's egg open onto a pan, and the contents sprawl in a disorganized mess. Crack it into water, and the egg will resume its spherical shape. —ADRIAN FORSYTH, "Shell Game: The Beauty and the Logic of the Well-Engineered Egg"

Persuasive writing aims to sway the reader's opinions or attitudes, arouse the reader to action, or in some other way bring about a particular response. Persuasive writing relies especially on the use of evidence and logical reasoning (see also Section **31**). The reader's perception of the writer's honesty and fair-mindedness is crucial. Persuasive writing may also depend on the skilful use of language to evoke an emotional response. For example, a defence lawyer's summation to a jury will rely on documented evidence from which the lawyer draws logical conclusions, and it may also cite the testimony of authorities, and employ words and phrases that appeal to the jurors' emotions and sense of morality. Not least in this arsenal of techniques is the lawyer's stance as a seeker of truth and justice. Some other examples of persuasive writing are advertisements, political speeches, and editorials.

In the following example, Margaret Laurence aims to persuade the reader to accept her belief that the preservation of life on earth is the responsibility of each individual living on the planet:

> Dr. Helen Caldicott speaks of "psychic numbing," the temptation to shut out from our minds and hearts all the terrifying things in our world. To think that the problems may just possibly go away if we ignore them. To feel that we are totally helpless, and so . . . why bother trying to do anything? What Dr. Caldicott calls "psychic numbing" I would call "despair," and although I would take issue with the early Church Fathers on many things, I would agree that despair is rightly placed as one of the deadly sins. The problems of our world will not go away if we ignore them. It is not all happening on TV. It is happening on our earth, and we, humankind, are the custodians of that earth. We cannot afford passivity. We must take on responsibility for our lives and our world and we must be prepared to make our government listen to and hear us. Our aim must be no less than human and caring justice, and peace . . . *for all people that on earth do dwell.* —MARGARET LAURENCE, "My Final Hour"

Although the purpose of college and university writing is often informative, it may also be expressive or persuasive. Whenever you write, understand which aim a writing situation calls for. You might write an expressive essay on the impact of a personal encounter with poverty for an English course, an informative paper on the causes of poverty for an economics class, and a persuasive paper arguing for measures to eliminate poverty in a political science course. If you maintain an awareness of your purpose and your reader throughout the writing process, your writing will be clearer and more successful.

■ **Exercise 1**   Select two of the following subjects and explain how you could treat each (1) as expressive writing, (2) as informative writing, and (3) as persuasive writing.

a. finding an apartment
b. buying a car
c. applying for a job
d. accepting responsibilities
e. preserving the environment

33b
Find an appropriate subject.

If you are assigned a subject to write about or if your situation clearly dictates a subject—as in most business writing, for example—you can move directly to a consideration of your audience, of the particular aspect of the subject you will emphasize and of the ways you might organize your discussion. Especially in college and university writing, however, you will sometimes be expected to choose a subject for yourself.

Often the best subject may be one drawn from your own experience—your personal knowledge, interests, and beliefs. Do you play a musical instrument? Climb mountains? Like to travel? Do you have a job? What classes are you taking? Can you think of a particular place that is important to you? An interesting character you have met? Something unusual about your family? What ambitions do you have for yourself? What strong convictions do you hold? When you are free to choose a subject, you can write an interesting paper on almost anything you care about.

Sometimes you will need to choose a subject outside your own experience because you want to extend your knowledge of a subject or because the situation dictates that you do so. If you have to write a term paper for a microbiology course, you may be free to write on any aspect of that discipline that interests you, but the instructor making the assignment wants a paper demonstrating your command of information, not your personal feelings about or experiences with microbes. No less than with writing about personal experience, however, you should take some trouble to find a subject that interests you. You can often find a subject by looking in your textbook, particularly in the sections listing suggestions for further reading and study. You can go through your lecture notes, examine books and articles in the library, scan the subject catalogue, or refer to encyclopedias. Sometimes talking to other students or to your instructor will help you find a subject.

Finally, remember that most writing situations have built-in constraints. For instance, the choice of a subject for a sociology paper may be up to you, but the instructor may specify a length of ten to twelve pages. Obviously, a subject you can develop fully in two or three pages won't do. Or you may have free choice of a subject for a political science paper, but the paper may be due in a week. You will do well to choose a subject you already know something about rather than one on which you have to do extensive research. Choose a subject you can handle in the situation.

■ **Exercise 2**   Be prepared to discuss in class one of the following:

1. Choose a personal experience you might want to write about. How was the experience meaningful to you? What reasons can you think of for sharing this experience with others?
2. Find a controversial subject you are interested in, one that you would like to know more about. What are the issues involved? What would you need to look up to write about it? What are the main points for it? Against it?

33c
Analyze your audience.

Before you begin to write, think as specifically as you can about who will read your writing—your audience. Understanding your audience will help you not only to define your subject and establish its scope but also to decide how technical you can be, what kinds of details you will use, and what tone you will adopt. You can distinguish between at least two kinds of audience, specialized and general.

SPECIALIZED AUDIENCES

A specialized audience has considerable knowledge of the subject about which you are writing and a keen interest in it. For example, if your subject is a new skiing technique, a group of ski instructors would obviously constitute a specialized audience. So would readers of *Ski* magazine, though in writing for this audience you would allow for a greater variation in knowledge and interest. (A specialized audience for one subject would be a general audience for another; the ski instructor, unless also a gifted chef, would probably constitute a general audience for an essay on cooking with a wok.)

It is often easier to write for specialized audiences because you have a specific idea of how much and what kinds of information, as well as what methods of presentation, are called for. You can adjust your tone and the kind of language you use as you tailor your presentation to their expertise and attitudes. The following example from the *Annual Review of Astronomy and Astrophysics* is written for a specialized audience that understands mathematical notation and expects scientific jargon to provide shortcuts to explanations.

> It is now generally believed that a cometary nucleus consists of some sort of conglomerate of ice and meteoric material, as was envisioned by Whipple (1950, 1951). As the comet nears the Sun, the ices are sublimated, and the resultant gas and released meteoric dust become available for forming the coma and tail. Reaction of the comet to the ejection of this material then provides an explanation for the nongravitational effects in the motions of comets. The prevalence of strong outward radial components of the nongravitation forces ($A_1 \approx 10 \mid A_2 \mid$) is precisely to be expected from the icy-conglomerate model. The fact that there is any transverse component at all follows from the comet's rotation and a lag between the direction of maximum mass ejection and the subsolar meridian: $A_2 > 0$ corresponds to direct rotation of the comet, $A_2 < 0$ to retrograde rotation.
>
> —BRIAN G. MARSDEN, "Comets"

GENERAL AUDIENCES

Think of a general audience as a reader or readers not expert on your topic but presumably willing to read what you have to say about it. It is possible to identify certain characteristics even in a general audience so that you can shape your presentation accordingly. For example, the audience for which your instructor usually wishes you to write is one made up of educated adults, intellectually alert and receptive to ideas (but with many different special interests of their own). This assumed audience is not very different from the one for which the articles in a general encyclopedia are written. Consider the following description from such an encyclopedia.

> A comet is a generally nebulous celestial body of small mass revolving around the Sun. Its appearance and brightness vary markedly with its distance from the Sun. A comet far from the Sun is very faint, appears starlike, and consists of a small body or group of bodies reflecting sunlight, called the nucleus. As the comet approaches the Sun, a nebulosity called the coma develops around the nucleus; with the nucleus it constitutes the head of the comet. The coma contains dust and gas released from the nucleus through the action of solar radiation. When close enough to the Sun, a tail may develop, sometimes very long and bright, directed away from the Sun. Such a comet shines partly by scattering of solar radiation on dust particles and partly be re-emission of the gas of absorbed solar radiation (through processes called resonance or fluorescence).
>
> —ENCYCLOPAEDIA BRITANNICA

General audiences may be of quite different kinds. Consider the following passage from a fifth-grade science textbook. It describes a comet by using details (such as "flying frozen gravel pits") that appeal to ten-year-old readers and by using simple words in short, uncomplicated sentences.

> Comets may be no more than a few miles across. They are made of bits of frozen gas and dust. They can be thought of as flying frozen gravel pits. Much of a comet's matter changes to vapor when the comet travels near the sun. As the comet "head" absorbs the sun's energy, the gas of the comet expands. So the comet takes up more space. A "tail" is formed. The tail may be as much as 500 million miles long. The matter of a comet is spread very thin.
>
> —GEORGE MALLINSON et al., *Science: Understanding Your Environment*

When you are writing for a general audience, a useful technique is to imagine one specific reader whose background and expectations are typical; then adjust your choice of details and your tone accordingly.

MIXED AUDIENCES

Although in work-related writing you will probably write most often for a specialized audience, occasionally you will need to write for a mixed audience of specialized and general readers. For example, an engineer may prepare a technical report for an immediate supervisor who is also an engineer and therefore represents a specialized audience. But the report will also be read by executives who are not engineers. The engineer, therefore, has to design the report so that it conveys specialized information to the supervisor but is clear to others. Often in such situations it is simply not possible to serve all the members of a mixed audience equally well; a writer must then determine who the primary audience is and write mainly to that audience, doing the best he or she can for the others.

■ **Exercise 3**   Choose an experience you have had recently and write letters about it to all three of the following: (1) your parents or your employer, (2) your best friend, (3) *Maclean's* magazine.

TONE

A clear sense of audience is essential in determining the tone you should take when you write. What is your relationship to your reader? What is the reader's perception of the relationship? How do you want your reader to react? The answers to such questions will help to determine whether you should be formal or informal, humorous, serious, or indignant. Suppose that as you were driving your new automobile down a busy street your brakes locked and caused you to slide into a parked car. In complaining to the company that manufactured your car with defective brakes, you would be writing to an unfamiliar audience, and your tone might reflect your indignation that the brakes were faulty. If you wrote to your insurance company to explain what happened, it would be inappropriate for you to take an indignant tone, though you would probably be serious and formal. A letter to your best friend would have an entirely different flavour. You might decide to express your indignation, even to do so humorously, but your tone would probably be informal.

The control of tone can be a subtle thing. Notice in the following essay how the author's serious, matter-of-fact approach to the subject and her stance as a person eager to be helpful to her reader contribute to the humorous effect.

Heat on the Hoof

1   As fuel costs continue to spiral upwards, the householder must continue his search for a reasonable and effective means of heating his establishment. Solar, or "passive," heating and woodburning stoves are popular alternatives to oil- and coal-burning systems; however, no discussion of modern heating methods would be complete without mention of the horse.

2   Horses may be used in a variety of ways as heating units. All of these are simpler than existing mechanical methods, and surprisingly effective. The average 1,200 pound horse has a caloric production rate of 600 therms per minute, and double that if he is angry or unsettled. The fuel-calorie conversion rate is extremely favorable, being about one to eight, which means that the standard four-bedroom house, with snacking center and media room, can be heated by one healthy horse and eight bales of hay per week: an appealing statistic and a soothing prospect. As there are a number of horse-heating methods available, it is wise to examine each to determine which will fit your particular needs the best.

3   One common practice is the installation of a very large horse (a Percheron or other heavy draft type is popular) in

the basement of the house. Hot air ducts lead off the Percheron and act as conduits throughout the house. This is a safe and reliable method, as Percherons are mild and ruminative by nature, and fond of basements. In the event that your basement has been turned into a family recreation center, this should not adversely affect your Percheron system: many Percherons are ardent ping-pong spectators, and some are interested in taking up the game themselves. If the prospect of a blue-roan gelding playing round-robin in your basement unsettles you, remember this: even the most ineffectual efforts on the Percheron's part to join in family ping-pong games will raise the heat production in your home by a tremendous factor. Encouraging the horse in any sort of physical activity, even charades, should enable your entire family and the close neighbors of your choice to take hot showers as a result.

4   A drawback of the central-heating Percheron is that it heats the entire house regardless of which rooms are being used, and some homeowners prefer a more adaptable system which will heat only the rooms that are routinely occupied. Many people find that stationing Thoroughbred mares throughout the house is an attractive alternative to the heavy draft cellar horse. The Thoroughbred is an extremely energetic breed, and its heat production is enormous, owing to its highly developed capillary system, which is a relatively new feature in equine design. The dainty Thoroughbred foot, another hallmark of this fine breed, ensures minimum damage to your flooring and fine carpets. Thoroughbreds are, however, emotionally unstable, and more care and attention must be paid them than the placid draft horse. This maintenance may be more than the average homeowner is willing to provide: soothing words must be used, idle or vicious gossip must be eschewed, and a friendly greeting must be offered daily, incorporating the correct name of the horse (not some jocular substitute), to maintain psychic order. Failure to follow these rules may result in "sulk-outs," and a general lowering of the temperature. Mares are more effusive than geldings, and they make particularly good heat producers, but they tend to shy at mice and vio-

lence, so geldings are recommended for kitchen and TV room use.

5   A third, and highly recommended, plan is to give each member of the family a Shetland pony of his own. These tiny ponies are docile creatures, with thick coats and long manes which will double as bathmats. If properly trained, these nimble creatures will follow their receptors eagerly and unselfishly about the house, producing a steady stream of therms. They can be trained as well to make beds and wash sweaters; the drawback is, of course, that they are such terrible liars.

6   Besides the practical attractions of the horse, there is his great aesthetic appeal. Durably made and skillfully designed, the horse is available in a handsome selection of coordinated earth tones, ranging from white to black and including brown. He also comes in a wide assortment of body styles, from the trim and compact Shetland, through the rugged, all-purpose Quarter horse, whose stylish white trim and abstract patterning make him a popular favorite with decorators, to the massive, heavy-duty Percheron or Clydesdale, who can heat an entire convention without moving a fetlock.

7   The horse is clean, docile, thrifty, and cheerful. He is biodegradable, non-carcinogenic, and produces no long-term side effects. His own needs are modest: he requires only sweet sun-cured timothy hay and a double handful of dry oats daily. Clearly, the record of the horse as a reliable and valuable helpmate to man continues, and the horse takes his place beside the stove, the sun, and the furnace.

—ROXANNA BARRY

33d
Explore and focus the subject.

When you have a subject in mind—whether it is one assigned by an instructor, one dictated by some other situation, or one you have chosen for yourself—you will often need to explore the subject further to discover all the particular aspects of it that may be worth developing. And almost certainly you will benefit—make your writing task easier and the finished composition more effective—by taking at least a few minutes to limit the subject and get it sharply in focus before you start writing.

(1) Explore your subject.

Writers use many methods to explore a subject. Some especially useful methods are listing, questioning, applying different perspectives, and surveying the possible development strategies. Use whatever methods seem to be productive for you. Different methods may work best for different subjects: if you run out of ideas using one method, switch to another. Sometimes, especially for an assigned subject remote from your own interests and knowledge, you may need to use several methods.

Listing   Your mind already holds a variety of ideas about any subject you choose to write on. One way to dig these ideas out is to make an informal list. Jot down any ideas that come to you while you are thinking about your subject. Don't worry if the ideas seem to come without any kind of order, and don't worry about the form in which you write them down—grammar, spelling, and diction are not concerns at this stage. You can devote as much time to making your list as necessary—perhaps five minutes, perhaps an entire evening. The point is to collect as many ideas as you can about your subject.

If you are thinking about writing on home computers, you might make a list like the one below. This one took a student about five minutes.

> reasons people want home computers
> playing games
> keeping track of money

helping to organize daily tasks
what should you look for when you choose one?
what size and price?
what do you want it to do for you?
what kinds of programs are available for it?
cost of programs
ease of use—programs and computer
any gadgets to attach—like printers, disk drives?
what about monitors—colour, monochrome?
can you use your TV?
what kind of storage is best?
what do you have to know before you can use one?
do you need to know math?
where can you learn?
any hidden costs—higher electrical bills, repairs, etc.?
do they break frequently?
where do you get them fixed?
where should you buy one?
keeping records—addresses, Christmas cards, spending habits, tax

If you study this list, you can see that the writer was keeping her mind open, sometimes letting one idea lead to another, sometimes making a jump in an entirely new direction. Occasionally the greatest value of such a list is that it allows an idea to surface that can become the subject of a new list; consider, for example, the last item on the list and the fifth from the last.

Questioning   Another useful way to explore a subject is to ask yourself questions about it. The journalists' questions *who? what? when? where? how?* and *why?* are easy to use and can help you discover ideas about any subject. Using journalists' questions to explore the subject of home computers could lead you to think about *how* computers affect people, *what* they are, and *what* kinds are available, *when* and *how* they were developed, *where* they are used or *who* uses them, *why* people want home computers, *how* computers work or *how* to decide which one to buy.

Applying perspectives Sometimes it is helpful to consider a subject in three quite different ways—as static, dynamic, and relative. A *static* perspective would focus your attention on what a home computer is. You might define it, describe its physical characteristics, analyze its parts or its main uses, or give examples of home computers.

The *dynamic* perspective focusses on action and change. Thus, you might examine the history or development of the computer, its workings or the processes involved in using it, and changes of all sorts resulting from its use.

The *relative* perspective focusses on relationships, on systems. You might examine relationships of the computer to other things and to people. You can view the home computer as a system in itself or as a part of a larger system of information management. You can also analyze it in relation to other kinds of computers such as mainframe computers, or to other kinds of information management tools such as library catalogues.

Surveying development strategies The various development strategies (more fully discussed in **32d**) represent natural thinking processes and so are especially useful for generating ideas about a subject. Here are some thoughts a writer might jot down using these strategies.

> *Narration*—Tell about my first experience using a home computer.
> *Process*—How do you buy one? How does it work?
> *Cause and Effect*—Why were home computers developed? What effects do they have on other things?
> *Description*—What does a home computer look like? What is a typical owner like?
> *Definition*—What is a home computer?
> *Analysis*—What are the parts of a computer? What are the various tasks it can do?
> *Classification*—What kinds of people buy these computers?

What types are on the market?

Example—Computers save time—name several ways.

Comparison and Contrast—What similarities and differences are there between kinds of home computers? What are the differences between managing information with a computer and without? How is a computer like a library or like an office?

(2) Limit and focus the subject.

No matter how well you have explored your subject, almost certainly you will need to limit and focus it before you write. As you do so, keep your purpose and your audience in mind. A simple analogy helps explain why limiting and focussing are so important. When you take a picture of something, you decide what it is you want to photograph, and you aim your camera in that direction. But that's not all you do: you also look through the viewfinder to make sure the subject is correctly framed and in focus. You may decide to move in closer to eliminate distracting elements from the frame, and you may change your angle, using light and shadow to emphasize some features of your subject over others. You need to do something very similar when you write. When you have generated enough ideas about your subject, look at them carefully to see how to frame your subject and to make sure it is clearly in focus.

For example, "home computers" is too large and general a subject to make a good writing topic. However, some of the items that appear on the list about the home computer in **33d(1)** can be grouped to form a writing topic that might be manageable. Items about cost can be grouped, as can items about programs, about things the computer can do, or about learning to use the computer. Conceivably, an essay focussing on any one of these groups—eliminating all the other, irrelevant items—might be both workable and interesting.

Chances are, however, that still more focussing will be required. Suppose you have narrowed "home computers" to "learning to use a home computer." This is still a very big topic, one on which sizable books are written. For a short paper you would do better to focus on, for example, the ways such knowledge can be acquired. You might examine the relative merits of college courses, training sessions given by dealers, and self-instruction through reading manuals and other publications. Or you could focus your paper on the specific kinds of knowledge that are needed: how to turn the computer on and off, how to use disk drives, how to save information you have put into the computer, and so forth. The exact focus you finally choose will be determined by your purpose, your audience, and the time and space available.

■ **Exercise 4** Taking one of the subjects from Exercise 2, explore it by using the journalists' questions (*who? what? when? where? why? how?*). Next explore the same subject using the three perspectives: What is it? How does it change or act? What is it related to—part of, different from, or like? Then explore the subject by surveying development strategies. Decide how you would limit and focus this subject.

33e
Construct a focussed, specific thesis statement containing a single main idea.

An effective thesis statement satisfies your reader's natural desire to know—usually early in the paper—what the central point or idea will be and how you are likely to go about presenting it. It contains a single idea clearly focussed and specifically stated.

A good thesis statement is useful to you as the writer as well as to your reader. It will help you maintain unity and will guide many decisions about what details to include.

Sometimes you have information about your subject that is interesting but does not really help you make your point. When you are tempted to include such material simply because it is interesting, looking at your thesis statement can help you decide to leave it out. You can also use the thesis statement to guide your search for additional information that you may need to make your point.

As you write, refer to your thesis statement from time to time to see if you have drifted away from your main idea. Do not hesitate to change your thesis, however, if you find a more productive path, one you would rather pursue. Make whatever adjustments you need to ensure a unified essay.

A good thesis statement is often a declarative sentence with a single main clause—that is, either a simple or complex sentence. If your thesis statement announces two or more co-ordinate ideas, as a compound sentence does, be sure you are not in danger of having your paper lose direction and focus. If you wish to sharpen the thesis statement by adding information that qualifies or supports it, subordinate such material to the main idea. Beware of vague qualifiers such as *interesting, important,* and *unusual.* Often such words signal that you have chosen a subject that does not interest you much and you would do better to rethink your subject to come up with something you care about. In a thesis statement such as "My education has been very unusual" the vague word *unusual* may indicate that the idea itself is trivial and unproductive and that the writer needs to find a more congenial subject. Conversely, this kind of vague thesis may disguise an idea of real interest that simply needs to be made specific: "Unlike most people, I received my high school education from my parents on a boat." Sometimes thesis statements containing such vague words can be made more effective by simply replacing the bland words with other, more meaningful ones. The following examples show ways to focus, clarify, and sharpen vague thesis statements.

VAGUE	Rock collecting can be an interesting hobby.
BETTER	Rock collecting fills empty time, satisfies a yen for beauty, and brings in a little extra cash.
VAGUE	I have trouble making decisions.
BETTER	Making decisions is difficult for me, especially when money is involved, and most of all when such decisions affect other people.
VAGUE	Summer is an interesting season.
BETTER	Summer is an infuriating season.

Thesis statements appear most often in the first paragraph, although you may put them anywhere that suits your purpose—occasionally even in the conclusion. The advantage, however, of putting the thesis statement in the introductory paragraph is that your reader knows from the beginning what you are writing about and where the essay is going. If the thesis statement begins the introductory paragraph, the rest of the sentences in the paragraph usually support or clarify it with more specific information.

> Whether we like it or not—and many may disagree with my thesis because painting, or music, or some other art is more important to them—the art of the moving picture is the only art truly of our time, whether it is in the form of the film or television. The moving picture is our universal art, which comprises all others, literature, and acting, stage design and music, dance and the beauty of nature, and, most of all, the use of light and color.
>
> —BRUNO BETTELHEIM, "The Art of Moving Pictures"

> If it be true that Victoria is the City of Gardens, as those who live there so happily assert, then equally it could be said that British Columbia is Canada's first province of flowers. B.C.'s extraordinarily diverse climate—from the snowy slopes of the Rocky Mountains to the warm, wet regions of the coast, to the boglands, the alpine meadows, the prairies, river valleys and the dry country between—makes for an amazing variety of flora unequalled anywhere else in Canada. —PETER SYMCOX, "Land of Bouquet"

Frequently, you will want to give your reader some background on your subject, or to place it in a particular context, before stating your thesis.

> Joan of Arc (1412–1431), the extraordinary sixteen-year-old daughter of a French peasant family, defied almost every tradition of the peasant woman's world. She disobeyed her parents, importuned those above her station for help, and insisted that she must act outside accepted female roles. Joan told everyone that she had been sent by God to join the army of the King of France and to raise the English siege of the town of Orléans. Everything about her manner, her demands, and her actions was unorthodox. In normal circumstances, the very personification of the insubordinate, disobedient female, she would have been left to the reprimands of her mother and father. But in the midst of the Hundred Years War, the secular and religious leaders of fifteenth-century France listened to the unorthodox. They came to agree with Joan's vision of herself as the young virgin granted access to God through her voices. They came to perceive her as a heroine: the holy maiden warrior, zealous and strong, sent for the salvation of the kingdom. So perceived, Joan's passion, energy, persistence, and ingenuity gained her power and success in roles traditionally reserved to men and to men of higher caste as well.
> —BONNIE S. ANDERSON and JUDITH P. ZINSSER, *A History of Their Own: Women in Europe from Prehistory to the Present*

Sometimes an essay has no explicit thesis statement. This is especially common in writing that is primarily narrative or descriptive. (The essay "Ice," pages 408–409, has none.) Sometimes, even in the kinds of writing where a thesis is most often explicitly stated (persuasive and informative), there may be special reasons for leaving the thesis statement out. Yet even when your thesis is implied, your readers should be able to sense a clear direction and focus in your paper. You can make sure that they will by writing a thesis statement of your own and then testing each paragraph to make sure it is relevant to the thesis. What is important is to think about your thesis even if you never intend your readers to see it.

■ **Exercise 5** Construct a clear and precise thesis statement for the subject you limited in Exercise 4.

33f
Choose an appropriate method or combination of methods of development for arranging ideas, and prepare a working plan.

The strategies discussed and exemplified in **32d** are more than simply methods for developing a paragraph and exploring a subject (see **33d**). They are the methods by which writers organize and develop longer pieces of writing as well.

Your choice of a particular method of development will depend to a great extent on other choices you have already made—purpose, subject, focus, thesis. Whether your aim is expressive, informative, or persuasive, one of these methods or a combination of them can be used for organizing your paper: exemplification, narration, process, cause and effect, classification, definition, description, analysis, and comparison and contrast.

Most writers find that they need some kind of written working plan to keep their writing on course. Many think that making a formal outline interferes with the flow of their ideas, generally preferring to use lists or other kinds of jottings. Others find a formal outline useful, particularly when the project is long or when they have to produce their composition under pressure. Choose a plan that works for you.

INFORMAL WORKING PLANS

An informal working plan need be little more than an ordered list that suggests a way of organizing your information. Such plans often grow out of lists similar to those used to explore subjects (see **33d**). A student who chose to write a paper on student life in the nineties made the following list as she was exploring ideas.

a different life today from life in the past

common misconceptions about the life among members of the public

difficult challenges—financial, academic, psychological

high tuition fees

strict admissions requirements

difficulties of going from high school to post-secondary institutions

classrooms in the nineties

the need to get involved, to develop critical skills

the heavy demands of reading, labs, midterms, etc.

getting along with fellow students

recognizing the benefits and privileges of the life

college and university life

romanticized images of student life

When you make a list such as this, ideas often overlap. Some are general, some specific. They appear in no particular order. But you have the beginning of a plan. Examine your list carefully to see if any items are repeated and if any particular plan suggests itself.

The student writing on student life in the nineties examined her list and noticed that the misconceptions about and challenges of student life these days kept coming into her mind. Choosing to limit her essay to that observation and to train her attention on the lives of post-secondary students, she noticed that one item on her list gave her a focus for her composition: for all its benefits and privileges, student life in the nineties presents difficult challenges. She formulated a thesis statement and decided that a climactic

organization would present her arguments effectively—
student life is a privileged one compared with the lives of
others, but in the nineties, it presents greater financial, psychological, and academic challenges than it once did. She
then prepared an informal working plan of how her paper
would be organized:

Thesis Statement: Students today face obstacles in gaining
entrance to colleges and universities, and once they win
the opportunity to pursue their studies, they have a lot to
learn: in order to succeed, they must teach themselves to
meet the psychological and academic demands of student
life.

1. Problems of gaining entrance.
2. Problems of adjustment.
3. Problems of learning.

FORMAL OUTLINES

A formal outline uses indention and numbers to indicate
various levels of subordination. Thus, it is a kind of
graphic scheme of the logic of your paper. The main points
form the major headings, and the supporting ideas for each
point form the subheadings.

Thesis:
    I. Major idea
       A. Supporting idea
          1. Example or illustration for supporting idea
          2. Example or illustration for supporting idea
            a. Detail for example or illustration
            b. Detail for example or illustration
       B. Supporting idea
    II. Major idea

Headings and subheadings stand for divisions, and a division denotes at least two parts. Therefore, to be logical, each outline should have at least two main headings, I and II. If it has a subheading marked A, it should also have a subheading marked B; if it has a 1, it should also have a 2. Any intelligible system of notation is acceptable.

The types of outlines most commonly used are the topic outline and the sentence outline. When you write a topic outline, you express the major headings (those numbered I, II, III, and so on) and subdivisions in phrases. In topic outlines, the phrases that make up the major headings (I, II, III, and so on) should be grammatically parallel (see Section **26**), as should each group of subheadings. But it is unnecessary to strive for parallel structure between different groups of subheadings—for example, between A, B, and C under I and A, B, and C under II. When you write a sentence outline, you do not have to be concerned about parallel structure. Instead, express your headings and subdivisions in complete sentences.

The advantage of a sentence outline is that it helps ensure that you become specific about your subject rather than simply generalizing. The advantage of the topic outline, besides its brevity, is that its parallel structure reveals the logic you will follow in your paper. But regardless of what type of outline you choose, you will need to have enough major headings to develop your topic fully within the boundaries established by your thesis statement.

Sentence Outline

Thesis Statement: Students today face obstacles in gaining entrance to colleges and universities, and once they win the opportunity to pursue their studies, they have a lot to learn: in order to succeed, they must teach themselves to meet the psychological and academic demands of student life.

I. Post-secondary students today frequently discuss problems of entrance to universities and colleges.
    A. Decreased government funds mean increased tuition fees.
    B. Colleges and universities have stricter admissions standards.
II. Students new to post-secondary studies face psychological adjustments.
    A. They miss the security of high school life.
    B. They must make special efforts to make friends and to fit in.
III. Post-secondary students must meet the academic demands of life in college or university.
    A. Students should seize the opportunity to learn new lessons.
    B. They sometimes fail to learn when they are intimidated by what they don't know.
    C. They must develop methods of learning huge volumes of material.
    D. They must become active learners who are fully involved in discussion and debate.
    E. They must balance their studies with the demands of life.

Topic Outline

Thesis Statement: Students today face obstacles in gaining entrance to colleges and universities, and once they win the opportunity to pursue their studies, they have a lot to learn: in order to succeed, they must teach themselves to meet the psychological and academic demands of student life.

I. Gaining entrance to colleges and universities
    A. Problems of increased tuition fees
    B. Problems of stricter admissions standards

II. Facing psychological adjustments to college and university
   A. Leaving high school behind
   B. Making friends and fitting in
III. Meeting the academic demands of college and university
   A. Seizing the opportunity to learn new lessons
   B. Coping with feelings of intimidation about learning
   C. Developing effective study skills
   D. Becoming active learners
   E. Balancing studies with the demands of everyday life

■ **Exercise 6** Follow your instructor's directions as you develop a working plan or an outline for the subject you limited in Exercise 4.

33g
Write the composition.

As you write the first draft of your composition, keep your plan in mind, but put your ideas on paper quickly without much concern for matters such as spelling, punctuation, and usage. Remember, you are the only one who will read this draft. If you realize you have veered from your plan, you may find it helpful to stop drafting and reread what you have written to reorient yourself. If you find yourself stuck and uncertain where to go next, referring to your plan should help you discover how to continue. When you complete your draft, set it aside for a time, several days if possible.

Some writers find that they work best by writing chunks or blocks of their essay without worrying about the order in which the chunks will finally appear. For example, if writing the introduction is difficult for you, try starting with one of the supporting ideas you feel sure of and draft that idea through to a stopping point. You may find that once you are actually writing, your thinking processes will operate more efficiently. If that happens, you can move on to any part of the composition you think will be easy to write next—another paragraph presenting a supporting idea, even the introduction or conclusion. What is important is to begin writing and to write as quickly as you can. One word of caution: if you find that writing in chunks works best for you, you will later need to give special care to ensuring that you have clear transitions.

(1) Write effective introductions and conclusions.

An effective introduction arouses the reader's interest and indicates what the composition is about (see also pages 426–30). Introductions have no set length; they can be as brief as a phrase or as long as a paragraph or more. To arouse interest, you might begin your introduction with a startling event, a cleverly phrased statement, or an anecdote. The first introductory paragraph below begins with an arresting sentence that makes you want to read more. The second introductory paragraph engages your attention with an interesting anecdote.

> Everyone has fantasies. Mine are historical daydreams, a way of playing Rip van Winkle in reverse. I slide deep into my armchair, a heavy tome growing heavier in my hands, and let myself nod off. Then I wake up in Paris, at the height of the Revolution, aroused by a kiss. At times it is the kiss of death, at times the kiss of love, a little love, love lost amid the passions of the past: *le baiser de Lamourette*.
>
> —ROBERT DARNTON, *The Kiss of Lamourette:*
> *Reflections in Cultural History*

> The patient had not spoken a word for years. But all of a sudden, while in Justine Sergent's office at the Montreal

Neurological Institute and Hospital one day, he began to sing along with a radio. When the music stopped, he did too, and he has not spoken a word since. For Sergent, it was more evidence that perhaps the neural networks controlling words and music are distinct, a suspicion the Montreal neurologist has since proved true by mapping the place of music in the brain. —MERILYN SYMONDS MOHR, "Musical Spheres"

Sometimes an interesting fact or unusual detail makes an introduction effective.

Twenty-eight percent of the occupations that will be available to children born in 1976 were not in existence when those children were born.

Many introductions simply begin with general information as background about the subject and then focus specifically on the thesis.

Chinese speakers use words of one syllable, or *zi,* as building blocks for polysyllabic words, phrases, and sentences. When compared with many other languages, including English, Chinese places very few sounds at the disposal of its speakers. Mandarin allows four hundred spoken one-syllable words, approximately; Cantonese makes about twice that number available. With so few building blocks, how can Chinese construct linguistic structures equal to the complexities of human life?
—RAYMOND CHANG and MARGARET SCROGIN CHANG,
Speaking of Chinese

If your essay is persuasive, you may want to begin with the proposition for which you intend to argue.

The Chinese have never accounted for more than 1 per cent of Canada's population, but their role in Canadian history and society has been disproportionately significant. Unfortunately, this role has consisted largely of being the victims of racist abuse. Of all the immigrant groups seeking a new life in this country, only the Chinese had to pay a head tax—a fee for permission to settle in Canada. In 1923, the Chinese became the first and only people to be excluded from Canada on the basis of race. These early examples of institutional racism have been obscured by the commonly held myth that Canada is a "tolerant" nation, unlike, say, the United States with its "black problem."

—ANTHONY B. CHAN, *Gold Mountain: The Chinese in the New World*

Avoid using a cliché in an introduction unless you can give it a fresh twist (see **20c**). Also avoid unnecessary definitions, such as "Webster's dictionary defines *hate* as. . . ." Finally, apologies generally have no place in an introduction. You may not know as much as you would like to about your subject or you may find it difficult to write about, but apologizing for that fact will only undermine the effectiveness of your paper.

A composition should finish, not merely stop. Some effective conclusions, especially those that introduce a question for further thought or suggest directions for future study of the topic, do encourage the reader to continue thinking about the subject. To maintain the unity of your essay, however, avoid introducing a completely new subject in the conclusion. Other effective conclusions summarize, restate, or evaluate the information in the essay without encouraging the reader to think beyond the discussion. But avoid simply repeating your thesis in the conclusion. If a summary of your thesis is useful, try to rephrase it to avoid unnecessary repetition.

Linda McQuaig's conclusion to her essay criticizing the Canadian government's drift toward the American government's policies on social welfare evaluates the information she has presented but does not direct the reader beyond the discussion.

In many ways, the most chilling aspect of the U.S. poverty problem is the fact that many Americans have become so

desensitized to the poor that they no longer care whether a family of three can survive on $120 a month. After all, the poor can always sell their blood. For Canadians, this spectacle should make us pause before we dismantle our social welfare programs and make ourselves more like the [U.S.] "dinosaur." —LINDA McQUAIG, *The Wealthy Banker's Wife:*
The Assault on Equality in Canada

Farley Mowat's conclusion directs the reader's attention to the lessons to be taken by all human beings from the stranding of a single whale in Aldridges Pond, Newfoundland.

The whale was not alone in being trapped. We were all trapped with her. If the natural patterns of her life had been disrupted, then so had ours. An awesome mystery had intruded into the closely circumscribed order of our lives; one that we terrestrial bipeds could not fathom, and one, therefore, that we would react against with instinctive fear, violence, and hatred. This riddle from the deeps was the measure of humanity's unquenchable ignorance of life. This impenetrable secret, which had become the core of our own existence in this place, was a mirror in which we saw our own distempered faces . . . and they were ugly.

—FARLEY MOWAT, *A Whale for the Killing*

Conclusions often clinch or stress the importance of the central idea by referring in some way to the introduction, as U.S. vice-president Al Gore's does in the next example.

INTRODUCTION   One of the clearest signs that our relationship to the global environment is in severe crisis is the floodtide of garbage spilling out of our cities and factories. What some have called the "throwaway society" has been based on the assumptions that endless resources will allow us to produce an endless supply of goods and that bottomless receptacles (i.e., landfills and ocean dumping sites) will allow us to dispose of an endless stream of waste. But now we are beginning to drown in that stream. Having relied for too long on the old strategy of "out of sight, out of mind," we are now running out of ways to dispose of our waste in a manner that keeps it out of either sight or mind.

CONCLUSION

Believing ourselves to be separate from the earth means having no idea how we fit into the natural cycle of life and no understanding of the natural processes of change that affect us and that we in turn are affecting. It means that we attempt to chart the course of our civilization by reference to ourselves alone. No wonder we are lost and confused. No wonder so many people feel their lives are wasted. Our species used to flourish within the intricate and interdependent web of life, but we have chosen to leave the garden. Unless we find a way to dramatically change our civilization and our way of thinking about the relationship between humankind and the earth, our children will inherit a wasteland. —AL GORE, "The Wasteland," in *Earth in the Balance: Ecology and the Human Spirit*

As in an introduction, avoid apologizing in a conclusion. Finally, in very short essays where all the points can easily be kept in mind, a conclusion is often unnecessary because it is likely to unbalance the essay and, in any case, there is little more to be said.

(2) Develop a good title.

First impressions are important, and usually the first thing your reader sees is your title. An appropriate title fits the subject matter of the paper. Sometimes the title announces the subject simply and directly: "Ice," *Colombo's Concise Canadian Quotations*, Virginia Woolf's "Professions for Women." A good title may also arouse the reader's curiosity, as do X.J. Kennedy's "Who Killed King Kong?" and Russell Hoban's "Thoughts on a Shirtless Cyclist, Robin Hood and One or Two Other Things." Sometimes a clever title, such as Farb and Armelagos' *Consuming Passions: The Anthropology of Eating*, will reflect the writer's attitude and approach. A good way to begin developing a title is to try condensing your thesis statement without becoming too vague or general. Try to work in some indication of the attitude and approach you have taken in the paper. Consider the following possible titles for the essay beginning on page 419:

GENERAL   A New Method of Heating [only vague indication of subject, no indication of attitude or approach]

ADEQUATE   The Horse as Heater [clearer indication of subject but still no suggestion of attitude or approach]

BETTER   Heat on the Hoof [sharply focussed, indicates subject, attitude and approach, and tone]

33h
Revise the composition.

In one way or another you revise throughout the writing process. For example, even in the earliest planning stages, as you consider a possible subject and then discard it in favour of another, you are revising. Similarly, after choosing a subject, if you decide to change your focus to emphasize some new aspect of it, you are revising. And of course you are revising when, as you draft your paper, you realize that a sentence or a paragraph you have just written does not belong where it is and you pause to strike it out or mark it to be moved to an earlier or later place in the paper. But once you have finished a draft, you should set it aside for a time (preferably overnight) so that you will be able to see it freshly and objectively, and then you should revise it carefully and systematically as a whole. In scheduling your work, allow plenty of time for revising.

Consider large matters before you turn to smaller ones. Attending to the larger matters first is an efficient approach because as you revise paragraphs or reorganize the essay you often change or eliminate smaller elements—sentences, words, punctuation, mechanics, and so forth. Check to be sure that you have stuck to your purpose and your subject and that you have not lost sight of your audience anywhere in the draft. Is your focus consistent? Is everything governed by the central idea, or thesis? Are the major ideas in the most effective order? Is the reasoning logical?

Is every paragraph unified, coherent, and well developed? Is every sentence related to the paragraph's central idea? Are the sentences presented in the most natural and effective order? Are transitions adequate between paragraphs and between sentences?

Next, look at sentence structure. Are all of your sentences clear? Do short sentences give your essay a choppy, unconnected movement? Consider combining some of them. Rework long, overly complicated sentences. Do too many of your sentences begin with the same kind of grammatical structure? For example, if your essay contains many sentences that begin with prepositional phrases, try to rework some of those into other patterns. Have you avoided needless shifts in grammatical structures, tone, style, or point of view?

Examine your diction. Do you find vague words like *area, interesting,* or *unusual* where more precise words would be more effective? Watch for clauses and sentences in the passive voice. The active voice usually, though by no means always, makes your writing more direct and forceful. Is your writing wordy and repetitive? Cut any non-essential words, phrases, and sentences to make your writing tighter and more emphatic. Make sure sentences are grammatically correct. Check spelling, punctuation, and mechanics.

Sometimes while revising sentences you will find that you still have work to do on your paragraphs. Fuzzy sentences often obscure faults in reasoning or lapses in unity or coherence. Don't be discouraged. Many writers wrestle with the same problems. Keep in mind that many professionals consider revision the most important part of their writing. As one observed, "I'm not a very good writer, but I'm a terrific reviser!" You will probably find that you too will need to revise your compositions several times, sharpening, rewriting, inserting, and deleting again and again to communicate with your reader and achieve your purpose as effectively as you can.

WORD PROCESSING

Access to a computer with word-processing capability puts a powerful revision tool at your fingertips. If you need to correct, change, or rearrange any part of your writing—from inserting or deleting a single letter to reorganizing large blocks of materials—word-processing programs such as *Microsoft Word* or *WordPerfect* (to name two of many) can help you do that. With these programs you can even delete or insert whole paragraphs or pages. Furthermore, you can rearrange words and blocks of writing by moving them to a part of the composition where you think they will be most effective. And word processing allows you to do this without having to retype anything. The computer simply makes room on the screen where you need it and takes space away where you don't.

When you have completed your drafting and revision, many word-processing programs will help you check spelling and even grammar before you finally print what you have written. Style-checking programs that can help you make your composition more unified and coherent are also becoming available. Such programs usually operate by high-lighting or otherwise isolating on the screen any part of your composition that may contain a problem. You are offered the chance to reconsider what you have written and revise it if necessary. A word of caution: word-processing programs are only a mechanical means for manipulating language that you create yourself. They cannot think for you; they only remind you to think for yourself, and they make revision faster and easier. A further caution: because they are so easy to use, word processing systems can also reinforce natural but undesirable tendencies, making a wordy writer even wordier, for example, or a terse writer even less fluent.

AN ESSAY UNDERGOING REVISION

Following are two drafts of an essay on student life in the nineties by Cami Tong, the first marked with Tong's notes for revision. Compare the drafts and observe all the ways in which Tong has made the final version more effective than the first.

First Draft and Revisions

A Lot to Learn — Student Life in the Nineties

~~Student Life in the Nineties~~

To the members of Canada's work force, who pour millions of tax dollars into the country's educational institutions every year, the life of a post-secondary student must seem ~~to be an~~ idyllic ~~one.~~

To those in our country who are homeless, or who are living from paycheque to paycheque, ~~or~~ struggling to survive in the shantytowns and refugee camps of the world, the life of a Canadian college or university student must seem nothing short of ~~a~~ an impossible or even cruel dream. Viewed comparatively, ~~paradise or a utopia. Comparatively speaking,~~ the lives of those who attend this country's colleges and universities ~~is one that provides~~ afford tremendous opportunities and privileges. ~~satisfaction if not ease.~~ We study the great ideas of the past, present, and ~~and future~~ with academics who are experts in their fields; we have the time, ~~to and~~ the resources, and the freedom to speculate about solutions to difficult problems and to debate ~~great and~~ controversial issues of the day with students from other parts of the country and from other countries of the world; we have the luxury of learning and planning for bright futures ~~and~~ socializing all at the same time. We can work toward educational goals that, if they do not guarantee us ~~a~~ satisfying and high-paying jobs upon graduation, immediately can nevertheless prepare us to meet the changing world with more

understanding, ~~and more~~ preparation, and ~~more~~
versatility than many ~~less fortunate people~~ *others* in
this country or this world are able to have.
We have ~~little~~ *few* ground*s* for complaint, many
would say. And they would be right.

This view of student life is one that
~~students themselves~~ *we as students* can hardly quarrel with.
Life is good to us in more ways than we can
count. And yet, *I would guess that* a national survey of *today's* college
and university students ~~today~~ would ~~surely~~
reveal ~~a~~ considerable unrest, ~~unease,~~ and
uncertainty among the men and women ~~currently~~
attending the nation's post-secondary
institutions. Our lives ~~may not be~~ *are neither bleak nor* impossible,
as those of others are, but getting a higher
education in the last decade of the twentieth
century is not without its difficulties, no
matter how the situation may appear to those
on the outside looking in. Students today face
obstacles in gaining entrance to colleges and
~~university,~~ *universities,* and once they win the opportunity
to pursue their studies, they have a lot to
learn: *in order to succeed,* they must teach themselves to meet the
psychological and academic demands of student
life.

Whenever students get together to talk seriously about the facts of post-secondary life, the related topic ~~s~~ access and of ~~money~~ are ~~is~~ never far from the top of the agenda. After the boom years of the seventies and the eighties, when money for college and university operating budgets flowed quite ~~seemed to flow~~ freely, the nineties ~~seem to~~ have produced a drought in educational funding.

~~Whenever students get together to talk seriously about the facts of post-secondary education these days, the discussion invariably turns to the past.~~ *(No new ¶)* We may not have studied the evolution of education in a scholarly way, but we know that sometime between the 1960s and the 1990s, colleges and universities changed from open and relatively inexpensive academies ~~institutions~~ to institutions whose gates were closed to a number of applicants whose bank accounts could not fund their tuition fees. ~~for long periods of time.~~ In effect, the open university or college of the past has become ~~became~~ the more expensive and ~~the~~ more exclusive institution of the present as tuition fees have increased ~~were raised~~ to help meet growing deficits in post-secondary budgets. Thus, many students I know must take out student loans and work one or two part-time jobs in order to meet their expenses. Others must rely on their

parents for support, and still others must

leave their studies for one or two years when

~~money problems become too great for them to~~ manage without a steady paycheque.

~~handle.~~ ⌐¶ For better and for worse, the ~~would~~ would-be

college and university students of this decade

must~ also face the fact that their ~~high school~~ past academic

performances must be much stronger than those

of their counterparts of a decade or two ago

if they are to have ~~a~~ the chance ~~of continuing~~ to continue

their education further.~ ~Before~ For example, high school students in my

own home province of British Columbia can hope

to gain admission to ~~a university~~ one of B.C.'s universities, they must

present academic transcripts that show consistently high grade-point averages. ~~have won the battle of the high grade-point averages.~~ And if they decide to apply to one

of the province's community colleges, they

will find themselves in stiff competition with

tens of thousands of other men and women with

the same idea. It seems to many of us these

days that we are very fortunate if a~ single college

or a university chooses us, whereas our older

brothers, ~~and~~ sisters, and friends and our

parents tell us of times when they ~~choose~~ could choose from

among~ any number of acceptance letters from any number of

universities and colleges. The effect of these

tighter financial and academic requirements is

that young students must begin saving money

and building strong ∧scholastic records some three or four

years before they are ready to embark on a

post-secondary education. ∧Thus, The times have

changed and we have had to change with ~~the~~
them
~~times~~ or face being shut out or left behind

altogether in this decade of restraint and

retrenchment.

    Once today's students ~~passes through~~ win

acceptance ~~at~~ to a college or a university, they

enter into a new life just as surely as

immigrants to a new country do. And just like

the newcomers to a new land, they sometimes

have a ~~tough~~ difficult time letting go of ~~the~~ their past.

Students in their first year at college ~~and~~ or

university ~~spend much~~ have been known to spend time looking back to the

security of the high school life--to a time

and a place where they had individual

identities, where teachers knew their names,

where they couldn't walk along a ~~pathway~~ corridor

without meeting friends and a͓quaintances who

would greet them and make them feel that they

belonged.

    Well, college and university life ~~aren't~~ isn't

like that--at least not at first. In those

first weeks and months, ~~the~~ newcomer ^s^ ~~is~~ are on

^their^ ~~his~~ own some of the time. For the first time

in a long time, they may find themselves in

classrooms where they know no one. Only with

^openness and^ ~~time, humour, and~~ patience will they begin to

make friends of those ~~among~~ ^in^ that sea of

anonymous ~~faces.~~ ^people.^ But when the time comes, they

~~may well~~ ^will^ find ~~people~~ ^friends and adversaries^ who will challenge their

unexamined ideas and share their

^victories with them. What newcomers must^ disappointments and ~~triumphs The trick is to~~ ^learn is to hold on until that time comes.^ ~~hold on until that time comes.~~

What happens inside college and university

classrooms these days? Beyond the grade-point

averages, the tuition fees, the lineups ^to enroll in classes,^ to buy

textbooks ^and to order lunch,^ colleges and

universities are still places where learning

goes on. Students can be treated to lectures,

discussions, and debates on every topic from

genetic engineering to situational ethics, to

political correctness. They can have their own

ideas examined and sharpened by some of the

country's best minds ^;^ they can come into

contact with the most challenging new ideas,

theories, and applications ^in any number of disciplines.^

Students have
~~There is~~ so much to learn that learning itself becomes intimidating to them sometimes. *On my own campus,* ₐIt is not uncommon to find students leaving a class frustrated that they don't already know in advance what has been presented to them in that day's lecture. They sometimes seem insecure about learning what they don't know; they seem to want to have what they've learned *With everything else they have to adjust to,* before repeated and confirmed. ~~In short,~~ they *also* ₐneed to adjust to what it means to be a student these days--to be an individual who lives quite comfortably with uncertainty, healthy skepticism, and energetic inquiry into what we <u>need</u> to learn as opposed to what we <u>already</u> know.

④The weight of what we don't know becomes more apparent to *us* ~~students~~ at college and university than it may be at any other time in our lives. In an average academic year, thousands of words crowd themselves into our *vocabularies;* ~~vocabulary;~~ our eyes travel over dozens of chapters, hundreds of pages, and millions of *sentences.* ~~words.~~ We struggle to master complex chemical *formulae,* ~~formulas,~~ *intricate* ~~complex~~ political and economic debates, and challenging problems in every field from architecture to med~~e~~*i*cine to ecology.

As ideas crowd around ~~them, students~~ *us, we* must
~~design~~ *devise* methods by which to organize what ~~they~~ *we*
learn. ~~They~~ *We* must confront the demands of time
and learn that it is not enough to memorize
important facts and ~~sitting~~ *sit* quietly with our
hands folded in our laps as others engage in
lively debate about the issues of the day, of
days past, or of days to come. Learning at
college and university is less neat and tidy
~~and simple~~ than that. If we are to make the
most of our time ~~there,~~ we must learn *to express ourselves,*
real problems,~~,~~ *and* to exercise a healthy
skepticism about any ideas presented to us as
dogma~~, or doctrine.~~ If any student finishes
college or university without asking a probing
question, or changing *a single one of* his or her own long-
cherished ~~view,~~ *views,* or ~~expressing~~ *voicing* sincere
skepticism about the views of others, then he
or she has failed--no matter what ~~his or her~~ *the*
academic ~~record~~ *records* may say.

Learning to juggle the a*c*quisition of
knowledge with the living of a good, happy
life is one of the greatest challenges of all
for students in the nineties. The pressure of

part-time jobs,
reading assignments, lab reports, research

essays, and midterms that seem to stretch from

beginning to end of *a* term can make ~~a student~~ *students who are*

determined to excel too driven--too *and*

introspective. *for their own good.* It is not healthy to withdraw

or to brood over ~~the~~ *a* disappointing grade on a

term paper or ~~the~~ *a* less-than-perfect score on

~~the~~ *a* mid-term test. Perhaps now more the*a*n

ever--when the competition is so fe*i*rce and

demands on time, energy, and finances seem so

great--students must make reasonable time for
Such diversions as
exercise, relaxation, and relationships. Young
men
~~man~~ and women must not put real life on hold

while they strive to prepare for real life:
makes
such a strategy ~~would make~~ little logical or

psychological sense.

    At one time, college and university

campuses may have been oases of calm or havens
frantic
from the harsh and ~~busy~~ world. Perhaps

scholars once did reside in refuges known as
And
ivory towers. ~~C~~ampuses may once have fit those

romantic movie images in which intense young

people lingered long over debates in ~~smoke-~~

~~filled~~ coffee houses, strolled in leisurely

fashion along tree-lined paths to ~~wood-panelled~~

First Draft and Revisions   453

lecture halls filled with other young people
who knew their names, and never seemed to
spend much time hunched over notebooks or
slouched in front of keyboards squeezing out
the last term paper as the hands of the clock
~~signal~~ signalled the end of yet another ⸰all nighter.⸰
Students today don't live the coddled lives of
their fictional counterparts in the celluloid world. They are more
fortunate than many, no doubt, but they do not
live entirely sheltered lives sequestered from
the world they are about to join. ~~The ivory
tower may exist, but then again it may not.~~
Those of us who are students these days don't
live in or even visit ~~ivort~~ ivory towers; we just
dream about them every once in a while.

Final Draft

A Lot to Learn--Student Life in the Nineties

    To the members of Canada's work force, who
pour millions of tax dollars into the
country's educational institutions every year,
the life of a post-secondary student must seem

idyllic. To those in our country who are homeless or who are living from paycheque to paycheque, and to those struggling to survive in the shantytowns and refugee camps of the world, the life of a Canadian college or university student must seem nothing short of an impossible or even cruel dream. Viewed comparatively, the lives of those who attend this country's colleges and universities afford tremendous opportunities and privileges. We study the great ideas of the past and present with academics who are experts in their fields; we have the time, the resources, and the freedom to speculate about solutions to difficult problems and to debate controversial issues of the day with students from other parts of the country and from other countries of the world; we have the luxury of learning, socializing, and planning for bright futures all at the same time. We can work toward educational goals that, if they do not guarantee us satisfying and high-paying jobs immediately upon graduation, can nevertheless prepare us to meet the changing world with more understanding, preparation, and versatility than many others in this country or this world are able to have. We have few grounds for complaint, many would say. And they would be right.

This view of student life is one that we as students can hardly quarrel with. Life is good to us in more ways than we can count. And yet, I would guess that a national survey of today's college and university students would reveal considerable unrest and uncertainty among the men and women attending the nation's post-secondary institutions. Our lives are neither bleak nor impossible, as those of others are, but getting a higher education in the last decade of the twentieth century is not without its difficulties, no matter how the situation may appear to those on the outside looking in. Students today face obstacles in gaining entrance to colleges and universities, and once they win the opportunity to pursue their studies, they have a lot to learn: in order to succeed, they must teach themselves to meet the psychological and academic demands of student life.

Whenever students get together to talk

seriously about the facts of post-secondary life, the related topics of access and money are never far from the top of the agenda. After the boom years of the seventies and the eighties, when money for college and university operating budgets flowed quite freely, the nineties have produced a drought in educational funding. We may not have studied the evolution of education in a scholarly way, but we know that sometime between the 1960s and the 1990s, colleges and universities changed from open and relatively inexpensive academies to institutions whose gates were closed to a number of applicants whose bank accounts could not fund their tuition fees. In effect, the open university or college of the past has become the more expensive and more exclusive institution of the present as tuition fees have increased to help meet growing deficits in post-secondary budgets. Thus, many students I know must take out student loans and work one or two part-time jobs in order to meet their expenses. Others must rely on their parents for support, and still others must leave their studies for one or two years when money problems become too great for them to manage without a steady paycheque.

For better and for worse, the would-be college and university students of this decade must also face the fact that their past academic performances must be much stronger than those of their counterparts of a decade or two ago if they are to have the chance to continue their education further. For example, before high school students in my own home province of British Columbia can hope to gain admission to one of B.C.'s universities, they must present academic transcripts that show consistently high grade-point averages. And if they decide to apply to one of the province's community colleges, they will find themselves in stiff competition with tens of thousands of other men and women with the same idea. It seems to many of us these days that we are very fortunate if a single college or university chooses _us_, whereas our older brothers, sisters, and friends and our parents tell us of times when _they_ could choose from among any number of acceptance letters from any number of universities and colleges. The effect of these tighter financial and academic requirements is that young students must begin saving money and building strong scholastic records some three or four years before they are ready to embark on a post-secondary education. Thus, the times have changed and we have had to change with them or face being shut out or left behind altogether in this decade of restraint and retrenchment.

Once today's students win acceptance to a college or a university, they enter into a new life just as surely as immigrants to a new country do. And just like the newcomers to a new land, they sometimes have a difficult time letting go of their past. Students in their first year at college and university have been known to spend time looking back to the security of the high school life--to a time and a place where they had individual identities, where teachers knew their names, where they couldn't walk along a corridor without meeting friends and acquaintances who would greet them and make them feel that they belonged.

Well, college and university life is not

like that--at least not at first. In those
first weeks and months, newcomers are on their
own some of the time. For the first time in a
long time, they may find themselves in
classrooms where they know no one. Only with
openness and patience will they begin to make
friends of those in that sea of anonymous
people. But when the time comes, they will
find friends and adversaries who will
challenge their unexamined ideas and share
their disappointments and victories with them.
What newcomers must learn is to hold on until
that time comes.

What happens inside college and university
classrooms these days? Beyond the tuition
fees, the grade-point averages, the line-ups
to enroll in classes, to buy textbooks, and to
order lunch, colleges and universities are
still places where learning goes on. Students
can be treated to lectures, discussions, and
debates on every topic from genetic
engineering to situational ethics to political
correctness. They can have their own ideas
examined and sharpened by some of the
country's best minds; they can come into

contact with the most challenging new ideas, theories, and applications in any number of disciplines.

Students have so much to learn that learning itself becomes intimidating to them sometimes. On my own campus, it is not uncommon to find students leaving a class frustrated that they don't already know in advance what has been presented to them in that day's lecture. They sometimes seem insecure about learning what they don't know; they seem to want to have what they've learned before repeated and confirmed. With everything else they have to adjust to, they also need to adjust to what it means to be a student these days--to be an individual who lives quite comfortably with uncertainty, healthy skepticism, and energetic inquiry into what we <u>need</u> to learn as opposed to what we <u>already</u> know.

The weight of what we don't know becomes more apparent to us at college and university than it may be at any other time in our lives. In an average academic year, thousands of words crowd themselves into our vocabularies;

our eyes travel over dozens of chapters, hundreds of pages, millions of sentences. We struggle to master complex chemical formulae, intricate political and economic debates, and challenging problems in every field from architecture to medicine to ecology.

As ideas crowd around us, we must devise methods by which to organize what we learn. We must confront the demands of time and learn that it is not enough to memorize important facts and sit quietly with our hands folded in our laps as others engage in lively debate about the issues of the day, of days past, or of days to come. Learning at college and university is less neat and tidy than that. If we are to make the most of our time, we must learn to express ourselves, to solve real problems, and to exercise a healthy skepticism about any ideas presented to us as dogma. If any student finishes college or university without asking a probing question, or changing a single one of his or her own long-cherished views, or voicing sincere skepticism about the views of others, then he or she has failed--no matter what the academic records may say.

Learning to juggle the acquisition of knowledge with the living of a good, happy life is one of the greatest challenges of all for students in the nineties. The pressure of part-time jobs, reading assignments, lab reports, research essays, and midterms that seem to stretch from beginning to end of a term can make students who are determined to excel too driven--and too introspective for their own good. It is not healthy to withdraw or to brood over a disappointing grade on a term paper or a less-than-perfect score on a midterm test. Perhaps now more than ever--when the competition is so fierce and demands on time, energy, and finances seem so great-- students must make reasonable time for such diversions as exercise, relaxation, and relationships. Young men and women must not put real life on hold while they strive to prepare for real life: such a strategy makes little logical or psychological sense.

At one time, college and university campuses may have been oases of calm or havens from the harsh and frantic world. Perhaps scholars once did reside in refuges known as ivory towers. And campuses may once have fit those romantic movie images in which intense young people lingered over debates in coffee houses, strolled in leisurely fashion along tree-lined paths to lecture halls filled with other young people who knew their names, and never seemed to spend much time hunched over notebooks or slouched in front of keyboards squeezing out the last term paper as the hands of the clock signalled the end of yet another all nighter. Students today don't live the coddled lives of their fictional counterparts in the celluloid world. They are more fortunate than many, no doubt, but they do not live entirely sheltered lives sequestered from the world they are about to join. Those of us who are students these days don't live in or even visit ivory towers; we just dream about them every once in a while.

Reviser's Checklist

The Essay as a Whole

1. Does the whole essay stick to the purpose (see **33a**) and the subject (see **33b**)?

2. Have you kept your audience clearly in mind? Is the tone appropriate and consistent? See **33c**. Do any terms require definition?

3. Is the focus consistent (see **33d**)? Do the ideas in the essay show clear relationships to the central idea, or thesis?

4. Is the central idea or thesis sharply conceived? Does your thesis statement (if one is appropriate) clearly suggest the position and approach you are taking? See **33e**.

5. Have you chosen an effective method or combination of methods of development? See **33f**.

6. Is the essay logically sound both as a whole and in individual paragraphs and sentences? See Section **31**.

7. Will the introduction arouse the reader's interest? Does it indicate what the paper is about? See **33g**.

8. Does the essay come to a satisfying close? See **33g**.

Paragraphs

1. Are all the paragraphs unified? Are there any ideas in any paragraph that do not belong? See **32a**.

2. Is each paragraph coherent? Are sentences within each paragraph in a natural and effective order? Are the sentences connected by repetition of key words or ideas, by pronoun reference, by parallel structure, or by transitional expressions? See **32b**.

3. Is the progression between paragraphs easy and natural? Are there clear transitions where needed? See **32b(6)**.

4. Is each paragraph adequately developed? See **32c**.

Sentences and Diction

1. Have you used subordination and co-ordination to relate ideas effectively? See Section **24**.

2. Are there misplaced sentence parts or dangling modifiers? See Section **25**.

3. Do you find any faulty parallelism? See Section **26**.

4. Are there any needless shifts in grammatical structures, in tone or style, or in viewpoint? See Section **27**.

5. Does each pronoun refer clearly to its antecedent? See Section **28**. Does your choice of pronouns reflect the need for gender-neutral language?

6. Are ideas given appropriate emphasis within the sentence? See Section **29**.

7. Are the sentences varied in length? in type? See Section **30**.

8. Are there any fragments? comma splices or fused sentences? See Sections **2** and **3**.

9. Do all verbs agree with their subjects? pronouns with their antecedents? See Section **6**.

10. Have you used the appropriate form of the verb? See Section **7**.

11. Are any words overused? used imprecisely? vague? See Section **20**.

12. Have all unnecessary words and phrases been eliminated? See Section **21**. Have any necessary words been omitted? See Section **22**.

Punctuation, Spelling, Mechanics

1. Are commas (see Section **12**) and semicolons (see Section **14**) used where required by the sentence structure? Have superfluous commas been removed (see Section **13**)?

2. Is any end punctuation omitted? See Section **17**.

3. Are apostrophes (see Section **15**) and quotation marks (see Section **16**) placed correctly?

4. Are all words spelled correctly? See Section **18**.

5. Are capitals (see Section **9**), italics (see Section **10**), and abbreviations used correctly?

6. Is your manuscript in an acceptable form? Have all words been divided correctly at the ends of lines? See Section **8**.

33i

Write well-organized answers to essay tests; write effective in-class essay examinations.

(1) Write clear, concise, well-organized answers on essay tests.

When you write an answer to an essay question, you are conveying information, but you are also proving to your audience—the examiner—that you have mastered the information and can work with it. In other words, your purpose is both informative and persuasive. There are several things you can do in preparing for and taking an essay examination to ensure that you do the best job you can.

Prepare trial questions.

Perhaps the best way to get ready for an essay examination is to prepare yourself from the first day of class. Try to decide what is most important about the material you have been learning and pay attention to indications that your instructor considers certain material especially important. As you assimilate facts and concepts, attempt to work out questions that your instructor is likely to ask. Then plan how you would answer such a question.

Plan your time.

Although you will be working under severe pressure of time, take a few minutes to plan your time and your answer. Determine how many minutes you can devote to each answer. Answer the questions that are worth the most points first (unless your mind is a blank about them at that moment).

Read instructions and questions carefully.

During your examination, first read the question carefully. Most essay examination questions are carefully worded and contain specific instructions about how as well as what you are to answer. Always answer exactly the question asked without digressing to related areas unless they are called for. Furthermore, if you are asked to define or identify, do not evaluate. Instead, give clear, concise, and accurate answers. If you are asked to explain, you must demonstrate that you have a depth of understanding about the subject. If you are asked to evaluate, you must decide what is important and then measure what you plan to say against that yardstick. If you are asked to compare and contrast, you will need to have a thorough knowledge of at least two subjects and you will need to show efficiently how they are similar and/or different.

Plan your answer.

Jot down the main points you intend to make as you think through how you plan to respond. This list of main points can serve as a working plan to help you stay on target.

State main points clearly.

State your thesis in the first paragraph so that the instructor will know what you intend. Make your main points stand out from the rest of the essay by identifying them in some way. For instance, you can use transitional expressions such as *first, second, third;* you can underline each main point; or you can create headings to guide the reader.

Support generalizations.

Be sure that you support any generalizations that you make with specific details, examples, and illustrations. Write with assurance to help convince the instructor that you have a thorough knowledge of the subject. Make sure your answers are complete; do not write one- or two-sentence answers unless it is clearly specified that you should. Do not, however, pad your answers in an effort to make the instructor think you know more than you do. A clearly stated, concise, emphatic, and complete answer, though somewhat brief, will impress a reader much more than a fuzzy answer that is much longer.

Stick to the question.

Sometimes you may know more about a related question than you do about the question asked. Do not wander from the question asked by trying to answer a question that you think you could handle better. Similarly, make sure that you follow your thesis as you answer the question and do not include material that is irrelevant.

Revise or proofread.

Finally, save a few minutes to reread your answer. Make whatever corrections and revisions you think are necessary. It is much better to cross out a paragraph that is irrelevant (and to replace it with a relevant one if time permits) than to allow it to stand. Similarly, consider whether your sentences are clear and correct. Check sentence structure, spelling, and punctuation; clarify any illegible scribbles.

(2) Write well-organized, clear in-class essays.

Writing an in-class essay is much like writing any other essay except that you are usually given the topic and you must produce the finished essay during one class period. Because the writing process is so compressed, you must plan to make the best use of your time that you can. Reserve a few minutes at the end of the class period for revising and proofreading. Take a few minutes at the beginning of the class period to consider your main idea, or thesis, and make at least a mental plan.

As you draft the essay, keeping your plan in mind will help you stay on track. Pace yourself so that you can cover all your major points. Don't forget transitions. It is just as important to support your generalizations and to stick to the point in an in-class essay as in an essay test or in an essay you write at home.

In the time you have saved for revision and proofreading, check your essay for unity and coherence. Strike out any unrelated matter and make any needed insertions. Unless you are instructed to do so, it is best not to use your revising time to make a clean copy of the essay. Make your revisions as neatly and clearly as possible (see also page 113). Proofread carefully.

■ **Exercise 7** Write and revise a composition from the work you did in Exercises 4 through 6.

■ **Exercise 8** Carefully read the following composition in preparation for a class discussion of (1) its title and thesis, (2) its purpose and audience, (3) its arrangement and development of main points, (4) its beginning and ending. Also be prepared to discuss how the choice of words and the use of specific details contribute to the tone of the essay.

Can One Person Make a Difference?

Human beings are mysterious: that is an axiom of life. One of the greatest mysteries confronting individual human beings of the past and the present is the one contained in the perennial question, "Does society determine the individual, or does the individual determine society?" Many of us in North America today have grown up with the assumption that the individual is simply a product of the environment; we believe that we can't fight city hall and that we as single solitary men, women, and children can't change the world. But even a brief survey of the great inventors, the great thinkers, and the great leaders of the past suggests that individuals have made a difference. Acting alone, they have proved that one individual can change society.

Consider just a few of the inventors who have moved our species from the caves of prehistory to the skyscrapers of today. The individuals who gave us fire to cook by, light to read by, and vehicles to travel in were not robotic prisoners of the societies in which they lived. They were somehow able to think beyond the way things were to imagine better and different worlds. Their individual imaginations permitted them—even compelled them—to step out and change the conventional order of things.

In addition to the inventors who have given the world the tools and technologies of human progress, society has been determined by great thinkers who have moved our species forward through the power of their insights. No anonymous conglomerate or artificial intelligence gave us the great ideas that so influence the way that we think today. It was Socrates and not some nameless cartel who gave his "students" and students of all ages the idea of the question—the Socratic method—as a means of learning. It was Charles Darwin and not some faceless bureaucracy who gave us a fuller understanding of our place on this planet. It was Sigmund Freud and not the committees and parliaments of the late nineteenth and early twentieth centuries who gave us the thought-provoking premises about human character and sexuality that first formed the basis of the psychology that we study and debate today.

Even great leaders, who seem to be so tightly tied to and determined by the masses to whom they owe their mandates, are more often shapers of society than they are products of it. The world may be short of visionary and creative leadership at this very moment, but today is not forever. We need only look back a few decades in this century to find a shining example of individual leadership in the figure of Mahatma Gandhi. He preached and lived the philosophy of nonviolence; he moved India out of bondage and hatred and into independence by refusing to eat until the bloodshed had stopped. And although his life was ended by an assassin's bullet, his philosophy has continued to influence human rights movements from the United States to Poland to South Africa. Aren't the Gandhis of this world proof that one individual can determine an entire society?

So the individual does have power—if only he or she will recognize it and use it. We are not clones or pawns in some gigantic and incomprehensible social machine. If we use our minds to invent, to think, or to lead, we can and do make a difference. We do matter, and no amount of cynicism or shoulder-shrugging can change that simple fact of life.

—ALEXANDRA ATKINSON

The Research Paper

34

Learn how to use the library and how to write a research paper.

If you have read Section **33** on the whole composition and have written even a few essays, you are ready to begin the special kind of essay known as the research paper (or term paper). Planning, drafting, and revising a research paper involve the skills you have already developed. The distinctive feature of the research paper assignment is that it requires you to find and use information in library books and periodicals and to acknowledge your sources properly. Section **34** will help you develop these additional skills.

One of the best ways to begin a research assignment is with a question, with something you want to find out. You may also begin with a tentative *thesis* (**33e**), but if you do you must be willing to revise it if your research findings do not support it (see also **31a**). Once you have done some digging in your sources, you will be in a position to decide whether the *purpose* (**33a**) of your paper will be chiefly informative (to report, analyze, or explain) or persuasive (to prove a point). Your *audience* (**33c**) may or may not be an expert on your subject (this will depend on the assignment), but you may safely envision a reader who is intelligent, fair-minded, and interested in finding out what you have to say, and so your tone should be objective and businesslike.

A word of caution: scheduling your time is especially important because the research paper assignment usually spans several weeks and the temptation to procrastinate is strong. Divide the amount of time you are given into blocks for various stages of completion: choosing a subject, preparing a preliminary bibliography, taking notes, drafting, and revising.

34a
Choose a subject for a research paper and limit it appropriately. See also **33b** and **33d**.

Occasionally, you may be assigned a specific subject. If so, you are ready to begin your search for sources (**34b**). Often, however, choosing a subject will be up to you. An inquiring mind is the best equipment you can bring to this task: choose a subject you would enjoy knowing more about. If you are stuck for an idea, consider some of the resources mentioned in **33b.** Four reference works in the library may be especially helpful for research paper subjects: try scanning the *Library of Congress Subject Headings* (see pages 478–79) or the subject categories in the *Readers' Guide to Periodical Literature,* the *Canadian Periodical Index,* and the *New York Times Index* (see pages 479–80).

Once you have a subject in mind, your exploration of it will evolve naturally as you do your research, but the exploration methods discussed in **33d**—listing, questioning, considering perspectives, surveying development strategies—will almost certainly help you limit your subject and find an interesting focus. Limiting is especially important with the research paper since one of your main objectives is to show that you can treat a subject in some depth within the constraints of time and (usually) a specified length. One basic test of any subject you may have in mind is the amount of pertinent material in the library. If you find dozens of relevant sources, you may be getting in over your head and you should probably narrow the subject to one with a more manageable scope. Conversely, if you find only two or three sources, chances are that your subject is too narrow and needs to be more inclusive.

■ **Exercise 1** Select a subject that would be suitable for a research paper. Then check the availability of materials. (If you cannot find enough books, periodicals, and so on, try another subject.) As you skim through the information, perhaps beginning with an encyclopedia, single out facets of the subject that you would like to investigate further. Finally, limit the subject so that you can develop it in a paper of the assigned length.

34b
Learn to find the library materials you need and to prepare a working bibliography.

College and university libraries are organized to make research as efficient as possible. Most provide a map or diagram—either printed for handing out or posted in a prominent place—to show you where various kinds of materials are located. Reference books, encyclopedias, and indexes—materials that cannot usually be checked out of the library—are located in the *reference collection.* Other books are located in the *stacks* or at the *reserve desk* and may be checked out for a specified length of time. If your library has a closed-stack policy, you request the books you need by call number in the *main catalogue* (on cards, in microform, or on a computer). If the stacks are open, however, you may find it useful to browse among the books shelved near those you have located through the catalogue. *Periodicals* (magazines, journals, newspapers) and their indexes are usually stored in a special section of the library. Also bear in mind that many colleges and universities, especially those in the same geographic area, have arrangements for the exchange of books between libraries. You may also be entitled to use the facilities of other college and university libraries in your area. If you have difficulty locating or using any research materials, do not hesitate to ask a *reference librarian* for help.

(1) Learn to find books and periodicals.

Books

The first place to look is usually the *main catalogue.* This may be a traditional card catalogue, or it may be in microform or on a computer. Long-established libraries with extensive collections may combine these, so it is always wise to find out how the collections are catalogued.

The Card Catalogue   The card catalogue lists all books and, usually, all periodicals in the library's collection. In many libraries one general catalogue lists all books owned by the college or university and shows whether a book is in the general library or in a special collection in another building.

The card catalogue consists of cards arranged alphabetically in drawers. For each book, cards are filed alphabetically in at least three ways: by author, by title, and by subject or subjects. Major libraries may also have a location file to indicate where the book is kept or whether it is available in several locations. For example, a university library may have separate collections (sometimes in buildings spread across a large campus) for such fields as medicine, law, forestry, engineering, and music. Author and title cards are often filed separately. These cards are identical except that the title card and the subject card have extra headings (See the following illustration for an example.)

SAMPLE CATALOGUE CARD

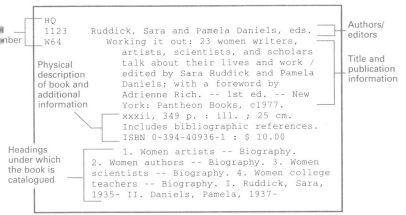

```
HQ
1123      Ruddick, Sara and Pamela Daniels, eds.
W64          Working it out: 23 women writers,
               artists, scientists, and scholars
               talk about their lives and work /
               edited by Sara Ruddick and Pamela
               Daniels; with a foreword by
               Adrienne Rich. -- 1st ed. -- New
               York: Pantheon Books, c1977.
             xxxii, 349 p. : ill. ; 25 cm.
             Includes bibliographic references.
             ISBN 0-394-40936-1 : $ 10.00
             1. Women artists -- Biography.
          2. Women authors -- Biography. 3. Women
          scientists -- Biography. 4. Women college
          teachers -- Biography. I. Ruddick, Sara,
          1935- II. Daniels, Pamela, 1937-
```

Call number — HQ 1123 W64

Physical description of book and additional information

Headings under which the book is catalogued

Authors/editors

Title and publication information

This example is an author card. Cards filed by title and by subject will have the same information under different headings.

The Microfilm or Microfiche Catalogue As book collections have grown, some libraries have turned to the microfilm or microfiche catalogue, essentially the card catalogue information reproduced in miniature on film, which is read on a special magnifying viewer. As with the card catalogue, you need to find out if author, title, and subject entries are alphabetized in the same listing or in separate listings.

The Computer Catalogue Today, more and more college and university libraries are computerizing their catalogues. Students use terminals (located in the library and often elsewhere on campus) to query the computer. By pressing a few lettered keys, users have instant access to information about an author, a title, a subject, an editor, and so on.

Some libraries also subscribe to commercial data-base services that transfer information from printed indexes, abstracts, government documents, and other such material to computer files that give users immediate access to this information. Data-base searches offer the advantages of speed and comprehensiveness. However, they have the disadvantage of expense (the user is charged a fee), and much of the material listed may not be available to you except on interlibrary loan.

The following illustration shows a title entry from a computer catalogue.

```
UBC Library Public System

:1   TITLE:        The integrated circus: the New
                   Right and the restructuring of
                   global markets. / M. Patricia
                   Marchak.
     NAMES:        Marchak, M. Patricia, 1936-
     CALL NUMBER:  HM 211 M37 1991
     LOCATION:     Main Stacks
                   Sedgewick Library has c.2

     STATUS:
         HM 211 M37 1991 [mn]    SEDGEWICK 04Sep92

     SOURCE:       Montreal: McGill-Queen's
                   University Press, 1991.
     DESCRIPTION:  xiv, 320p. ; 24cm.
     SUBJECTS:     Free enterprise.
                   Conservatism.
     NOTES:        Includes bibliographical
                   references (p.[289]-308) and
                   index.
                   For RELated works, enter REL
     Enter a command (or HELP):
```

Library of Congress Subject Headings   If your library uses Library of Congress numbers for cataloguing books, there is an easy way to find out quickly what books your library has in your subject area. First, look for your subject in the *Library of Congress Subject Headings*. If your subject is indexed by that catalogue, you will find a specific catalogue number for books on your subject as well as cross-references to related subject areas that may help you sharpen your focus. If you find a number indexed, write it down; then find that number in your library's own *shelf list*, which lists all the books in the library by call number. The first part of a call number indicates the subject of a book (for example, TJ163.5). Therefore, when you look up the call number of only one book, you will find adjacent to it call numbers of other books the library owns on that subject.

Other Indexes   You may wish to consult other standard references. The *Cumulative Book Index* lists books by author and subject. The standard references for books in print in Canada, Britain, and the United States are *Canadian Books in Print, Whittaker's Books in Print* (British), and *Books in Print* and *Paperbound Books in Print* (American). All are arranged by author and title. All are updated annually, and all list publishers' addresses in their respective countries. In addition, a *Subject Index* and a *Subject Guide* are available for the Canadian and American catalogues.

Periodicals

Since periodicals (magazines, journals, newspapers) are published frequently (and much more quickly than books), they often contain the most recent information on your subject. A variety of the periodical indexes (usually located in the reference section of the library) do for articles what the main catalogue does for books. You may need to consult a number of these indexes to find the information you need, since each index includes some publications not listed in the others.

General-Interest Periodicals   If your subject is one that may have been dealt with in popular or general-interest magazines or in newspapers, you will want to consult the

Readers' Guide to Periodical Literature, published from 1900 to the present, the *Canadian Periodical Index,* and newspaper indexes, the best known of which is the *New York Times Index,* published since 1913.

The front pages of each issue of the *Readers' Guide* provide an explanation of a sample entry as well as a key to abbreviations.

SUBJECT ENTRY

> **ETHNIC CLEANSING**
> Commission on Human Rights: 'ethnic cleansing' condemned. *UN Chronicle* 29:22 D '92
> "Ethnic cleansing". C.A. White. *Canada and the World* 58:5–7 S '92
> Murder at Ugar Gorge. J.L. Graff. il *Time* 140:62 O 12 '92
> Original virtue, original sin [Bosnian Muslims in Banja Luka] D. Rieff. *The New Yorker* 68:82–8+ N 23 '92
> Walcott blasts 'ethnic cleansing' in Europe during Nobel ceremony. il pors *Jet* 83:24 D 28 '92–Ja 4 '93
> Watching rights [ethnic cleansing by Serbs] A. Neier. *The Nation* 255:765 D 21 '92
> Why are the camps still full? [survivors of Serb camps in Bosnia qualify as political refugees] C. Lane. il *Newsweek* 120:37 N 9 '92
> Why does the world ignore "ethnic cleansing" in Africa? W. Soyinka. il *New Perspectives Quarterly* 9:52–3 Fall '92

This subject entry on the form of genocide known as "ethnic cleansing" appears in the *Readers' Guide* quarterly cumulative index issued in February 1993. It lists items published between 9 October 1992 and 14 January 1993. The first item listed in this entry is an unsigned article entitled "Commission on Human Rights: 'Ethnic Cleansing' Condemned." The article was published in Vol. 29 of the periodical *UN Chronicle,* on page 22 of the December 1992 issue.

PERSONAL NAME ENTRY

> **GOULD, STEPHEN JAY, 1941–**
> The confusion over evolution [cover story] il *The New York Review of Books* 39:47–54 N 19 '92
> Dreams that money can buy. il *The New York Review of Books* 39:41–5 N 5 '92

What is a species? il *Discover* 13:40+ D '92
  about
When the human urge to collect takes over a life. J.P. Wiley, Jr.
  il *Smithsonian* 23:92–9 O '92

This entry for biologist Stephen Jay Gould also appears in the February 1993 issue of the *Readers' Guide.* It first lists three articles written by Gould and then one article about him. One of the articles written by Gould, "The Confusion over Evolution," is an illustrated cover story appearing in Vol. 39 of the *New York Review of Books,* the 19 November 1992 issue, on pages 47–54. The article written about Gould, "When the Human Urge to Collect Takes over a Life," is an illustrated piece by J.P. Wiley, Jr. It appears in Vol. 23 of *Smithsonian,* on pages 92–99 of the magazine's October 1992 issue.

For older articles of general interest you can consult *Poole's Index,* 1802–1907, or *Nineteenth Century Readers' Guide,* 1890–99.

Special-Interest Periodicals   Virtually every specialized field has its own periodicals. Some of the most useful indexes to them are listed below.

Applied Science and Technology Index. 1958–. Formerly *Industrial Arts Index.* 1913–57.
Art Index. 1929–.
Biography Index. 1946–.
Biological and Agricultural Index. 1964–. Formerly *Agricultural Index.* 1916–64.
Business Periodicals Index. 1958–.
Canadian Essay and Literature Index. 1973–.
Canadian Index. 1993–. Formerly *Canadian Business Periodicals Index.* 1975–80. *Canadian Business Index.* 1980–92. *Canadian News Index.* 1980–92.
Current Index to Journals in Education. 1969–.
Education Index. 1929–.
Engineering Index. 1884–.
Government of Canada Publications/Publications du Gouvernement du Canada. (Revised quarterly)

Humanities Index. 1974–. Formerly *Social Sciences and Humanities Index.* 1965–73. *International Index.* 1907–65.
Index to Legal Periodicals. 1908–.
Microlog: Canadian Research Index. 1979–. (Canadian research index, includes Canadian federal, provincial, and local government publications; bilingual; revised monthly.)
Music Index. 1949–.
Public Affairs Information Service (Bulletin). 1915–.
Social Sciences Index. 1974–. Formerly *Social Sciences and Humanities Index.* 1965–73. *International Index.* 1907–65.
United States Government Publications (Monthly Catalogue). 1895–.
See also the various abstracts, such as *Chemical Abstracts,* 1907–; *Abstracts of English Studies,* 1958–; *Abstracts of Popular Culture,* 1976–82.

Reference Books

For a detailed list of reference books, with a short description of each, consult *Canadian Reference Sources: A Selected Guide* by Dorothy E. Ryder, *Guide to Basic Reference Materials for Canadian Libraries,* edited by Claire England, *Guide to Reference Books* (with supplements) by Eugene P. Sheehy, and *American Reference Books Annual (ARBA),* edited by Bohdan S. Wynar and Anna G. Patterson. A few of the most important reference books are listed on the following pages (with abbreviated bibliographical information).

Another useful research tool is *Microform Research Collections: A Guide,* edited by Suzanne Cates Dodson. This book lists, in detail, available microform resources and describes each set as well as any associated indexes and bibliographies.

General dictionaries (unabridged)

A Dictionary of American English on Historical Principles. 4 vols. 1938–44.
Century Dictionary and Cyclopedia. 12 vols. 1911. 3 vols. 1927–33.

New Standard Dictionary of the English Language. 1947, 1952, 1966.

The Oxford English Dictionary. 20 vols. 1989. Originally issued as *A New English Dictionary on Historical Principles.* 10 vols. and supp. 1888–1933. Supplements.

The Random House Dictionary of the English Language. 2nd ed. 1987.

Webster's Third New International Dictionary. 1986.

Special dictionaries: language

Avis, Walter, et al. *A Dictionary of Canadianisms on Historical Principles.* 1967.

Cassidy, Frederic G. *Dictionary of American Regional English.* Vol. 1 (A–C). Vol. 2 (D–H). 1985–.

Chapman, Robert L., ed. *New Dictionary of American Slang.* 1986.

Cowie, A.P., and R. Mackin. *Oxford Dictionary of Current Idiomatic English.* Vol. I–. 1975–.

Fowler, H.W. *Dictionary of Modern English Usage.* 2nd ed. Rev. Sir Ernest Gowers. 1965.

Hayakawa, S.I., and the Funk and Wagnalls dictionary staff. *Modern Guide to Synonyms and Related Words.* 1968.

Mawson, C.O.S. *Dictionary of Foreign Terms.* 2nd ed. Rev. Charles Berlitz. 1975.

Morris, William, and Mary Morris. *Harper Dictionary of Contemporary Usage.* 2nd ed. 1985.

New Dictionary of American Slang. Ed. Robert L. Chapman. 1986.

Onions, C.T. *Oxford Dictionary of English Etymology.* 1967.

Partridge, Eric. *Dictionary of Catch Phrases.* 1979.

——. *Dictionary of Slang and Unconventional English.* 8th ed. 1984.

Random House Thesaurus. College ed. Ed. Jess Stein and Stewart Berg Flexner. 1984.

Roget's Thesaurus. New ed. Ed. Betty Kirkpatrick. 1987.

Roget's 21st Century Thesaurus in Dictionary Form. Ed. Barbara Kipfer. 1992.

Vinay, Jean-Paul. *The Canadian Dictionary: French-English/ English-French.* 1962.

General encyclopedias

Academic American Encyclopedia. 21 vols. 1984.
Collier's Encyclopedia. 24 vols. 1988.
Encyclopaedia Britannica. 32 vols. 1990.
Encyclopedia Americana. Intl. ed. 30 vols. 1989.
Encyclopedia Canadiana. 10 vols. 1977.

Special encyclopedias and dictionaries

Adams, James T. *Dictionary of American History.* Rev. ed. 8 vols. 1976.
Cambridge Encyclopaedia of Astronomy. Ed. Simon Mitton. 1977.
Canadian Encyclopedia. 2nd ed. 4 vols. 1988.
Colombo, John Robert. *Colombo's Canadian References.* 1976.
Dictionary of the History of Ideas. Ed. Philip P. Wierner et al. 5 vols. 1973.
Encyclopedia of American Foreign Policy. Ed. Alexander DeConde. 3 vols. 1978.
Encyclopedia of Computers and Data Processing. Vol. I–. 1978–.
Encyclopedia of Philosophy. Ed. Paul Edwards et al. 4 vols. 1973.
Encyclopedia of Psychology. 2nd ed. Ed. Hans Jurgen Eysenck et al. 1979.
Encyclopedia of World Art. 17 vols. 1959–68. Supplements.
Flanders, Stephen A., and Carl N. Flanders. *Dictionary of American Foreign Affairs.* 1992.
Focal Encyclopedia of Photography. Rev. ed. 1980.
Grzimek's Animal Life Encyclopedia. 13 vols. 1972–75.
International Encyclopedia of Higher Education. Ed. Asa K. Knowles. 10 vols. 1977.
International Encyclopedia of the Social Sciences. Ed. D.E. Sills. 17 vols. 1968. Supplements.
Kallmann, Helmut, et al. *Encyclopedia of Music in Canada.* 2nd ed. 1992.
Klein, Barry, and D. Icolari. *Reference Encyclopedia of the American Indian.* 6th ed. 1992.
Kurian, George Thomas. *Encyclopedia of The Third World.* 3 vols. 1987.

McGraw-Hill Encyclopedia of Science and Technology. 20 vols. 7th ed. 1992.

Munn, Glenn G., Ferdinand L. Garcia, and Charles J. Woelfel. *The St. James Encyclopedia of Banking and Finance.* 9th ed. 1991.

The New Grove Dictionary of Music and Musicians. Ed. Stanley Sadie. 20 vols. 1980.

Stierlin, Henri. *Encyclopaedia of World Architecture.* 2 vols. 2nd ed. 1979.

Story, Norah. *Oxford Companion to Canadian History and Literature.* 1967. Supplement, 1973.

Thompson, Oscar. *International Cyclopedia of Music and Musicians.* 11th ed. [Ed. Bruce Bohle.] 1985.

Atlases

Commercial Atlas and Marketing Guide (Rand McNally). 1992.
Cosmopolitan World Atlas (Rand McNally). 1992.
Historical Atlas of Canada. 2 vols. 1990.
National Atlas of Canada. 5th ed. 1985.
National Geographic Atlas of the World. 6th ed. 1990.
The Times (London) Atlas of the World: Comprehensive Edition. 1992.
Today's World: A New World Atlas from the Cartographers of Rand McNally. 1992.
U.S. Department of the Interior Geological Survey. *The National Atlas of the United States of America.* 1970.

Yearbooks—current events

Americana Annual. 1923–.
Annual Register. 1758–.
Britannica Book of the Year. 1938–.
Canada Year Book. 1867–.
Canadian Almanac and Directory. 1847–.
Canadian Global Almanac. 1992–.
Canadian News Facts. 1967–.
Facts on File. 1940–.
Information Please Almanac. 1947–.
Pears Cyclopaedia. 1898–.
Quick Canadian Facts. 1945–.

Reader's Digest Almanac and Yearbook. 1966–.
Statesman's Year-Book. 1864–.
Statistical Abstract of the United States. 1878–.
World Almanac and Book of Facts. 1868–.

Biography

Canadian Who's Who. 1875–.
Contemporary Authors. 1962–.
Current Biography. 1940–.
Dictionary of American Biography. 16 vols. and index. 1927–80. Supplements.
Dictionary of Canadian Biography. 12 vols. and index (vols. 1–12). 1966–.
Dictionary of National Biography (British). 22 vols. 1882–1953. Rpt. 1981. Supplements.
Dictionary of Scientific Biography. 18 vols. 1970–90.
International Who's Who (London). 1935–.
Macmillan Dictionary of Canadian Biography. 4th ed. 1978.
McGraw-Hill Encyclopedia of World Biography. 12 vols. 1973.
Webster's Biographical Dictionary. 1980.
Who's Who in America. 1899–. [See also *Marquis Who's Who Publications: Index to All Books* (revised annually).]

Literature

Bartlett's Familiar Quotations. 15th ed. 1981.
Benét's Reader's Encyclopedia. 3rd ed. 1987.
Cambridge History of American Literature. 3 vols. in 1. 1943.
Canadian Essay and Literature Index. 1973–.
Carpenter, Humphrey, and Mari Pritchard. *Oxford Companion to Children's Literature.* 1984.
Colombo, John Robert. *Colombo's Canadian Quotations.* 1974.
Drabble, Margaret. *Oxford Companion to English Literature.* 5th ed. 1985.
Essay and General Literature Index. 1900–.
Evans, Bergen. *Dictionary of Quotations.* 1968.
Fiction Catalog. 12th ed. 1991. Supplements.
Granger's Index to Poetry. 8th ed. 1986.
Hamilton, Robert M., and Dorothy Shields. *Dictionary of Canadian Quotations and Phrases.* 2nd ed. 1982.

Hart, James D. *Oxford Companion to American Literature.*
  5th ed. 1983.
Harvey, Sir Paul, *Oxford Companion to Classical Literature.*
  2nd ed. 1937. Rpt. 1989.
Hirsch, E.D., Joseph E. Kett, and James Trefil. *Dictionary of
  Cultural Literacy.* 1988.
Holman, C. Hugh. *Handbook to Literature.* 6th ed. 1992.
Klein, Leonard G. *Encyclopedia of World Literature in the 20th
  Century.* 2nd ed. 4 vols. 1981–84.
Klinck, Carl F., et al. *Literary History of Canada.* 2nd ed. 4 vols.
  1990.
New Cambridge Bibliography of English Literature. 5 vols.
  1969–77.
Oxford Dictionary of Quotations. 4th ed. 1992.
Patterson, Margaret C. *Literary Research Guide.* 2nd ed. 2nd rev.
  ptg. 1984.
Play Index (Wilson). 5 vols. 1949–.
Seymour-Smith, Martin. *Funk and Wagnalls Guide to Modern
  World Literature.* 1975.
Short Story Index (Wilson). 1953. Supplements.
Smith, Horatio. *Columbia Dictionary of Modern European
  Literature.* 2nd ed. 1980.
Spiller, Robert E., et al. *Literary History of the United States.*
  4th ed. 2 vols. 1974.
Toye, William. *Oxford Companion to Canadian Literature.* 1983.
Watters, Reginald Eyre. *A Checklist of Canadian Literature and
  Background Materials, 1628–1960.* 1972.
Watters, Reginald Eyre, and Inglis Freeman Bell. *On Canadian
  Literature, Its Authors and Language.* 1973.

(2) Prepare a working bibliography.

A working, or preliminary, bibliography contains information (titles, authors, dates, and so on) about the materials
you think you might use. Write down the most promising
sources you can find. Put each on a separate card (preferably 7.6 cm × 12.7 cm [3 × 5 inches]) so that you can readily drop or add a card and can arrange the list alphabeti-

cally without recopying it. Follow consistently the bibliographical form you are instructed to use. Following that
style from the start will save you valuable time later, when
you must compile a formal list of works cited to appear at
the end of your paper.

The style illustrated by the samples on the next page follows the 1988 guidelines of the Modern Language
Association (MLA). On pages 506–520 are examples of all
the kinds of entries you are likely to need.

BIBLIOGRAPHY CARDS

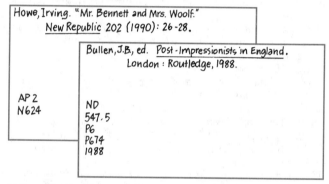

■ **Exercise 2**   Select a subject (the one you chose for Exercise 1
on page 475 or a different one) and prepare a working bibliography. Often you will find helpful bibliographies in the books that
you consult, especially in encyclopedias and other reference
books.

34c
Evaluate and take notes on your sources.

As you take notes on your readings, learn how to find and
evaluate useful passages with a minimum of time and
effort. Seldom will a whole book, or even a whole article,
be of use as subject matter for any given research paper. To

get what is needed for your paper, you will find that you must turn to many books and articles, rejecting most of them altogether and using from others only a section here and there. You cannot always take the time to read each book completely. Use the table of contents and the index of a book, and learn to skim the pages until you find the passages you need.

One important consideration always is the reliability of the source. Do others speak of the writer as an authority? As you read, do you find evidence that the author is competent, well informed, not prejudiced in any way? Is the work recent enough to provide up-to-date information? Is the edition the latest one available? The *Book Review Digest,* which contains convenient summaries of critical opinion on a book, may help you make decisions about which sources in your bibliography are most dependable.

As you take notes, be especially careful to indicate clearly on each note card what part of the information is your own idea and what came from the source; write down exactly where an idea or a quotation appears in the source and check the bibliographical information to be sure it is accurate. Scrupulous care now can prevent a multitude of problems later on—such as your having to go back to the library to check the accuracy of a quotation or to look up additional bibliographic information about a source when you are actually drafting your paper.

One of the best ways to take notes is on cards of uniform size, preferably 10 cm × 15 cm (4 × 6 inches). Each card must show the source of the note, including the exact page from which it is drawn. When information is taken from more than one page, be sure to indicate in your notes exactly where one page ends and another begins. It is a good idea to put a single note, or closely related ideas from a single source, on one card with a heading—a key word or phrase. You can then easily arrange your note cards as you make changes in organization.

BIBLIOGRAPHY CARD WITH SOURCE

> Dunn, Jane. <u>A Very Close Conspiracy</u>: Vanessa Bell and
>   <u>Virginia Woolf</u>. London : Jonathan Cape, 1990.

SOURCE (from page 149)

> The painterly qualities in Virginia Woolf's work provide enough speculation and example for a study in themselves. Everywhere there is evidence of how fertile for Virginia were the painters' preoccupations and explorations at this time. Sentences, she realised, were like brush-strokes, they had a rhythm and a shape that were distinctive to the artist who made them. Her acute visual sense suffused her writing, giving the sense on countless occasions that she was creating a picture, painting with the pared-down boldness and simplicity of a Post-Impressionist.

NOTE CARD

> <u>Post-Impressionism in Woolf's fiction</u>
> (Dunn 149)
>
> Woolf's work reflected the "preoccupations and explorations" of painters.
>
> How? "Her sentences were like brush strokes" in their style. Her work was visual in the same ways that Post-Impressionist paintings were.
>
> "The painterly qualities in Virginia Woolf's work provide enough speculation and example for a study in themselves."

For other examples of note cards, see pages 536, 538, 562.

Another way to take notes is to use photocopies of short excerpts from materials you think you may quote directly. On a photocopy you may mark quotable material and jot down your own ideas as you study the source.

PHOTOCOPIED SOURCE WITH NOTES

from Vol. I A Woman's Essays : Selected Essays V. Woolf
(85)

MR BENNETT AND MRS BROWN

WOOLF ON HER
CONTEMPORARIES

controlling/central
idea - possible title
for my essay?

{ quotable!
Woolf's
squeamishness?}

with an aunt for the weekend rolls in the geranium bed out of sheer desperation as the solemnities of the sabbath wear on. The more adult writers do not, of course, indulge in such wanton exhibitions of spleen. Their sincerity is desperate, and their courage tremendous; it is only that they do not know which to use, a fork or their fingers. Thus, if you read Mr Joyce or Mr Eliot you will be struck by the indecency of the one, and the obscurity of the other. Mr Joyce's indecency in *Ulysses*[28] seems to me the conscious and calculated indecency of a desperate man who feels that in order to breathe he must break the windows. At moments, when the window is broken, he is magnificent. But what a waste of energy! And, after all, how dull indecency is when it is not the overflowing of a super-abundant energy or savagery, but the determined and public-spirited act of a man who needs fresh air! Again, with the obscurity of Mr Eliot. I think Mr. Eliot has written some of the loveliest single lines of modern poetry. But how intolerant he is of the old usages and politeness of society—respect for the weak, consideration for the dull!

Direct quotations

Any quotations that you use in your paper should be convincing and important ones. They should be made an integral part of your text. (For examples of ways this can be done, see pages 529, 535.) When you discover a quotable passage in your reading, you should take it down verbatim—that is, copy every word, every capital letter, and every mark of punctuation exactly as in the original. Be sure to enclose the quoted passage in quotation marks. When you are quoting, quote accurately. When you are not quoting, use your own sentence structure and wording, not a slightly altered version of your source. Any quotation (except well-known or proverbial passages) of the words of another person should be placed inside quotation marks (or indented if over four lines in length), and exact sources should be cited.

> In <u>Hamlet's Mother and Other Women</u>, Carolyn Heilbrun observes that "in their separate ways, Joyce and Woolf divide the modern genius between them" (66).

[Quotation marks enclose copied words, and internal documentation indicates the source.]

For other examples of the use and the documentation of direct quotations, see the sample research paper on pages 527–71.

As you write your research paper, keep a few guidelines in mind when you are quoting the exact words of another writer. Pay close attention to form, punctuation, and spacing: see **16a**. Use ellipsis points appropriately to indicate omissions: see **17i**. But do not use ellipsis points before quotations that are only parts of sentences. To avoid ellipsis points at the beginning of a quotation (especially one that begins a paragraph), use a word like *that* or an introductory word group before the quotation.

Paraphrase

A paraphrase is a restatement of the source in about the same number of words. As you compare the source on the next page with the paraphrase that follows, notice differences in sentence structure and word choice.

SOURCE   (from the introduction to *Post-Impressionists in England,* edited by J.R. Bullen)

In 1910 many people in Britain thought they were witnessing a break in the artistic continuity of European art and the arrival of so-called Post-Impressionist painting in England served to polarise attitudes to both the function and status of art in contemporary life.

PARAPHRASE

> J.R. Bullen states that people living in
> Britain in 1910 believed that they were faced
> with the rejection of principles of European
> art; the exhibition of Post-Impressionist
> paintings seemed to stimulate a debate over
> the role and place of art in this context (1).

For further examples of the use and documentation of paraphrases, see pages 532–37.

Summary

A summary is a concise restatement (shorter than the source). When you paraphrase or summarize, avoid not only copying the actual words but also imitating the writer's style or sentence structure. If you cannot do this and you need the material, quote it directly.

SOURCE   (from "Mr Bennett and Mrs Brown" by Virginia Woolf)

> My first assertion is one that I think you will grant—that every one in this room is a judge of character. Indeed it would be impossible to live for a year without disaster unless one practised character-reading and had some skill in the art. Our marriages, our friendships depend on it; our

business largely depends on it; every day questions arise which can only be solved by its help. And now I will hazard a second assertion, which is more disputable perhaps, to the effect that in or about December 1910 human character changed.

SUMMARY

As Woolf observed in "Mr. Bennett and Mrs. Brown," we are all required to engage in "character-reading." We must evaluate the characters of others in our private, public, and professional lives, and we must read character in answering many of the questions we face in our daily lives. Woolf went on to argue that the human character we all must learn to read changed "in or about December 1910" (70).

■ **Exercise 3**   Carefully read paragraphs 1 (pages 369–70) and 38 (page 397) in Section **32**. First write a paraphrase of one of these paragraphs. Then write a summary of the same paragraph. Unless you are quoting directly, avoid using the sentence patterns of the source. To convey the ideas in the source exactly, choose your words carefully.

Plagiarism

You must acknowledge all material quoted, paraphrased, or summarized from any work. Failing to cite a source, deliberately or accidentally, is plagiarizing—presenting as your own work the words or ideas of another. As the *MLA Handbook* (New York: Modern Language Assn., 1988) states,

The most blatant form of plagiarism is to repeat as your own someone else's sentences, more or less verbatim. . . . Other forms of plagiarism include repeating someone else's particularly apt phrase without appropriate acknowledgment, paraphrasing another person's argument as your own, and presenting another's line of thinking as though it were your own. (sec. 1.6)

After you have done a good deal of reading about a given subject, you will be able to distinguish between common knowledge in that field—facts, dates, and figures—and the distinctive ideas or interpretations of specific writers. When you use the ideas or information that these writers provide, be sure to cite the exact source of the material used.

NOT In <u>Post-Impressionists in England</u>, Post-Impressionist painting is described as polarizing attitudes to both the function and status of art. [undocumented copying]

BUT In <u>Post-Impressionists in England</u>, J.R. Bullen comments that Post-Impressionism "served to polarise attitudes to both the function and status of art" (1). [Quotation marks enclose copied words, and the page number in parentheses cites the source.]

NOT Virginia Woolf wrote with the pared-down boldness and simplicity of a Post-Impressionist. [an undocumented idea from the work of another writer]

BUT Virginia Woolf's writing has been compared to Post-Impressionist painting (Dunn 149).

OR

Jane Dunn states that Virginia Woolf wrote "with the pared-down boldness and simplicity of a Post-Impressionist" (149).

If you are in doubt about whether you need to cite a source, the best policy is to cite it.

34d
Make a working plan or outline.

After completing a working bibliography and taking notes on your subject, make a working plan for your paper. Be careful, though, not to adhere too rigidly to this plan. No plan or outline should be regarded as complete until the research paper has been finished. As you write the paper, you will probably revise your original plan frequently, adding points, changing points, and perhaps dropping points you had originally intended to cover.

It is sometimes useful, especially if your paper is long or complicated, to have a detailed outline before you actually begin to write. If you work best with a formal outline, decide whether to use a topic outline or a sentence outline. A topic outline presents information in parallel phrases or single words (see pages 434–35 and 524–25). A sentence outline presents the same ideas in declarative statements (see page 434). If your instructor has asked you to submit a formal outline of your paper before you begin to draft, prepare a topic or sentence outline as you are directed.

When you have finished drafting your paper, a good way to check your organization is to correlate the ideas in your text with those in an outline and to make any needed revisions. Also check the form of your outline; see **33f**, pages 434–35. As you study the sample research paper on pages 527–71, notice that the arrangement of paragraphs accords with that of the divisions of the topic outline.

34e
Draft and revise the research paper. Use an acceptable form for your citations and prepare a list of works cited.

After you have taken notes and organized your material, you should be ready to begin writing. Using the headings on your note cards (see page 489), arrange your notes in the order of your working plan or outline and then use them as the basis of your paper. Naturally you will need to expand some parts, cut others, and provide transitions. As you draft the paper, remember that it is *your* paper. Write it in your own words, your own style. Integrate your source material—paraphrases, summaries, quotations—with your own statements rather than making the paper a patchwork of other people's comments.

(1) Citations

Since the material in your research paper comes largely from the work of others, you will need to give proper credit by citing your sources. Traditionally, such citations took the form of notes numbered consecutively throughout the paper and placed either at the bottom of the appropriate pages (footnotes) or all together at the end of the paper (endnotes). For examples of the endnote (or footnote) style and the APA system for citation, see pages 572–77 and 578–80. Beginning in 1984, however, the practice recommended by the Modern Language Association is to place citations of sources directly in the text, in parentheses. Numbers in the text refer to supplementary or explanatory comments (see the notes on page 565). Parenthetical citations refer the reader to a list of works cited at the end of the paper.

The basic elements of the citation are the author's last name, a shortened but easily understood form of the title (with, if necessary, the volume number), and the page number of the material used from the source. However, only enough information to guide the reader to the appropriate source is necessary. In other words, the author's name and the title of the source can be omitted from the parenthetical citation if they are clearly identified outside the parentheses nearby in the text of the paper.

Furthermore, if only one work by a given author is listed in "Works Cited," the work's title can be omitted from the parenthetical citation. As you study the following examples, observe that common sense rather than hard and fast rules determines the information that must be included in a parenthetical citation.

A work by one author

The following examples from the research paper on pages 527–71 provide enough information to refer readers to the appropriate pages of the works listed alphabetically in the list of works cited at the end of the paper.

```
Virginia Woolf's writing has been compared to

Post-Impressionist painting (Dunn 149).
```

In this citation, the author is not identified in the text, and her name therefore appears within parentheses. Because only one work by Dunn is included in the list of works cited, there is no need to use the title in the parentheses. However, the reference to a specific passage and not to the Dunn work as a whole requires citing the page number.

```
Woolf described the public reaction to the

1910 exhibition of Post-Impressionist paintings

at the Grafton Gallery in the following words:

"The public in 1910 was thrown into paroxysms

of rage and laughter. They went from Cézanne

to Gauguin and from Gauguin to Van Gogh, they

went from Picasso to Signac, and from Derain

to Friesz, and they were infuriated" (Roger

Fry 153-54).
```

In this citation, Woolf has been identified in the text of the paper as the source of the quotation and need not be named in the citation. However, since Woolf is the author of two works in the list of works cited, the title (shortened) is necessary.

Both citations supply only the information the reader needs to identify the source, but suppose that the quotations were combined and worded differently, as in the following example. Notice the information that must change for the citations to be complete.

> Post-Impressionism arrived in England in dramatic fashion when members of the public visited an exhibit of Post-Impressionist paintings at the Grafton Galleries. They responded with "rage and laughter. They went from Cézanne to Gauguin and from Gauguin to Van Gogh, they went from Picasso to Signac, and from Derain to Friesz, and they were infuriated" (Roger Fry 153-54). Whereas the public reaction was hostile, the reaction of a writer like Virginia Woolf was profound and positive. Biographer Jane Dunn has observed that Woolf's writing took on the features of the Post-Impressionist painting (149).

Observe that although the same sources as before are cited, Woolf must now be identified as the author of the direct quotation, and Dunn, now named in the actual text of the fifth sentence, needs no further mention in the citation.

Suppose that the text of the second sentence of this example had been written differently and provided additional information about the source, as in the following version.

In Roger Fry, her biography of the man who
brought the work of Post-Impressionist
painters to London in 1910, Woolf records the
public reaction to the Grafton Galleries'
exhibit as one of "rage and laughter. They
went from Cézanne to Gauguin and from Gauguin
to Van Gogh, they went from Picasso to Signac,
and from Derain to Friesz, and they were
infuriated" (153-54).

Because author and title are clear from the context, the citation is simply a page number.

A work by two authors

By cleverly manipulating carefully selected
facts, propagandists today either ignore or
play down any evidence that might effectively
refute their one-sided arguments--the old
card-stacking trick (Cantril and Hart).

Both authors are included in the parenthetical citation. Note, incidentally, that this citation of an encyclopedia article does not require a page reference, since encyclopedias are arranged alphabetically and a reader would have no trouble locating the source.

A work by three authors

If you are citing a source by three authors, supply the names of all three.

> Polarized two-party systems provide the
>
> simplest form of political competition in
>
> electoral democracies. Each of the two parties
>
> offers the electorate a clear set of policy
>
> orientations and issue positions and the party
>
> closest to the preferences of the voting
>
> majority wins (Blake, Carty, and Erickson
>
> 122).

More than three authors

If you are citing a source of more than three authors, supply the name of the first author and follow the name with *et al.*, the Latin abbreviation for "and others."

> During World War II, both Canada and Japan
>
> engaged in forms of hostage-taking in pursuit
>
> of military and political goals (Roy et al.).

The absence of a page number in this citation indicates that the reference is to an entire work rather than to a specific passage.

Works by different authors with the same last name

Occasionally your list of works cited will contain sources by two authors with the same last name—for example, K. Patricia Cross and Wilbur Cross. In such cases, whenever mention of an author's name is required, you must use the first name as well as the last.

```
Educator Wilbur Cross has suggested that the
situation of the mature student has excited
considerable interest in academic circles
(8-9). Other commentators explore the ways
that academe can serve these students
(K. Patricia Cross 32, 41).
```

Notice also in these examples the treatment of references to more than one page: 8–9 identifies the continuous pages; 32, 41 indicates that the reference is to two separate pages.

Poetry, drama, and the Bible

When you refer to poetry, drama, and the Bible, you must often give numbers of lines, acts, and scenes, or of chapters and verses, rather than page numbers. This practice enables a reader to consult an edition other than the one you are using. Nonetheless, your list of works cited should still identify your edition.

Act, scene, and line numbers (all Arabic) are separated by periods with no space before or after them. Biblical chapters and verses are treated similarly. In both cases, the progression is from larger to smaller units.

The following example illustrates a typical citation of lines of poetry.

```
Emily Dickinson concludes "I'm Nobody! Who Are
You?" with a characteristically bittersweet stanza:
```

> How dreary to be somebody!
>
> How public, like a frog
>
> To tell your name the livelong June
>
> To an admiring bog! (5-8)

The following citation shows that Hamlet's "To be, or not to be" soliloquy appears in Act 3, Scene 1, lines 56–89 of *Hamlet*.

> In <u>Hamlet</u> Shakespeare presents the most famous
>
> soliloquy in the history of the theatre: "To
>
> be, or not to be . . . " (3.1.56-89).

The following reference to the Bible indicates that the account of creation in Genesis extends from chapter 1, verse 1, through chapter 2, verse 22.

> The Old Testament creation story (Gen.
>
> 1.1-2.22), told with remarkable economy,
>
> culminates in the arrival of Eve.

Notice that the names of books of the Bible are neither underlined (italicized) nor enclosed in quotation marks and that abbreviation is desirable.

Punctuation and mechanics

Commas are used to separate authors' names and titles (Woolf, *Roger Fry*) and to indicate interruptions in a sequence of pages or lines (44, 47). Hyphens are used to indicate continuous sequences of pages (44–47) and lines (1–4). Colons separate volume and page numbers (*Essays* 2: 41). A space follows the colon. Periods separate acts, scenes, and lines in drama (3.1.56–89) and chapters and verses in the Bible (Gen. 1.1).

Citations should, wherever possible, appear just before punctuation in the text of the paper.

> Wilbur Cross speaks of adult learners who "range in age from the mid-twenties to the upper sixties, and vary in background from nurses, teachers, business people and government employees to truck drivers, police officers and `just ordinary family people'" (116), whereas K. Patricia Cross views adult learners as a class of students disproportionately young, white, and affluent (45).

Wilbur Cross's citation falls just before a comma, K. Patricia Cross's just before a period. In a sentence such as the following, however, the citations cannot precede punctuation.

> Wilbur Cross (116) and K. Patricia Cross (45) speak of different kinds of adult learners.

In quotations set off from the text (see **16a**), citations follow the final punctuation.

As Marshall and Eric McLuhan observe in <u>Laws of Media: The New Science</u>:

> To the Inuit, truth is given, not by "seeing is believing," but through oral tradition, mysticism, intuition, all cognition--in other words, not simply by measurement of physical phenomena. To the Inuit, the ocularly visible apparition is not clearly so common as the purely auditory one; "hearer" would be a better name than "seer" for their holy men. (67)

(2) List of works cited

When you are ready to make the final version of your paper, you will know which sources from your working bibliography you have actually used and cited in your paper. Now eliminate the bibliography cards for the works that you do not cite, and arrange the remaining cards in alphabetical order by authors' last names. You are now ready to prepare the list of works cited that will conclude your paper. As you make your final revision, you will be checking your citations against this list to ensure that they are complete and correct. Other documentation styles handle this list differently and have different names for it.

In MLA style the list of works cited is arranged alphabetically by author and is double-spaced throughout. The first line of each entry is flush with the left margin; subsequent lines are indented to leave five spaces. If you use more than one work by the same author, list the works alphabetically by title. Give the author's name with the first title, but substitute three hyphens for the name in subsequent entries.

Berton, Pierre. <u>The Great Depression 1929-1939</u>.

    Toronto: McClelland, 1990.

---. <u>Niagara: A History of the Falls</u>. Toronto:

    McClelland, 1992.

Bibliographical entries often consist of only three units, which are separated by periods:

Findley, Timothy. <u>Headhunter</u>. Toronto:

    HarperCollins, 1993.

1. *Name of the author.* Give the last name first. Your final list of works cited will be arranged alphabetically by authors' last names.

2. *Title of the book.* Underline (italicize) the title, and capitalize it in accordance with **9c**. Always include the book's subtitle, and underline it as well.
3. *Publication data.* Include the place of publication, the publisher, and the latest copyright date, as shown on the copyright page. Give a shortened form of the publisher's name as long as it is clear.

Some entries, however, require more than three units and must be given special treatment. As you study the following MLA-style bibliographical entries, which cover most of the special problems you are likely to encounter, observe both the punctuation and the arrangement of information. See also pages 520–23 for a list of abbreviations that are permissible in bibliographies, notes, and tables. Note that the MLA style favours Arabic numbers throughout and that such abbreviations as *vol.* and *sec.* are not capitalized.

Sample Bibliographical Entries

Books

One author

Gwyn, Sandra. <u>Tapestry of War: A Private View of Canadians in the Great War</u>. Scarborough, ON: HarperCollins, 1992.

Notice that a colon is used before a subtitle and before the publisher's name; note, too, that the underlining of the complete title is continuous. Always give the city of publication to help in identifying the book. In this case, the province is also included for readers unfamiliar with the location of Scarborough or for readers who might confuse Scarborough, Ontario, with Scarborough, England.

Galbraith, Kenneth. <u>The Culture of Contentment</u>.

    Boston: Houghton, 1992.

The publisher's name (in this instance, Houghton Mifflin) is shortened as much as possible while remaining clearly identifiable.

Two authors

Granatstein, J.L., and David Bercuson. <u>War and</u>

    <u>Peacekeeping: From South Africa to the Gulf--</u>

    <u>Canada's Limited Wars</u>. Toronto: Key Porter,

    1991.

Note that a comma follows the first author's name (inverted order) and that the second author's name is not inverted.

Three authors

Kinneavy, James L., William J. McCleary, and Neil

    Nakadate. <u>Writing in the Liberal Arts</u>

    <u>Tradition: A Rhetoric with Readings</u>. New

    York: Harper, 1985.

Note that the names of the second and third authors are given in the usual order (rather than surname first) and that commas are used after both the first and second names.

More than three authors

Baumol, William J., et al. <u>Economics: Principles</u>

    <u>and Policy</u>. 3rd Can. ed. Toronto: Harcourt,

    1991.

---. <u>Economics: Principles and Policy</u>.

    <u>Macroeconomics</u>. 3rd Can. ed. Toronto:

    Harcourt, 1991.

In the first entry, a comma follows the first author's name (inverted order); *et al.* is not underlined. Note the indication of an adaptation of a text for a Canadian audience. Note also the use of three hyphens and a period to indicate the second citation for the same author or authors.

Corporate author

St. John Ambulance. <u>Heart Start: One-rescuer CPR</u>:

    <u>Adult Casualty</u>. Ottawa: STJA, 1989.

Edition after the first

Novak, Mark. <u>Aging and Society: A Canadian</u>

    <u>Perspective</u>. 2nd ed. Scarborough, ON: Nelson,

    1993.

Editors

Strong-Boag, Veronica, and Anita Clair Fellman,

    eds. <u>Rethinking Canada: The Promise of</u>

    <u>Women's History</u>. 2nd ed. Toronto: Copp, 1991.

Wynne, Graeme, and Timothy Oke, eds. <u>Vancouver and</u>

    <u>Its Regions</u>. Vancouver, UBC Press, 1992.

A translation

Havel, Vaclav. <u>Summer Meditations: On Politics</u>,

    <u>Morality and Civility in a Time of Transition</u>.

    Trans. Paul Wilson. London: Faber, 1992.

An "edition"

```
Brooke, Frances. The History of Emily Montague.

    1769. Ed. Mary Jane Edwards. Ottawa:

    Carleton UP, 1990.
```

The term *edition* indicates a work by one author that has been prepared for print by an editor. Historical works and literary works of authors no longer living (for example, Shakespeare, Austen, Tennyson) usually list the editor on the title page. The original date of publication is given, followed by a period and two spaces.

Note: In this case as in others, the publisher's name (Carleton University Press) is shortened as much as possible. There is no period after the *U* for *University* or the *P* for *Press.*

Literary work from an anthology

```
Rosen, Sheldon. Ned and Jack. Twenty Years at

    Play: A New Play Centre Anthology. Ed. Jerry

    Wasserman. Vancouver: Talon, 1990. 45-81.
```

The title of the play is underlined, as it would be if the text were printed separately. Cite the inclusive pages for the work at the end of the entry, following the date and period.

```
Webb, Phyllis. "The Days of the Unicorns." Poetry

    by Canadian Women. Ed. Rosemary Sullivan.

    Toronto: Oxford, 1989. 127-28.
```

The title of the poem is put in quotation marks.

Non-literary work from an anthology

```
Said, Edward. "The Politics of Knowledge."

        Debating P.C.: The Controversy over Political

        Correctness on College Campuses. Ed. Paul

        Berman. N.Y.: Laurel-Dell, 1992. 172-89.
```

Note: Publishers sometimes use different imprints to identify particular types or lines of books they publish, as, for example, the Laurel imprint in the Dell title above. In such cases, give the imprint, followed by a hyphen and the publisher's name (for example, New Canadian Library-McClelland, Viking-Penguin).

```
McLuhan, Marshall. "The Role of New Media in

        Social Change." Antigonish Review 74-75

        (1988): 43-49. Rpt. in The Canadian Essay.

        Ed. Gerald Lynch and David Rampton. Toronto:

        Copp, 1991.
```

For previously published non-literary works, give both the original publication data and the publication data for the anthology.

Reprint

```
Lowry, Malcolm. October Ferry to Gabriola. New

        York: World Publishing, 1970. Vancouver:

        Douglas and McIntyre, 1988.
```

If the book has been reprinted by a publisher that did not print the original, give the dates of both the original edition and the reprint. In the foregoing example, the original hard-cover edition was published by World Publishing eighteen years earlier than the Douglas and McIntyre paperback.

A History of Canadian Journalism in the Several
    Portions of the Dominion. Canadian Press
    Association, 1908; rpt. New York: AMS, 1993.

In this example, the reprint information signals that this book is of historic interest. The first edition was published by the Canadian Press Association in 1908; the reprint was published by AMS Press in 1993.

A non-English work

Hébert, Anne. Le premier jardin. Montréal:
    Éditions du Seuil, 1988.

In general, treat non-English works as you would any English book, but provide a translation of the title in square brackets (Le premier jardin [The First Garden]) if it needs clarification. Note that capitalization practices differ from language to language. Here, only the first word of the title is capitalized, in keeping with conventional practice for French: in both titles and subtitles, only the first words and proper nouns are capitalized (for example, *La route d'Altamont* for *The Road Past Altamont*). Copy non-English titles exactly as printed. For guidance with non-English bibliographic entries, consult the *MLA Handbook.*

A work in more than one volume

Halpenny, Frances G., and Jean Hamelin, eds. The Dictionary of Canadian Biography. 12 vols. Toronto: U of Toronto P, 1966-91.

The multivolume work above was published over a period of years.

Sandburg, Carl. Abraham Lincoln: The War Years. 4 vols. New York: Harcourt, 1939.

The work above consists of four volumes published in the same year.

A work in more than one volume with a separate volume title

Pelikan, Jaroslav. Reformation of Church and Dogma (1300-1700). Vol. 4 of The Christian Tradition: A History of the Development of Doctrine. Chicago: U of Chicago P, 1985.

A work in a series

Morton, Desmond. Labour in Canada. Focus on Canadian History Series. Toronto: Grolier, 1982.

Strong-Boag, Veronica. The Canadian Campaign for Woman Suffrage. Canada's Visual History Series 30. Ottawa: National Museum of Man and National Film Board, 1977.

In the foregoing entry, the volume number is given in Arabic numerals (*30*) and without the abbreviation *vol.*

Green, Otis Howard. <u>The Literary Mind of Medieval and Renaissance Spain</u>. Introd. John E. Keller. Studies in Romance Langs. 1. Lexington: UP of Kentucky, 1970.

Notice that a separate author wrote the introduction.

A foreword, preface, introduction

Atwood, Margaret. Foreword. <u>Charles Pachter</u>. By Bogomila Welsh-Ovcharov. Toronto: McClelland, 1992.

Government Publications

Canada. Department of External Affairs and International Trade. <u>NAFTA: What's It All About</u>? Ottawa: Minister of Supply and Services, 1993.

British Columbia. <u>Clayoquot Sound Land Use Decision: Background Report</u>. Victoria: Queen's Printer, 1993.

United States. Department of Labor. <u>Valuing Cultural Diversity</u>. Washington: GPO, 1992.

Notice the sequence of data given for a government publication: government, agency (if given), title—each followed by a period and two spaces. The publisher in the last example is the U.S. Government Printing Office.

Conference and Symposium Proceedings

```
Umar, Y.K., ed. Conference on George Grant and the
        Future of Canada: Proceedings. Calgary, AB:
        U of Calgary P, 1992. Conference held
        2-3 Mar. 1992 in Calgary.
```

Enter the published proceedings of a conference as you would a book. If the title does not include pertinent details about the conference, add them.

```
Gavora, J.S. et al., eds. Animal Breeding: Recent
        Advances and Future Prospects. Ottawa:
        Animal Research Centre, Agriculture Canada.
        [1988]. Presented in part at the symposium
        "Genetics in Agriculture" at the 1983
        Annual Meetings of the Genetics Society of
        Canada.
```

In the example above, no date of publication appears in the printed proceedings. This information, obtained from the library catalogue, should be added in square brackets.

Magazines, Journals, and Newspapers

Unsigned articles

```
"The Economics of European Disintegration." The
        Economist 22 May 1993: 56-57.
```

Note: As a rule, the names of months except May, June, and July are abbreviated.

Daily Newspaper

```
Lacey, Liam. "MuchMusic Dances to a More Political
        Beat." Globe and Mail 22 May 1993, weekend
        ed.: C3.
```

When not part of the publisher's name, the city's name should be given in square brackets after the title: *Straits Times* [Singapore]. For nationally published newspapers (*Globe and Mail, New York Times*), the city may be omitted. Column numbers are not used. If a specific edition is named on the masthead, it is specified, preceded by a comma, after the date: `16 Mar. 1993, late ed., sec. A: 14.`

Note that *The* should not be included in citing the newspaper's name (*Winnipeg Free Press,* not *The Winnipeg Free Press*).

Weekly magazine or newspaper

```
Turbide, Diane. "Canadians Shine on Broadway."
        Maclean's 24 May 1993: 37.
Mihill, Chris. "`Global Emergency' Brings TB
        Vaccination Plea." Manchester Guardian
        Weekly 2 May 1993: 8.
```

Volume numbers are unnecessary because specific dates are given. Notice that words in quotation marks in the title are put into single quotation marks.

Monthly magazine

Collins, Anne. "The Battle over <u>The Valour and the</u>

<u>Horror</u>." <u>Saturday Night</u> May 1993: 44+.

Note: When a title requiring underlining (for example, the title of a television program) appears within a title enclosed in quotation marks, retain the underlining in the citation. In the example above, Anne Collins' article focusses on the controversy surrounding the CBC television documentary entitled <u>The Valour and the Horror</u>.

Note on magazine pagination Sometimes a magazine article is printed on pages that are separated by other articles; for example, in Collins' article, the first part appears on pages 44–49, the balance on pages 72–76. In such cases, give only the first page number followed by a plus sign: 44+.

Journal—continuous pagination through year

Chen, Xiaomei. "The Poetics of `Misunderstanding':

An Ahistorical Model of Cross-Cultural

Literary History." <u>Canadian Review of</u>

<u>Comparative Literature</u> 19 (1992): 485-506.

If the pages of a journal are numbered continuously, by volume, throughout each year, only the volume number, followed by the year in parentheses, is required; the issue number and the month may be omitted.

Journal—separate pagination

Allen, Richard. "Representation, Illusion, and the

Cinema." <u>Cinema Journal</u> 32.2 (1993): 21-48.

If the pages of a journal are numbered separately (starting with page 1) in each issue, both the volume and issue number must be included. Note that an issue number follows a volume number, separated by a period.

Bök, Christian. "Sibyls: Echoes of French Feminism

in The Diviners and Lady Oracle." Canadian

Literature 135 (1992): 80-93.

Some journals, such as *Canadian Literature* in the example above, use only issue numbers (rather than volume numbers). In such cases, cite the issue number (135 in this example) as you would a volume number.

Editorials, signed and unsigned

Robinson, Bart T. "A Short Note of Gratitude."

Editorial. Equinox 57 (1991): 7.

"Drug War Casualties." Editorial. The Vancouver

Sun 25 May 1993, sec. A: 14.

Book review

Compton, Valerie. "Narrating Anew." Rev. of Green

Grass, Running Water by Thomas King. Quill

and Quire Mar. 1993: 46.

Encyclopedias and Almanacs

Entry signed with name or initials

Eichler, Margrit. "Women's Studies." Canadian

Encyclopedia. 1988 ed.

Full publication information is not required for a familiar reference work.

Sc[himmel], An[nemarie]. "Islam." <u>Encyclopaedia</u>

    <u>Britannica: Macropaedia</u>. 1990 ed.

Square brackets enclose the added parts of the name. A list of contributors is ordinarily supplied in the index volume or in the front matter of an encyclopedia.

Entry unsigned

"Somalia." <u>The Economist World Atlas and Almanac</u>.

    1989 ed.

In this almanac, main sections (like "Language") are arranged alphabetically in the text.

"Utrecht, Peace of." <u>New Columbia Encyclopedia</u>.

    1975 ed.

The title indicates that the article is listed under *U*.

"Broadcasting Stations in Canada." <u>Canadian</u>

    <u>Almanac and Directory</u>. 1993 ed. 1-223-1-281.

Notice that page numbers may be supplied for ease of reference, though the front matter of this almanac does list topics alphabetically.

Pamphlets and Bulletins

<u>Earthquakes</u>. Ottawa: Minister of Supply and

    Services, 1991.

Women and AIDS: Choices for Women in the Age of
<u>AIDS</u>. Ottawa: Minister of Supply and
Services, 1991.

Titles of pamphlets are italicized (underlined).

Unpublished Dissertation

Drover, Jane Louise. "<u>Frankenstein; or the Modern</u>
<u>Prometheus</u> and the Inoculated Reader."
Diss. McMaster, 1991.

Micropublications

Document a book or periodical photographically reproduced in miniature form as though the work were in its
original form. Refer to a microform as such in a list of
works cited only if that is the original form.

Non-print Sources

Motion picture

<u>Much Ado about Nothing</u>. Dir. Kenneth Branagh.
Alliance-Goldwyn, 1993.

Television or radio program

Williams, Tennessee. <u>Cat on a Hot Tin Roof</u>. Dir.
Jack Hofsiss. American Playhouse. PBS.
KCET, Los Angeles. 24 June 1985.
Gzowski, Peter. <u>Morningside</u>. CBC, Toronto. 16 Mar.
1993.

Stage play

<u>Democracy</u>. By John Murrell. Dir. Graham Harley.

Manitoba Theatre Centre, Winnipeg. 18 Mar.

1993.

Recording

Gould, Glenn. <u>Bach: Goldberg Variations</u>. CBS US,

37779, 1982.

Lecture

Webb, Phyllis. "Poetry and Psychobiography."

Vancouver Institute Lecture. UBC,

Vancouver. 13 Mar. 1993.

Interview

Chiang, Li-Po. Personal interview. 13 Jan. 1993.

Additional non-print sources

For samples of citations of other non-print sources—such as microforms, games, globes, filmstrips, microscope slides, and transparencies—consult Eugene B. Fleischer's *A Style Manual for Citing Microform and Nonprint Media* (Chicago: American Library Association, 1978).

COMMON ABBREVIATIONS

The following is a list of abbreviations commonly used in bibliographies, tables, or notes (but not the text) of research papers. For a more complete list see the *MLA*

Handbook for Writers of Research Papers, 3rd ed. New York: Modern Languages Assoc., 1988.

abr.	abridged, abridgement
Acad.	Academy
adapt.	adaptation, adapted by
anon.	anonymous
app.	appendix
Apr.	April
Assn.	Association
Aug.	August
biog.	biography, biographer, biographical
bk., bks.	book, books
bull.	bulletin
c.	*circa,* "about" (for example, "c. 1966")
cf.	compare
ch., chs.	chapter, chapters
col., cols.	column, columns
Coll.	college
comp.	compiled by, compiler
cont.	contents; continued
DAB	*Dictionary of American Biography*
DCB	*Dictionary of Canadian Biography*
Dec.	December
dept.	department
dir.	directed by, director
diss.	dissertation
div.	division
DNB	*Dictionary of National Biography*
ed., eds.	edition(s) OR editor(s)
enl.	enlarged (as in "rev. and enl. ed.")
et al.	*et alii,* "and others"
Feb.	February
fig.	figure
front.	frontispiece
fwd.	foreword, foreword by
gen. ed.	general editor
govt.	government

GPO	Government Printing Office
HMSO	Her (His) Majesty's Stationery Office
i.e.	*id est,* "that is"
illus.	illustrated by, illustrator, illustration
inc.	incorporated, including
Inst.	Institute, Institution
intl.	international
introd.	[author of] introduction, introduced by
Jan.	January
jour.	journal
mag.	magazine
Mar.	March
ms., mss.	manuscript, manuscripts
n, nn	note, notes (used immediately after page number: 6n3)
natl.	national
NB	*nota bene,* "take notice," "mark well" (always in upper case)
n.d.	no date [of publication]
no., nos.	number [of issue], numbers
Nov.	November
n.p.	no place [of publication], no publisher
n. pag.	no pagination
Oct.	October
OED	*Oxford English Dictionary*
op.	*opus,* "work"
P	Press (used in documentation; see "UP")
p., pp.	page, pages (omitted before page numbers unless reference would be unclear)
pref.	preface, preface by
proc.	proceedings
prod.	produced by, producer
pseud.	pseudonym
pt., pts.	part, parts
pub.	published by, publisher, publication
rept.	reported by, report
rev.	revision, revised, revised by OR review, reviewed by
rpt.	reprinted, reprint

sec., secs.	section, sections
Sept.	September
ser.	series
sic	"thus," "so" (in square brackets)
Soc.	Society
supp.	supplement
trans.	translated by, translator, translation
U	University (used in documentation; see "UP")
UP	University Press (used in documentation: Oxford UP)
vol., vols.	volume, volumes (omitted before volume numbers unless reference would be unclear)

(3) Final revisions and proofreading

After writing and carefully documenting the first draft of your paper, make needed revisions. To make your writing as clear and effective as possible, you will probably need to rewrite some sentences and strike out or add others. Use the Reviser's Checklist on pages 465–67. (You may wish to review pages 441–43 of Section **33**.) Refer to **8b** and especially to the sample research paper on pages 527–71 as you put your paper in final form. Even when writing final copy, you will probably continue to make changes in word choice and to correct occasional errors in spelling, mechanics, or grammar. Type or write legibly. Proofread your final revision before handing it in.

Some instructors ask their students to submit outlines, notes, and drafts along with the final paper. Other instructors require a title page and a final outline along with the text of the paper. A title page usually gives the title of the paper, the author, the name of the course and its section number, the instructor's name, and the date—all attractively centred on the page: see the example on page 572. MLA recommends using no title page and giving the identification on the first page before the title of the paper: see page 527.

When submitted with the text of a research paper, the final outline serves as a table of contents. The following sample is a topic outline. (If your instructor specifies a sentence outline, see the sample on page 434.) Some instructors ask students to make the introduction and conclusion numbered headings. Others require an outline only of the main discussion and suggest that references to introduction and conclusion be omitted from the outline.

Outline

Thesis: Virginia Woolf made a perceptive comment when she said that human character changed at the beginning of this century. In the first years of the Modern Age, Woolf and a handful of artists in the worlds of painting, drama, and literature became individuals in search of a new human character.

Introduction: The context of Woolf's comment; the exhibit of Post-Impressionist paintings that inspired it; the reactions to this new way of depicting human character

Body:

 I. The new ways of seeing in the world of painting

  A. The contributions of the Post-Impressionists

   1. Cézanne

   2. Gauguin

   3. Van Gogh

  B. Reactions against the Post-Impressionists

C. Support for Post-Impressionists among young artists

II. The new ways of seeing in the world of theatre

   A. The attempts of censors to stifle freedom in the theatre

   B. The contributions of Chekhov to a new view of human character on the stage

III. The new ways of seeing in the world of literature

   A. The literary establishment and the portrayal of character

     1. H.G. Wells

     2. Arnold Bennett

   B. The portrayal of character by "window-breaking" writers

     1. Conrad

     2. Joyce

     3. Woolf

Conclusion: Woolf may have been mischievous, but she wasn't deluded when she announced the change in human character in 1910.

Sample Research Paper

A sample research paper follows. The left-hand pages contain passages from sources, some note cards, and comments on content and form.

◼ **Exercise 4** Prepare for a class discussion of the strengths and weaknesses of the following research paper.

COMMENTS

1. The identification, double-spaced, begins 2.5 cm from the top of the page and flush with the left margin. A double space precedes the title of the paper. A margin of about 2.5 cm is provided at the left, right, and bottom of the page.
2. Four spaces separate the centred title from the first line of the text. A title consisting of two or more lines is double-spaced, and each line is centred. For example:

```
            The Window Breakers:

 Several Artists in Search of Human Character
```

3. All pages (including the first page) are numbered with Arabic numerals in the upper right-hand corner, about 1.25 cm from the top. Notice that no period follows page numbers.
4. The essay begins with an epigraph from "Resolving the Contradictions of Modernity and Modernism," an article by Daniel Bell that appeared in the journal *Society* in March 1990. An epigraph can serve to establish major themes of a research essay, especially when it presents comments in clear and memorable language. Present epigraphs in block quotation form and single-spaced.
5. The epigraph is followed by four substantial paragraphs of introduction. To explain Virginia Woolf's cryptic comment about the change in human character and to establish the cultural and historical context in which she made the comment, the writer provides a somewhat longer introduction than would usually be required. (See pages 429, 437.)
6. In paragraph 1, Michael Nguyen uses the superscript number 1 to refer readers to an endnote that supplies additional information: see page 565.
7. In the two citations from "Mr Bennett and Mrs Brown," Nguyen includes a reference to Woolf's *A Woman's Essays* because the paper cites other works by Woolf. He does not include Woolf's name because it is clear from the context that Woolf is the author.

1

Michael Nguyen
English 290.02
Dr. Sihota
26 March 1993

The Window Breakers:
Several Artists in Search of Human Character

> What defines the modern is a sense of
> openness to change, of detachment from
> place and time,... and a readiness, if
> not eagerness, to welcome the new, even
> at the expense of tradition and the past.
> (Bell 43)

1   Virginia Woolf must have been a mischievous
person. Writing at the beginning of what we now
refer to as the Modern Age, she seemed to
enjoy producing essays that provoked thought
and lively debate. One such essay, "Mr Bennett
and Mrs Brown," published in several different
versions in 1923 and 1924,[1] contained a comment
guaranteed to produce thought and debate among
those who stopped to think about it then and
those who stop to think about it now. In
arguing for the vital importance of "reading
character" in everyday life as well as in the
writing and reading of fiction, she stopped to
observe that "in or about December 1910 human
character changed" (Woolf, <u>A Woman's Essays</u> 70).

2   No doubt, human character has changed again
and again over time. But what could Woolf have
meant when she announced that the human
character had changed suddenly and perhaps
irreversibly in a single month at the end of
a single year at the beginning of our century?

COMMENTS

1. All pages after the first page give a shortened form of the author's name (usually the last name preceded by an initial) and the page number. This information is placed in the upper right-hand corner, about 1.25 cm from the top. A double space separates the writer's name from the first line of the text.

2. Notice that the paraphrase of Samuel Hynes' interpretation of Woolf's comments begins with a reference to his credentials. You should try to establish the credibility of sources your readers may not know well by introducing them in the way that Michael Nguyen has done here.

3. The direct quotation from Virginia Woolf's biography of her friend Roger Fry includes an emendation: [the members of the public]. Nguyen has added this editorial comment after the pronoun "they" to prevent the possibility of any ambiguity in the pronoun reference and to make the quotation fit into his sentence.

4. The quotation from Bullen exceeds four lines, and so it is fully indented. Note that such quotations are not ordinarily enclosed in quotation marks and that the final punctuation precedes the parenthetical reference.

SOURCE

For Woolf quotation:

> It is difficult in 1939, when a great hospital is benefiting from a centenary exhibition of Cézanne's works, and the gallery is daily crowded with devout and submissive worshippers, to realise what violent emotions those pictures excited less than thirty years ago. The pictures are the same; it is the public that has changed. But there can be no doubt about the fact. The public in 1910 was thrown into paroxysms of rage and laughter. They went from Cézanne to Gauguin and from Gauguin to Van Gogh, they went from Picasso to Signac, and from Derain to Friesz, and they were infuriated.

Cultural historian Samuel Hynes has interpreted Woolf's comment to mean that a sweeping change in the artist's perception of human character--a change that profoundly affected Western culture's definition of what it means to be human--arrived at Britain's door in 1910. It arrived with the opening of a controversial exhibit of paintings entitled "Manet and the Post-Impressionists," and it developed in the weeks of action and reaction that followed (Hynes 325-26). Woolf herself described the public's response to the Grafton Gallery exhibit as one of

> rage and laughter. They [the members of the public] went from Cézanne to Gauguin and from Gauguin to Van Gogh, they went from Picasso to Signac, and from Derain to Friesz, and they were infuriated. (Woolf, Roger Fry 153-54)

3   The exhibit, it seems, became a symbol of unwelcome change for many Britons. It represented an invasion from abroad, and an outrageous one at that. One writer has speculated that

> in 1910 many people in Britain thought they were witnessing a break in the artistic continuity of European art and the arrival of so-called Post-Impressionist painting in England served to polarise attitudes to both the function and status of art in contemporary life. (Bullen 1)

COMMENTS

1. The last two sentences of paragraph 4 present Michael Nguyen's thesis. They also contain references to "window breakers" and to the artist's search for human character—ideas that appear in the essay's title and subtitle.
2. Paragraph 4 also provides examples of two sorts of citations: the direct quotation from Jane Dunn and the paraphrase of Virginia Woolf's metaphor of the artist as window breaker in "Mr Bennett and Mrs Brown."
3. Paragraph 5 contains a paraphrase of the definition of Post-Impressionism appearing in an unsigned article in *The Encyclopaedia Britannica: Micropaedia.* Note that such citations do not ordinarily include page references, since the articles they refer to can be easily located in the encyclopedia's alphabetical arrangement. In this case, however, Nguyen has included the reference to emphasize that "Postimpressionism" is part of a citation and not some other parenthetical comment. The encyclopedia's editors have chosen to present the title of the article unhyphenated, and this variant is preserved in Nguyen's paper.

SOURCE

For the paraphrase of Woolf:

> Thus, if you read Mr Joyce and Mr Eliot you will be struck by the indecency of the one, and the obscurity of the other. Mr Joyce's indecency in *Ulysses*[28] seems to me the conscious and calculated indecency of a desperate man who feels that in order to breathe he must break the windows. At moments, when the window is broken, he is magnificent. But what a waste of energy! And, after all, how dull indecency is when it is not the overflowing of a super-abundant energy or savagery, but the determined and public-spirited act of a man who needs fresh air!

4   Whereas many of her fellow citizens seemed
ready to resist Post-Impressionism and all
it represented with all their might, Woolf
embraced it. Although not a painter herself,
she understood the ways in which the ideas,
techniques, and impulses of one art could
influence another. Her writing came to be
compared to Post-Impressionist painting in its
"pared-down boldness and simplicity" (Dunn 149).
And so, in the first years of the period that
we in the Post-Modern Age call the Modern Age,
Woolf and a handful of artists in the worlds
of painting, drama, and literature became
individuals in search of a new human character.
They became what Woolf playfully referred to in
"Mr Bennett and Mrs Brown" as window breakers--
stifled by the ways of the past and eager
to let fresh air into a world that had been
living according to Victorian values for too
long (Woolf, <u>A Woman's Essays</u> 85).

5   These window-breaking artists had at least
two things in common: they worked alone, and
they consciously rejected the traditions of the
previous generation ("Postimpressionism"
639-40). The painters whose works were reviled
in London in 1910 provided the inspiration and
the impetus for these individuals determined to
invigorate their art with a few blasts of fresh
air. Cézanne, Gauguin, and Van Gogh were all
three dead when their paintings came to the
Grafton Gallery, but their ghosts were alive
and well and giving shape to new images of
human character in their work. One art   ·
historian has described these three figures

1. Paragraphs 5 through 15 develop the first major point of the essay. They focus on the distinctive ideas and paintings produced by three eminent Post-Impressionist painters—Cézanne, Gauguin, and Van Gogh—and explain the positive and negative reactions to their work.

2. As you read the sources below, notice how Nguyen has tailored each passage to serve his purposes by including only those sections he has found relevant. Note that the four ellipsis points in the Earp quotation indicate that Nguyen has omitted material between two sentences, whereas the three ellipsis points in the Jalard quotation indicate that he has omitted material from within a sentence.

SOURCES

From Earp, *The Modern Movement in Painting* (19–20)

For Post-Impressionism was not a school, but an impulse. Its leaders were isolated personalities, all showing a dynamic force of expression, but with very little in common beyond dissatisfaction with official tradition. They all started from Impressionism, but each developed beyond it on independent lines. Seurat, the scientist of technique, influenced a phase of Van Gogh's work. For a short time Van Gogh, the apostle of emotion in painting, and Gauguin, the electric, reciprocally contributed to the perfecting of each other's style. Gauguin, again, was aware of Cézanne's efforts in the simplification of form; though the Provençal painter, who was to mean so much to a later generation, was for his contemporaries the least regarded of them all.

It was as individuals, and not with conscious unity, that they brought a fresh vision to their art and enlarged the range of its expression. Not only in the method of their treatment, technically speaking, but in their method of confronting the visible world before them, they effected a revolutionary change. By their ardent concentration, and the spirit of analysis which reinforced it, it may even be said that they invented a new way of seeing. Previously, with the exception of the impressionist protest, the artist had regarded his subject with a ready-made plan of traditional picturesque in his head, to which, willy-nilly, it had to conform. The post-impressionists gave the subject its freedom, allowed it to rise before them altogether apart from any pre-arranged conception of it. They enriched Nature with a new wonder.

from Jalard, *Post-Impressionism* (14)

Cézanne's painting is not just the poetry of sight; it is also the poetry of sensation, or of a colour system. As Cézanne said to Joachim Gasquet*: "There is only one road to take in order to convey and translate everything: colour. Colour is, as it were, biological. Colour is alive, and only colour can make things live.

COMMENT

In paragraph 7, Michael Nguyen makes the first of several references to particular Post-Impressionist paintings. Note that he has underlined the title of each work of art he describes and discusses; he also provides a parenthetical reference in each case to the book or the catalogue in which he has found a plate of the work.

M. Nguyen 4

in paradoxical terms as

> leaders [who were] isolated personalities,
> all showing a dynamic force of expression,
> but with very little in common beyond
> dissatisfaction with official tradition....
> By their ardent concentration, and the
> spirit of analysis which reinforced it, it
> may even be said that they invented a new
> way of seeing. (Earp 19-20)

6   For Paul Cézanne, the Impressionist turned
Post-Impressionist, the new way of seeing had
everything to do with colour. He seems to have
looked at his paints one day and decided that
colour was an organic thing. So he seemed to
suggest in a comment to his friend Émile
Bernard: "There is only one road to take in
order to convey and translate everything:
colour. Colour is ... biological. Colour is
alive, and only colour can make things live"
(Jalard 14).

7   Although it is true that many of Cézanne's
best paintings were landscapes and still lifes
that had little to do with the presentation of
human character, he did paint portraits, and
they were very different from the posed,
complacent-looking figures found in the works
that London gallery goers had been used to
seeing before 1910. His 1879 Self-Portrait
in a Hat (The Complete Paintings of Cézanne
Plate IX), for example, seemed to demonstrate
Cézanne's belief that "the artist must scorn
all judgment that is not based on an intelligent
observation of character" (Nochlin 92).

COMMENT

Paragraphs 8 and 9 continue the development of point I of the outline (see page 524–25) with a focus on the artistic philosophy and practice of Paul Gauguin. Michael Nguyen draws on Robert Goldwater's work on Gauguin for his discussion in paragraph 8.

BIBLIOGRAPHY CARD FOR GOLDWATER

> Goldwater, Robert. <u>Paul Gauguin</u>.
>   New York: Abrams, 1928.

NOTE CARD USED FOR PARAGRAPH 8

> Gauguin's Aesthetic Views
>   (Goldwater 92)
>
> Goldwater portrays Gauguin as a conscious rebel against tradition.
> He quotes Gauguin here to reinforce his argument.
>
> "All I have learnt from others has been an impediment to me." (92)
>   [How so?]

The face in the self-portrait is a fascinating
one. It is not an impassive mask; it is a
shrewd and almost scowling head that seems to
entice the viewer to wonder about the mind
that it contains. When art critic Charles
Lewis Hind saw this painting hanging in the
Grafton Gallery, he saw something

> fatigued yet eager, as of a soul struggling
> for release, the paint a means not an end,
> the idea everything, the real man grown
> old searching for that which can never
> be wholly found. (qtd. in Bullen 190)[2]

8   If Cézanne was the father of Post-
Impressionism, Paul Gauguin was the young Turk
of the movement. Of the Impressionists he was
reacting against, he said: "They need only the
eye, and neglect the mysterious centres of
thought, so falling into merely scientific
reasoning" (Goldwater 92). In the true spirit
of a window breaker, he issued a declaration
of artistic independence when he said: "All I
have learnt from others has been an impediment
to me. It is true I know little, but what I do
know is my own" (Goldwater 35).

9   There was more to Gauguin than rhetoric,
however. Two paintings in particular show that
he was dedicated to exploring human character
on canvas in ways that it had not been
explored before. In his 1892 <u>Spirit of the
Dead Watching</u> (Goldwater 115), there is plenty
of human mystery in the figure of the young
Tahitian woman lying tensely on a bed; the
fear on her face is not explained by the
inscrutable female figure in the background

COMMENTS

1. The discussion of Post-Impressionist painters continues, with Michael Nguyen moving from an examination of Paul Gauguin in paragraph 10 to his examination of Vincent Van Gogh in paragraphs 11 through 14.

2. In paragraph 11, Nguyen provides an indirect reference to a source when he presents the words of Van Gogh as quoted in Jalard's book *Post-Impressionism*. He has adopted this strategy because he has not been able to find the original source in the libraries to which he has access. Whenever possible, writers of research papers should attempt to trace quotations to their original sources, but when that proves impossible, they may use the "quoted in" citation instead.

NOTE CARD

Notice that Nguyen's own ideas are placed in square brackets in the card below.

[Van Gogh as a Symbolic Figure for Modernists?]

Sweetman calls him "the isolated, rejected prophet of modern art" (Sweetman 2).

Earp called him an "apostle of emotion" (20).

Van Gogh himself wrote and spoke about his painting as the expression of thought and hope (Jalard 103).

[Is Van Gogh a twentieth-century figure even though he died ten years before the century began?]

seated rigidly on a chair. This is a painting
calculated to arouse curiosity about
character: the viewer's eyes are drawn back
and forth between the face of that terror-
stricken girl and that stoic old woman.

10   Gauguin's 1891 <u>Reverie</u> (Goldwater 103) is
a different picture of human character. The
Tahitian woman in this portrait is one of
Gauguin's waiting figures: she sits in a
rocking chair lost in some undisclosed thought.
Colour may be one clue to the mood behind that
face with the downcast eyes. The deep blue
wall behind her and the deep pink of her robe
are intense and sad rather than vibrant and
bright. They intensify the viewer's feeling
that she may be mourning a loss, and they
reinforce the sense that Gauguin must have
believed that a human being's sadness, like
his or her fear, was a fit subject for art.

11   Vincent Van Gogh ended his life a decade
before this century began, and yet there is no
disputing that he, even more than Cézanne or
Gauguin, has been viewed as "the isolated,
rejected prophet of modern art" (Sweetman 2).
More than any of his contemporaries, he was
"the apostle of emotion in painting" (Earp 20),
and that meant he was keenly interested in the
human character. He described his technique as
an attempt

> to express the thought of a brow by the
> radiance of a light tone against a sombre
> background, to express hope by some star,
> the ardour of a soul by a sunset
> radiance. (Jalard 103)

COMMENTS

1. Paragraphs 12 through 14 continue the discussion of Van Gogh; paragraph 15 begins a transition to a discussion of the impact of Post-Impressionism on young British painters seeking alternatives to the status quo in their nation's painting.

2. Paragraphs 13 and 14 present Michael Nguyen's own conclusions about specific works of Van Gogh, which he has obviously studied quite carefully.

3. Paragraph 15 contains a reference to "character reading," an idea first introduced and cited in paragraph 1. Because the reference to Woolf is clear, and because the reader should remember the earlier reference, a parenthetical citation is unnecessary here.

12   Van Gogh seemed to recognize the new
feelings of ambivalence that became so much a
part of modern art. He was the artist who could
paint sunflowers vibrating with life and then
turn around and fill a canvas with menacing
skies bursting with quivering, whirling stars.

13   Van Gogh's portraits reveal his intense
interest in capturing what it meant to him to
be a human being. <u>Sorrow</u> (Frankfurter 39), an
1882 pencil portrait of Christine, a street
girl with whom Van Gogh lived for almost two
years, is a very striking nude. It is the
study of a girl crouched, her breasts sagging
and her head buried in her thin little arms.
She is not classically beautiful, but she is
poignant; she represents Van Gogh's fascination
with failure. This same fascination with
failure was later to become a frequent theme
of window-breaking art.

14   <u>Dr. Gachet</u> (Bonafoux 128) is Van Gogh's
1890 portrait of the doctor who cared for him
during his time at the sanitarium at Saint-Remy.
In this painting, the doctor sits beside a
table on which rests a vase of dying flowers.
And the striking thing--the thing that
captivates the eye--is the man's face. It
seems torn; it wears "the heartbroken expression
of our time" (Van Gogh, <u>The Complete Letters</u>
286-87).

15   Cézanne, Gauguin, and Van Gogh led the
search for human character because they were
so intensely involved in what Woolf called
"character reading." They discovered that human
beings in their solitude, sitting quietly and

COMMENT

Paragraph 16 focusses on the artistic establishment's strong reaction against the new way of seeing in painting and contrasts it with the more positive response of young artists. To illustrate the ferocity of the establishment's reaction, Michael Nguyen decides to present quite a lengthy quotation—a departure from his usual practice of presenting short quotations and paraphrases of sources. In this case, he has quoted Wilfrid Blunt at length because he believes that only Blunt's words can do full justice to the point he is trying to make.

M. Nguyen 8

doing nothing, were worthy of attention; they discovered that their energies were not wasted when they attempted to portray the loneliness that is part of the human experience.

16   The Post-Impressionists had a positive impact on young British painters looking for a new way of seeing. By 1912, Duncan Grant, Vanessa Bell, and Wyndham Lewis were exhibiting their works in the Grafton Gallery's second Post-Impressionist show. Still, the prevailing view was one of "militant Philistinism" (Woolf, <u>Roger Fry</u> 157), expressed most indignantly and most entertainingly by poet and diplomat Wilfrid Blunt, when he wrote in his diary:

> The exhibition [the first Post-Impressionist exhibit] is either an extremely bad joke or a swindle. I am inclined to think the latter, for there is no trace of humour in it. Still less is there a trace of sense or skill or taste, good or bad, or art or cleverness. Nothing but that gross puerility which scrawls indecencies on the walls of a privy. The drawing is on the level of that of an untaught child of seven or eight years old, the sense of colour that of a tea-tray painter, the method that of a schoolboy who wipes his fingers on a slate after spitting on them.... Apart from the frames, the whole collection should not be worth £5, and then only for the pleasure of making a

COMMENTS

1. Paragraph 17 puts the focus on the second major section of the body of the essay (see page 525): the impact of the new way of seeing human character on the British theatre.

2. Notice that Michael Nguyen includes a synopsis of an argument presented by Samuel Hynes in five pages of his book. This synopsis appears in paragraph 17. Note also that Nguyen relies once again on Hynes as his source in his comments on the strong reaction against renewal in the theatre (see paragraph 18).

REVISION OF AN EARLIER DRAFT—WITH A PURPOSE

The following revisions to Nguyen's first draft of paragraph 17 provide more sentence variety and stronger transitions between ideas. Such transitions show the reader that the writer is concerned about connecting the many details and ideas he has uncovered in what appears to have been extensive research.

```
Wilfrid Blunt had his counterparts in the world
of British theatre. Their names were Redford and
                These two members of the old guard
Brookfield. Redford and Brookfield did not just
                              ① +
wield critical power. Theirs was the power of
          Each of them      in the post of      P
censorship. They served as Examiner of plays.
The Examiner was responsible to the Lord
Chamberlain, who was accountable to the King for
the quality of drama presented in Britain's
licensed theatres at the beginning of this
                              Of the Examiner it has been written that
century (Hynes 212-16). "He had a hangman's
power over the London stage at a time when
English drama was beginning to show signs of
life" (Hynes 218).
```

M. Nguyen 9

bonfire of them. . . . They are the works
of idleness and impotent stupidity, a
pornographic show. (qtd. in Hynes 328–29)

17   Wilfrid Blunt had his counterparts in the
world of British theatre. Their names were
Redford and Brookfield. These two members of
the old guard did not just wield critical
power; theirs was the power of censorship.
Each of them served in the post of Examiner
of Plays. The Examiner was responsible to the
Lord Chamberlain, who was accountable to the
King for the quality of drama presented in
Britain's licensed theatres at the beginning
of this century (Hynes 212–16). Of the
Examiner it has been written that "he had a
hangman's power over the London stage at a
time when English drama was beginning to show
signs of life" (Hynes 218).

18   The antics of Redford and Brookfield
would have been funny if they were not so
dangerous and infuriating. The mere fact
that they could demand changes in a script
or prevent the production of a play without
explanation must have made the work of
Britain's playwrights very difficult. The
ever-present threat could only have had a
chilling effect. And thanks to Redford and
Brookfield, Edwardian audiences were protected
from such scandalous works as the Oberammergau
Passion Play, the "incestuous" Oedipus
Tyrannus, and the politically objectionable
Mikado (Hynes 214–18).

COMMENT

Read paragraphs 17–23 and carefully observe inter-relations, a few of which are indicated by arrows below.

II. The New Ways of Seeing in the World of Theatre

¶17 a reference to opposition and censorship of new theatre

    Hynes: a summary of censorship practices with reference to two Examiners of Plays: Redford and Brookfield

    Hynes: the "hangman's power" of the Examiner

    opposition

¶18 a paragraph of specific illustration the censorship of three specific works:
    (1) the Oberammergau Passion Play
    (2) Oedipus Tyrannus
    (3) the Mikado (Hynes 214-18)

¶19 a transitional paragraph moving from the censors to the influence of Chekhov's window-breaking drama (focus on the 1911 production of The Cherry Orchard)

    transition

¶20 the effects of Chekhov's work and a comparison of Chekhov with Cézanne

¶21 specific discussion of Chekhov's ideas about stagecraft
    the stage/setting as a metaphor

¶22 Chekhov's new way of seeing character compared with Van Gogh (see Sorrow) reference to failures in The Cherry Orchard

    contribution

¶23 Chekhov's new way of seeing human relationships
    examples from The Cherry Orchard
    Chekhov's tendency to turn traditional relationships (mother-daughter, master-servant) upside down

M. Nguyen 10

19   With the exception of Bernard Shaw,
dramatists in this closely monitored theatrical
world produced very little that would last. It
took a second invasion from abroad, that of
Anton Chekhov's <u>Cherry Orchard</u> in 1911, to break
the windows and reinvigorate British drama with
a needed gust of fresh air.

20   Once again, the old guard laughed at the
new art. The critic for the <u>Times</u> described
the London production of Chekhov's play as
"something queer, outlandish, even silly" (qtd.
in Hynes 338). Still, Chekhov's work had its
effect, as it influenced playwrights looking
for a new way of seeing to abandon the cup-and-
saucer drama of the turn of the century and
to use the stage in the same spirit that the
Post-Impressionist painters used colour. Like
Cézanne, who saw colour as an organic thing,
these playwrights saw the stage as organic,
and they began to use it as a metaphor for the
world they saw crumbling around them.

21   Chekhov's stage communicated with an
audience before any of his characters ever said
a word. The first act of <u>The Cherry Orchard</u> is
set, like the last act, in an unused nursery--
a metaphor for an infertile world in which
adult nostalgia for childhood is a major
preoccupation. The cherry orchard outside the
Ranyevskaia mansion is a hopeful symbol of
growth, but it blooms next to a graveyard, and
it is continually threatened with the axe until
it is sold and cut down in the play's final act.

COMMENTS

1. Notice Michael Nguyen's extensive discussion of Anton Chekhov's *The Cherry Orchard,* a play that he has studied quite carefully in the course for which he is writing this paper. He does not quote the text of the play at any point in this section, but he does present his analysis of Chekhov's use of character. The references to the play in this part of the essay entitle Nguyen to include it in the "Works Cited" section of his paper.

2. Note that Nguyen is careful to avoid plot summary of *The Cherry Orchard.* He knows that his audience has read and studied the text, and so he does not make the mistake of retelling the plot when he needs to be analyzing the text.

3. Notice Nguyen's attempts to knit the parts of the paper together in his comparisons of Chekhov's work with the work of Van Gogh, which he has discussed earlier in the paper.

22   Not only did Chekhov find a new way of
seeing his medium, he also joined in the search
for a new kind of character. Those who live in
the world of The Cherry Orchard are men and
women who, in their laughable, poignant, and
often absurd behaviour, suffer from the
powerlessness that seems to be a chronic
disease of the modern character. Like the
defeated girl in Van Gogh's Sorrow, they are
studies in failure. Madame Ranyevskaia is an
aging beauty who spends her time yearning for
her childhood and mismanaging her money; Gayev
is an ineffectual man who talks to bookcases,
plays imaginary billiards, and speaks when his
mouth is full of boiled sweets. Varia and
Lopakhin cannot make their romance work, and
Trofimov is just a verbal revolutionary whose
rhetoric gives no promise of action.

23   The convulsions that seem to shake the
characters in some of Van Gogh's paintings also
shake Chekhov's characters--none of whom know
where they fit. Charlotta, Yepihodov, and
Dooniasha spend their lives searching for who
they are and where they belong. Ania and Madame
Ranyevskaia are mother and daughter, but as The
Cherry Orchard develops, the audience begins to
see that the mother-daughter relationship has
been turned upside down and that Ania takes
care of her hapless mother. Similarly, Chekhov
turns the master-servant relationship upside
down when the old servant, Feers, treats his
master, Gayev, in a paternalistic manner.

24   The window breaking that was going on in
the visual and performing arts in the first

COMMENT

1. Paragraphs 24–27 are comparable to paragraphs 17–20 in their focus on the reactions of members of the old guard to changes in the arts. Michael Nguyen is working to make the three major sections of the body of the essay parallel in their treatment and arrangement of content.

SOURCE

from *"The Author's Craft" and Other Critical Writings of Arnold Bennett* (244)

> Supposing a young writer turned up and forced me, and some of my contemporaries—us who fancy ourselves a bit—to admit that we had been concerning ourselves unduly with essentials, that we had been worrying ourselves to achieve infantile realisms? Well, that day would be a great and a disturbing day—for us. And we should see what we should see.

years of the century was also under way in
literature. The reaction against the new ways of
seeing was fierce. Words that Arnold Bennett,
Virginia Woolf's nemesis, wrote in 1910 after
seeing the Post-Impressionist exhibit are
prophetic in forecasting the kind of warfare
that erupted in literary circles when certain
writers decided to break a few windows and let
in a little fresh air. He wrote:

> Supposing a young writer turned up and
> forced me, and some of my contemporaries--
> us who fancy ourselves a bit--to admit that
> we had been concerning ourselves unduly
> with essentials, that we had been worrying
> ourselves to achieve infantile realisms?
> Well, that day would be a great and a
> disturbing day--for us. And we should see
> what we should see. (Bennett, "The Author's
> Craft" and Other Critical Writings 244)

25   Those young writers did appear, and they did
cause great and disturbing days among the
members of the literary establishment. The
reaction was predictable. Self-appointed censors
banded together in Britain's National Vigilance
Society to exert pressure on circulating
libraries to withdraw books deemed offensive.
Publishing houses were pressured to refuse
publication to suspect authors. In this
atmosphere, Émile Zola's publisher, Henry
Vizetelly, was jailed for printing Soil:
A Realistic Novel, and James Joyce was forced

COMMENT

Paragraphs 26 and 27 offer specific discussion of two texts that Michael Nguyen has read as background for his English class. He refers to both *Tono-Bungay* and *The Old Wives' Tale* to illustrate his point about the depiction of character in early twentieth-century British fiction. He quotes passages of character description from both texts, which he has found in his university's library.

SOURCE *TONO-BUNGAY* (61–62)

He whisked out of his shop upon the pavement, a short figure in grey and wearing grey carpet slippers; one had a sense of a young fattish face behind gilt glasses, wiry hair that stuck up and forward over the forehead, an irregular nose that had its aquiline moments, and that the body betrayed an equatorial laxity, an incipient "bow window" as the image goes.

into an eight-year search for a publisher for
<u>Dubliners</u>.

26   Those who resisted the new way of seeing,
writers such as H.G. Wells and Arnold Bennett,
had been writing well-crafted but unadventurous
fiction. Although they might have agreed with
Virginia Woolf that the creation of character
was the essence of fiction, they did not see
the need for new kinds of characters that
Woolf did. Wells seemed content to follow in
Dickens' footsteps and Bennett to follow in
Thackeray's, and neither seemed interested in
breaking any windows when addressing Britain's
reading public. Readers of Wells' <u>Tono-Bungay</u>
would find characters who were caricatures--
full of Dickensian eccentricities:

> He whisked out of his shop upon the
> pavement, a short figure in grey and
> wearing grey carpet slippers; one had a
> sense of a young fattish face behind gilt
> glasses, wiry hair that stuck up and
> forward over the forehead, an irregular
> nose that had its aquiline moments, and
> that the body betrayed an equatorial
> laxity, an incipient "bow window" as the
> image goes. (61-62)

27   In Arnold Bennett's fiction, characters are
the puppets of their creators, much as they
are in Thackeray's stories. His narrators
are obsessed with minute details; they also
maintain a distance between themselves and
the characters they describe. The narrator's

COMMENTS

1. Paragraph 28 acts as a transition to the discussion of fiction writers who rejected the old order and adopted a new way of seeing. It begins with a comparison and contrast of established and new writers; it points back to ideas raised in the previous paragraphs and points forward to upcoming arguments. This strategy provides coherence as the essay moves into the last section of the body.

2. Notice that in his references to *Lord Jim,* Nguyen cites the edition that he and his classmates used in English 290.

M. Nguyen 14

first cool look at the protagonists of <u>The Old
Wives' Tale</u> demonstrates Bennett's approach:

> Constance's nose was snub, but agreeably
> so. Sophia had a fine Roman nose; she was
> a beautiful creature, beautiful and
> handsome at the same time. They were both
> of them rather like racehorses, quivering
> with delicate, sensitive, and luxuriant
> life; exquisite, enchanting proof of the
> circulation of the blood; innocent, artful,
> roguish, prim, gushing, ignorant, and
> miraculously wise. (7)

28   The window breakers did not compare their
protagonists with racehorses or describe them in
long lists of adjectives. They were not content
to look at characters from the outside; for
them, the exploration of the mind took the
place of the fascination with appearance. Two
writers who led the way in the invigoration of
literature were, like the Post-Impressionists
and Chekhov, outsiders. Joseph Conrad was a
Polish expatriate for whom English was a third
language, and James Joyce was an Irish exile
whose work reflected his ambivalence about
things English.

29   Joseph Conrad's <u>Lord Jim</u> broke new ground
in the search for character. It is the study
of character above all else, as Conrad himself
suggested in his "Author's Note" to the work
(1). Jim, like the cast of characters in
<u>The Cherry Orchard</u>, lives in a constant state
of ambivalence. His fanatical dedication to the

COMMENTS

1. In paragraphs 29–31, Michael Nguyen demonstrates his knowledge of the literary texts he has studied in his course. He has analyzed his audience well enough to know that he should not use this part of the essay to summarize plots. Instead, he uses details of the texts to support his arguments about the portrayal of character in fiction. Although he does not quote or paraphrase a number of the novels he refers to, he will include them in his "Works Cited" pages as texts he has referred to in developing his thesis.

2. Notice Nguyen's reference to "window breakers" in paragraph 30. After you have finished reading the whole paper, go back and read it again, but this time note the number of times Nguyen has used the metaphor of "window breaking" to unify his composition. Discuss the effectiveness of this strategy as you consider the strengths and weaknesses of the paper.

M. Nguyen 15

sailor's code of honour does not keep him
from jumping from his ship at a time when
he should be tending to the safety of its
other passengers. And alongside this central
character, who remains inscrutable no matter
how hard the narrator or the reader tries to
figure him out, Conrad placed a new type--the
mysterious minor character who seems to hold
the secret of life but who never quite
divulges it. Stein, the mysterious butterfly
collector who understands Jim better than
anyone else, has his counterparts in E.M.
Forster's Godbole and Virginia Woolf's August
Carmichael, but there are no such figures in
the fiction of Wells and Bennett.

30   James Joyce was the leading window breaker
as far as Virginia Woolf was concerned. Her
comments in "Mr Bennett and Mrs Brown" suggest
that she didn't entirely approve of his
methods (85). But what he did with character
was invigorating. He did not manipulate his
creatures as a puppeteer would; he did not
distance himself so much from them that he saw
only the exterior as Bennett did. Instead,
he climbed inside a character's mind, looked
through his or her eyes, and saw the world as
one living on the margins of life would see
it. The characters in <u>Dubliners</u>--Eveline and
Maria, Lenehan, Mr. Doran, Little Chandler,
and Mr. Duffy--all live on the sidelines,
acutely self-conscious, yearning for adventure
and yet afraid to act, faintly ridiculous and
yet always poignant.

COMMENTS

In paragraphs 32–35, Michael Nguyen moves to the last part of the body of his essay. Paragraph 32 functions as a transition from Joyce to Woolf and uses a quotation from an authoritative source—critic Carolyn Heilbrun—to support a comparison of the two writers. Note the way in which Nguyen uses both paraphrase and quotation in his references to Heilbrun in paragraph 32.

SOURCE (*HAMLET'S MOTHER AND OTHER WOMEN*, 67)

> almost all notice of commerce between them has been confined to a dismissal of Woolf's "snobbish" response, in her diary, to her first reading of *Ulysses,* and to accusations that she copied Joyce. Joyce's views on Woolf are nowhere, to my knowledge, mentioned, but *The Voyage Out* was among the books in his Trieste library in 1920. Joyce had stamped his name in it.

31   Joyce's characters are not social
butterflies or garrulous storytellers. Their
solitude, their silence, and their failures
make them interesting to readers. Much as Joyce
chose to exile himself from his country and his
family and his culture, he makes his characters
exiles in Dublin. For the Dubliners, failure
and solitude have become a way of life. Gabriel
Conroy cannot make love to Gretta when she
is thinking of a childhood sweetheart; Little
Chandler, lost in dreams of grandeur, can
neither soothe his baby son nor please his
angry wife; James Duffy wants companionship,
but something in him cringes at the touch of
Mrs. Sinico's hand.

32   Joyce practised his new way of seeing
in relative isolation. And although he and
Virginia Woolf were contemporaries (they
were born within a few days of each other),
Woolf's tone in her references to Joyce was
disapproving, whereas Joyce did not write a
single word about her (Heilbrun 67). Still, a
close study of their fiction supports critic
Carolyn Heilbrun's view that "Joyce and Woolf
divide the modern genius between them" (66).

33   In her life as an essayist, Woolf looked
at the painters, playwrights, and novelists
of her time and saw a Great Divide separating
many of them. From her vantage point, it must
have seemed that the changes sweeping over her
generation and her nation were lasting--perhaps
even permanent. Those of us living in the
Post-Modern Age who see ourselves tugged

COMMENTS

1. Note the citation of a passage from an editorial in the last sentence of paragraph 33.

2. Note the reference to a comment in a book review in the last sentence of paragraph 34.

3. Notice that Nguyen has underlined the phrase *Boeuf en Daube* in sentence 3 of paragraph 36. He is following the practice of underlining or italicizing words drawn from languages other than English (see **10b**).

SOURCES

from the editorial "Off the Post" (2)

> A friendly editor recently remarked on the annoying prevalence of the slash/solidus/virgule in my writing. Why not, I thought? And then, later, why? One answer, one self-justification, lies in an appeal to the *times*. The post-modern climate is either/or, and both at the same time. Many of us are on this knife-edge in our criticism and our writing, between a nostalgia for the order and sense of the New Criticism in which we were trained, and the lure of creative word-playing in semiotic/deconstructionist methods.

from the review entitled "Issuing" (170)

> She may begin by declaring that the answer to the question of how to resist authority and change tradition, in literature and society, "without establishing a new (alternative, oppositional, counter) tradition, which can become just as restrictive, repressive, authoritative," is not to be found "in reconciling, balancing or choosing between two positions"; but, by Chapter Two, it takes her only a paragraph to prove that "the problem [of an apparent contradiction] is capable of resolution."

M. Nguyen 17

between "a nostalgia for . . . order and . . . the lure of creative methods" (Ricou 2) know that she was wrong about that.

34 Woolf was clearly amazed and amused by the window breaking going on all around her, but her comments in "Mr Bennett and Mrs Brown" do not indicate that she ever saw herself as one of those leading the charge to shatter the glass. Perhaps she was being modest or mischievous in leaving herself out, but a look at her fiction and her characters shows that she was as much engaged in trying to answer "the question of how to resist authority and change tradition" (Hulcoop 170) as others were.

35 The Mrs. Ramsay of Woolf's <u>To the Lighthouse</u> hardly seems to be of the same species as the Constance and Sophia of Bennett's <u>The Old Wives' Tale</u>. Unlike Bennett, who spent a great deal of time describing his characters' exteriors, Woolf does little more than suggest Mrs. Ramsay's outer beauty. Readers may feel that she is beautiful, but most would have difficulty finding concrete details in the text to support that impression.

36 Woolf, like Conrad, Joyce, and others, concentrated on the interiors of her characters. Like her children and her husband and her summer guests, Mrs. Ramsay spends much of her day living the life of the mind. She is lost in thought as she knits a stocking for the lighthouse keeper's boy, or comforts her son, or sits with her husband, or serves out portions of <u>Boeuf en Daube</u> during the evening meal. Woolf's

COMMENT

Note the strategies that Michael Nguyen has used in concluding his essay. Unlike the introduction, which is four paragraphs long, the conclusion is presented in a single paragraph. Notice the methods Nguyen uses to tie his conclusion to his introduction by means of deliberate repetition of the phrases and the metaphors he has used to maintain unity and coherence throughout his paper.

NOTE CARDS FOR PARAGRAPH 37

Window-breaking artists ①

Woolf refers to Eliot and Joyce as artists eager to (desperate to) break the windows in order to let in some fresh air (85, Essays).

[a metaphor for the need to reinvigorate art and culture in Britain]
[Woolf and others share a similar impulse]

Window-breaking artists — post-modern views ③

A number of sources (Hulcoop, Ricou, Heilbrun, Halperin) suggest that today the modernist view may seem as stifling as the [pre-modern] view seemed to Woolf and her contemporaries.

Window breaking : how it became apparent ②

Woolf, Essays 70 : "in or about December 1910 human character changed "

M. Nguyen 18

characters experience moments of triumph or harmony
that Conrad's and Joyce's characters may not
experience, but they are as different from
what has gone before as the faces in the
canvasses of Cézanne, Gauguin, and Van Gogh
were from the faces in hundreds and thousands
of portraits preceding them. Critic John
Halperin has described Woolf's original
presentation of character in this way:

> Virginia Woolf had the capacity to
> enter into her creations body and soul,
> a capacity for a sort of negative
> capability. . . . She lived fully in her
> art and there was very little of her left
> over for . . . her real life. (436-37)

37   Woolf and the window-breaking artists who
engaged in the search for human character
in the first decades of this century made
contributions that some today might disparage.
Some artists in these times might feel that
modernism is stifling; some might feel the
need to break a few windows themselves and
to let in a new blast of fresh air. Still,
in just a few well-chosen words, Woolf
captured for all who have come after her
what it felt like to be living and working
in a time of dramatic change. She might have
been mischievous, but she wasn't deluded when
she announced the change in human character
in the dying days of 1910.

COMMENT

Two endnotes provide supplementary information that is not directly related to the thesis but that might be of interest to readers.

M. Nguyen 19

Notes

[1]"Mr Bennett and Mrs Brown" appeared in some four different versions between December 1923 and October 1924. According to editor Rachel Bowlby, the essay appeared first in <u>Nation and Athenaeum</u> in December 1923. In its next incarnation, it was delivered as a lecture to the Cambridge Heretics in the spring of 1924; then it was published in the <u>Criterion</u> as "Character in Fiction" several months later. Finally, the essay was published by the Woolfs' Hogarth Press in the autumn of 1924 under the now-famous title, "Mr Bennett and Mrs Brown."

[2]"The Post-Impressionists," an essay on the 1910 Grafton Gallery exhibit, was written by Charles Lewis Hind and first published in 1910.

COMMENTS

1. All (and only) works cited as sources in the paper should be included in the list of works cited.

2. Alphabetization: Initial articles (*A, An, The*) are ignored in alphabetizing. For example, Bennett's *"The Author's Craft" and Other Critical Writings of Arnold Bennett* precedes *The Old Wives' Tale* (*A* before *O*).

3. Punctuation: Observe the use and placement of periods and commas, especially in relation to parentheses and quotation marks. A colon separates a title from a subtitle and the place of publication from the publisher's name. A colon precedes page numbers of articles from periodicals.

4. Note the treatment of editors in the entries for *"The Author's Craft" and Other Critical Writings of Arnold Bennett* and *Post-Impressionists in England.* If the editor's work is the focus of your essay, cite the editor's name first, followed by a comma and the abbreviation *ed.* Otherwise, cite the author first and add the editor's name after the title. The order of presentation in this case is *Ed.* and then the editor's first and last names, followed by a period.

5. Notice that an essay title appearing within the title of a book is enclosed in quotation marks and then underlined along with the rest of the title (see the first entry for Arnold Bennett).

6. Note the treatment of a translation in the Chekhov entry.

M. Nguyen 19

Works Cited

Bell, Daniel. "Resolving the Contradictions of
    Modernity and Modernism." Society 27.3
    (1990): 43-50.

Bennett, Arnold. "The Author's Craft" and Other
    Critical Writings of Arnold Bennett. Ed.
    Samuel Hynes. Lincoln: U of Nebraska P,
    1968.

---. The Old Wives' Tale. London: Dent, 1960.

Bullen, J.R., ed. Post-Impressionists in England.
    London: Routledge, 1988.

Cézanne, Paul. Self-Portrait in a Hat. Plate IX in
    The Complete Paintings of Cézanne. By Sandra
    Onenti. London: Weidenfeld and Nicolson,
    1970.

Chekhov, Anton. The Cherry Orchard. Plays. Trans.
    Elisaveta Fen. Harmondsworth: Penguin, 1951.

Conrad, Joseph. Lord Jim. Ed. Thomas Moser. New
    York: Norton, 1968.

Dunn, Jane. A Very Close Conspiracy: Vanessa Bell
    and Virginia Woolf. London: Jonathan Cape,
    1990.

Earp, T.W. The Modern Movement in Painting.
    London: The Studio, 1935.

Goldwater, Robert. Paul Gauguin. New York: Abrams,
    1928.

COMMENTS

1. The Hulcoop entry illustrates the treatment of a book review appearing in a journal with an issue number but no volume number. The Ricou entry shows the treatment of an editorial appearing in a different issue of the same journal.

2. Compare the entry for an article from a journal with separate pagination (see Bell) with the entry for an article from a journal with continuous pagination (see Halperin).

3. Annotation: If you are asked to submit an annotated bibliography, supply a brief description of each entry, as in this example:

```
Hynes, Samuel. The Edwardian Turn of Mind.

    Princeton: Princeton UP, 1968.

            Samuel Hynes, American scholar and

            cultural historian, discusses the

            state of British culture in the period

            that has come to be known as

            "Edwardian," the period from 1900 up

            to August 1914. Hynes' treatment of

            the conflicts between those who held

            to tradition and those who agitated to

            break from it is the focus of the

            book. Of particular interest is the

            discussion of the impact of censorship

            on the British theatre in the first

            years of this century.
```

M. Nguyen 20

Halperin, John. "Bloomsbury and Virginia Woolf:
Another View." Dalhousie Review 59 (1979):
426-42.

Heilbrun, Carolyn. Hamlet's Mother and Other
Women. New York: Ballantine, 1990.

Hulcoop, John. "Issuing." Rev. of Virginia Woolf
and Post-Modernism: Literature in Quest and
Question of Itself, by Pamela L. Caughie.
Canadian Literature 135 (1992): 169-71.

Hynes, Samuel. The Edwardian Turn of Mind.
Princeton: Princeton UP, 1968.

Jalard, Michel-Claude. Post-Impressionism. Trans.
Anne J. Cope. London: Heron, 1968.

Joyce, James. Dubliners. New York: Modern Library,
1954.

Nochlin, Linda. Impressionism and Post-
Impressionism: 1874-1904. Englewood Cliffs,
NJ: Prentice, 1966.

"Postimpressionism." Encyclopaedia Britannica:
Micropaedia. 15th ed. 1990.

Ricou, Laurie. "Off the Post." Editorial. Canadian
Literature 107 (1985): 2-4.

Sweetman, David. The Love of Many Things: A Life
of Vincent Van Gogh. London: Sceptre-Hodder
Stoughton, 1991.

Van Gogh, Vincent. The Complete Letters of Vincent
Van Gogh. 2nd ed. vol. 3. Trans. J. Van
Gogh-Bonger. Greenwich, CT: New York Graphic
Society, 1959.

---. Dr. Gachet. In Van Gogh. By Pascal Bonafoux.
Trans. Alexandra Campbell. London: Barrie and
Jenkins, 1990.

1. Note the treatment of the unsigned article on Post-Impressionism from the 15th edition of *The Encyclopaedia Britannica: Micropaedia.* Page numbers are not required.

2. Note that Michael Nguyen has cited three works by Virginia Woolf in his essay. He arranges them alphabetically by title.

M. Nguyen 21

---. <u>Sorrow</u>. In <u>Van Gogh</u>. Ed. Alfred Frankfurter.
New York: Art Foundation, 1953.

Wells, H.G. <u>Tono-Bungay</u>. London: Macmillan, 1912.

Woolf, Virginia. <u>Roger Fry: A Biography</u>. New York:
Harcourt, 1940.

---. <u>To the Lighthouse</u>. Harmondsworth: Penguin,
1974.

---. <u>A Woman's Essays: Selected Essays</u>. Vol. 1. Ed.
Rachel Bowlby. Harmondsworth: Penguin, 1992.

Note: If your instructor prefers that you include a title page, here is a model you can follow (unless a different style is specified).

```
                  The Window Breakers:
   Several Artists in Search of Human Character


                     Michael Nguyen
                     English 290.02
                       Dr. Sihota
                     26 March 1993
```

Endnote (or Footnote) Style

As you consult sources, you will notice that many of them use footnotes or endnotes rather than parenthetical citations in the text. Some instructors prefer this system. Footnotes and endnotes are identical except for their location: footnotes appear at the foot of the relevant page, whereas endnotes appear together at the end of the paper. Either way, reference to the notes is by consecutive superscript numbers at the appropriate points throughout the text of the paper.

The first page of Michael Nguyen's paper (see page 527) is shown on page 573 as it would appear with superscript references rather than parenthetical ones. Endnotes corresponding to all of Nguyen's parenthetical citations are presented in sequence on pages 574–77. (Notice that the discursive notes on page 565 are integrated, in consecutive order, with the endnotes.) The style followed in these sample notes is one of several currently deemed acceptable—see page 600–601.

In research papers that use footnotes or endnotes instead of parenthetical citations, a list of works cited (more commonly referred to in such cases as a *bibliography*) is usually, but not always, required. Check with your instructor.

1

Michael Nguyen
English 290.02
Dr. Sihota
26 March 1993

The Window Breakers:
Several Artists in Search of Human Character

> What defines the modern is a sense of
> openness to change, of detachment from
> place and time, . . . and a readiness, if
> not eagerness, to welcome the new, even
> at the expense of tradition and the past.[1]

1　　Virginia Woolf must have been a mischievous
person. Writing at the beginning of what we
now refer to as the Modern Age, she seemed to
enjoy producing essays that provoked thought
and lively debate. One such essay, "Mr Bennett
and Mrs Brown," published in several different
versions in 1923 and 1924,[2] contained a comment
guaranteed to produce thought and debate among
those who stopped to think about it then and
those who stop to think about it now. In
arguing for the vital importance of "reading
character" in everyday life as well as in the
writing and reading of fiction, she stopped to
observe that "in or about December 1910 human
character changed."[3]

M. Nguyen 19

Notes

¹Daniel Bell, "Resolving the Contradictions of Modernity and Modernism," <u>Society</u> 27.3 (1990): 43.

²"Mr Bennett and Mrs Brown" appeared in some four different versions between December 1923 and October 1924. According to editor Rachel Bowlby, the essay first appeared in <u>Nation and Anthenaeum</u> in December 1923. In its next incarnation, it was delivered as a lecture to the Cambridge Heretics in the spring of 1924; then it was published in the <u>Criterion</u> as "Character in Fiction" several months later. Finally, the essay was published by the Woolfs' Hogarth Press in the autumn of 1924 under the now-famous title "Mr Bennett and Mrs Brown."

³Virginia Woolf, <u>A Woman's Essays: Selected Essays</u>, ed. Rachel Bowlby, vol. 1 (Harmondsworth: Penguin, 1992) 70.

⁴Samuel Hynes, <u>The Edwardian Turn of Mind</u> (Princeton: Princeton UP, 1968) 325-26.

⁵Virginia Woolf, <u>Roger Fry: A Biography</u> (New York: Harcourt, 1940) 153-54.

⁶J.R. Bullen, ed., <u>Post-Impressionists in England</u> (London: Routledge, 1988) 1.

⁷Jane Dunn, <u>A Very Close Conspiracy: Vanessa Bell and Virginia Woolf</u> (London: Jonathan Cape, 1990) 149.

⁸Woolf, <u>A Woman's Essays</u> 85.

⁹"Postimpressionism," <u>Encyclopaedia Britannica: Micropaedia</u>, 1990 ed.

[10]T.W. Earp, <u>The Modern Movement in Painting</u> (London: The Studio, 1935) 19-20.

[11]Michel-Claude Jalard, <u>Post-Impressionism</u>, trans. Anne J. Cope (London: Heron, 1968) 14.

[12]Paul Cézanne, <u>Self-Portrait in a Hat</u>. Plate IX of <u>The Complete Paintings of Cézanne</u>, by Sandra Onenti (London: Weidenfeld and Nicolson, 1970).

[13]Linda Nochlin, <u>Impressionism and Post-Impressionism: 1874-1904</u> (Englewood Cliffs, NJ: Prentice, 1966) 92.

[14]"The Post-Impressionists," an essay on the 1910 Grafton Gallery exhibit, was written by Charles Lewis Hind and first published in 1910.

[15]Robert Goldwater, <u>Paul Gauguin</u> (New York: Abrams, 1928) 92.

[16]Goldwater 35.

[17]Paul Gauguin, <u>Spirit of the Dead Watching</u>, page 115 in <u>Paul Gauguin</u>, by Robert Goldwater (New York: Abrams, 1928).

[18]Goldwater 103.

[19]David Sweetman, <u>The Love of Many Things: A Life of Vincent Van Gogh</u> (London: Sceptre-Hodder Stoughton, 1991) 2.

[20]Earp 20.

[21]Jalard 103.

[22]Vincent Van Gogh, <u>Sorrow</u>, page 39 in <u>Van Gogh</u>, ed. Alfred Frankfurter (New York: Art Foundation, 1953).

[23]Vincent Van Gogh, <u>Dr. Gachet</u>, page 128 in <u>Van Gogh</u>, by Pascal Bonafoux, trans. Alexandra Campbell (London: Barrie and Jenkins, 1990).

[24]Vincent Van Gogh, <u>The Complete Letters of Vincent Van Gogh</u>, 2nd ed., vol. 3, trans. J. Van Gogh-Bonger (Greenwich, CT: New York Graphic Society, 1959) 287.

[25]Woolf, <u>Roger Fry</u> 157.

[26]Hynes 328–29.

[27]Hynes 212–16.

[28]Hynes 214–18.

[29]Anton Chekhov, <u>The Cherry Orchard</u>, <u>Plays</u>, trans. Elisaveta Fen (Harmondsworth: Penguin, 1951). All references to the text will be to this edition.

[30]Hynes 338.

[31]Arnold Bennett, <u>"The Author's Craft" and Other Critical Writings of Arnold Bennett</u>, ed. Samuel Hynes (Lincoln: U of Nebraska P, 1968) 244.

[32]H.G. Wells, <u>Tono-Bungay</u> (London: Macmillan, 1912). All references in the essay are to this edition.

[33]Arnold Bennett, <u>The Old Wives' Tale</u> (London: Dent, 1960) 7. All references in the essay are to this edition.

[34]Joseph Conrad, <u>Lord Jim</u>, ed. Thomas Moser (New York: Norton, 1968) 1. All references in the essay are to this edition.

M. Nguyen 22

[35]Woolf, <u>A Woman's Essays</u> 85.

[36]James Joyce, <u>Dubliners</u> (New York: Modern Library, 1954). All references in this essay are to this edition.

[37]Carolyn Heilbrun, <u>Hamlet's Mother and Other Women</u> (New York: Ballantine, 1990) 67.

[38]Heilbrun 66.

[39]Laurie Ricou, "Off the Post," editorial, <u>Canadian Literature</u> 107 (1985): 2.

[40]John Hulcoop, "Issuing," rev. of <u>Virginia Woolf and Post-Modernism: Literature in Quest and Question of Itself</u>, by Pamela L. Caughie, <u>Canadian Literature</u> 135 (1992): 170.

[41]Virginia Woolf, <u>To the Lighthouse</u> (Harmondsworth: Penguin, 1974). All references in the essay are to this edition.

[42]John Halperin, "Bloomsbury and Virginia Woolf: Another View," <u>Dalhousie Review</u> 59 (1979): 436–37.

34f
Draft and revise a research paper using APA-style documentation.

Text Citations in APA style

The documentation style recommended by the American Psychological Association (APA) is widely used for writing in the social sciences. In APA style, the basic elements of a parenthetical citation in the text are the author's last name, the year of publication, and the page number if the reference is to a specific passage in the source. If the author's name is mentioned in the text of the paper, give the date alone or the date and the page number within the parentheses. In the following examples, note the details of punctuation and the treatment of the page number.

A work by one author

> One writer has stated, "If we can measure intelligence, we can measure (also imperfectly) other types of behavior and observe how intelligence influences that behavior" (Walsh, 1991, p. 24).
>
> OR
>
> Walsh has stated, "If we can measure intelligence, we can measure (also imperfectly) other types of behavior and observe how intelligence influences that behavior" (1991, p. 24).
>
> OR
>
> Walsh (1991) has stated, "If we can measure intelligence, we can measure (also imperfectly) other types of behavior and observe how intelligence influences that behavior" (p. 24).

Note: APA style, unlike MLA style, requires the abbreviation *p.* (or *pp.* for "pages") before the page reference. Use commas to separate the author's name from the date and the date from the page reference.

A work by two authors

    Recent advances in genetic research require

    that scientists, governments, and members of

    the public ensure that genetic diversity is

    maintained in non-human and human species

    alike (Suzuki & Knudtson, 1989).

Note: The ampersand (&) is used to separate the authors' names.

A work by more than two authors

    According to one recent study, early

    intervention is essential in preventing the

    disintegration of poor families in urban

    centres and in reducing problems with drugs

    and delinquency following from family break-

    ups (Fanshel, Finch, & Grundy, 1992).

Cite all the authors in the first reference, but in subsequent references give only the last name of the first author followed by "et al." ("Fanshel et al." in this case). If a work has more than six authors, provide only the last name of the first author followed by "et al.," even in the first citation.

Anonymous works

Use a shortened version of the title to identify an anonymous work:

```
Deep-sea biologists will soon be able to

pursue research of the ocean floor using

battery-operated robots capable of surveying

and photographing the depths for months at a

time ("All alone," 1993).
```

In this case, the author has cited a short article identified in
the bibliography as "All alone in the deep."

Two or more works within the same parentheses

```
Advances in genetic research are producing

difficult ethical questions with no evident or

easy answers (Heyd, 1992; Suzuki & Knudtson,

1989).
```

Use a semicolon to separate different studies, and arrange
the studies in alphabetical order.

References in APA style

In APA style, the alphabetical list of works cited is called
"References." Make the first line of each entry flush with
the left margin, and indent subsequent lines three spaces.
The reference entries below follow the style of the 1983
edition of the APA *Publication Manual*. Observe all details
of indention, spacing, and mechanics.

Book by one author

```
Gould, S. J. (1991). Bully for brontosaurus:

    Reflections in natural history. New York: Norton.
```

Give the author's last name and use initials for first and middle names. (If two authors have the same last name and initials, spell out their first names and list the references in the alphabetical order of their first names.) Put the date in parentheses, followed by a period. Capitalize only the first word and any proper name in a book title and subtitle. Give only enough of the publisher's name to identify it clearly.

Book by two or more authors

Suzuki, D., & Knudtson, P. (1989). <u>Genethics: The</u>
<u>clash between the new genetics and human</u>
<u>values</u>. Cambridge, MA: Harvard University
Press.

Article in an edited book

Lawton, S. B. (1990). Current issues in the public
finance of elementary and secondary schools
in Canada. In Y. L. Lam (Ed.), <u>The Canadian</u>
<u>public education system: Issues and prospects</u>
(pp. 31-46). Calgary: Detselig.

Capitalize only the first word and any proper nouns in article titles, and do not put quotation marks around the title. (If the article has a subtitle, put a colon after the title, and capitalize the first word in the subtitle.) For an article in an edited book, provide both the title of the article and the title of the book in which it appears. Identify who edited the book and give the complete pages of the article.

Article in a journal with continuous pagination

Auslander, B. A., & Langlois, P. H. (1993).
Toronto tap water: Perception of its quality

and use of alternatives. <u>Canadian Journal of
Public Health, 84</u>, 99-102.

Note: The titles of journals are capitalized differently from
article or book titles. Underline the volume number so that
it will be distinct from the page reference (which is not
preceded by an abbreviation).

Article in a journal paginated separately

Moorhouse, A. (1993). User fees: Fair cost con-
tainment or a tax on the sick? <u>The Canadian
Nurse, 89</u>(5), 21-24.

Insert the issue number within parentheses immediately
after the volume number.

Article in a monthly magazine

Anderson, R. M., & May, R. M. (1992, May).
Understanding the AIDS pandemic. <u>Scientific
American</u>, pp. 58-61+.

For a weekly magazine, provide the exact date of issue:
(1993, January 12).

Article in a newspaper

Ip, G. (1993, June 23). Bank rate at 20-year low
may move mortgage levels. <u>Financial Post</u>,
p. 5.

For an anonymous article, place the article title where the
author's name would normally appear, and alphabetize by
the first important word in the title.

A government document

```
Employment and Immigration Canada. (1991) Project-
     based training: Guide for applicants (MP 43-
     255/1991). Ottawa: Minister of Supply and
     Services.
```

Treat the issuing agency as a corporate author when no author is specified. Include a document or contract number (but not a library's call number) if either number is printed on or in the document.

Note: If you use more than one work by the same author, list the works in order of publication date, earliest first. Repeat the author's name for each entry.

Sample Research Paper

For additional examples of APA-style documentation, see the following student essay and the commentary on it printed on the left-hand pages.

COMMENT

1. The title page should include the title, the author's full name, the course in which the paper is being submitted, the name of the instructor who is teaching the course, and the date the essay is submitted. The APA *Publication Manual* requires that a shortened version of the title, identified as "Running head," appear centred near the bottom of the title page. This heading is then used in the upper right-hand corner of every page, including the title page—which is counted as page 1. This format allows a reader to remove the title page and evaluate the paper without being influenced by prior knowledge of the author. (If you use this model for an MLA paper, do not number the title page and do not include a running head.)

Test Anxiety
1

Treatment for Test Anxiety
Sharon Johnson

Psychology 101, Section 7
Professor Marquez
4 May 1993

Running head: TEST ANXIETY

COMMENTS

1. An abstract is a short summary of a paper. The APA requires that an abstract be supplied on the second page of any essay that is to be submitted for publication. Check with your instructor to see if an abstract is required for your own assignment.

2. Sharon Johnson draws on personal experience in her opening paragraph to catch the interest of her audience. But she introduces her topic by the end of paragraph 1.

3. Paragraph 2 (report page 4) includes a citation to a specific page, a citation to an entire work, and a citation to several studies that reached the same conclusion. The data reported in this paragraph establish the purpose for the paper by demonstrating that test anxiety is a widespread problem.

4. Paragraph 3 (report page 5) defines "test anxiety" by showing how it differs from nervousness.

5. Paragraph 4 (report pages 5–6) surveys early research in this field and offers an explanation for disappointing results.

Abstract

The cause-and-effect relationship between test anxiety and poor academic performance is now well established. Although some researchers question whether reducing test anxiety will necessarily lead to higher grades, the most recent research in this field suggests that the grades of test-anxious students are raised when such students are provided with therapy that combines relaxation training and tutoring to improve study skills.

Treatment for Test Anxiety

1   Although my younger sister is very smart, she had trouble in school for many years. She would carefully do her homework and usually seem to have mastered her assignments when my parents or I helped her to review. Unfortunately, whenever Stacey had to take a test, she would freeze up and seem to forget everything she knew. Since her grades were based mostly on her tests, she usually received low grades that did not reflect how much she really knew. Everyone in the family could see that Stacey was nervous about taking tests, and we kept telling her to try to relax. What we did not realize was that Stacey was

suffering from a condition called "test anxiety," a psychological syndrome that has been the subject of much research since the early 1950s, when an important study on college students was conducted at Yale University (Mandler & Sarason, 1952).

2   Research reveals that my sister's problem is not unusual. It has been estimated that "4-5 million children in elementary and secondary schools experience strong debilitating evaluation anxiety" and that another 5 million experience "significant anxiety" (Hill & Wigfield, 1984, p. 110); moreover, as much as 25% of college students may suffer from this condition (McGrath, 1985; Wilson & Rotter, 1986). Although there is evidence that females may be more vulnerable than males to test anxiety (Couch, Garber, & Turner, 1983; Furst, Tennenbaum, & Weingarten, 1985; Hembree, 1988), the problem is widespread within both sexes, and it can be found at all levels of intelligence. One recent study suggests that students of Asian background may be especially likely to suffer from test anxiety because they come from cultures that emphasize the importance of scholastic excellence (Dion & Toner, 1988), but most research reports that test anxiety is not limited to students of any particular race or culture.

3   Test anxiety should not be confused with
simple nervousness. A student may be nervous
before a test but then be able to successfully
concentrate on taking the test once it is
under way; this same student may be relaxed
before another exam in a subject he or she
enjoys. In some cases, a little anxiety can
even be helpful, since some students are
motivated to excel when they are concerned
about performance. In other cases, anxiety may
be appropriate if a student has neglected
assignments and has no real hope of passing an
examination on material that has gone unread.
A student with test anxiety, however, is
likely to be dominated by negative feelings
(including anger, guilt, and frustration)
before almost <u>any</u> exam, and these feelings
will subsequently interfere with performance
after the test has begun. Students suffering
from test anxiety thus lose the ability to
concentrate on problem solving. Instead of
concentrating on the exam before them, they
are usually distracted by other concerns, such
as how poorly they are doing and what other
people will think of them if they fail.

4   Early research in this field demonstrated
that students who scored high in tests
designed to measure test anxiety consistently
did poorly in test situations (Mandler
& Sarason, 1952). But the tests used to

COMMENTS

1. Paragraph 5 includes evidence that will support Johnson's argument. Note that she was careful to avoid relying too heavily on Zitzow (which, as the reference list reveals, was a short article). When introducing the Hembree study, Johnson was careful to include background information that would enable her audience to recognize the value of this source.

2. Paragraph 6 (report page 7) includes a second citation to a source with more than two authors.

3. Paragraphs 7–10 (report pages 8–10) include recommendations for treatment. Note how paragraphs 9 and 10 begin with concessions likely to reassure a skeptical audience.

4. Note that the long quotation—a quotation of more than 40 words—in paragraph 8 (report page 9) is indented five spaces only, per APA style.

measure student anxiety may not be entirely
accurate. Some students may exaggerate
their defects (Davies, 1986), and the tests
themselves may be biased (Couch et al., 1983).
Faulty methods of measuring test anxiety may
account for the disappointing results of much
research in this field: many researchers have
reported successful reduction of student
anxiety levels without noting a corresponding
improvement in academic achievement (Lent,
Lopez & Romano, 1983; Ricketts & Galloway,
1984).

5   Evidence suggests, however, that there
is hope for students who suffer from test
anxiety. In one study, "grade improvements
were noted for over 70% of participants in
identified courses . . . " (Zitzow, 1983,
p. 565). Although a single study is
insufficient to prove anything conclusively,
a recent, exhaustive study is highly
persuasive. Reviewing the results of 562
separate studies of test anxiety (including
369 journal articles and 148 doctoral
dissertations) and subjecting them to
statistical analysis, a mathematician has
concluded, "Contrary to prior perceptions,
improved test performance and grade point
average (GPA) consistently accompany TA
reduction" (Hembree, 1988, p. 47). According to
this study, early researchers failed to detect

significant academic improvement because many of them based their observations on sample groups that were too small. Drawing the results of many studies together reveals that treatment for test anxiety improves students' test scores by an average of 6 points on a 100-point scale (p. 73). This may seem like a small improvement for a student who is failing a course, but a 6-point improvement can be significant in some cases. More important, even a 6-point improvement helps to prove that there is a cause-and-effect relationship between test anxiety and academic performance. If this is the case, then improved methods of treatment may produce greater academic improvement in the future.

6   For treatment to be effective, counsellors need to realize that test anxiety is a complex state involving two factors: "worry," which involves thinking about negative possibilities; and "emotionality," which describes the perception of such physiological phenomena as accelerated heart beat and sweating (Furst et al., 1985). Irwin G. Sarason, one of this country's foremost experts on test anxiety, has concluded that "worry" has an especially significant impact on academic performance (1985). Taking this research into account, it seems that therapy that does not address the problem of worry is unlikely to help

students do better on tests. A test-anxious
student needs something more than soft music
and deep-breathing exercises.

7   The best results seem to be achieved by
counselling programs that provide students
with more than one type of help. Many test-
anxious students devote insufficient time to
studying because they spend so much time
worrying (Davies, 1986) or because they have
given up in frustration. Such students often
need specific help in learning good study
habits in addition to receiving therapy to
reduce anxiety. Several experts recommend that
treatment for test anxiety be accompanied by a
tutoring program in study skills (Lent et al.,
1983; Wilson & Rotter, 1986; Zitzow, 1983).
Tutoring alone, however, is not likely to
provide much help for someone suffering from
test anxiety: "Study skills training is . . .
not effective unless another treatment style
is also present" (Hembree, 1988, p. 73).

8   One problem in the treatment of test
anxiety is that individual students respond
very differently to the same situation:
"The same test that seems to maximize the
performance of low anxious examinees results
in relatively poor performance by moderately
anxious examinees" (Rocklin & Thompson, 1985,
p. 371). A possible solution to this problem

would be to devise different tests for students
with different degrees of anxiety. Another
possibility would be to put students into
testing groups determined by anxiety levels.
According to I. G. Sarason,

> A highly test-anxious college student might
> simply become more tense before, during,
> and after tests by virtue of contacts with
> completely confident, effective, and
> seemingly worry-free models. On the other
> hand, opportunity to observe and perhaps
> interact with other students who are
> mildly fearful of tests but who are not
> immobilized by them . . . might have
> decidedly therapeutic results. (1972,
> p. 396)

9   Reorganizing classes to group together
students of similar anxiety levels may not be
feasible, however, since this would require
elaborate organization and registration
procedures. (This method might be considered,
however, when planning for special tests that
are of particular importance and are independent
of course work.) Within a classroom situation,
teachers can help reduce anxiety levels by
providing students in advance with clear
instructions about the nature of upcoming tests
and how to prepare for them (Davies, 1986).

Test Anxiety

10

Teachers should also realize that anxiety
levels in general increase when students are
undergoing a stressful life event such as the
transition from junior to senior high school
or from high school to college. Additional
support for students during these times has
been shown to be beneficial (Bloom, 1985).
One type of support that should be considered
is to reduce time pressure by allowing
students enough time to complete tests
(Hill & Wigfield, 1984).

10   It would be a mistake, however, to assume
that the responsibility for treating test
anxiety rests within the schools. Many schools
do not have the resources to undertake any
new special programs, and many teachers are
so overworked that it would be unrealistic
to expect them to give troubled students
the individualized attention they may need.
Parents should be alert to the problem of test
anxiety and take the initiative in seeking
therapeutic help for any child who seems
regularly immobilized by tests. And college
students should be prepared to seek such
help for themselves if they are certain that
anxiety--rather than lack of preparation--
causes them to do poorly on tests.

11   I now know that simply telling someone with
test anxiety to "try to relax"--as my parents and

COMMENTS

1. The conclusion, with its reference to "my sister," establishes a link with the introduction.

2. The reference section is organized alphabetically and begins on a new page. The last name is always given first, and initials are provided for first and middle names. The date of publication is always given parenthetically, immediately after the author's name.

3. Observe the use of periods and commas and the unusual capitalization in book and article titles (but not in journal titles). Underline book titles, journal titles, and volume numbers for periodicals. If citing material from more than one work by the same author, repeat the author's name (as in the Sarason, I. G., entry) before each work.

I used to tell my sister--is about as useful as telling someone with severe depression to "try to cheer up." Whatever the cause that triggers it, someone suffering from anxiety needs trained, professional help, and students with test anxiety are no exception. They also need to know that help is available. Although the evidence is not conclusive, and more research needs to be done, what we know about test anxiety suggests that it can be treated effectively: treatment that combines therapy with tutoring is likely to improve students' self-concepts and lead to higher scores on tests.

References

Bloom, B. L. (1985). <u>Stressful life event theory
and research: Implications for primary
prevention</u> (DHHS Publication No. ADM
85-1385). Rockville, MD: National Institute
of Mental Health.

Couch, J. V., Garber, T. B., & Turner, W. E.
(1983). Facilitating and debilitating test
anxiety and academic achievement.
<u>Psychological Record, 33</u>, 237-244.

Davies, D. (1986). <u>Maximizing examination
performance</u>. New York: Nichols.

Dion, K. L., & Toner, B. B. (1988). Ethnic
differences in test anxiety. <u>Journal of
Social Psychology, 128</u>, 165-172.

Furst, D., Tennenbaum, G., & Weingarten, G.
(1985). Test anxiety, sex, and exam type.
<u>Psychological Reports, 56</u>, 663-668.

Hembree, R. (1988). Correlates, causes, effects,
and treatment of test anxiety. <u>Review of
Educational Research, 58</u>, 47-77.

Hill, K. T., & Wigfield, A. (1984). Test anxiety:
A major educational problem and what can be done
about it. <u>Elementary School Journal, 85</u>, 105-126.

Lent, R. W., Lopez, F. G., & Romano, J. L. (1983).
A program for reducing test anxiety with
academically underprepared students. <u>Journal
of College Student Personnel, 24</u>, 265-266.

Test Anxiety

13

Mandler, G., & Sarason, S. (1952). Some correlates of test anxiety. <u>Journal of Abnormal and Social Psychology, 47</u>, 561-565.

McGrath, A. (1985, November 4). Mettle testing. <u>Forbes</u>, pp. 236-239.

Ricketts, M. S., & Galloway, R. E. (1984). Effects of three different one-hour single-session treatments for test anxiety. <u>Psychological Reports, 54</u>, 115-120.

Rocklin, T., & Thompson, J. M. (1985). Interactive effects of test anxiety, test difficulty, and feedback. <u>Journal of Educational Psychology, 77</u>, 368-372.

Sarason, I. G. (1972). Experimental approaches to test anxiety: Attention and the uses of information. In C. D. Spielberger (Ed.). <u>Anxiety: Current trends in theory and research</u> (Vol. 2, pp. 381-403). New York: Academic.

Sarason, I. G. (1985). Cognitive processes, anxiety and the treatment of anxiety disorders. In A. H. Tuma & J. Maser (Eds.) <u>Anxiety and anxiety disorders</u> (pp. 87-107). Hillsdale, NJ: Erlbaum.

Wilson, N., & Rotter, J. C. (1986). Anxiety management training and study skills counseling for students on self-esteem and test anxiety and performance. <u>School Counselor, 34</u>, 18-31.

Zitzow, D. (1983). Test anxiety: A trimodal strategy. <u>Journal of College Student Personnel, 24</u>, 564-565.

■ **Exercise 5** Compose a topic outline for Sharon Johnson's research paper on test anxiety.

34g
Vary your documentation style according to discipline.

Each department of a college or a university ordinarily suggests a particular style for bibliographies and citations. Use the style your instructor specifies. Instructors in the sciences, business, economics, and so forth may recommend a documentation from one of these manuals; study it carefully, and make sure your bibliography and notes correspond exactly to the examples it provides.

Style books and manuals

American Institute of Physics. Publications Board. *Style Manual for Guidance in the Preparation of Papers.* 3rd ed. New York: American Inst. of Physics, 1978.

American Chemical Society, *American Chemical Society Style Guide and Handbook.* Washington, D.C.: American Chemical Soc., 1985.

American Mathematical Society. *A Manual for Authors of Mathematical Papers.* 8th ed. Providence: American Mathematical Soc., 1984.

American Psychological Association. *Publication Manual of the American Psychological Association.* 3rd ed. Washington, D.C.: American Psychological Assn., 1983.

Associated Press. *The Associated Press Stylebook and Libel Manual: The Journalist's Bible.* Reading, MA: Addison, 1987.

Canada, Secretary of State: *The Canadian Style: A Guide to Writing and Editing.* Toronto: Dundurn, 1985. (Text in French and English)

The Canadian Press. *Canadian Press Stylebook: A Guide for Writers and Editors.* Toronto: CP, 1983.

The Chicago Manual of Style, 14th ed. Chicago: University of Chicago Press, 1993.

Council of Biology Editors. Style Manual Committee. *CBE Style Manual: A Guide for Authors, Editors, and Publishers in the Biological Sciences.* 5th ed. Bethesda: Council of Biology Editors, 1983.

Harvard Law Review: *A Uniform System of Citation.* 13th ed. Cambridge: Harvard Law Review Assn., 1981.

McGill Law Journal. *Canadian Guide to Uniform Legal Citation.* 2nd ed. Toronto: Carswell, 1988.

Turabian, Kate L. *A Manual for Writers of Term Papers, Theses, and Dissertations.* 5th ed. Chicago: University of Chicago Press, 1987.

United States: Government Printing Office. *Style Manual.* Rev. ed. Washington, D.C.: GPO, 1983.

Writing for Special Purposes

35

Write effective papers about fiction, poetry, and drama; write effective letters, résumés, memos, and reports.

You may be asked during one of your courses to read and analyze a work of literature and to write a paper about it. This task requires the kind of analytical skills necessary for any close reading and the kind of writing skills that involve exploration, development, and organization with an awareness of audience, purpose, and occasion. Its purpose is primarily persuasive as you attempt to support your viewpoint. Like all writing, it involves careful attention to the conventions of usage. Writing about literature is the focus of **35a.**

Business writing is the focus of **35b.** Whether it takes the form of a letter, memo, résumé, or formal report, business writing generally combines informative and persuasive aims (see **33a**); it gives necessary information and, at the same time, is designed to win a favourable response from the reader. Additionally, such documents—which sometimes have legal implications—often become important records for the company or organization and so should be objective, clear, and concise.

35a
Learn to read literature and write effective papers about fiction, poetry, and drama.

The research paper about literature requires you to go beyond your own reading of a work to critical analysis supported by library research (see **34b**). This discussion covers the kind of writing about literature that draws from the work itself for support of your own interpretation, analysis, or evaluation.

Writing about literature is like writing about other subjects inasmuch as you state a thesis and support it. Like all writing in specialized fields, literature has its own vocabulary that is used in talking and writing about texts. In learning this vocabulary you are not just learning a list of terms and definitions. You are grasping concepts that will help you to read and understand literature and to write about it as well. This section provides only the most basic guidelines for such concepts; ask your instructor for further help in reading and writing about literature.

(1) Use the principles of all good writing.

Consider the rhetorical situation: your audience, your purpose, and the occasion (**33a**). In addition to your instructor, envision an intelligent, educated general audience that has read the work. Your purpose, as mentioned earlier, is mainly to persuade since you are arguing for your own perspective or viewpoint. Finally, observe the conventions suggested by the occasion of your instructor's assignment.

Explore, limit, and focus your subject (see **33d**) as you read and write, and formulate a directed thesis statement that can be supported from the work itself (see **34e**). Reread the work to find ways to develop your thesis. Plan how you will arrange your ideas. Papers about literature often follow the arrangement of the work itself. For example, you might trace a certain character as he or she develops throughout a short story.

In your introduction (**33g**) state the name of the work, the author, and your thesis. You might also include a one- or two-sentence summary of the plot or story line, some background information about the author, or the historical context of the work. Make your conclusion brief, but you might also restate your thesis, evaluate the significance of the work for you as well as for a larger community, and analyze the success of the work in accomplishing its purpose (see **33g**).

As you write, new ideas may occur to you, or you may wish to go back to parts of the work to find support for a point. Be prepared to reread the work and revise and rewrite your paper. Finally, prepare a clean, neat manuscript for submission to your instructor.

(2) Read and reread with care.

Reading literature requires active participation and engagement with the work rather than the passive involvement of watching television. Read the work with such matters as plot, characters, and setting in mind.

First, analyze *how* the poem or story means what it says. What techniques has the author used? How might a story use setting or characters to express its meaning? How might a poem use metaphor to communicate its theme? How might a play use dialogue?

Second, read to discover *what* the work means to you. What is its theme? Every poem, story, and play has one or more themes—that is, general truths that it attempts to communicate through the medium of its component parts: its plot, characters, and setting (the time and place of the action). Not all readers agree on what a poem or story means. New interpretations may change or enrich older interpretations. But any interpretation must be supported by such evidence as short quotations or references to acts or events in the work itself.

Third, evaluate *how well* the work accomplishes its purpose in communicating its meaning. Do not confuse this question with whether or not you liked the work. Your reaction is, of course, important, but even more important is your analysis of why you liked or disliked it. Did it move you? Did it offer new insights? Or did you detect specific flaws in its plot or characterization?

As you read, take notes and jot down ideas. Trust your own first reactions. What characters do you admire? Why? Does the setting help the story along? How? Can you find reasons for your reactions within the work itself? Work toward a tentative thesis (**33d** and **33e**) that will enable other readers to share your response. As you develop an idea for a thesis, reread with that focus in mind, looking for evidence to support your tentative thesis. If you can't find such support, you may have to alter or abandon your thesis.

(3) Analyze, interpret, and evaluate.

There are different ways of reading and writing about literature. Look at a work by analyzing it, interpreting it, and evaluating it. A short paper may do only one of these, or a longer paper may do all three.

Analyze (see **32d[6]**) a work of literature by breaking it into its parts and examining how such parts as setting, characters, and plot combine to form the whole. How do the parts interact? For example, in her paper on *King Lear* (beginning on page 629), Susan Ferk demonstrates how the characters in the subplot comment on and intensify the main plot and theme.

Interpret a work by asking what it means—what its theme is. Support your interpretation by referring to elements in the work itself. For example, in her paper on

Frankenstein (page 613), Susan Suehring shows how Frankenstein's quest for knowledge and Walton's journey exemplify Shelley's theme. In poetry, this kind of paper is often called an explication. You might choose to concentrate on how one element, such as sound, develops the theme. For example, the "s" sounds in William Wordsworth's "A Slumber Did My Spirit Seal" reinforce the hushed feeling of sleep and death in the poem.

Evaluate a work by asking how successful the author is in communicating the meaning to the reader. In his paper "The Tulips" (beginning on page 621), James Dalgetty points out the many metaphors and images that reinforce the difference between the drugged, deathlike figure in the hospital bed and the bright, vital tulips. Finally, ask yourself if the work is of value to you. Does it reflect or enlighten your own experience? Would it reflect the experience of others? Would others also find it valuable? Are the subject and the theme worth writing about?

(4) Choose a subject and develop it.

Your instructor may give you a specific subject, such as a comparison of two characters in Margaret Atwood's novel *The Handmaid's Tale,* or a more general subject, such as characterization in *The Handmaid's Tale.* You must form a thesis for both assignments, but the second requires you to narrow the subject.

If you are asked to select your own subject, your first step is to determine the author's purpose. What is he or she trying to say to you? What is the theme? Then ask yourself what techniques the author uses to accomplish that purpose.

Try some of the methods suggested in **33d** to explore your subject. List ideas and topics that occur to you after that first reading. Then reread the work with the list in mind to see if any of the topics seem supportable.

Question as you read and apply perspectives (**33d**). Think of a character as *static* by describing her as she appears at one point in the work, or think of her as *dynamic* by analyzing how or why she changes. Finally, think of her as *relative* to other characters, to the setting, or to other elements in the work.

Also, apply strategies of development (**32d**). *Define and classify* a play as a comedy or a tragedy, or *describe* a setting that contributes to a work's meaning. Determine *cause-and-effect* relationships: Why, for example, does an important character marry the wrong man? *Compare and contrast* two characters or two poems about a similar subject.

(5) Writing about fiction

Although the events have not happened and the characters may never have existed, fiction expresses a general truth about the human condition through such components as setting, character, and plot. Before you start to write, ask yourself what the author is trying to say in the work. In the following short story, Grace Paley examines the human desire to escape reality through the main character, who retreats to an unreal world and lives vicariously.

Wants
Grace Paley

1   I saw my ex-husband in the street. I was sitting on the steps of the new library.

2   Hello, my life, I said. We had once been married for twenty-seven years, so I felt justified.

3   He said, What? What life? No life of mine.

4   I said, O.K. I don't want to argue when there's real disagreement. I got up and went into the library to see how much I owed them.

5   The librarian said $32 even and you've owed it for eighteen years. I didn't deny anything. Because I don't

understand how time passes. I have had those books. I have often thought of them. The library is only two blocks away.

6   My ex-husband followed me to the Books Returned desk. He interrupted the librarian, who had more to tell. In many ways, he said, as I look back, I attribute the dissolution of our marriage to the fact that you never invited the Bertrams to dinner.

7   That's possible, I said. But really, if you remember: first, my father was sick that Friday, then the children were born, then I had those Tuesday-night meetings, then the war began. Then we didn't seem to know them any more. But you're right. I should have had them to dinner.

8   I gave the librarian a check for $32. Immediately, she trusted me, put my past behind her, wiped the record clean, which is just what most other municipal and/or state bureaucracies will *not* do.

9   I checked out the two Edith Wharton books I had just returned because I'd read them so long ago and they are more apropos now than ever. They were *The House of Mirth* and *The Children,* which is about how life in the United States in New York changed in twenty-seven years fifty years ago.

10   A nice thing I do remember is breakfast, my ex-husband said. I was surprised. All we ever had was coffee. Then I remembered there was a hole in the back of the kitchen closet which opened into the apartment next door. There, they always ate sugar-cured smoked bacon. It gave us a very grand feeling about breakfast, but we never got stuffed and sluggish.

11   That was when we were poor, I said.

12   When were we ever rich? he asked.

13   Oh, as time went on, as our responsibilities increased, we didn't go in need. You took adequate financial care, I reminded him. The children went to camp four weeks a year

and in decent ponchos with sleeping bags and boots, just like everyone else. They looked very nice. Our place was warm in winter, and we had nice red pillows and things.

14 I wanted a sailboat, he said. But you didn't want anything.

15 Don't be bitter, I said. It's never too late.

16 No, he said with a great deal of bitterness. I may get a sailboat. As a matter of fact I have money down on an eighteen-foot two-rigger. I'm doing well this year and can look forward to better. But as for you, it's too late. You'll always want nothing.

17 He had had a habit throughout the twenty-seven years of making a narrow remark which, like a plumber's snake, could work its way through the ear down the throat, halfway to my heart. He would then disappear, leaving me choking with equipment. What I mean is, I sat down on the library steps and he went away.

18 I looked through *The House of Mirth,* but lost interest. I felt extremely accused. Now, it's true, I'm short of requests and absolute requirements. But I do want *something.*

19 I want, for instance, to be a different person. I want to be the woman who brings these two books back in two weeks. I want to be the effective citizen who changes the school system and addresses the Board of Estimate on the troubles of this dear urban center.

20 I *had* promised my children to end the war before they grew up.

21 I wanted to have been married forever to one person, my ex-husband or my present one. Either has enough character for a whole life, which as it turns out is really not such a long time. You couldn't exhaust either man's qualities or get under the rock of his reasons in one short life.

22 Just this morning I looked out the window to watch the street for a while and saw that the little sycamores

the city had dreamily planted a couple of years before the kids were born had come that day to the prime of their lives.

23   Well! I decided to bring those two books back to the library. Which proves that when a person or an event comes along to jolt or appraise me I *can* take some appropriate action, although I am better known for my hospitable remarks.

The elements of setting, plot, characters, point of view, and tone all combine to reinforce Paley's theme.

Setting   *Setting* involves time—not only historical time, but also the length of time covered by the action. It also involves place—not only the physical setting but also the atmosphere created by the author. The time sequence in Grace Paley's short story is brief—a chance meeting between a wife and her ex-husband. The library setting represents the unreal world of books, of fictional characters and settings, to which the wife escapes. At the end, the scene of "the little sycamores" represents a significant shift in the character's outlook, from the unreal world of fiction to the real world of the growing trees outside her window. Setting can be a determinant of action and character.

Plot   The series of events that make up the story is the *plot*. The plot of "Wants" is simple: a brief encounter between a woman and her ex-husband, the paying of a fine, a short conversation, a contemplation, and the returning of books to the library. Usually such events are arranged to produce a climax—the high point of the action toward which the plot builds and out of which the conclusion or solution evolves. The climax in this story comes with the husband's remark "You'll always want nothing," which makes the main character painfully aware of her tendency to avoid life, to live through her books, and to enjoy her breakfast only through the smells of the bacon cooking in the next apartment. This plot reveals the inner conflict within the wife and leads to the conclusion when she sees the growing sycamores for the first time in years and decides to return the books to the library. The nature and resolution of the conflicts often reveal the theme. Such conflicts can exist between characters; between characters and an opposing force, such as an institution or circumstances; and between different feelings within a single character, as in this short story.

Characters   The *characters* carry the plot forward and include a main character, called a protagonist, who is often in conflict with another character or institution or with herself, as in "Wants." In this story she is also in conflict with her husband's desire to embrace life. Whereas she liked the ponchos, sleeping bags, boots, and warm apartment, he longed for a sailboat—to strike out and to live life. You might choose to compare two characters in a story or to analyze one character's development on the basis of his or her actions or conversation. Support your thesis by referring to a description by the author-narrator or by what other characters say to or about him or her.

Point of view   The position from which the action is observed—the person through whose eyes the events are seen, the narrator who tells the story—is the *point of view.* The first-person narrator is a character within the work who tells the story but who may or may not be credible. Grace Paley relates the events from the point of view of the main character, who sees only her own actions and thoughts. The third-person narrator is not a character within the story and may be omniscient—that is, all-knowing. This narrator may know all or only some of the thoughts or actions of the characters. Such narrators are not always consistent throughout an entire work. But it is important to explore why such an inconsistency exists.

Tone *Tone* is the narrator's attitude toward the events and characters in the story or even, in some circumstances, toward the readers. In writing about the narrator, tone is an important concern. The tone of the narrator in "Wants" is naive and innocent, and she seems unaware of her own motivations. She is neither introspective nor reflective except in the most superficial way. This tone emphasizes her detachment from the real world. You might analyze why the author uses a particular narrative technique and tone to make the theme clear to the reader.

Symbolism A common characteristic of fiction, *symbolism* is used in all literature. A symbol is an object, usually concrete, that stands for something else, usually abstract. In writing about a particular symbol, first determine what it stands for. Then trace the incidents in the story that reinforce that idea. In Grace Paley's story, the books symbolize her escape from reality in the same way that the hole in the back of the kitchen closet symbolizes her "grand feeling" about breakfast without ever having to suffer the consequences of feeling "stuffed and sluggish." In avoiding the real breakfast, she is avoiding the real world. The books, especially *The Children,* and the "little sycamores" are additional symbols that reinforce the author's theme.

As you read and write, ask yourself the following questions: What is the theme? How does the author use setting, plot, characters, and symbolism to support the meaning? Who is telling the story? What is the tone of the narrator? Who is the protagonist? How is his or her character developed? How does one character compare with another? What symbols does the author use?

In the following paper, the student compares two characters from a longer piece of fiction—the novel *Frankenstein* by Mary Shelley.

SAMPLE STUDENT PAPER ABOUT FICTION

Suehring 1

Susan Suehring
Professor Rose
English 212
30 April 1993

Themes in <u>Frankenstein</u>

1   Romantic authors often wrote about subjects like the search for knowledge and the desire to know the unknown. In her book <u>Frankenstein</u>, Mary W. Shelley deals with these desires and their consequences. This theme is present early in the book as we are introduced to Robert Walton and learn of his forthcoming exploration into the Arctic. When Walton later meets Victor Frankenstein, the friendship they develop and the similarities and differences between the two men prepare the reader to analyze their unusual search for knowledge and their journeys into the unknown.

2   Shelley advances the idea that human beings have a strong desire to attain the unattainable and shows that sometimes that desire can have serious results. Although both men feel driven

to succeed and have noble goals--Walton's exploration of regions of the Arctic and Frankenstein's desire to give life back to the dead--Walton seems better prepared mentally and emotionally. Walton is impatient to begin his journey, but he still takes six years to make preparations and ready himself for the hardships he realizes he will encounter. In contrast, Frankenstein appears to plunge blindly forward. He has spent many years studying his craft, but upon discovery of the secret of life he blunders on, never giving a thought to what his creation will be like and what his responsibilities toward it will be. As the reader discovers later in the novel, his failure to consider these questions causes him his worst grief.

3   Chapters 2 and 4 of the novel concentrate on Frankenstein's quest for knowledge and his accomplishments at school. We learn of his early delights at finding the internal cause of things. "Curiosity, earnest research to learn the hidden laws of nature, gladness akin to rapture, as they were unfolded to me, are among

the earliest sensations I can remember" (22).
In his search for truth, Frankenstein comes
across the works of authors currently ridiculed
by modern scientists. Just as Frankenstein
studies works that are scorned, he later
creates a monster that he and others abhor.
Thus, persons may unconsciously protect
themselves by denying knowledge that will
lead them to answers they cannot handle.

4   Shelley's point is that Frankenstein spends
too much time learning and that he carries his
search into the unknown too far. We learn from
Frankenstein himself that as his understanding
at school increases, "I . . . soon became
so ardent and eager that the stars often
disappeared in the light of morning whilst I was
yet engaged in my laboratory" (35). His success
at school seems to drive him onward. What end
can there be for a man who conquers knowledge
and then goes in search of more? "A mind
of moderate capacity which closely pursues
one study must infallibly arrive at great
proficiency in that study," according to
Frankenstein (36).

5   The result of Frankenstein's efforts is, of
course, the creation of a monster whose unhappy
life is related throughout the remaining chapters.
Walton likewise encounters problems as he ventures
northward: men die in the bitter cold, and the
ship becomes entrapped by sheets of floating ice.
Unlike Frankenstein, however, Walton realizes that
he must end his journey before its completion,
since it is possible that he and his crew will
die. The crew threatens mutiny if Walton tries
to go north. Even so, Walton shows that he has
learned from Frankenstein's experience and
decides not to pursue his voyage.

6   Shelley shows us that at the end of
Frankenstein's life, he finally acknowledges the
disastrous results of his search for ultimate
knowledge. He tells Walton, "Learn from me, if
not by my precepts, at least by my example, how
dangerous is the acquirement of knowledge and how
much happier that man is who believes his native
town to be the world, than he who aspires to
become greater than his nature will allow" (38).

Work Cited

Shelley, Mary W. <u>Frankenstein</u>. 1818. New York:
    Bantam, 1981.

In this paper, Susan Suehring compares two characters' search for knowledge and the consequences of those searches—represented by Walton's Arctic exploration and Frankenstein's desire to restore life to the dead. In paragraph 2, she points out similarities and then moves to differences between the two characters in their approaches to their symbolic journeys. In paragraphs 3 and 4, she traces Frankenstein's drive for knowledge and concludes with the difference between Walton's and Frankenstein's reactions to the problems that they encounter, thus emphasizing Shelley's theme that acquiring knowledge has its dangers. Suehring traces the development of this theme throughout the novel by comparing and contrasting the two main characters and their searches.

■ **Exercise 1**   In one sentence, write the thesis of this paper. This is basically a comparison paper (see **32d[10]**). How does the author set up the comparison? List five references to the text that support the points she is making. What symbols does she suggest that Shelley uses? Be prepared to discuss your answers in class.

(6) Writing about poetry

Poetry shares many of the components of fiction. It too may contain a narrator with a point of view, and dramatic monologues and narrative poems may have plot, setting, and characters. Like all literature, poetry uses symbols. But poetry is primarily characterized by voice and tone and its concentrated use of connotative diction, imagery, figures of speech, symbols, sound, and rhythm. Before starting to write a paper about a poem, try to capture the literal meaning of the poem in a sentence or two; then analyze how the poet transfers that meaning to the reader through the use of the following poetic devices.

Voice   The speaker in the poem—the persona—is referred to as the *voice*. The first-person "I" in the poem is not necessarily the poet. Listen to the tone of the voice in a poem just as you do in conversation. Is it angry, joyful, melancholy, or fearful? What elements in the poem reinforce that impression? In Dylan Thomas's "Do Not Go Gentle into That Good Night," the tone of the voice, reinforced by diction and imagery, is one of rage and resistance against the inevitability of death.

Diction   The term *diction* means "choice of words," and the words in poetry connote meanings beyond the obvious denotative ones (see **20a[2]**). As you read, check definitions and derivations of key words in your dictionary to find meanings beyond the obvious ones. How do such definitions and derivations reinforce the meaning of the poem?

Imagery   The *imagery* in a poem is a word or phrase describing a sensory experience that reminds us of a feeling we have had. Notice the images in the following lines from the poem "Meeting at Night" by Robert Browning about a lover journeying to meet his sweetheart.

> Then a mile of warm sea-scented beach;
> Three fields to cross till a farm appears;
> A tap at the pane, the quick sharp scratch
> And a blue spurt of a lighted match,
> And a voice less loud, through its joys and fears,
> Than the two hearts beating each to each!

The feeling, the smell, and the sound of the beach; the sounds of the tap at the window, the scratch of a match being lighted, the whispers, and the hearts beating; and the sight of the two lovers in the match light, embracing—all give us the image of a young man, his senses fine-tuned with excitement and anticipation, travelling at night to his sweetheart's home, where they meet in secret.

Figures of speech   The words or phrases that depart from the expected thought or word arrangement, to emphasize a point or to gain the reader's attention, are known as *figures of speech.* Metaphor, simile, and personification are common in poetry (see **20a**). The richness of such figures, although fully felt, is often subtle and difficult to identify. Sir Walter Raleigh uses simile and metaphor in his tightly woven couplet (a pair of rhyming or rhythmic lines):

> Our graves that hide us from the searching sun
> Are like drawn curtains when the play is done.

The above simile equates life with the sun, and death with darkness, closure, endings, and separation, whereas the metaphor equates life with a drama. All of this is suggested in just two lines. As you read a poem, identify the figures of speech and then describe how they enrich the meaning by what they suggest.

Sound   *Sound* is an important element in poetry. *Alliteration* is the repetition of initial consonants, *assonance* is the repetition of vowel sounds in a succession of words, and *rhyme* is the repetition of similar sounds either at the end of lines or within a line (internal rhyme). When you encounter such repetitions, examine and analyze their connection to each other and to the meaning of a line or a stanza or a poem. For instance, notice how the repetition of the "w" and the "s" sounds in the following lines from Elinor Wylie's "Velvet Shoes" sounds like the soft whisper of walking in a snowstorm.

> Let us walk in the white snow
>   In a soundless space;

We are sensitive to sound in poetry because as we read poetry we unconsciously hear it.

Rhythm   The regular occurrence of accent or stress that we hear in poetry is known as *rhythm,* and the rhythm is commonly arranged in patterns called *metres.* Such metres depend on the recurrence of stressed and unstressed syllables in units commonly called *feet.* The most common metrical foot in English is the *iambic,* which consists of an unstressed syllable followed by a stressed one (procee̋d). A second common foot is the *trochaic,* a stressed foot followed by an unstressed one (fifty̆). Less common are the three-syllable *anapestic* (ŏvĕrcome) and the *dactylic* (paragraph). A series of feet make up a line to form a regular rhythm, as exemplified in the following lines from Coleridge's "Frost at Midnight."

> The Frost performs its secret ministry,
> Unhelped by any wind. The owlet's cry
> Came loud—and hark, again! loud as before.

Note the changes in rhythm and their significance—the ways in which rhythm conveys meaning. In the second line there is a pause (caesura), marked by the ending of the sentence, which adds special emphasis to the intrusion of the owlet's cry.

As you read and write, ask yourself the following questions: What is the meaning of the poem? How does the poet use diction? What words have strong connotations or multiple meanings? What images can you identify? What figures of speech does the poet use? How do these advance the meaning? How does the poet use sound, rhythm, and rhyme to reinforce the meaning?

The following is a student paper about a poem, "Tulips," by Sylvia Plath. The first-person narrator is in the hospital, and the tulips in her room intrude on her drugged state.

SAMPLE STUDENT PAPER ABOUT POETRY

Dalgetty 1

James Dalgetty
Professor Anderson
English 2
15 March 1993

The Tulips

1   The angry, intractable image of life in her
otherwise antiseptic, plastic existence, the
tulips push disturbing images of the potency
of life into Sylvia Plath's opiate-induced,
trancelike existence. The tulips seem more
alive than the author herself, and the imagery
associated with them becomes stronger and more
vital than the images of the author. This
constant struggle between the tulips and self-
image allows us to enter the disturbing world
of her nonexistence. In order to understand the
power of "Tulips," consider the pattern of the
imagery, the power of the specific metaphors,
and the dichotomy between the emotions of the
author and the emotions of the tulips.

2   The emotions of the tulips precipitate
our journey into the author's confined,
trancelike existence. "The tulips are too
excitable, it is winter here" (1). This first
line illustrates both the powerful emotions of
the personified tulips and the author's lack of
emotion about her world. From this initial
metaphor we then get a spatial introduction
into her fixed world. The first eighteen lines
are a description of her hospital stay,
confined to a bed with her head propped up
"like an eye between two white lids that
will not shut" (9). This narrative gives a
disturbing picture of the poet, the metaphors
associating her with images of a dazed
nonexistence. She pictures herself as "white,"
"winter," "peaceful," "nobody," and "a pebble."
All of these images translate into a picture of
a body with no name or identity: she is just
there for the ride.

3   Line 18 starts a tone of active involvement
in her experience; however, again this is a
disturbing portrait of a "lost soul." This is
the story of cutting ties with the past and

Dalgetty 3

present, a distinct set of images promoting
a loss of identity and dissociation. The
author pictures herself as "lost," "drowned,"
"nun," "pure," "empty," "dazed," "dead," and
finally "I have no face" (48). Lines 25
through 35 further reinforce these images
with a strong association of drowning and
then seem to indicate death as a favourable
state of affairs.

4   Into this "pleasant" state of oblivion
the tulips rear their heads. Their "excitable,"
glaring intrusion becomes more real and alive
than anything in the author's private limbo.
Their colour is too alive: "The tulips are too
red in the first place, they hurt me" (36).
The tulips become "like an awful baby," wrapped
in white swaddlings (38). They float in her
daze but try to "weigh me down" (40) like
"lead sinkers" (42) in an attempt to bring
her back down to earth and reality.

5   After their introduction, the tulips seem
to personify strong emotions of hunger and
life force. Lines 46 and 47 describe the
contrast between the author's self-image and

the ever-growing personality of the tulips.
"And I see myself, flat, ridiculous, a cut
paper shadow / Between the eye of the sun
and the eyes of the tulips." Line 47 also
illustrates the complete projection of
identity and personality to the tulips; by
equating the sun and the tulips as "eyes,"
the author endows them with the same image
that she gives herself in line 9.

6   The projection now complete, the tulips
assume an almost "dangerous" (58) character
to the author. The tulips disturb and anger
her and generate fear in her soul. They force
her attention to the real world of life and
beauty and strong emotion. "They concentrate
my attention, that was happy / Playing and
resting without committing itself" (55, 56).
The tulips fill her nonexistence like a "loud
noise" (52). Their presence fills the air,
which "snags and eddies round" them like
"a river." The power of their life force even
penetrates the walls (57). The final image
is perhaps the most potent: the tulips open
their collective maw like "dangerous animals,"

threatening to swallow the author's safe
oblivion and force her to face life and
reality.

7   As a most disturbing portrait of a woman
who is so lost that briefly blooming flowers
emote more tenacious life force than does
the author, the complex series of images
that comprise "Tulips" is both sinister
and compelling. It is an entrance into a
frightening world of self-induced oblivion
and nonexistence, with the compelling
portraits of the short-lived flowers
assuming more life, character, and tenacity
than the portrait of the author herself.

Dalgetty 6

Work Cited

Plath, Sylvia. "Tulips." <u>The Collected Poems
    of Sylvia Plath</u>. Ed. Ted Hughes. London:
    Faber, 1981. 160–62.

In this paper James Dalgetty compares the images and metaphors associated with the author or persona and those associated with the tulips. He follows the order of the poem itself, tracing these images throughout and supporting his comments with appropriate quotations from the poem. For example, Dalgetty supports his point about the contrast between the author's image and the "ever-growing personality of the tulips" by a line from the poem: "And I see myself, flat, ridiculous, a cut paper shadow / Between the eye of the sun and the eyes of the tulips."

■ **Exercise 2** In a single sentence, state the literal meaning of the following Shakespearean poem. Who is the persona? Find three images that the poet uses to convey that meaning. Be prepared to discuss your answers in class.

Sonnet 73

That time of year thou mayst in me behold
When yellow leaves, or none, or few, do hang
Upon those boughs which shake against the cold,
Bare ruined choirs, where late the sweet birds sang.
In me thou see'st the twilight of such day
As after sunset fadeth in the west;
Which by and by black night doth take away,
Death's second self, that seals up all in rest.
In me thou see'st the glowing of such fire,
That on the ashes of his youth doth lie,
As the deathbed whereon it must expire,
Consumed with that which it was nourished by.
This thou perceiv'st which makes thy love more strong,
To love that well which thou must leave ere long.

William Shakespeare

(7) Writing about drama

Although it is written to be filmed or performed on a stage, drama is also meant to be read, which is probably the way that you will encounter it in your course work. In a live performance, the director and the actors imprint the play with their own interpretations; in a book or script, you have only the printed word. Drama has many of the same elements as fiction and poetry, but they are presented differently.

Dialogue   *Dialogue* is the medium through which we see action and characterization in reading a play. Examine dialogue to discover inner thoughts, motives, and internal conflicts, as well as relationships.

Characters   Often identified briefly in a list at the beginning of the play, the *characters* are developed largely through what they say and what is said about them and to them. In Ibsen's "A Doll's House," Nora's growth from a child to a mature woman can be traced through her gestures and her speech. In writing about drama, you might compare characters or analyze their development and the significance of that development through their dialogue and their actions.

Plot   *Plot* in drama is similar to plot in fiction and is marked by climax and conflict. Although there may be time lapses between scenes, the story line must be developed within the more narrow time and place constraints of the play. Subplots similar to the one outlined in the sample student paper that follows may reinforce the theme of the main plot. In a paper you might examine how dialogue, characterizations, and stage directions for gesture and movement further the action.

As you read and write, ask yourself the following questions: What is the theme of the play? How does the dialogue move the action and support the meaning? How are the characters depicted through dialogue? through their gestures? through their actions?

The following student paper outlines the significance of the subplot in *King Lear* as intensifying the main plot and lending universality to the play.

Sample student paper about drama

Susan K. Ferk

Professor Dorgan

English 211

15 October 1993

The Subplot as Commentary in <u>King Lear</u>

1   To a careless eye, the subplot involving
Gloucester, Edgar, and Edmund in Shakespeare's
<u>King Lear</u> may appear to be trivial and
unnecessary, a simple restatement of the theme
of the main story. After close examination,
however, it is clear that Shakespeare has
skilfully introduced a second set of
characters whose actions comment on and
intensify the main plot and theme.

2   The first scene of <u>King Lear</u> sets up
comparison and contrast between Lear and
Gloucester. Gloucester jokes about his bastard
son while Lear angrily banishes his favourite
daughter. By the end of the second scene, we
realize how important their children are to
both men and yet how little they really know

them. Both are easily deceived: Lear by Goneril and Regan, who convince him of their love with flowery words, and Gloucester, who is convinced by very little evidence of Edgar's plot against his life. The audience is set up to accept Lear and Gloucester as old fools. Neither man takes responsibility for what has happened. Gloucester says "these late eclipses" (1.2.102) have brought about these changes, and Lear blames Cordelia for her losses. Neither realizes or acknowledges that his own foolishness has brought about these events.

3   Gloucester, however, does comment on Lear's actions in scene 2. He is amazed that the king has limited his power so suddenly. When Edmund suggests that when "sons [are] at perfect age, and fathers declined, the father should be as ward to the son, and the son manage his revenue" (1.2.72-74), Gloucester is enraged by what he thinks are Edgar's words. He calls Edgar unnatural, and since this is exactly the action taken by Lear with his daughters, we can assume that he thinks Lear's act was unnatural also.

Ferk 3

4   At Goneril's palace Lear foreshadows
Gloucester's fate when he says "Old fond eyes,
beweep this cause again, I'll pluck ye out"
(1.4.305-06). In the same way that Lear fears
for his eyes because of Goneril, so does
Gloucester lose his eyes because of Edmund.
At the end of act 1, Lear foreshadows his
own destiny, "Oh, let me not be mad, not mad,
sweet heaven!" (1.5.43).

5   Shakespeare brings together the two plots in
act 2 scene 2 when Regan, Cornwall, Gloucester,
and Edmund meet at Gloucester's castle.
Cornwall's offer of employment to Edmund on the
pretense of his royal service seems logical to
the audience, who knows the similarities of
their true natures. Gloucester calls Edmund his
"loyal and natural boy" (2.1.91), whereas Lear
calls Goneril a "degenerate bastard" (1.4.252).

6   Lear arrives at the castle and is outraged
when Cornwall and Regan do not meet him.
However, Lear decides that perhaps Cornwall is
ill and unable to come. Likewise, throughout
the remainder of act 2 Lear tries to imagine
that Regan and Cornwall love and respect him,

and he makes excuses for them when their actions do not conform to his expectations. Lear has more at stake here than Regan's love. If she proves as evil as Goneril (and she proves even more so), then Lear cannot deny that he was wrong in supposing these two daughters more loving than his banished Cordelia. Lear soon acknowledges that the disease of his daughters is in his own blood. The realization of his errors and his loss of power and Cordelia drive him to the madness seen in act 3.

7   Gloucester and Lear meet in scene 4 of act 3 in the midst of a raging storm, Lear's madness, and Gloucester's despair. Gloucester has not suffered the worst, but his words begin to echo those of Lear in earlier scenes. He says, "Thou sayest the King grows mad: I'll tell thee, friend, I am almost mad myself" (166–67). Gloucester helps the king into the hovel and cares for him like a child, much the same as Edgar later helps Gloucester after his eyes are plucked out.

8   Death begins in act 3 scene 7. A servant dies defending Gloucester, and Cornwall is

fatally wounded. In the confusion Gloucester realizes his mistakes and his former blindness. After losing his sight, he can now see. When he is turned out, his wanderings in the country remind us of Lear in the storm. Lear likewise in his despair now has learned to see.

9 Gloucester and Lear share many similarities at this point. Both men at the height of their afflictions desire the company of Tom O'Bedlam, who represents the wise man. They also acquire a sense of justice and care for less fortunate men. Lear looks after his fool in the storm, and Gloucester calls for clothes for Tom. Their similarities intensify the pain and change in each man. Also, Shakespeare's use of a king and a nobleman both suffering from their foolishness emphasizes the universality of human suffering. But they do not suffer in the same way. Gloucester does not lose his mind, and Lear does not try suicide.

10 In the end, the story comes full circle. Edgar tells Gloucester his identity and asks his father's forgiveness, thus causing

Gloucester's heart to break "'twixt two extremes of passion, joy and grief" (5.3.236). Lear also dies, with Cordelia in his arms, trying so hard to believe her alive that it strains his heart as well. These men have learned much, but as in real life, wisdom in old age and recognizing one's children for what they are do not always bring peace and happiness. The dismal final scenes of this play in which almost everyone dies serve to emphasize Shakespeare's intent to show two unfortunate characters who suffer from foolishness and Fortune's wheel.

Work Cited

Shakespeare, William. <u>The Tragedy of King Lear</u>. <u>The Folger Library General Reader's Shakespeare</u>. New York: Washington Square-Pocket, 1957.

Susan Ferk supports her thesis by comparing and contrasting the characters of Lear and Gloucester as they move through the play. In act 1, the plots are separate, but she points out how in act 2 they move together and proceed along parallel lines, crossing only occasionally. She traces this progression throughout the play, following the characters' actions and dialogue while emphasizing the significance of each plot in reinforcing and intensifying the other.

■ **Exercise 3** Select a recent film or television dramatization. In one sentence identify the theme. How do the plot and characters support that theme? Be prepared to discuss your answers in class.

(8) Use proper form in writing about literature.

See Section **34** for the conventions for a research paper. There are, in addition, certain special conventions for writing about literature.

Tense Use the present tense when analyzing the elements of a literary text, since those elements are present in your mind as you write about the text in present time.

> NOT   Earle Birney's poem "Vancouver Lights" *presented* images of Vancouver during wartime.
> BUT   Earle Birney's poem "Vancouver Lights" *presents* images of Vancouver during wartime.

Documentation Check with your instructor about the reference format he or she prefers. Ordinarily, you will be writing about a work from a book used in the course. In such cases you may not need to give the source and publication information of the book. However, you should always indicate if you are using another edition or an anthology. One way of doing so is to use the MLA form for works cited, as explained in **34e,** although in this case your bibliography might consist of only a single work. See the examples on pages 616, 625, and 634.

An alternative way of providing this information is by acknowledging the first quotation in an explanatory note at the end of the paper (see below) and then giving all subsequent references to the work in the body of the paper.

```
¹D.H. Lawrence, "Tickets, Please,"

The Norton Anthology of Short Fiction, ed.

R.V. Cassill (New York: Norton, 1986) 834.

All subsequent references to this work will

be by page number within the text.
```

If you use the note form, you may not need a works cited list to repeat the bibliographical information.

Whichever format you use, recall from **34e** that references to short stories and novels are by page number, references to poetry are by line number, and references to plays are usually by act, scene, and line numbers. The information in parentheses should be placed in the text immediately after the quotation, and the period or comma follows the quotation marks and the parentheses (see **16e**).

Plot Do not retell the plot. Refer to it only as necessary to support or clarify your thesis. Provide a brief summary of the plot, in two or three lines, only if you have reason to suspect that your audience may be unfamiliar with the work you are discussing, but do not take valuable space to describe the plot in great detail.

Poetry For *poems and verse plays,* type quotations of three lines or less within your text and insert a slash with a space on each side to separate the lines.

"Does the road wind uphill all the way?" / "Yes, to the very end"—Christine Rosetti opens her poem "Uphill" with this two-line question and answer.

Quotations of more than three lines should be indented ten spaces from the left margin with double-spacing between lines.

Author references   Use the full name in your first reference to the author of a work and only the last name in all subsequent references. Treat male and female authors the same: Dickens and Brontë, not Dickens and Miss Brontë.

35b
Write effective letters and résumés; use an acceptable format.

A knowledge of how to write business letters, application letters, and résumés can be useful to you not only in job-related situations but in your college or university and personal life as well. The three main formats for business letters—full block, modified block, and indented—can be used for any kind of business letter.

(1)   Use an acceptable business letter format.

Business letters are usually typed on only one side of white, unlined 21.6 × 27.9 cm (8½ × 11 inch) paper. Standard business envelopes measure about 9 cm × 16.5 cm (3½ × 6½ inches) or 10.15 cm × 25.5 cm (4 × 10 inches). Letterhead stationery and envelopes vary in both size and colour.

Check to see if your company or organization has a policy about letter format. Most companies use either full block, modified block, or indented formats for regular correspondence, though an indented format is often used for personal business correspondence such as thank-you notes, congratulations, and the like.

A business letter has six parts: (1) heading, (2) inside address, (3) salutation, (4) body, (5) closing, which consists of the complimentary close and signature, and (6) added notations.

The *heading* gives the writer's full address and the date. If letterhead stationery is used, the date is typed beneath the head, flush left, flush right, or centred, depending on your format. If plain stationery is used, the address of the writer followed by the date is placed toward the top of the page—the distance from the top arranged so that the body of the letter will be attractively centred on the page—flush with the left- or right-hand margin, as in the letters on pages 644 and 649. Notice that the heading has no end punctuation.

The *inside address,* typed two to six lines below the heading, gives the name and full address of the recipient.

The *salutation* (or greeting) is written flush with the left margin, two spaces below the inside address, and is followed by a colon (a comma is used after salutations in French).

When the surname of the addressee is known, it is used in the salutation of a business letter, as in the following examples.

Dear Dr. Davis:	Dear Mayor Campbell:
Dear Mrs. Greissman:	Dear Ms. Joseph:
Chère Mlle Desrosiers,	Chère Mme Gagnon,
Cher M. Paré,	Cher M. Roy,

Note: Use *Miss* or *Mrs.* if the woman you are addressing has indicated a preference for one of these titles. Otherwise, use *Ms.,* which is always appropriate and which is preferred by many businesswomen, whatever their marital status.

In letters to organizations, or to persons whose names and gender are unknown, such salutations as the following are customary:

Dear Sir or Madam: Dear Tilley Endurables:
Dear Subscription Manager: Dear Registrar:

For the appropriate forms of salutations and addresses in letters to government officials, military personnel, and so on, check an etiquette book or the front or back of your college dictionary.

The *body* of the letter should follow the principles of good writing. Typewritten letters are usually single-spaced, with double spacing between paragraphs. The first sentence of each paragraph should begin flush with the left margin (in full block or modified block) or should be indented five to ten spaces (in indented format). The subject matter should be organized so that the reader can grasp immediately what is wanted, and the style should be clear and direct. Do not use stilted or abbreviated phrasing:

NOT   The aforementioned letter
BUT   Your letter
NOT   Please send it to me ASAP.
BUT   Please send it to me as soon as possible.

The *closing* is typed flush with the left-hand margin in full-block style. In modified block and indented style, it is typed to the right of the letter, in alignment with the heading. Here are the parts of the closing:

Complimentary close: This conventional ending is typed, after a double space, below the last paragraph of the body of the letter. Among the endings commonly used in business letters are the following:

FORMAL   LESS FORMAL
Very truly yours,   Sincerely,
Sincerely yours,   Cordially,

Typed name: The writer's full name is typed three or four lines below the closing. A woman may choose to indicate her marital status or preferred title in parentheses.

Sylvia Tanazaki
Sylvia Tanazaki
(Mrs. Hiro Tanazaki)

Eloise Browne
(Ms.) Eloise Browne

Title of sender: This line, following the typed name, indicates the sender's position, if he or she is acting in an official capacity.

Manager, Employee Relations
Chairperson, Search Committee

Signature: The letter is signed between the complimentary close and the typed name.

Notations are typed below the closing, flush with the left margin. They indicate, among other things, whether anything is enclosed with or attached to the letter (*enclosure* or *enc., attachment* or *att.*); to whom copies of the letter have been sent (*cc: AAW, PTN*); and the initials of the sender and the typist (*DM/cll*).

MODEL BUSINESS LETTER

QUEEN CITY REGIONAL HEALTH SERVICES

1502 Regent Street   Regina, Saskatchewan S4N 1R9

2 March 1993

Dr. Nathan Boyko
Community Health Centre
433 Cheadle Street West   **INSIDE ADDRESS**
Swift Current, SK
S9H 0B1

Dear Dr. Boyko: **SALUTATION**

We have completed our study of the nutri-
tion education program being conducted by
the Community Health Centre. The findings
are encouraging. However, we believe that
awareness training for the staff, a few
schedule changes, and greater involvement
of the parents could significantly improve
the program.

Our final report, available by 30 March,   **BODY**
will explain these recommendations more
fully. Rachel Walsh, our Chief
Consultant, will be happy to work with
you if you would like her assistance.

We look forward to hearing from you soon.

Sincerely,   **Complimentary close**

Dorothy Muir

                    Signature   **CLOSING**

Dorothy Muir,   **Typed name**
Director   **Title**

DM/ewl   **NOTATION**

BUSINESS ENVELOPES

The address that appears on the envelope is identical to the inside address, with one exception: whereas the traditional abbreviations for provinces or states are still often used in the inside address, the modern two-letter postal abbreviation (*not* followed by a period) should always be used on the envelope. The traditional and the current postal abbreviations for the provinces and territories are as follows:

Alta.	B.C.	Man.	N.B.	Nfld.	N.S.
AB	BC	MB	NB	NF	NS

N.W.T.	Ont.	P.E.I.	Que.	Sask.	Y.T.
NT	ON	PE	PQ	SK	YT

The return address regularly gives the full name and address of the writer, including the postal code (or U.S. zip code).

MODEL ADDRESSED ENVELOPE

```
Marielle Gagnon
2002 rue St Hubert
Montréal, PQ
H2L 3Z5

                    Mr. Adam Troikos
                    Personnel Manager
                    Echo Electronics
                    1726 Macdonald Street
                    Vancouver, BC
                    V6K 1M5
```

Note that the postal code may appear either on a separate line or on the same line as the city and province.

(2) Write effective application letters and résumés.

Application letters and résumés are essential parts of applying for a job. In both, your main concern is to emphasize your strong points, to present yourself in the best light so that a prospective employer will grant you an interview. Usually written to draw the reader's attention to the résumé, the letter of application should indicate the job you want and state your qualifications briefly. In the last paragraph you should indicate when you are available for an interview. The résumé (pages 646–47) that accompanies the letter of application gives more information about you than your letter can. Ordinarily, your letter should be no longer than one typed page, and your résumé should not exceed two pages.

A résumé is a list of a person's qualifications for a job and is enclosed with a letter of application. It is made up of four basic categories of information:

1. Personal data: name, mailing address, telephone number
2. Educational background
3. Work experience
4. References

If appropriate or requested, information concerning awards, honours, personal achievements, or extracurricular activities related to the position may also be included.

Make your résumé look professional. Like the letter of application, the résumé is a form of persuasion designed to emphasize your qualifications for a job and to get you an interview. Since there is usually more than one applicant for every job, your résumé should make the most of your qualifications. Consider devising a résumé especially tailored to each job you apply for so that you can present your qualifications in the strongest light. After reading all the letters and résumés received, a potential employer usually decides to interview only the best-qualified candidates.

APPLICATION LETTER

2002 rue St Hubert
Montréal, PQ
H2L 3Z5
3 April 1993

Mr. Adam Troikos
Personnel Manager
Echo Electronics
1726 Macdonald Street
Vancouver, BC
V6K 1M5

Dear Mr. Troikos:

Please consider me for the position of Assistant Director of Employee Benefits in the Personnel Division of Echo Electronics.

As you can see from my résumé, my major was Administrative Management with an emphasis in personnel management. Whenever possible, I have found jobs and campus activities that would give me experience in dealing with people. As an assistant at UBC's Gage Towers Conference Services, I dealt with visitors to campus, made conference arrangements, and co-ordinated tours. The position required good organizational skills, as well as an understanding of people.

As an administrative intern with Echo last summer, I learned a great deal about the management of a company. Through first-hand experience, I was able to gain a firmer grasp of the contribution that personnel management makes to the overall objectives of the company.

I would very much like to put my interests and my training to work for Echo Electronics, and I am available for an interview at your convenience.

Sincerely,

Marielle Gagnon

Marielle Gagnon

Writing a résumé requires the same planning and attention to detail that writing a paper does. First, make a list of the jobs you have had, the activities and clubs you have been part of, and the offices you have held. Amplify these items by adding dates, job titles and responsibilities, and a brief statement about what you learned from each of them. Arrange these items with the most recent first. Activities that may not seem relevant to the job you want can often be explained to show that you learned important things from them. The résumé on pages 646–47 illustrates the following tips on résumé writing.

TIPS ON RÉSUMÉ WRITING

1. Don't forget to include your name, address, and telephone number; unless relevant to the job, personal data such as age and marital status are better left out.

2. Mention your degree, college or university, and pertinent areas of special training.

3. Think about career goals but generally reserve mention of them for the application letter or interview (and even then make sure they enhance your appeal as a candidate). Match your qualifications to the employer's goals.

4. Even if an advertisement asks you to state a salary requirement, any mention of salary should usually be deferred until the interview.

5. Whenever possible, make evident any relationship between the jobs you have had and the job you are seeking.

6. Use an acceptable format and make sure the résumé is neat, orderly, and correct to show that you are an efficient, well-organized, thoughtful person.

RÉSUMÉ

RÉSUMÉ

MARIELLE GAGNON
2002 rue St Hubert
Montréal, Québec
H2L 3Z5
(514) 845-8328

EDUCATION   <u>Administration</u>. Bachelor of Arts,
Concordia University (May 1993);
major in Administrative Management;
minor in Personnel Management;
additional course work in Corporate
Economy and in Entrepreneurship and
Small Business Management.
Arts One Programme, University of
British Columbia, 1987-88

RELATED EXPERIENCE

Summers

1992   <u>Intern</u>, <u>Echo Electronics</u>. Learned
about pension plans, health-care
benefits, employee associations,
and work regulations as they affect
employee relations and personnel
management.

1991   <u>Conference Assistant</u>. Gage Towers,
UBC. Assisted campus visitors and
conference delegates. Co-ordinated
local tours, travel arrangements,
and shuttle service to the airport.
Also served as translator for
Francophone visitors.

1989-90   <u>Orientation Leader</u>. Student
Counselling Office, Concordia
University. Met with prospective
students and their parents, conducted tours of campus, answered
questions, and wrote reports for
each orientation meeting.

1988   <u>Volunteer Worker</u>. Crane Library for
the Blind, UBC. Preparation of

```
taped materials for the Crane Library.
Provided assistance and orientation for visu-
ally impaired students arriving in the summer.

HONOURS      Copely-Starr Bursary
             (Administrative), 1992
             TELEBANK Business Writing Prize,
             1991

LANGUAGES    English, Swedish, and conversa-
             tional French

REFERENCES   Gage Towers Conference Services
             University of British Columbia
             1875 East Mall, Vancouver, BC
             V6T 1W5
             (604) 822-3219

             Ms. Jocelyne Lauré
             Student Counselling Office
             Concordia University
             8812 Sherbrooke Street West
             Montréal, Québec
             H4B 1R6
             (514) 845-4083
```

You may find it helpful to consult one of the following books for further information about application letters, résumés, and interviews:

Angel, Juvenal L. *The Complete Resume Book and Job-Getter's Guide.* 3rd ed. New York: Pocket Books, 1989.

Bolles, Richard N. *What Color Is Your Parachute? A Practical Manual for Job-Hunters and Career-Changers.* Rev. ed. Berkeley: Ten Speed Press, 1989.

Komar, John J. *The Job Game.* New York: New Century, 1988.

Smith, Michael H. *The Resumé Writer's Handbook.* Rev. ed. New York: Barnes and Noble, 1987.

University Career Planning Association. *The Résumé.* Rev. ed. Toronto: U. of Toronto Career Counselling Service, 1982.

(3) Write effective business letters.

LETTER OF INQUIRY

Essentially a request for information, a letter of inquiry should first explain your reasons for writing—both why you are seeking the information and why you think your reader is the person to supply the information. If you need the information by a certain date, mention that fact in the introduction along with your explanation of why you are writing.

Next, state the questions you need answered. You will be more likely to get a response if your questions are specific and detailed. Finally, since you have asked someone to take time to answer your questions, express appreciation, and if the answers will help you with some project, offer to share the results. (See the sample letter of inquiry on the following page.) It is courteous to send a stamped, self-addressed envelope with the request (if you are not a potential customer.)

If you are asked to respond to an inquiry and you can provide the information, follow the order for your responses that was used for the questions. When appropriate, number your responses the same way the questions were numbered. If you cannot provide the information requested, explain why you cannot help and, if possible, offer to help with future requests.

SAMPLE LETTER OF INQUIRY

20 March 1993

High Flyers Angling Club
275 Malaspina Street
Nanaimo, BC V6R 2R4

Mr. Mark Blodgett, Secretary
Miramichi Atlantic Salmon Society
1106 Shoreview Road
Chatham, NB E1N 3V7

Dear Mr. Blodgett:

I understand your society can provide
information about streams in northern
New Brunswick and adjacent Quebec. I am
chairing a committee our local anglers' club
has formed to prepare--by July--a booklet
listing good fly-fishing locations in your
area. Also, many members have questions about
the effects of industrial pollution on the
streams and rivers in that area.

We are particularly interested in the answers
to two questions:

1. Who gathers information about Atlantic
   salmon populations in the Restigouche
   and streams in the area?
2. Has the ongoing study of the Miramichi
   found any increased toxicity?

We will very much appreciate any help you
can give us in collecting this information.
And if you are interested, we will be happy
to send you a copy of our booklet when it
is completed.

Sincerely,

Richard James
Chair, Booklet Committee

RJ/lh

CLAIM AND ADJUSTMENT LETTER

The more specifically and exactly the claim and adjustment letter describes what is wrong, the easier and quicker it will be to correct the situation. If an airline has lost your suitcase, describe it fully and include the flight number, date, and destination. If an appliance is faulty, identify the brand, style, model, and serial number. A company will often do exactly what you request, if it can. The more reasonable and courteous your request, the better your chance of getting the adjustment you want.

SAMPLE CLAIM AND ADJUSTMENT LETTER

Box 293
Legal, AB
T0G 1L0
11 February 1993

Mr. Norman Huckley
Huckley Electronics, Inc.
235 Central Avenue
Edmonton, AB
T0G 1M0

Dear Mr. Huckley:

A week ago today I bought a 48 cm Supersonic colour television set from you, model number 0300-B, serial number 0137-8112-77. All week the set has worked perfectly, but when I turned it on today, nothing happened. The trouble is not with the electrical outlet, which I checked by plugging in another appliance.

I would like to bring the set in for on-the-spot repair on Saturday, 18 February. I trust you will honour the conditions of sale and either repair it free of charge or replace it with another 48 cm Supersonic. My telephone number is 689-4140, and you can call me any day from noon to 5:00 P.M.

Sincerely,

Thomas McNally

Thomas McNally

THANK-YOU LETTER

Thank-you letters are written often in private life, and they are also used in business. If a representative of a company has been helpful or done more than you expected, a thank-you letter or note is an appropriate way of showing appreciation. A gift, recommendation, award, or prize should also be acknowledged with a letter of thanks.

Usually, thank-you letters are in the indented style. It is not necessary to include an inside address, and a comma replaces the colon after the salutation. Some think thank-you letters should be handwritten, but typewritten ones are equally correct.

SAMPLE THANK-YOU LETTER

```
                        12 Cardinal Knoll
                        Brantford, ON
                        N3R 6C9
                        26 October 1992
```

Dear Dean Rutledge,

    Thank you very much for recommending me for the Young Forester's Bursary. I'm happy to tell you that I am the recipient of the 1993 bursary. I have already received a letter from the Awards Office advising me that the Foresters' Association has released funds for my second-term fees. I am very pleased to be so honoured.

                Sincerely,

                Norman R Ahrends

                Norman R. Ahrends

35c
Write effective memos.

Generally, memos are used for communicating a variety of information within an organization—directives on policy or procedures, requests and responses to requests for information, trip reports and monthly action summaries, and informal reports such as field reports or lab reports. Whereas the length of the memo varies according to its purpose, the basic format is relatively standardized, though companies often have specially printed forms for the first page. Usually, memos identify the person or persons to whom the memo is addressed in the first line, the person who wrote the memo in the second line, and subject of the memo in the third line.

> To: J. Karl Meyer, Managing Editor
> From: Lee Dawson, Project Editor
> Subject: Status Report on Books in Production

If the memo is long, it sometimes begins with a *statement of the purpose,* and then gives a *summary* of the discussion. This summary helps a manager or executive, who may receive thirty or forty memos a day, decide which ones to read carefully and which to skim. The *discussion* is the main part of the memo. If it is more than a page long, it may benefit from the use of headings to highlight the main parts. If appropriate, the memo closes with *recommendations* for action to be taken. Clearly state in this part of the memo who is to do what and when it is to be done.

The tone of a memo can be casual, informal, or formal, depending on its purpose and audience. Naturally, a trainee would use a relatively formal tone in a memo addressed to a supervisor, but a more casual tone in one addressed to co-workers. Whatever the tone, the memo should be clear, concise, and correct. Notice the format and the tone of the sample memos. The first is from a member of a marketing group to a member of a sales group. The second was sent by an executive to the people he supervises. In the first memo, the tone is casual; in the second, it is more formal, but not stilted. Both are clear and concise.

MEMO

EASTGATE PHARMACEUTICALS, INC.   **MEMORANDUM**

A SUBSIDIARY OF HALL-CHURCH COMPANY

TO _____ Jack Hammond _____

FROM _____ Sharon Lincoln _____

DATE _____ 26 March 1993 _____

SUBJECT ___ SunSafe _____

Thanks for the comments and ideas on the SunSafe sales display.

We are out of the consumer pamphlets we used with the displays. I can, however, send the pamphlets intended for use in doctors' offices. How many do you need?

I am also exploring, with John Seto of our agency, your suggestion about designing a SunSafe reference card for pharmacists. I like the idea. The timing may be a problem for 1993, but if it is, I'll include the idea in the 1994 plans. I'll keep you posted on my progress. I appreciate your interest and suggestions.

SRL/js

cc: Neil Thomlinson
     District Managers

35c wri

INTERNAL MEMO

To: All Field Personnel

From: R.W. Morgan
               Vice-President, Field Operations

Date: 7 October 1993

Subject: PICCOLO 973 SOFTWARE DIRECTORY

The first issue of the PICCOLO 973 SOFTWARE
DIRECTORY is attached. It lists CP/M-compatible
software products that are on the market now
for people with Z80-based microcomputer systems
such as the Piccolo 973.

We are trying to list only those products that
we have seen demonstrated on the 973 or that
a vendor, dealer, or distributor claims will
run on the 973; but we make no guarantees.

Please note: Inclusion in the directory does
not imply that Piccolo endorses the products
or suppliers or recommends them in preference
to others not listed. Further, Piccolo does
not warrant that these products are compatible
with Piccolo systems. The buyer is solely
responsible for determining application and
suitability.

Although this directory can be copied for
distribution to others, it is a temporary
listing intended primarily for your own use.
In late November it will be revised and
published in booklet form as a stock item.

Approximately 250 vendors have already been
contacted for information on software products
that might be appropriate in the directory.
A Software Vendor Listing Form is included
in the back of the directory for additional
vendors to whom you may wish to give copies.

RWM/jh

35d
Write effective reports.

Formal reports differ from informal memo reports in length and tone, and in the addition of such elements as a letter of transmittal, title page, abstract, executive summary, table of contents, glossary, and appendix (although not all reports include all of these elements). Writing a formal report often requires many of the same skills and basic techniques as writing a research paper (see Section **34**). Many organizations have a format guide for formal reports; in the absence of such a guide, you might begin by studying several successful reports from the company files.

An *abstract* is a brief summary of the material in the report, usually in language similar to that of the report (whether technical or non-technical). The abstract enables prospective readers to determine whether the report will be useful and whether they need to read all of it or only parts of it. If a report intended for technical personnel will also be read by non-technical management, it often includes an *executive summary,* in non-technical language, in addition to an abstract.

A *table of contents* provides a guide to the structure of the report and makes finding the exact section of the report needed easier for readers. If you have used effective and accurate headings in the body of your report, the simplest way to create a table of contents is to list them.

A *glossary* is an alphabetical list defining terms used in the report. Using a glossary lets you continue your discussion without having to stop to define terms. Generally, a glossary appears at the end of a report, but it may also be placed after the table of contents.

An *appendix* contains information that is relevant to the report but is too detailed or extensive to be included in the discussion. For example, an appendix might contain data tables, maps, supplementary diagrams, or a list of references. An appendix usually appears last.

You may find it helpful to consult one of the following books for further information about letters, memos, and reports.

Brusaw, C.T., G.J. Alred, and W.E. Oliu. *Handbook of Technical Writing*. 3rd ed. New York: St. Martin's, 1987.

Damerst, William A., and Arthur H. Bell. *Clear Technical Communication: A Process Approach*. 3rd ed. New York: Harcourt, 1989.

MacGregor, A.J. *Graphics Simplified: How to Plan and Prepare Effective Charts, Graphs, Illustrations, and Other Visual Aids*. Toronto: U of Toronto P, 1979.

Mathes, J.C. *Designing Technical Reports*. 2nd ed. New York: Macmillan, 1991.

Rodman, Lil. *Technical Communication: Strategy and Process*. Toronto: Harcourt, 1991.

■ Exercise 4

1. Prepare a résumé, and then write a letter of application for a position you are competent to fill.
2. Write to a former teacher to express appreciation for recommending you for a summer job.
3. Call the attention of your representative in city government to repairs needed on neighbourhood streets.
4. Write to a record company complaining about the technical quality of a compact disc you ordered from it.

Grammatical Terms

This glossary presents brief explanations of frequently used grammatical terms. Consult the index for references to further discussion of most of the terms and for a number of terms not listed.

absolute phrase   A grammatically unconnected part of a sentence—generally a noun or pronoun followed by a participle (and all the words associated with it). Some absolute phrases have the meaning (but not the structure) of an adverb clause. See **24a** and **30b(4)**. See also **phrase** and **sentence modifier.**

> We will have a cookout, **weather permitting.** [noun + present participle]
> COMPARE   We will have a cookout *if the weather permits.* [adverb clause: subordinator (*if*) + subject + predicate]

> **The national anthem sung for the last time,** the old stadium was closed. [noun + past participle with modifier]
> COMPARE   *After the national anthem had been sung for the last time,* the old stadium was closed. [adverb clause]

> The two of us worked on the homecoming float—**Tom in the morning and I at night.** [Note the use of *I,* the subjective case.]
> COMPARE   *Tom worked in the morning, and I worked at night.*

abstract noun   A word referring to a quality, concept, or emotion (*sweetness, honesty, justice, ratio, hatred*) rather than to a concrete reality perceptible by one or more of the senses (*candy, trees, sleet*). See **20a(3).**

active voice   The form of a transitive verb indicating that its subject performs the action the verb denotes: "Emily *sliced* the ham." See **29d.** See also **voice** and **verb.**

adjectival   A clause, phrase, or word (especially one without degrees of comparison) used to modify a noun or pronoun: *a Revenue Canada* audit, *Nancy's end-of-term* jitters, the search *for truth*, films *I like*. See **4d** and **18f(1).** See also **comparison.**

adjective A part of speech regularly used to modify a noun or a pronoun. Limiting adjectives restrict the meaning of the words they modify; descriptive adjectives usually have degrees of comparison; proper adjectives are derived from proper nouns. See **4b, 4c, 12c(2)**, and **9a(3)**. See also **comparison** and **predicate adjective**.

LIMITING	**that** cheese, **a** boy, **its** roots, **both** steps
DESCRIPTIVE	**newer** car, **green** one, **beautiful** eyes
PROPER	**Christlike** figure, **Irish** humour, **Roman** candle

adjective clause A subordinate clause used as an adjective: people *who bite their fingernails.* An adjective clause is either restrictive or non-restrictive. See **12d(1)** and **25a(3)**. See also **clause**.

adverb A part of speech regularly used to modify (describe, limit, or qualify) a verb, an adjective, or another verb: *slowly* ate, *too* tall, left *very quietly.* See **4a, 4c**, and **30b(1)**. An adverb may also modify a verbal, a phrase or clause, or the rest of the sentence.

> **Naturally,** the villain succeeds at first by **completely** outwitting the hero. [*Naturally* modifies the rest of the sentence; *completely* modifies the gerund *outwitting.*]

adverb clause A subordinate clause used as an adverb. An adverb clause may indicate time, place, cause, condition, concession, comparison, purpose, or result. See **12b** and **30b(1)**. See also **clause** and **conditional clause**.

> **If parents are too demanding** [condition], their children may behave like hermits or rebels.
> **Although he is usually quiet** [concession], everyone listens to him **when he speaks** [time] **because he makes good suggestions** [cause].

adverbial A clause, phrase, or word (especially one without degrees of comparison) used as an adverb. See **12b**. See also **adverb**.

> **When the hail started,** we ran **into the library.** [adverb clause and prepositional phrase]
> **Wow,** I forgot to ask; **however,** I'll see him **Friday.** [interjection, conjunctive adverb, and adverbial noun]

adverbial conjunction See **conjunctive adverb**.

agreement   The correspondence in the form of one word with another to indicate number/person/gender. See Section **6**.

> this type, these types, that girl, those girls [number]
> I ask, a boy asks, boys ask, they ask [person and number]
> the woman herself, the man himself [gender and number]

antecedent   A word or word group that a pronoun refers to. The antecedent usually precedes (but may follow) the pronoun. See **6b** and Section **28**.

> **Greg** paid his bills before he left town. [*Greg* is the antecedent of *his* and *he.*]
> Ask a **person** who owns an IBM, not an Apple. [*Person* is the antecedent of *who.*]
> Like their trainers, **pets** can be polite or rude. [The pronoun *their* precedes the antecedent *pets.*]

appositive   A noun (or nominal) placed next to or very near another noun (or nominal) to identify, explain, or supplement its meaning. Appositives may be restrictive or non-restrictive. See **12d(1)**, **24a**, **30b(4)**, and **30c(3)**. See also **nominal.**

> Our guide, a **Mr. Davis,** did not see the grizzly. [The appositive refers to and identifies the noun *guide.*]

> A **preservative** used in many canned goods, salt is not only tasty but nutritious. [The appositive (with its modifier, a participial phrase) supplements the meaning of *salt.*]

article   *The, a,* or *an,* used adjectivally before nouns: *the* cups, *a* cup, *an* extra cup. *The* is a definite article. *A* (used before consonant sounds) and *an* (used before vowel sounds) are indefinite articles. See **9f**.

auxiliary   A form of *be, have,* or *do* (or a modal, such as *will, should*) used with a verb. An auxiliary, or helping verb, regularly indicates tense but may also indicate voice, mood, person, number. See **6a** and Section **7**.

is eating	**did** eat	**will be** eating
have eaten	**should** eat	**had been** eaten

Modal auxiliaries—*will, would, shall, should, may, might, must, can, could*—do not take such inflectional endings as *-s, -ing*.

case   The form or position of a noun or pronoun that shows its use or relationship to other words in a sentence. The three cases in English are the *subjective* (or nominative), the *possessive* (or genitive), and the *objective* (sometimes called the accusative). See Section **5** and **15a**.

clause   A sequence of related words within a sentence. A clause has both a subject and a predicate and functions either as an independent unit (*main clause*) or as a dependent unit (*subordinate clause,* used as an adverb, an adjective, or a noun). See Section **24**. See also **sentence**.

SENTENCES
Only a few stars were visible. The moon was bright.
I know Herb. He will run for office.

MAIN CLAUSES
Only a few stars were visible, for **the moon was bright.**
I know Herb; he **will run for office.**
  [sentences connected by using the co-ordinating conjunction *for* and by using a semicolon and lower case for *he*]

SUBORDINATE CLAUSES
Only a few stars were visible **because the moon was bright.**
  [adverb clause]
I know Herb, **who will run for office.** [adjective clause]
I know **that Herb will run for office.** [noun clause—direct object]
  [sentences converted to subordinate clauses by using the subordinating conjunctions *because* and *that* and the relative pronoun *who,* a subordinator]

Elliptical clauses have omitted elements that are clearly understood: see **elliptical construction.**

collective noun   A noun singular in form that denotes a group: *flock, jury, band, public, committee.* See **6a(7)**.

common gender   A term applied to words that can refer to either sex, feminine or masculine (*parent, instructor, salesperson, people, human beings, anyone, everyone*), rather than to only one of the sexes (*mother, father, waitress, waiter*). See also **6b(1).**

common noun   A noun referring to any member or all members of a class or group (*woman, city, apples, holidays*) rather than to a specific member (*Kay Macpherson, Toronto, Winesap, New Year's Day*). See **9f.**

comparative   See **comparison.**

comparison   The inflection or modification of an adjective or adverb to indicate degrees in quality, quantity, or manner. There are three degrees: positive, comparative, and superlative. See **4c.**

POSITIVE	COMPARATIVE	SUPERLATIVE
good, well	better	best
high	higher	highest
quickly	more quickly	most quickly
active	less active	least active

complement   A word or words used to complete the sense of a verb. Although the term may refer to a direct or an indirect object, it usually refers to a subject complement, an object complement, or the complement of a verbal like *to be.*

> The lasagna tasted **delicious.** [subject complement]
> We made the ferret our **mascot.** [object complement]
> To be a good **leader,** one must learn how to listen. [complement of the infinitive *to be*]

complete predicate   A simple predicate (a verb or verb phrase) along with any objects, complements, or modifiers: "We *ate the fresh homemade pie before the salad.*" See also **predicate.**

complete subject   A simple subject (a noun or nominal) along with any modifiers: "*Everyone at the picnic* liked the pie." See also **subject.**

complex sentence   A sentence containing one main clause and at least one subordinate clause. See Section **24** and **30c(1).** See also **clause.**

Someone in the neighbourhood noticed a stranger [main clause]
who looked suspicious [subordinate clause].

compound-complex sentence   A sentence containing at least
two main clauses and one or more subordinate clauses. See also
clause.

When the lights went out [subordinate clause], we had no flashlight
or candles [main clause], so we sat outside and gazed at the stars
[main clause].

compound predicate   Two or more predicates having the same
subject: "Canada's Nursing Sisters *cared for the wounded during
World War II* and *won the nickname 'the bluebirds' for their distinctive dress.*" See **2a** and **30c(2)**. See also **predicate**.

compound sentence   A sentence containing at least two main
clauses and no subordinate clause. See **12a** and **14a**. See also
clause.

The water supply was dwindling, so rationing became mandatory.
[Pattern: Main clause, *so* main clause.]

compound subject   Two or more subjects of the same verb.
See **5a** and **6a**. See also **subject**.

Either **Phil** or **she** has to stay with Danny.
Women, men, and **children** call the crisis centre.

concrete noun   A non-abstract word referring to something
material or to specific realities that can be perceived by one or
more of the senses (*cologne, sunset, onions, thorns*) rather than
to a quality or concept (*humanity, essence, truth, envy*). See
20a(3).

conditional clause   An adverb clause (beginning with such
conjunctions as *if, unless, whether,* or *provided*) expressing a
real, imagined, or non-factual condition. See **7c**. Sentences with
conditional clauses often follow this pattern:

If . . . [condition stated], **then** . . . [consequence/conclusion].
If she does a good job, then I will promote her.
If everyone were a millionaire, we would all be poor.

conjugation A set or table of the inflected forms of a verb that indicate tense, person, number, voice, and mood. A conjugation of the irregular verb *see* follows.

PRINCIPAL PARTS: *see, saw, seen*

INDICATIVE MOOD
Active Voice   *Passive Voice*

PRESENT TENSE

Singular	*Plural*	*Singular*	*Plural*
1. I see	we see	I am seen	we are seen
2. you see	you see	you are seen	you are seen
3. one (he/she/it) sees	they see	one (he/she/it) is seen	they are seen

PAST TENSE

1. I saw	we saw	I was seen	we were seen
2. you saw	you saw	you were seen	you were seen
3. one saw	they saw	one was seen	they were seen

FUTURE TENSE

1. I shall see	we shall see	I shall be seen	we shall be seen
2. you will see	you will see	you will be seen	you will be seen
3. one will see	they will see	one will be seen	they will be seen

PRESENT PERFECT TENSE

1. I have seen	we have seen	I have been seen	we have been seen
2. you have seen	you have seen	you have been seen	you have been seen
3. one has seen	they have seen	one has been seen	they have been seen

PAST PERFECT TENSE

1. I had seen	we had seen	I had been seen	we had been seen
2. you had seen	you had seen	you had been seen	you had been seen
3. one had seen	they had seen	one had been seen	they had been seen

FUTURE PERFECT TENSE (seldom used)

1. I shall have seen	we shall have seen	I shall have been seen	we shall have been seen
2. you will have seen	you will have seen	you will have been seen	you will have been seen
3. one will have seen	they will have seen	one will have been seen	they will have been seen

SUBJUNCTIVE MOOD
Active Voice   *Passive Voice*

PRESENT TENSE

Singular: if I, you, one see   if I, you, one be seen
Plural: if we, you, they see   if we, you, they be seen

PAST TENSE

Singular: if I, you, one saw   if I, you, one were seen
Plural: if we, you, they saw   if we, you, they were seen

PRESENT PERFECT TENSE

Singular: if I, you, one have seen   if I, you, one have been seen
Plural: if we, you, they have seen   if we, you, they have been seen

PAST PERFECT TENSE
(Same as the indicative)

IMPERATIVE MOOD

PRESENT TENSE
see   be seen

conjunction   A part of speech (such as *and* or *although*) used to
connect words, phrases, clauses, or sentences. There are two
kinds of conjunctions: co-ordinating and subordinating.

The co-ordinating conjunctions—*and, but, or, nor, for, so,
yet*—connect and relate words and word groups of equal grammatical rank. See Section **26**. See also **correlatives**.

> Dick **and** Mario sang beautifully, **for** their host had paid them well.
> Colour-blind people can usually see blue, **but** they may confuse red
> with green **or** with yellow.

Subordinating conjuctions (such as *although, if, when*—see
the list on page 24) mark a dependent clause and connect it with
a main clause. See Section **24**.

> **When** Frank sulks, he acts **as if** he were deaf.

conjunctive adverb   A word (*however, therefore, nevertheless*—
see the list on page 45) that serves not only as an adverb but also
as a connective. See **3b, 14a,** and **32b(4)**.

connective   A word or phrase that links and relates words,
phrases, clauses, or sentences, such as *and, although, otherwise,
finally, on the contrary, which, not only . . . but also.* Conjunctions,

conjunctive adverbs, transitional expressions, relative pronouns, and correlatives function as connectives. See also **32b(4).**

construction A grammatical unit (a phrase, clause, or sentence) or the arrangement of related words in a grammatical unit.

co-ordinating conjunction One of seven connectives: *and, but, for, or, nor, so,* or *yet.* See **12a** and Section **26.** See also **conjunction.**

co-ordination The use of identical constructions (such as adjectives, prepositional phrases, or noun clauses): the *cool, clear, sparkling* water; *what they do* and *what they say.* See **12c, 24b,** and Section **26.**

correlatives Connectives used in pairs: *both . . . and, either . . . or, neither . . . nor, not only . . . but also, whether . . . or.* Correlatives link grammatically equal constructions: *both* Jane *and* Fred, *not only* in Peru *but also* in Mexico. See **26c.**

dangling modifier An adjectival or an adverbial that modifies nothing in a sentence or does not clearly refer to another word or word group in the sentence. Not a dangler, an absolute phrase modifies the rest of the sentence. See **25b.**

> DANGLING **Racing to class,** the running tap went unnoticed.
> [*Racing* modifies nothing in the sentence. The reader expects *racing* to modify the subject—which is *tap.*]
>
> REVISED **Racing** to class, **I** did not notice that running tap.
> [*Racing* clearly refers to the subject *I.*]
>
> COMPARE *The running tap going unnoticed,* I ran right past it on my way to class. [absolute phrase]

declension A set or table of inflected forms of nouns or pronouns: see the examples on page 61.

demonstratives Four words that point out: *this, that, these, those.*

> **Those** are as good as **these.** [pronouns]
> **Those** curtains have never been cleaned. [adjective]

dependent clause A subordinate clause: see **clause.**

determiner   A word (such as *a, an, the* or *my, their*) that signals the approach of a noun: **the** newly mown *hay*.

direct address   A name or descriptive term (set off by commas) designating the one (or ones) spoken to.

> Falstaff enters and exclaims, "Well said, **Hal**!"
> Don't forget, **backseat passengers,** to use those seatbelts.

direct object   A noun (or nominal) naming *whom* or *what* after a transitive active verb: "Emily sliced the *ham*." See also **object**.

direct quotation   A repetition of the exact spoken or written words of others. See **16a** and **34c** (pages 491–92).

DIRECT QUOTATIONS	John asked, **"Shamim, where are you going?"**
	"Where an opinion is general," writes Jane Austen, **"it is usually correct."**
INDIRECT QUOTATIONS	John asked **Shamim where she was going.**
	According to Jane Austen, **a general opinion, as a rule, is correct.**

double negative   A non-standard construction containing two negatives and having a negative meaning: "We can*not* do *nothing* about the weather." See **4e**.

elliptical construction   A construction in which words are omitted but clearly understood.

> The curtains are newer than the carpet [is].
> Whenever [it is] possible, get a full night's sleep.
> His hair is black; his face [is] deeply tanned.

expletive   The word *there* or *it* used as a structural filler and not adding to the meaning of the sentence.

> There were only a few ballet tickets left. [Compare "Only a few ballet tickets were left."]
> It is obvious that they do not like us. [Compare "That they do not like us is obvious."]

faulty predication The use of a predicate that does not logically belong with a given subject. See **23d**.

> FAULTY   One superstition is a black cat.
> REVISED   One superstition **has to do with** a black cat.

finite verb A verb form that can function as the only verb in the predicate of a sentence: "They *ate* a can of pork and beans." Verb forms classified as gerunds, infinitives, or participles cannot. See also **predicate**. Contrast **verbal**.

form change See **inflection**.

function words Words (such as prepositions, conjunctions, auxiliaries, and articles) that indicate the functions of other words (*vocabulary words*) in a sentence and the grammatical relationships between them. See also **vocabulary (lexical) words**.

gerund A verbal (non-finite verb) that ends in *-ing* and functions as a noun. Gerunds may take objects, complements, or modifiers.

> He escaped by *swimming* **rapidly.** [The gerund *swimming* is the object of the preposition *by* and is modified by the adverb *rapidly*.]
> *Borrowing* **money** is a mistake. [The gerund phrase—the gerund *borrowing* and its object, *money*—serves as the subject of the sentence.]

A possessive noun or pronoun before a gerund may be classified either as an adjectival (modifying the noun element of the verbal) or as the subject of the gerund.

> **His borrowing** money is a mistake. [Compare "*his* action" and "He *borrowed* the money."]

helping verb See **auxiliary**.

imperative See **mood**.

indefinites The article *a* or *an* (*a* cigar, *an* idea) as well as pronouns (*anybody, everyone*) and adjectives (*any* book, *few* friends, *several* pages) that do not specify distinct limits. See **6a(1)** and **6b(1)**.

independent clause   A main clause: see **clause**.

indicative   See **mood**.

indirect object   A word (or words) naming the one (or ones) affected—but not directly affected—by the action of the verb: "Emily sliced *me* some ham." See also **object**.

indirect quotation   A report of the written or spoken words of another without the use of the exact words of the speaker or writer: "The registrar said *that my cheque for tuition was returned to her.*" See also **direct quotation**.

infinitive   A verbal (non-finite verb) used chiefly as a noun, less frequently as an adjective or an adverb. The infinitive is usually made up of the word *to* plus the present form of a verb (called the *stem* of the infinitive), but the *to* may be omitted after such verbs as *let, make,* and *dare.* Infinitives may have subjects, objects, complements, or modifiers.

> Hal wanted **to open** the present. [*Present* is the object of the infinitive *to open;* the whole infinitive phrase is the object of the verb *wanted.*]
> The work **to be done** overwhelms me. [The infinitive is used adjectivally to modify the noun *work.*]
> **To tell** the truth, our team almost lost. [The infinitive phrase is used adverbially to modify the rest of the sentence.]

inflection   A change in the form of a vocabulary or lexical word to show a specific meaning or grammatical relationship to some other word or group of words. See **4c, 15a,** and **18d** and Sections **5, 6,** and **7**.

VERBS	drink, drinks, drank, drunk; grasp, grasps, grasped
PRONOUNS	**I, my** life, a gift for **me**
NOUNS	dog, dogs; dog's, dogs'
ADJECTIVES	a **good** one, a **better** one, the **best** one
ADVERBS	carefully, **more** carefully, **most** carefully

intensifier A modifier used for emphasis: *very* boring, *so* pleased, *certainly* did. See also **qualifier.**

intensive/reflexive pronoun The *-self* pronouns (such as *myself, himself, themselves*). The intensive is used for emphasis:

> The teenagers **themselves** had the best idea.

The reflexive is used as an object of a verb, verbal, or preposition:

> He blames **himself.**   She bought a present for **herself.**

Note that an intensive or reflexive pronoun always refers to another noun or pronoun that denotes the same individual or individuals.

interjection A word (one of the eight parts of speech) expressing a simple exclamation: *Whew! Ouch!* When used in sentences, mild interjections are set off by commas. See **17c.**

interrogatives Words like *which, whose,* or *why* used to ask a question.

> **Which** did he choose? [pronoun]   **Whose** car is it? [adjective]
> **Why** is real estate a good investment? [adverb]

intransitive verb A verb (such as *appear* or *belong*) that does not take an object. See also **verb.**

inversion A change in the usual word order of a sentence: "In the middle of the lake is a small island." See **29f.**

irregular verb A verb not inflected in the usual way—that is, by the addition of *d* or *ed* to the present form (or the stem of the infinitive). Below are the principal parts of five common types of irregular verbs. See **7a.**

> swim, swam, swum [vowels changed]
> beat, beat, beaten [*en* added]
> feel, felt, felt [vowel shortened, *ee* changed to *e*]

send, sent, sent [*d* changed to *t*]
set, set, set [no change]

lexical words   See **vocabulary (lexical) words**.

linking verbs   A verb that relates the subject complement to the subject. Words commonly used as linking verbs are *become, seem, appear, feel, look, taste, smell, sound,* and forms of the verb *be.* See **4b** and **5f**.

She **is** a pharmacist.   The music **sounds** brassy.

main clause   An independent clause: "When I explored the Black Hills, *I found many rocks to add to my collection.*" See **12a** and **14a**. See also **clause**.

misplaced modifier   An adjectival or adverbial in an awkward position—usually far away from what it modifies. Sometimes a misplaced modifier confuses the reader because it could qualify either of two words. See **25a**.

MISPLACED	I heard how to make ketchup flow out of the bottle **on the radio.**
REVISED	I heard *on the radio* how to make ketchup flow out of the bottle.

MISPLACED	To do one's best **sometimes** is not enough.
REVISED	To do one's best is **sometimes** not enough.
	OR It is not enough to do one's best **sometimes.**

modal auxiliary   See **auxiliary**.

modifier   A word or word group that describes, limits, or qualifies another: a *true* statement, walked *slowly,* yards *filled with rocks,* the horse *that jumped over the barrel.* See Sections **4** and **25**.

mood   The way a speaker or writer regards an assertion—that is, as a declarative statement or a question (*indicative* mood), as a command or request (*imperative*), or as a supposition, hypothesis, recommendation, or condition contrary to fact (*subjunctive*). Verb forms indicate mood. See **7c** and **7d**.

INDICATIVE	Joe **was** a winner.
	Does he drop by?
IMPERATIVE	**Be** a winner.
	Do drop by!
SUBJUNCTIVE	Joe talked as though he **were** a loser.
	I recommend that he **do** this soon.

nominal A clause, phrase, or word (a noun but especially a pronoun or gerund) used as a noun. See also **noun**.

> **Repairing that machine** was not easy.
> He contends **that selfless love is power.**

nominative See **case**.

non-finite verb A verb form used as a noun, an adjective, or an adverb. A non-finite verb cannot stand as the only verb in a sentence. See **2a**. See also **verbal**.

> Listeners call **to express** their opinions. [infinitive]
> Elisa delights in **facing** new challenges. [gerund]
> The help **offered** at that time was refused. [participle]

non-restrictive Non-essential to the identification of the word or words referred to. A word or word group is non-restrictive (parenthetical) when it is not necessary to the meaning of the sentence and may be omitted. See **12d**.

> My best friend, **Pauline,** understands me. [word]
> That airplane, **now being manufactured in large numbers,** is of immense commercial value. [phrase]
> That airplane, **which is now being manufactured in large numbers,** is of immense commercial value. [clause]

noun A part of speech that names a person, place, thing, idea, animal, quality, or action: *Mary, Europe, apples, justice, goose, strength, departure*. A noun usually changes form to indicate the plural and the possessive case, as in *man, men; man's men's*.

TYPES OF NOUNS

| COMMON | a **man,** the **cities,** some **trout** [general classes] |
| PROPER | **Mr. Park,** in **Venice,** the **Forum** [capitalized, specific names] |

COLLECTIVE	a **flock**, the **jury**, my **family** [groups]
CONCRETE	an **egg**, the **bus**, his **ear**, two **trees** [tangibles]
ABSTRACT	**honour, jealousy, pity, hatred** [ideas, qualities]
COUNT	one **dime**, ten **dollars**, a **job**, many **times** [singular or plural—often preceded by adjectivals telling how many]
MASS	much **money**, more **work**, less **time** [singular in meaning—often preceded by adjectivals telling how much]

FUNCTIONS OF NOUNS

SUBJECT OF FINITE VERB   **Dogs** barked.

OBJECT OF FINITE VERB OR PREPOSITION   He gave **Marcelle** the **key** to the **house.**

SUBJECT COMPLEMENT (PREDICATE NOUN)   She is a **lawyer.**

OBJECT COMPLEMENT   They named him **Jonathan.**

SUBJECT OF NON-FINITE VERB   I want **Ivan** to be here.

OBJECT OF NON-FINITE VERB   I prefer to drive a **truck.**

APPOSITIVE   Moses, a **prophet,** saw the Promised Land.

ADVERBIAL   **Yesterday** they went **home.**

ADJECTIVAL   The **magazine** article highlighted **Saskatchewan** winters.

DIRECT ADDRESS   What do you think, **Angela?**

KEY WORD OF ABSOLUTE PHRASE   The **food** being cold, no one really enjoyed the meal.

noun clause   A subordinate clause used as a noun. See also **clause.**

> **Whoever comes** will be welcome. [subject]
> I hope **that he will recover.** [direct object]
> I will give **whoever comes first** the best seat. [indirect object]
> Spend it on **whatever seems best.** [object of a preposition]
> This is **what you need.** [subject complement]
> I loved it, **whatever it was.** [appositive]
> **Whoever you are,** show yourself! [direct address]

number   The inflectional form of a work that indicates singular (one) or plural (more than one): *river—rivers, this—those, he sees—they see.* See Section **6** and **18d(5).**

object   A noun or noun substitute governed by a transitive active verb, by a non-finite verb, or by a preposition.

A *direct object,* or the *object of a finite verb,* is any noun or noun substitute that answers the question *What?* or *Whom?* after a transitive active verb. A direct object frequently receives, or is in some way affected by, the action of the verb.

> William raked **leaves.**
> **What** did he say?
> The Andersons do not know **where we live.**

As a rule, a direct object may be converted into a subject with a passive verb: see **voice**.

An *object of a non-finite verb* is any noun or its equivalent that follows and completes the meaning of a participle, a gerund, or an infinitive.

> Washing a **car** takes time.
> He likes to wear a **tie.**
> Following the **truck,** a bus rounded the bend.

An *indirect object* is any noun or noun substitute that states *to whom* or *for whom* (or *to what* or *for what*) something is done. An indirect object ordinarily precedes a direct object.

> He bought **her** a watch.
> I gave the **floor** a second coat of varnish.

It is usually possible to substitute a prepositional phrase beginning with *to* or *for* for the indirect object.

> He bought a watch for her.

An *object of a preposition* is any noun or noun substitute that a preposition relates to another word or word group.

> Cedars grow tall in these **hills.** [*Hills* is the object of *in.*]
> **What** am I responsible for? [*What* is the object of *for.*]

object complement   A word that helps to complete the meaning of such verbs as *make, paint, elect, name.* An object complement refers to or modifies the direct object. See **4b.** See also **complement**.

They painted the cellar door **blue.**
If it's a girl, they will name her **Kiyo.**

objective See **case.**

parenthetical element Non-essential matter (such as an aside or interpolation) usually set off by commas but often by dashes or parentheses to mark pauses and intonation. A word, phrase, clause, or sentence may be parenthetical. See **12d, 17e,** and **17f.**

> **Granted,** over 80 million people, **according to that estimate,** did watch one episode.
> **In fact,** the parachute ride—**believe it or not**—is as safe as the ferris wheel.

participle A verb form that may function as part of a verb phrase (was *laughing,* had *finished*) or as an adjectival (a *finished* product OR the players, *laughing* at their mistakes).

The present participle ends in *-ing* (the form also used for verbal nouns: see **gerund**). The past participle of regular verbs ends in *-d* or *-ed;* for past participle forms of irregular verbs, see **7a.** See also **irregular verb.**

Functioning as adjectivals in *participial phrases,* participles may take objects, complements, and modifiers. See **25b(1)** and **30b(2).**

> The prisoner *carrying* **the heaviest load** toppled forward. [The participle *carrying* takes the object *load;* the whole participial phrase modifies *prisoner.*]
> The telephone operator, **very *confused* by my request,** suggested that I place the call later. [The participle *confused* is modified by the adverb *very* and by the prepositional phrase *by my request;* the participial phrase modifies *telephone operator.*]

parts of speech The eight classes into which most grammarians group words according to their form changes and their position, meaning, and use in the sentence: *verbs, nouns, pronouns, adjectives, adverbs, prepositions, conjunctions,* and *interjections.* Each of these is discussed separately in this glossary. See also **1c.**

passive voice   The form of the verb that shows that its subject does not act but is the object or the receiver of the action: "The ham *was sliced* by Emily." See **29d**. See also **voice**.

person   Changes in the form of pronouns and verbs denoting or indicating whether one is speaking (*I am*—first person), spoken to (*you are*—second person), or spoken about (*it is*—third person). In the present tense, a verb changes its form to agree grammatically with a third-person singular subject (*I eat, a bird eats*). See **6a** and **27b**.

personal pronoun   Any one of a group of pronouns—*I, you, he, she, it,* and their inflected forms—referring to the one (or ones) speaking, spoken to, or spoken about. See Section **5**.

phrasal verb   A unit consisting of a verb and one or two uninflected words like *after, in, up, off,* or *out* (particles) and having the force of a single-word verb.

> We **ran out on** them. [Compare "We deserted them."]
> He **cut** me **off** without a cent. [Compare "He disinherited me."]

phrase   A sequence of grammatically related words without a subject and a predicate. See **2a** and **30c(4)**.

TYPE OF PHRASE

NOUN	A **young stranger** stepped forward.
VERB	All day long they **had been worrying**.
PREPOSITIONAL	**By seven o'clock** the lines stretched **from the box office to the corner**.
GERUND	**Building a sun deck** can be fun.
INFINITIVE	Do you want **to use your time that way**?
PARTICIPIAL	My friends **travelling in Italy** felt the earthquake.
APPOSITIVE	I introduced her to Bob, **my roommate**.
ABSOLUTE	**The game over**, we shook hands.

positive   See **comparison**.

possessive   See **case**.

predicate   A basic grammatical division of a sentence. A predicate is the part of the sentence comprising what is said about the subject. The *complete predicate* consists of the main verb along with its auxiliaries (the *simple predicate*) and any complements and modifiers.

> We *used* a patriotic theme for our celebrations that year. [*Used* is the simple predicate. *Used* and all the words that follow it make up the complete predicate.]

> *Had* the team **already** *been preparing* itself **psychologically?** [The simple predicate is the verb phrase *had been preparing*.]

predicate adjective   An adjective used as a subject complement: "The bread tastes *sweet*." See **4b**. See also **linking verbs**.

predicate noun   A noun used as a subject complement: "Bromides are *sedatives*." See **4b**. See also **linking verbs**.

predication   See **faulty predication**.

preposition   A part of speech that links and relates a noun or nominal to some other word in the sentence. See page 16 for a list of words commonly used as prepositions.

> The paintings hung **in** the hall. [The preposition *in* connects and relates *hall* (its object) to the verb *hung*.]

prepositional phrase   A preposition with its object and any modifiers: *in the hall, between you and me, for the new van*. See also **preposition**.

principal parts   The forms of any verb from which the various tenses are derived: the present infinitive (*take, laugh*), the past (*took, laughed*), and the past participle (*taken, laughed*). See **7a**.

progressive verb   A verb phrase consisting of a present participle (ending in *-ing*) used with a form of *be* and denoting continuous action. See the synopsis on page 88.

> **I have been playing** tennis all afternoon.

pronoun   One of the eight parts of speech. Pronouns take the position of nouns and function as nouns do. See Sections **5** and

28 and **6b.** See also **noun** and the separate entries for the types of pronouns listed below.

PERSONAL	**She** and **I** will see him in Tokyo.
RELATIVE	Leslie is the one **who** likes to bowl.
INDEFINITE	**Each** of you should help **someone.**
INTENSIVE	I **myself** saw the crash.
REFLEXIVE	Roy blames **himself.**
DEMONSTRATIVE	**Those** are riper than **these.**
INTERROGATIVE	**Who** are they? **What** is right?

proper adjective   An adjective (such as *Scottish*) derived from a proper noun (*Scotland*). See **9a(3).**

proper noun   A noun (beginning with a capital letter) referring to a particular or specific member of a class or group (*Wayne Gretzky, Lake Nipigon, November, God*) rather than to any member or all members (*man, lake, months, gods*). See **9a.**

qualifier   Any modifier, descriptive, limiting, or qualifying. Frequently, however, the term refers only to those modifiers that restrict or intensify the meaning of other words. See also **intensifier.**

Many thieves lie. **Almost** all of them do. [Compare "Thieves lie."] **Sometimes** children are **too** selfish to share.

quotation   See **direct quotation.**

reciprocal pronoun   One of two compound pronouns expressing an interchangeable or mutual action or relationship: *each other* or *one another.*

reflexive pronoun   See **intensive/reflexive pronoun.**

regular verb   A verb that forms its past tense and past participle by adding *-d* or *-ed* to the present form (or the stem of the infinitive): *love, loved; laugh, laughed.* See **7a.**

relative clause   An adjective clause introduced by a relative pronoun: the suits *that they wore.* See also **relative pronoun.**

relative pronoun   One of a small group of noun substitutes (*who, whom, whose, that, which, what, whoever, whomever, whichever, whatever*) used to introduce subordinate clauses. See **5b, 5c,** and **6a(5).**

> He has a son ***who* is a genius.** [adjective clause introduced by the relative pronoun *who*]
> ***Whoever* wins the prize** must have talent. [noun clause introduced by the relative pronoun *whoever*]

restrictive   Essential to the identification of the word or words referred to. A word, phrase, or clause is restrictive when it is necessary to the meaning of the sentence and cannot be omitted. See **12d.**

> The word ***interest*** is a synonym for *concern*. [restrictive appositive]
> Every drug **condemned by doctors** should be taken off the market. [restrictive phrase]
> Every drug **that doctors condemn** should be taken off the market. [restrictive clause]

sentence   A grammatically independent unit of expression. A simple sentence contains a subject and a predicate. See Section **1.** Sentences are classified according to structure:

SIMPLE	We won. [subject—predicate]
COMPOUND	They outplayed us, but we won. [two main clauses]
COMPLEX	Although we did win, they outplayed us. [subordinate clause, main clause]
COMPOUND-COMPLEX	I know that they outplayed us, but we did win. [two main clauses—the first of which contains a subordinate clause]

Sentences are also classified according to their purpose.

DECLARATIVE	We will fly to Montreal. [statement]
IMPERATIVE	Fly to Montreal. [command]
INTERROGATIVE	Shall we fly to Montreal? [question]
EXCLAMATORY	Would we like to fly to Montreal! [exclamation]

sentence modifier   An adverbial that modifies all the rest of the sentence, not a specific word or word group in it.

> **Yes,** the plane arrived on time.
> **To tell the truth,** a few are takers, not givers.
> **All things considered,** Yellowknife is a good place to live.

structure words   See **function words**.

subject   A basic grammatical division of a sentence. The subject is a noun or nominal about which something is asserted or asked in the predicate. It usually precedes the predicate. (Imperative sentences have subjects that are not stated but are implied.) The *complete subject* consists of the *simple subject* and the words associated with it.

> **The dog locked in the hot car** needed air. [*Dog* is the simple subject. *The dog locked in the hot car* is the complete subject.]

subject complement   A word (or words) that completes the meaning of a linking verb and that modifies or refers to the subject. See **4b**. See also **linking verb**.

> The old car looked **expensive.** [predicate adjective]
> The old car was an **eyesore.** [predicate noun]

subjective   See **case**.

subjunctive   See **mood**.

subordinate clause   A dependent clause: "Her cough vanished *after she had quit smoking.*" See also **clause**.

subordinating conjunction   a connective such as *although, if,* or *when:* see the list on page 24. See also **conjunction**.

subordination   The use of dependent structures (phrases, subordinate clauses) lower in grammatical rank than independent ones (simple sentences, main clauses). See Section **24**.

subordinator   A connective (such as *unless, whose, that, why*) that marks the beginning of a subordinate (dependent) clause: see page 24.

suffix   An added sound, syllable, or group of syllables attached to the end of a base or root (or another suffix). Suffixes change meanings, create new words, and indicate grammatical functions. See also **inflection**.

| the plays | play**er** | play**er's** | play**ing** |
| play**ed** | play**ful** | play**fully** | play**fulness** |

superlative   See **comparison**.

syntax   Sentence structure. The grammatical arrangement of words, phrases, clauses.

tense   The form of the verb that denotes time. Inflection of single-word verbs (*pay, paid*) and the use of auxiliaries (*am paid, was paid, will pay*) indicate tense. See Section **7**.

transitive   See **verb**.

verb   part of speech denoting action, occurrence, or existence (state of being). Inflections indicate tense (and sometimes person and number) and mood of a verb: see **inflection, mood, voice,** and Section **7**.

A *transitive verb* is a verb that requires an object to complete its meaning. Transitive verbs can usually be changed from the active to the passive voice: see **object** and **voice**.

Sid **hung** a wreath on his door. [direct object: *wreath*]

An *intransitive verb* is a verb (such as *go* or *sit*) that does not have an object to complete its meaning. Linking verbs, which take subject complements, are intransitive.

She **has been waiting** patiently for hours.
I **was** sick last Christmas.

The same verb may be transitive in one sentence and intransitive in another.

TRANSITIVE   Dee **reads** novels. [direct object: *novels*]
INTRANSITIVE   Dee **reads** well.

verbal   A non-finite verb used as a noun, an adjective, or an adverb. Infinitives, participles, and gerunds are verbals. Verbals (like finite verbs) may take objects, complements, modifiers, and sometimes subjects. See also **non-finite verb** and **gerund, infinitive, participle**.

Mr. Nelson went *to see* his daughter. [*To see,* an infinitive, functions as an adverb modifying the verb *went.* The object of the infinitive is *daughter.*]

Cars *parked* in the loading zone will be towed away. [*Parked,* a participle, modifies *cars.*]

Studying dialects in our area was fun. [*Studying,* a gerund, heads the phrase that is the subject of the verb *was.*]

verb phrase   See **phrase.**

vocabulary (lexical) words   Nouns, verbs, and most modifiers—those words found in vocabulary-building lists. See also **function words.**

voice   The form of a transitive verb that indicates whether or not the subject performs the action denoted by the verb. A verb with a direct object is in the *active voice.* When the direct object is converted into a subject, the verb is in the *passive voice.* A passive verb is always a verb phrase consisting of a form of the verb *be* (or sometimes *get*) followed by a past participle. See **29d.**

ACTIVE   Priscilla **chose** Jorge. [The subject (*Priscilla*) acts.]
PASSIVE   Jorge **was chosen** by Priscilla. [The subject (*Jorge*) does not act.]

Speakers and writers often omit the *by*-phrase after a passive verb, especially when the performer of the action is not known or is not the focus of attention.

Those flowers **were picked** yesterday.
The guilty ones **should be punished** severely.
We just heard that a new secretary **was hired.**

word order   The arrangement of words in sentences. Because of lost inflections, modern English depends heavily on word order to convey meaning.

Nancy gave Henry $14 000.
Henry gave Nancy $14 000.

Tony had built a barbecue pit.
Tony had a barbecue pit built.

Credits

Every reasonable effort has been made to find and acknowledge sources for all material used in this text. Any errors and omissions called to the publisher's attention will be corrected in future printings.

ANDERSON, BONNIE S., and JUDITH P. ZINSSER, from *A History of Their Own: Women in Europe from Prehistory to the Present,* Volume 1, Harper & Row, Publishers, New York, 1988.

BARRY, ROXANNA, the essay "Heat on the Hoof." Reprinted by permission of *Patent Trader.*

BEHRENS, PETER, from "Refugee Dreams," in *Saturday Night* 105, No.3, April 1990.

BERGER, THOMAS, from *Northern Frontier, Northern Homeland,* Revised Edition, Douglas & McIntyre, Vancouver, 1988.

BIRNEY, EARLE, from *Spreading Time,* Véhicule Press, Montreal, 1989.

BLAKE, DONALD E., R.K. CARTY, and LYNDA ERICKSON, from *Grassroots Politicians: Party Activists in British Columbia,* UBC Press, Vancouver, 1991.

BOOTH, DAVID, from *Censorship Goes to School,* Pembroke Publishers Ltd., Markham, Ontario, 1992.

BROWNMILLER, SUSAN, from *Femininity,* Ballantine Books, New York, 1985.

BRYSON, BILL, from *The Mother Tongue: English and How It Got That Way,* Avon Books, New York, 1990.

CARR, EMILY, from *Heart of a Peacock,* Irwin Publishing, Concord, Ontario, 1986.

CHAN, ANTHONY B., from *Gold Mountain: The Chinese in the New World,* New Star Books, Vancouver, 1983.

CHANG, RAYMOND, and MARGARET SCROGIN CHANG, from *Speaking of Chinese,* W.W. Norton & Company, New York, 1978.

DALGETTY, JAMES, the essay "The Tulips."

DARNTON, ROBERT, from *The Kiss of Lamourette: Reflections in Cultural History,* W.W. Norton & Company, New York, 1990.

DE MILLE, AGNES, from *Dance to the Piper,* Da Capo Press, New York, 1951.

DICKINSON, EMILY, lines from "I'm Nobody! Who Are You?" Reprinted by permission of the publishers and the Trustees of Amherst College. From *The Poems of Emily Dickinson,* ed., Thomas H. Johnson, Harvard U. Press, Cambridge, Mass., 1983.

EGOFF, SHEILA, from "Children's Literature in English," in *The Oxford Companion to Canadian Literature,* ed. William Toye, Oxford University Press, Toronto, 1983.

ERICKSON, ARTHUR, from "To Understand the City We Make," In *Vancouver Forum: Old Powers, New Forces,* ed. Max Wyman, Douglas & McIntyre, Vancouver, 1992.

FARB, PETER, from *Humankind,* Houghton Mifflin Company, Boston, 1978.

FARB, PETER, and GEORGE ARMELAGOS, from *Consuming Passions: The Anthropology of Eating,* Washington Square Press, New York, 1983.

FERK, SUSAN, the essay "The Subplot as Commentary in *King Lear.*"

FINDLEY, TIMOTHY, from *Inside Memory: Pages from a Writer's Workbook,* HarperCollins, Publishers Ltd., Toronto, 1990.

FLEISCHER, ARTHUR, GEOFFREY C. HAZARD, and MIRIAM Z. KLIPPER, from *Board Games: The Changing Shape of Corporate Power,* Little, Brown and Company, Boston, 1988.

FLEMING, WILLIAM, from *Arts and Ideas,* Seventh Edition, Holt, Rinehart and Winston, Inc., 1986.

FORSYTH, ADRIAN, from "Shell Game: The Beauty and the Logic of the Well-Engineered Egg," in *Equinox,* Number 68, March/April 1993.

FROST, ROBERT, "Fire and Ice," from *The Complete Poems of Robert Frost.* Copyright 1916, 1947 Holt, Rinehart and Winston. Copyright last renewed 1962 by Robert Frost. Copyright renewed 1964 by Lesley Frost Ballantine. Holt, Rinehart and Winston, New York, 1964.

FRYE, NORTHROP, from *The Well-Tempered Critic,* Indiana University Press, Bloomington, 1963.

GALBRAITH, JOHN KENNETH, from *Economics in Perspective: A Critical History,* Houghton Mifflin Company, Boston, 1987.

GROEN, RICK, from "Two Talk-Show Kings and a Tale of Two Countries," the *Globe and Mail,* Toronto, 19 June 1990.

GZOWSKI, PETER, from *The Morningside Papers.* Used by permission of the Canadian Publishers, McClelland & Stewart, Toronto, 1985.

HARDISON, O.B., JR., from *Disappearing through the Skylight: Culture and Technology in the Twentieth Century,* Viking Penguin, New York, 1989.

HOAGLAND, EDWARD, from "The Courage of Turtles," in *Heart's Desire: The Best of Edward Hoagland,* Summit Books, New York, 1988.

_____ , from "To the Point: Truths Only Essays Can Tell," in *Harpers' Magazine,* March 1993.

HODGINS, JACK, from *The Invention of the World,* Macmillan Canada, Toronto, 1977.

IRVING, JOHN, from "Why I Like Charles Dickens; Why Some People Don't" from "The King of the Novel" in *Trying to Save Piggy Sneed,* copyright © 1993 by John Irving, Alfred A. Knopf Canada, Toronto, 1993. Reprinted by permission of Alfred A. Knopf Canada.

JENISH, D'ARCY, from "Prime-Time Violence," *Maclean's,* 7 December 1992.

JOHNSON, SHARON, the essay "Treatment for Test Anxiety."

KUBLER-ROSS, ELISABETH, from *AIDS: The Ultimate Challenge,* Collier Books, Macmillan Publishing Company, New York, 1987.

LAURENCE, MARGARET, from "Down East," in *Heart of a Stranger,* Seal Books, McClelland-Bantam, Inc., Toronto, 1980.

_____ , from "My Final Hour," in *Canadian Literature,* Number 100, Spring 1984.

Credits

LIVESAY, DOROTHY, from "All Aboa-r-rd!" in *Canadian Literature,* Number 100, Spring 1984.

MACLENNAN, HUGH, from "On Living in a Cold Country," in *The Other Side of Hugh Maclennan,* Macmillan Canada, Toronto, 1978.

McLUHAN, MARSHALL, and ERIC McLUHAN, from *Laws of Media: The New Science,* University of Toronto Press, Toronto, Buffalo, London, 1988.

MERTON, THOMAS, from *The Seven-Storey Mountain,* Harcourt Brace Jovanovich, New York, 1990.

MILLER, J.R., from *Skyscrapers Hide the Heavens: A History of Indian-White Relations in Canada,* University of Toronto Press, Toronto, 1989.

MOHR, MERILYN SIMONDS, from "Musical Spheres," in *Equinox,* Number 68, March/April 1993.

MONAGAN, CHARLES, from *The Reluctant Naturalist: An Unnatural Field Guide to the Natural World,* Atheneum, New York, 1984.

MORRIS, JAN, from *City to City,* Macfarlane Walter & Ross, Toronto, 1990.

MORTON, W.L., and L.F. HANNON, from *This Land, These People: An Illustrated History of Canada,* Gage Publishing, Toronto, 1977.

MOWAT, FARLEY, from *This Rock Within the Sea,* McClelland & Stewart, Toronto, 1968.

_____ , from *A Whale for the Killing,* McClelland & Stewart, Toronto, 1972.

NEWMAN, PETER C., from *Caesars of the Wilderness: Company of Adventurers,* Volume II, Penguin Books Canada Ltd., Toronto, 1987.

NGUYEN, MICHAEL, the essay "The Window-Breakers: Several Artists in Search of Human Character."

NOWLAN, ALDEN, from *Miracle at Indian River,* Clarke, Irwin & Company, Toronto, 1968.

ONDAATJE, MICHAEL, from *Running in the Family,* McClelland & Stewart, Toronto, 1982.

ORWELL, GEORGE, from *Down and Out in Paris and London,* Secker & Warburg, London 1986.

PALEY, GRACE, "Wants," from *Enormous Changes at the Last Minute,* Farrar Strauss and Giroux, New York, 1987. Copyright by Grace Paley.

PEARCE, JOSEPH CHILTON, from *Exploring the Crack in the Cosmic Egg: Challenging Constructs of Mind and Reality,* Julian Press, New York, 1980.

PETROSKI, HENRY, from *The Pencil: A History of Design and Circumstance,* Alfred A. Knopf, New York, 1990.

PLATH, SYLVIA, for nine lines of "Tulips," from *The Collected Poems of Sylvia Plath,* ed. Ted Hughes, Faber, London, 1981.

PRESTON, RICHARD M., the essay "Ice."

RANDOM HOUSE, INC., definitions for "empty" and "empty-handed" from *Random House College Dictionary,* Revised Edition, copyright © 1991, 1988 by Random House, Inc. Reprinted by permission of Random House, Inc.

_____ , entry for "empty" from *Random House Thesaurus,* College Edition, copyright © 1984 by Random House, Inc. Reprinted by permission of Random House, Inc.

Index

Boldface numbers refer to rules; other numbers refer to pages.

Index

Composition (the whole). *See also*
    Research paper
    arranging ideas, **33f:** 430-35
    audience, 413, **33c:** 415-21
    background information, **33e:** 429
    checklist for revision of, **33h:**
        465-67
    choosing a subject, **33b:** 413-15
    conclusions, **33g:** 438-40
    drafts, 435, 444
    example of essay under revision,
        33h: 445-64
    exploring the subject (before
        writing), **33d:** 422-25
    focussing the subject, **33d:** 421-26
    formal outlines, **33f:** 432-35
    informal working plans for, **33f:**
        430-32
    introductions, **33g:** 436-40
    introductory paragraph of, **33e:**
        428
    leaving material out, **33e:** 427
    making list of relevant ideas, **33f:**
        431
    outlines, **33f:** 430-35
    purpose of, **33a:** 410-13
    revising, **33h:** 441-67
    thesis statement, **33e:** 426-30
    titles for, **33g:** 440-41
    tone, **33c:** 418-19
    word processors and, **33h:** 443-44
    writing, order of, approaches to,
        33g: 435-41
Compound-complex sentences, 28,
    174
    defined, 662
Compound predicate, **30c:** 356
    defined, 662
Compound sentence, 662
Compound subject, 662
Computer catalogue, **34b:** 477-78
Conclusions
    to compositions, **33g:** 438-40
    in deductive reasoning, **31b:**
        363-64
    in inductive reasoning, **31a:**
        362-63
Concrete words, **20a:** 275-77
    nouns, 662
Conditional clause, 662

Conference proceedings,
    bibliographical entry, 514
Conjugation, 663-64
Conjunctions, 13, 17
    co-ordinating, 40, 151
    defined, 664
    for linking sentences in paragraphs,
        32b: 385
    omitting, **22a:** 296-97
    subordinating, 24, 664
Conjunctive adverbs, 17
    beginning sentences with, **30b:**
        353
    defined, 664
    use of semicolon before, **3b:** 44-46
Connective, 664
Connotation, **20a:** 273
conscious, conscience, **19j:** 257
consensus of opinion, **19j:** 257
Constructions
    defined, 665
    mixed, **23c:** 305
Contractions
    apostrophe in, **15b:** 184
    in informal English, 244
    not, 5
Contrast
    paragraph development strategy,
        32d: 399-401
    transitional connective, **32b:** 385
Contrasted elements, comma with,
    12d: 162-63
Co-ordinate adjectives, **24:** 310
    commas and, **12c:** 158
Co-ordinating conjunctions
    beginning sentences with, **30b:**
        353
    comma use and, 151
    defined, 665
    linking main clauses, **3a:** 40-44,
        151
    parallel structure and, **26:** 322
    semicolons and, **14a:** 174
    sentences linked by, **24:** 310
    superfluous commas and, **13b:**
        169
Co-ordinating connectives, **24b:** 313
Co-ordination
    defined, **24:** 309, 665
    equal emphasis and, **24b:** 313

692

Index

Index

Index

Index

Index

markers, 4
meaning of tense forms, **7b:** 94-98
misuse of principal parts of, **7a:** 89-94
modified by adverbs, **4a:** 50-51
non-finite, 671
omission of, **22b:** 297-98
passive, 87
phrasal, 5-8
as predicate, 3, 89, 90
progressive, 4, 87
recognizing, **1a:** 3-8
regular, 86, 677
relation of to actual time, 94, **7b:** 96
single-word, 89, 94
spelling errors in, 92
subjects and objects of, **1b:** 8-12
subjunctive mood and form of, **7c:** 98-100
suffixes, 13-14
tenses of, 87-88. *See also* Tense(s)
transitive, 93, 680
very, **19j:** 267
Viewpoint, shifts in, **27e:** 331
Vocabulary (lexical) words, 681
Voice
active, for emphasis, **29d:** 343-44
avoiding shifts in, **27a:** 328
defined, 681
passive, **29d:** 343-44
in poetry, **35a:** 618
Volume, **11d:** 142
MLA-style bibliographical entry, 512
multivolume works, 512

want in, want out, **19j:** 267
ways, **19j:** 267
what, verb agreement and, **6a:** 77
where, **19j:** 268
where at, where to, **19j:** 268
whether...or, parallel structure, **26c:** 326
which, **19j:** 268
which or *that,* 160
Whole-by-whole comparison, **32d:** 400
who or *whoever,* **5b:** 64
who or *whom,* **5b:** 65, 68

whose vs. *of which,* 61
-wise, **19j:** 268
with regards to, **19j:** 268
woman, pronoun-antecedent agreement, **6b:** 80
Word division (line-breaks), **8d:** 109-110
abbreviations and acronyms, **8d:** 111
automatic hyphenation, **8d:** 110
in college dictionaries, 109
consonants and vowels, **8d:** 110
hyphenated words, 110
-ing words, **8d:** 110
misleading, **8d:** 110
one-letter syllables, **8d:** 110
one-syllable words, **8d:** 110
two-word endings, **8d:** 110
Wordiness, **21:** 286-94
combining sentences to avoid, **21b:** 289
defined, **21:** 286
examples of, **21a:** 287
Word order, 10-12
defined, 681
inverting for emphasis, **29f:** 346-47
WordPerfect, 443
Word-processed papers
automatic hyphenation, **8d:** 111
general practices for, **8a:** 106-107
justification, 109
laser printers, 109
revision and, **33h:** 443-44
Word processors
page layout and, **8g:** 116
search function, **8g:** 115
spell-checker, **8g:** 115-16
style-checking programs, **8g:** 115
usefulness in revising, **8g:** 115-16
Words. *See also* Dictionaries; Usage; Words (choice of)
basic meaning of, 238
cognate, 238
frequently confused, **18b:** 216-17
frequently misspelled, **18e:** 224-29
function type vs. structure, 13
parallel structure in, **26a:** 323
placement of for emphasis, **29a:** 339-40

READER REPLY CARD

We are interested in your reaction to *Harbrace College Handbook for Canadian Writers, 4/e*. You can help us to improve this book in future editions by completing this questionnaire.

1. What was your reason for using this book?
   - ❏ university course
   - ❏ college course
   - ❏ continuing education course
   - ❏ professional development
   - ❏ personal interest
   - ❏ other _____

2. If you are a student, please identify your school and the course in which you used this book.

3. Which chapters or parts of this book did you use? Which did you omit?

4. What did you like best about this book? What did you like least?

5. Please identify any topics you think should be added to future editions.

6. Please add any comments or suggestions.

7. May we contact you for further information?
   Name: _____
   Address: _____
   _____
   _____
   Phone: _____

LISTS FREQUENTLY CONSULTED	OTHER CORRECTION SYMBOLS